Grand Blue Dreaming 5

PRESENTED BY KENJI INOUE & KIMITAKE YOSHIOKA

The Colorful Cast of Grand Blue Dreaming

Diving Club Peek-a-Boo (PaB)

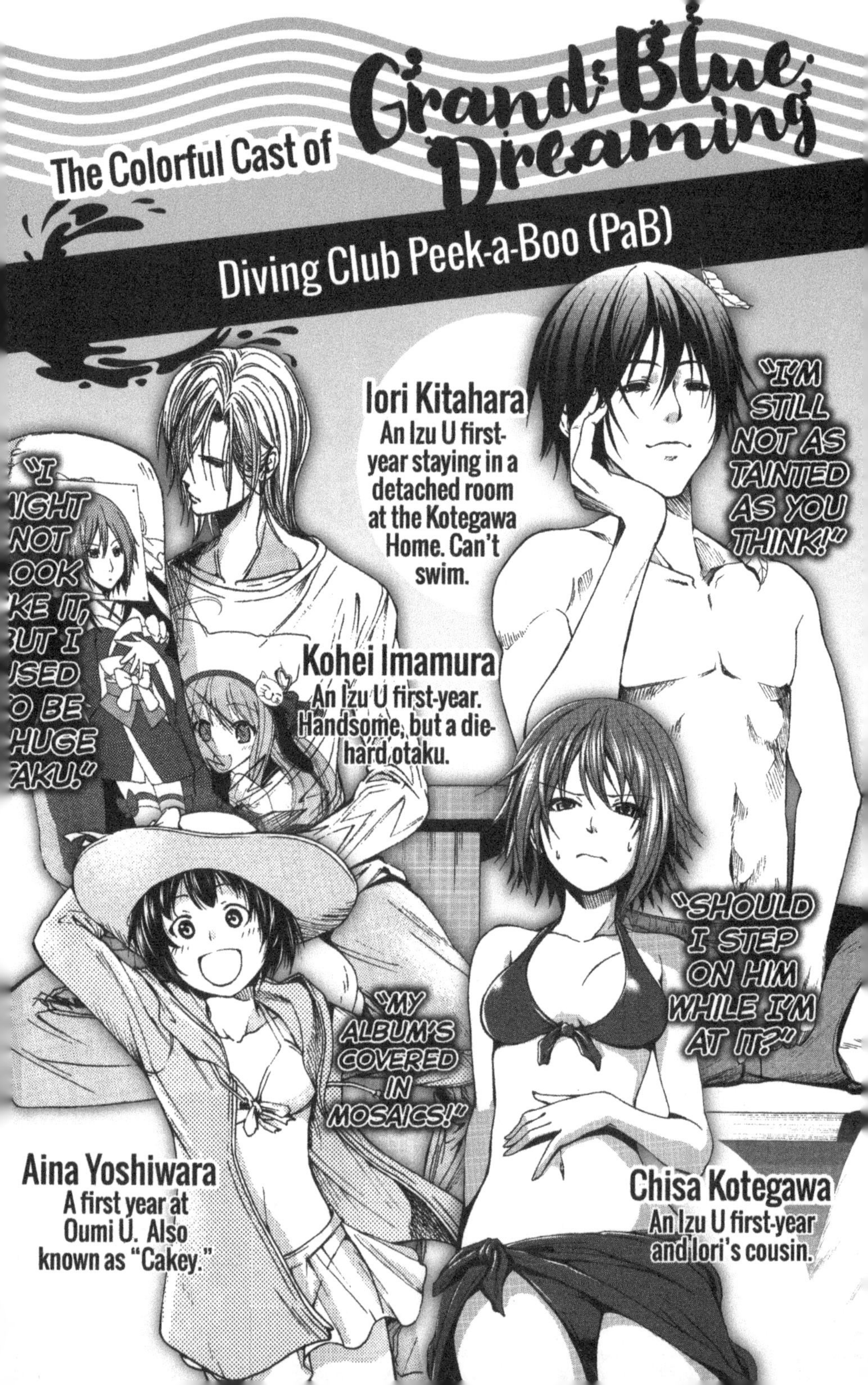
"I'M STILL NOT AS TAINTED AS YOU THINK!"
Iori Kitahara
An Izu U first-year staying in a detached room at the Kotegawa Home. Can't swim.
"I
IGHT
NOT
OOK
KE IT,
UT I
USED
O BE
HUGE
AKU."
Kohei Imamura
An Izu U first-year. Handsome, but a die-hard otaku.
"SHOULD I STEP ON HIM WHILE I'M AT IT?"
Chisa Kotegawa
An Izu U first-year and Iori's cousin.
"MY ALBUM'S COVERED IN MOSAICS!"
Aina Yoshiwara
A first year at Oumi U. Also known as "Cakey."

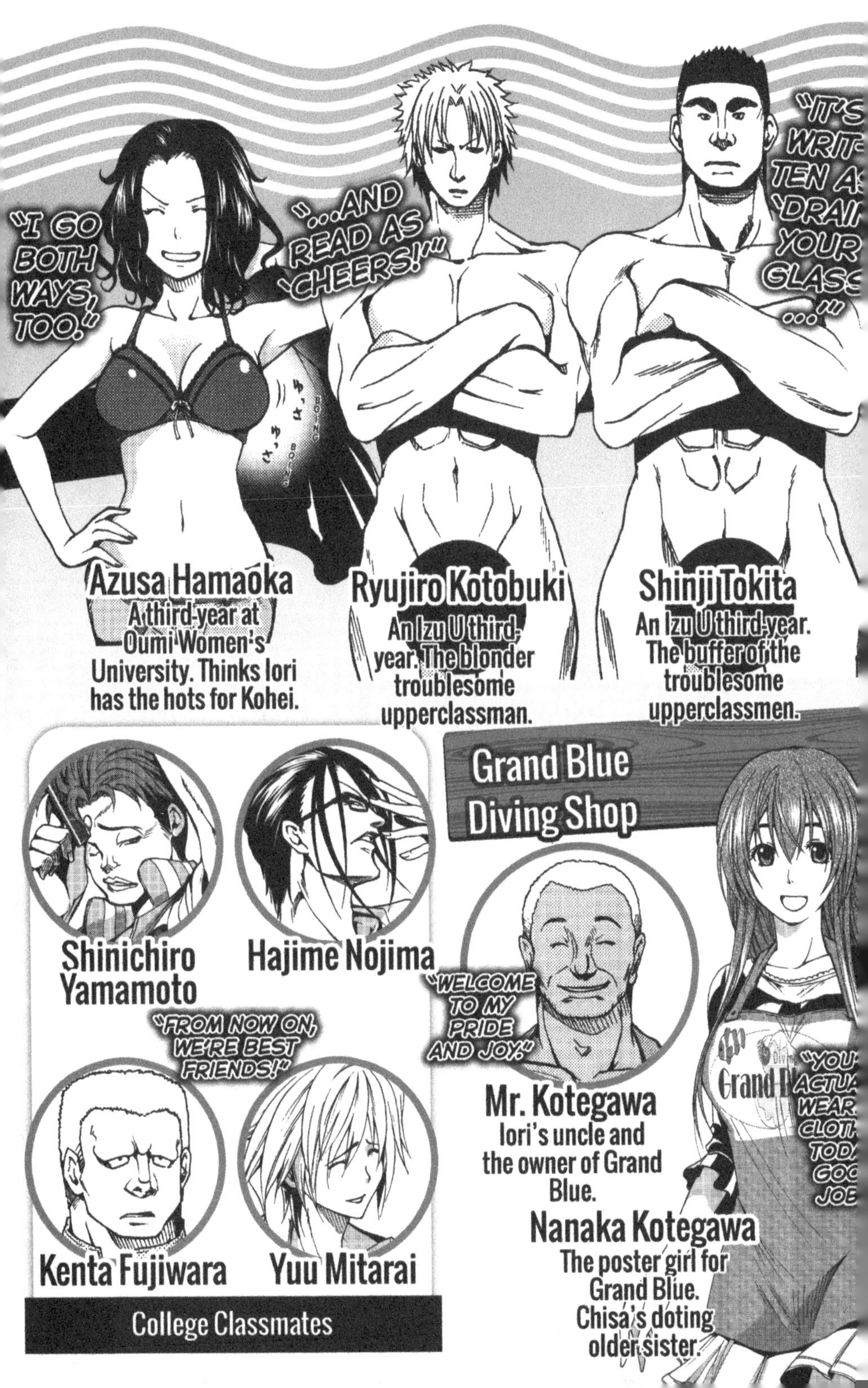
"IT'S WRIT- TEN AS 'DRAI YOUR GLAS ...!'"
Shinji Tokita
An Izu U third-year. The buffer of the troublesome upperclassmen.
"...AND READ AS 'CHEERS!'"
Ryujiro Kotobuki
An Izu U third-year. The blonder troublesome upperclassman.
"I GO BOTH WAYS, TOO."
BOING BOING
ゆっさ ゆっさ
Azusa Hamaoka
A third-year at Oumi Women's University. Thinks Iori has the hots for Kohei.
Grand Blue Diving Shop
"YOU ACTUA WEAR CLOTH TODA GOO JOB"
Grand Bl
"WELCOME TO MY PRIDE AND JOY."
Mr. Kotegawa
Iori's uncle and the owner of Grand Blue.
Nanaka Kotegawa
The poster girl for Grand Blue. Chisa's doting older sister.
Hajime Nojima
Shinichiro Yamamoto
"FROM NOW ON, WE'RE BEST FRIENDS!"
Yuu Mitarai
Kenta Fujiwara
College Classmates

PREVIOUSLY ON GRAND BLUE DREAMING

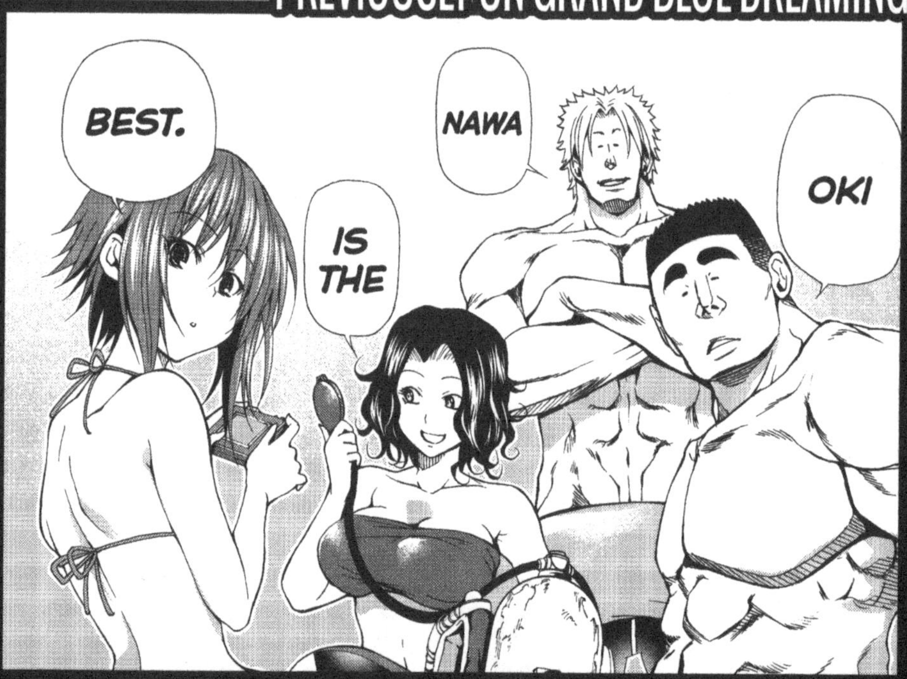
OKI
NAWA
IS THE
BEST.

The license exam is on in Okinawa and everyone's having a great time, however...

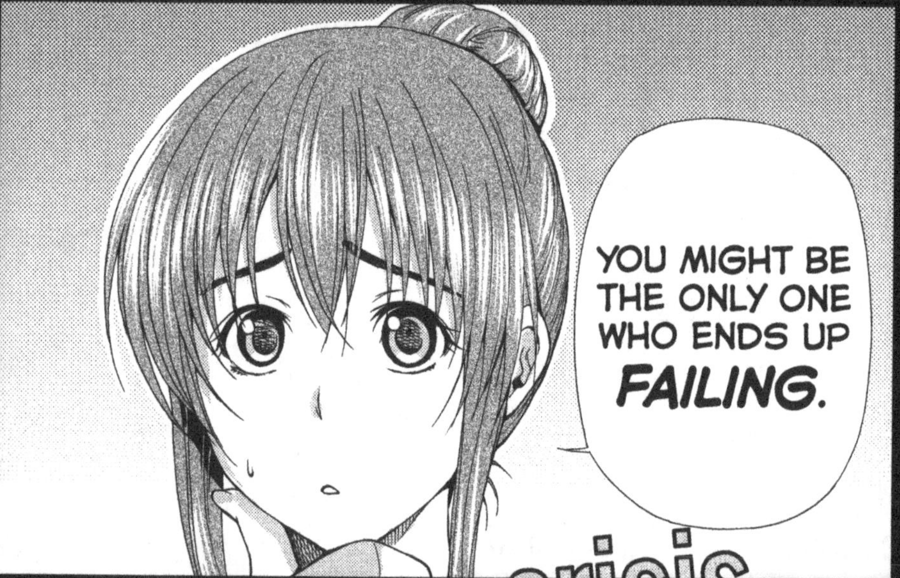
YOU MIGHT BE THE ONLY ONE WHO ENDS UP *FAILING*.

Iori is struck by a crisis!

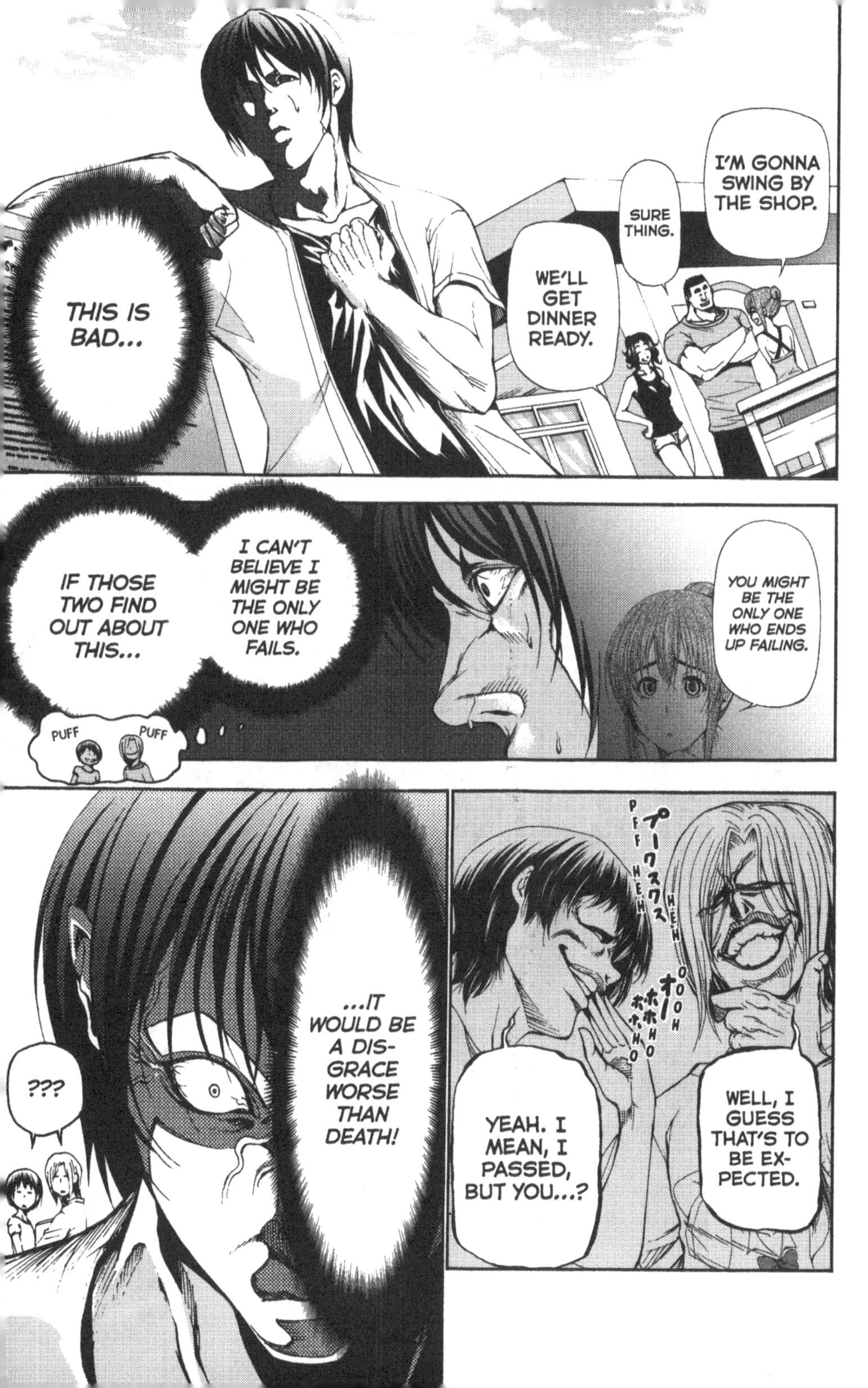
I'M GONNA SWING BY THE SHOP.
SURE THING.
WE'LL GET DINNER READY.
THIS IS BAD...
YOU MIGHT BE THE ONLY ONE WHO ENDS UP FAILING.
I CAN'T BELIEVE I MIGHT BE THE ONLY ONE WHO FAILS.
IF THOSE TWO FIND OUT ABOUT THIS...
PUFF
PUFF
プークスクス
PFF HEH HEH
オーホホホホ
OOOH HOHOHO
WELL, I GUESS THAT'S TO BE EXPECTED.
YEAH. I MEAN, I PASSED, BUT YOU...?
...IT WOULD BE A DISGRACE WORSE THAN DEATH!
???

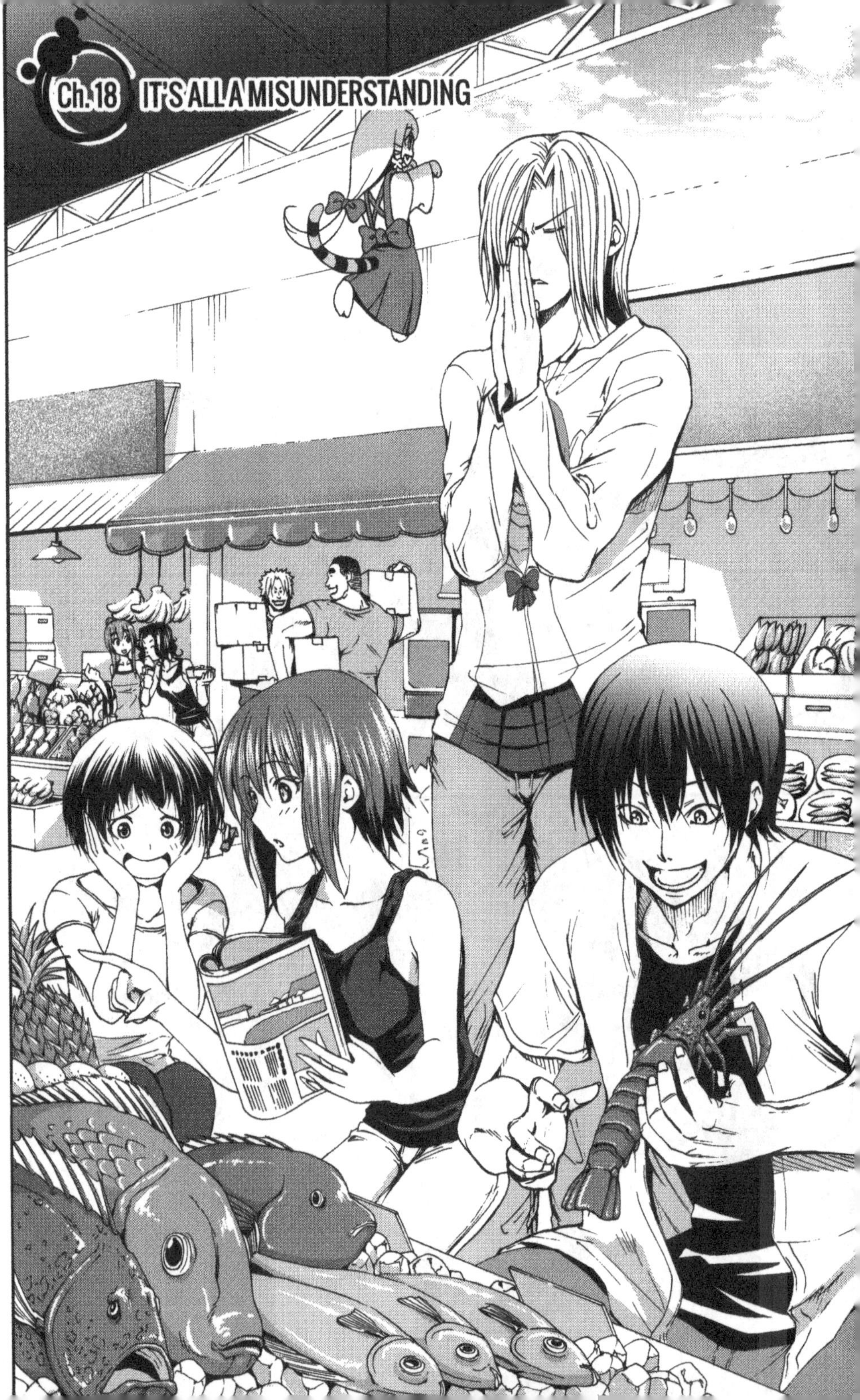
Ch. 18 IT'S ALL A MISUNDERSTANDING

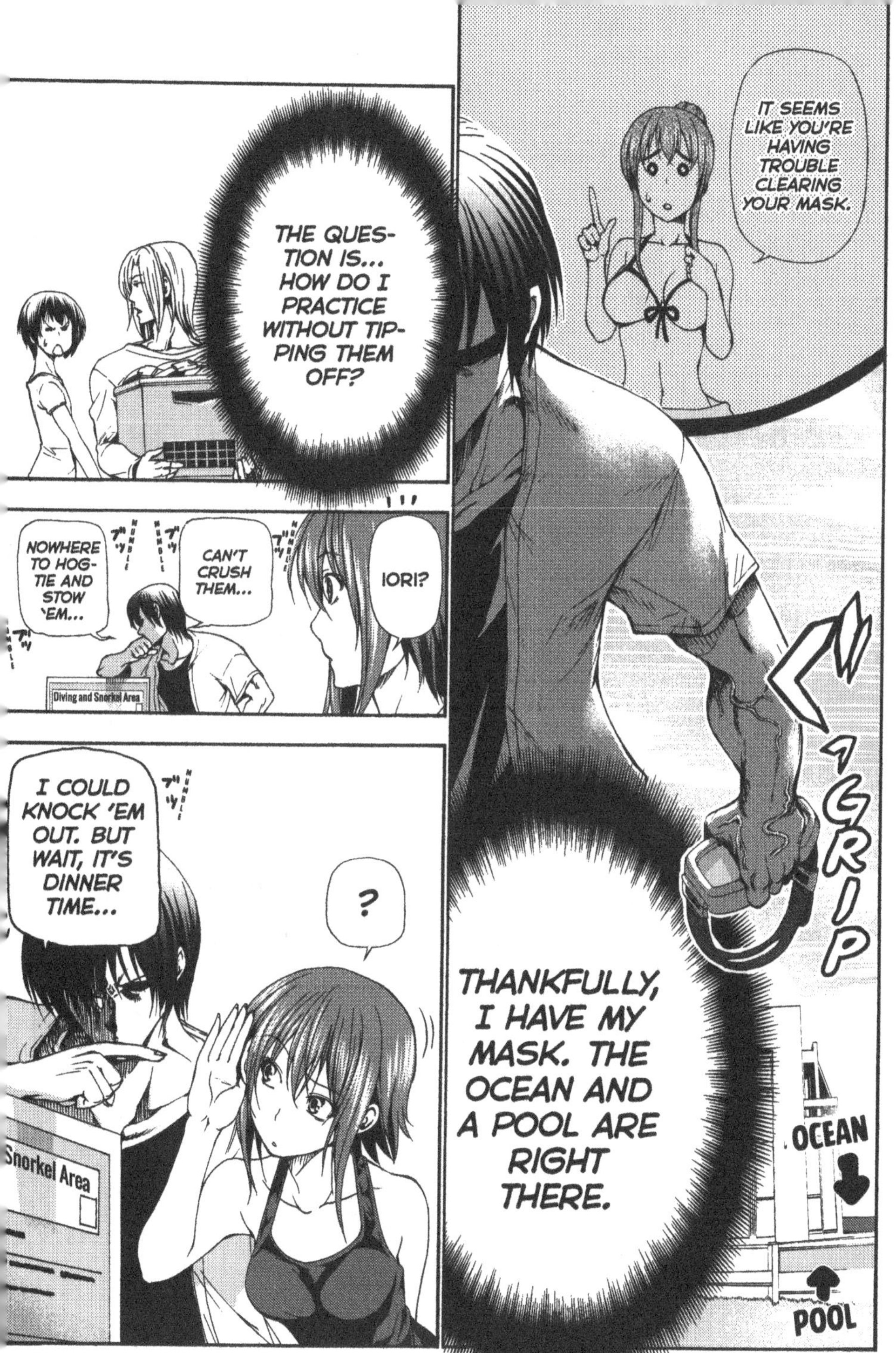

IT SEEMS LIKE YOU'RE HAVING TROUBLE CLEARING YOUR MASK.
GRIP
THANKFULLY, I HAVE MY MASK. THE OCEAN AND A POOL ARE RIGHT THERE.
OCEAN
POOL
THE QUES-TION IS... HOW DO I PRACTICE WITHOUT TIP-PING THEM OFF?
IORI?
CAN'T CRUSH THEM...
NOWHERE TO HOG-TIE AND STOW 'EM...
Diving and Snorkel Area
?
I COULD KNOCK 'EM OUT. BUT WAIT, IT'S DINNER TIME...
Snorkel Area

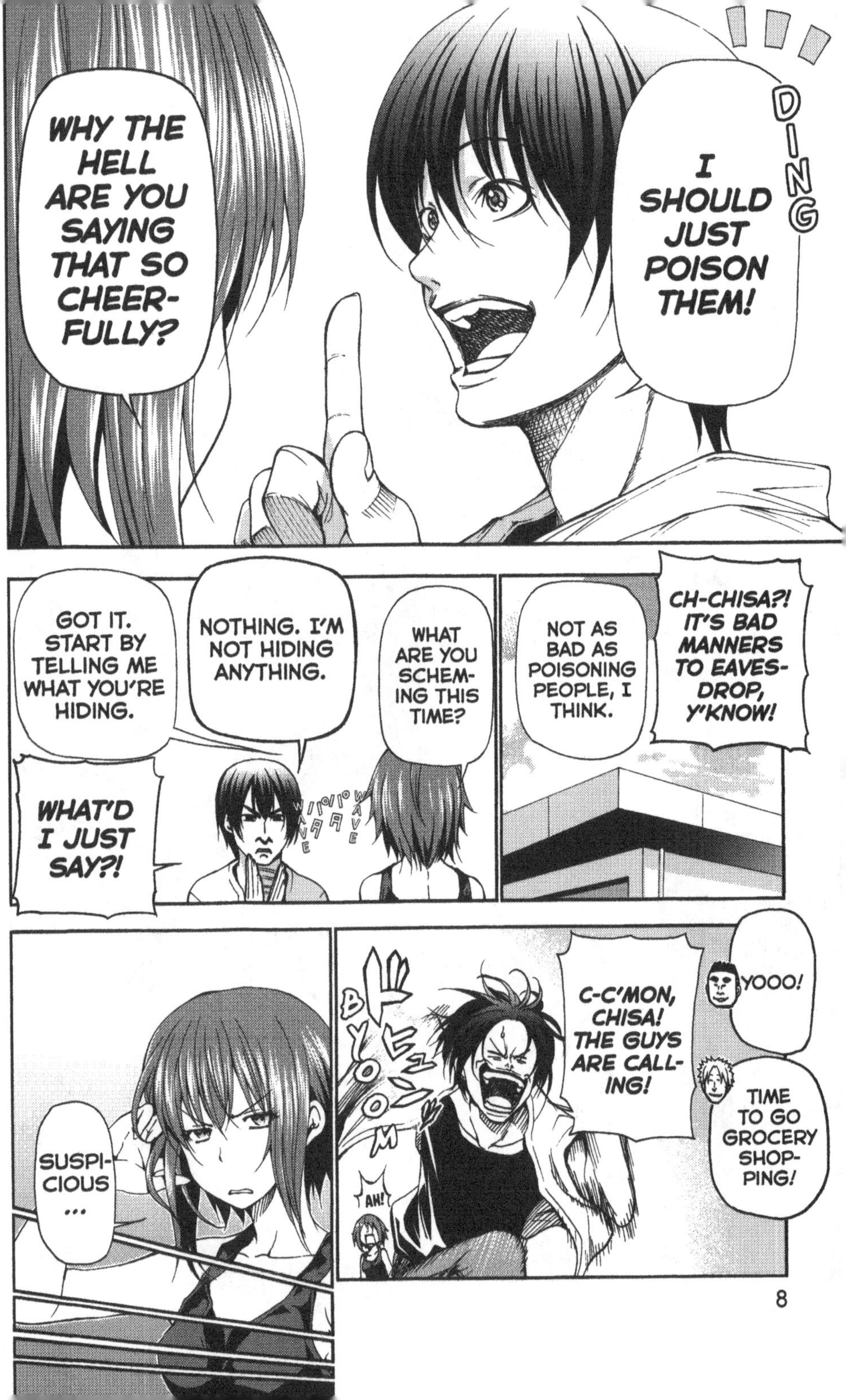
DING
I SHOULD JUST POISON THEM!
WHY THE HELL ARE YOU SAYING THAT SO CHEERFULLY?
CH-CHISA?! IT'S BAD MANNERS TO EAVESDROP, Y'KNOW!
NOT AS BAD AS POISONING PEOPLE, I THINK.
WHAT ARE YOU SCHEMING THIS TIME?
NOTHING. I'M NOT HIDING ANYTHING.
GOT IT. START BY TELLING ME WHAT YOU'RE HIDING.
WAVE
WHAT'D I JUST SAY?!
YOOO!
TIME TO GO GROCERY SHOPPING!
C-C'MON, CHISA! THE GUYS ARE CALLING!
BYOOOM
AH!
SUSPICIOUS...

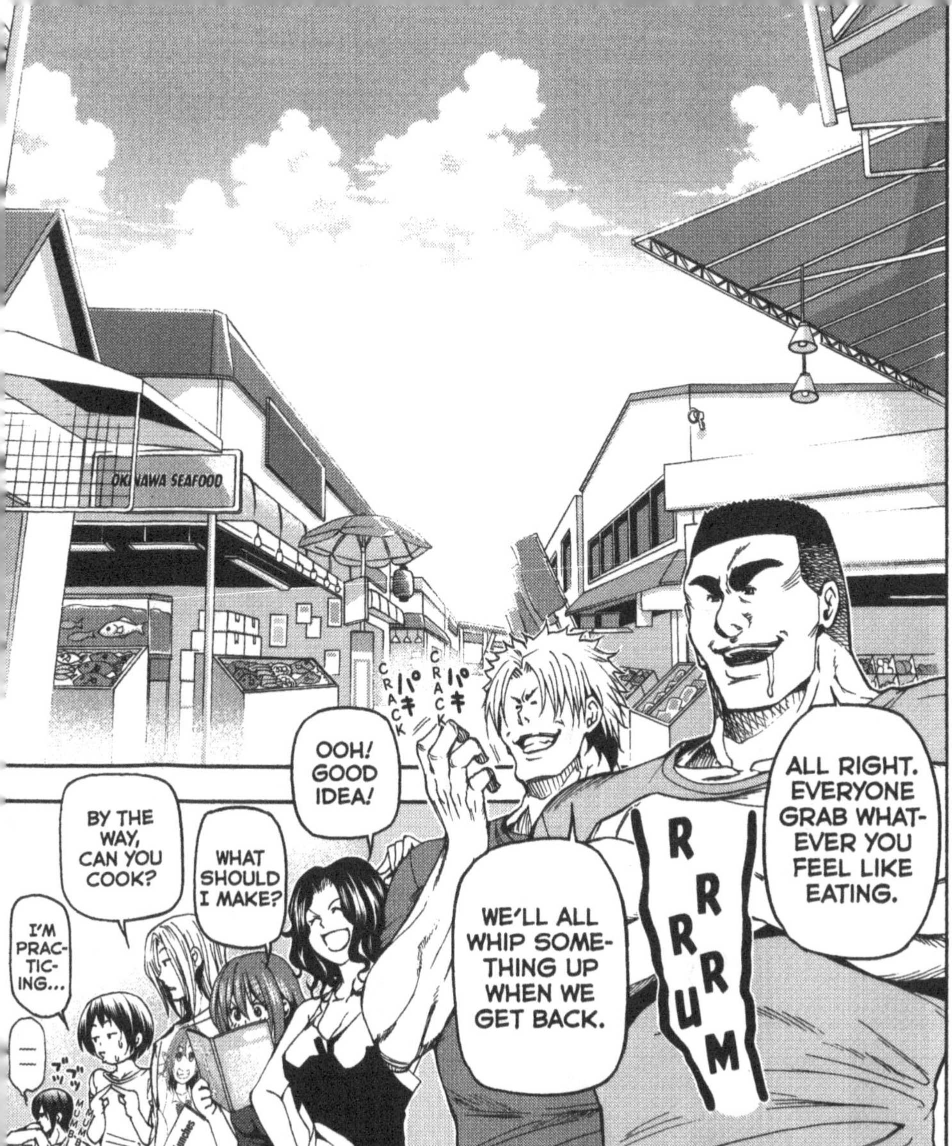
OKINAWA SEAFOOD
ALL RIGHT. EVERYONE GRAB WHAT-EVER YOU FEEL LIKE EATING.
RRRRUM
WE'LL ALL WHIP SOME-THING UP WHEN WE GET BACK.
パキ CRACK
パキ CRACK
OOH! GOOD IDEA!
WHAT SHOULD I MAKE?
BY THE WAY, CAN YOU COOK?
I'M PRAC-TIC-ING...
—
ブツブツ MUMBLE
Moe Lunches
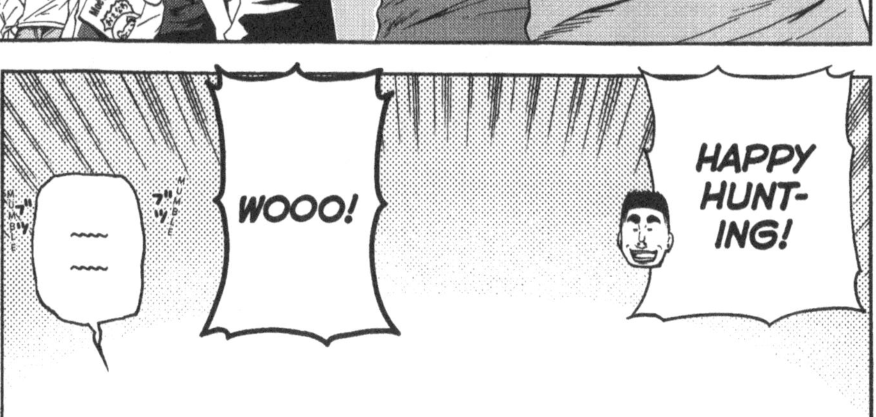
HAPPY HUNT-ING!
WOOO!
ブツ MUMBLE
ブツ MUMBLE
~~~
~~~

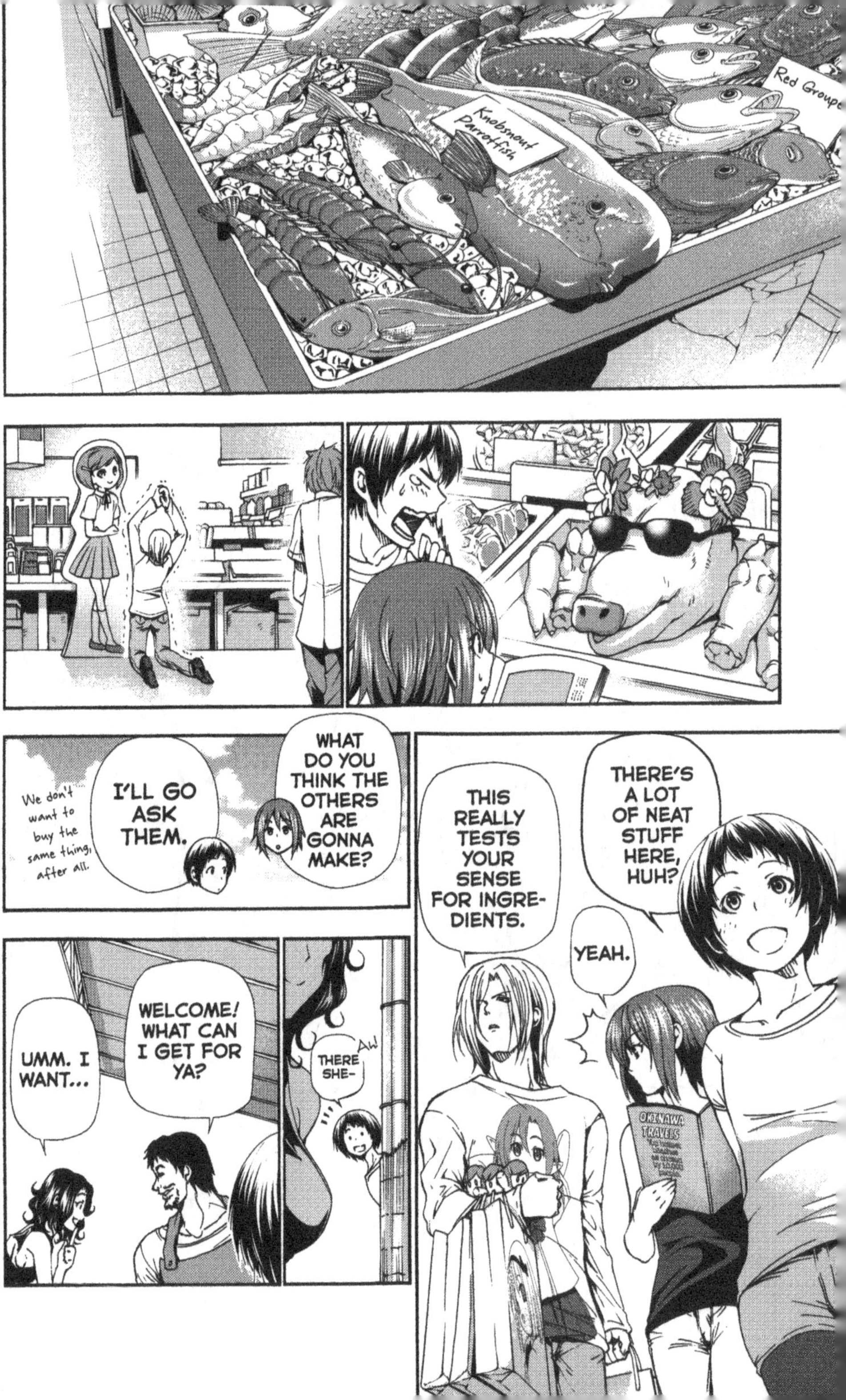
Red Groupe
Knobsnout Parrotfish
THERE'S A LOT OF NEAT STUFF HERE, HUH?
THIS REALLY TESTS YOUR SENSE FOR INGRE-DIENTS.
YEAH.
OKINAWA TRAVELS
WHAT DO YOU THINK THE OTHERS ARE GONNA MAKE?
I'LL GO ASK THEM.
We don't want to buy the same thing, after all.
THERE SHE-
AW!
WELCOME! WHAT CAN I GET FOR YA?
UMM. I WANT...

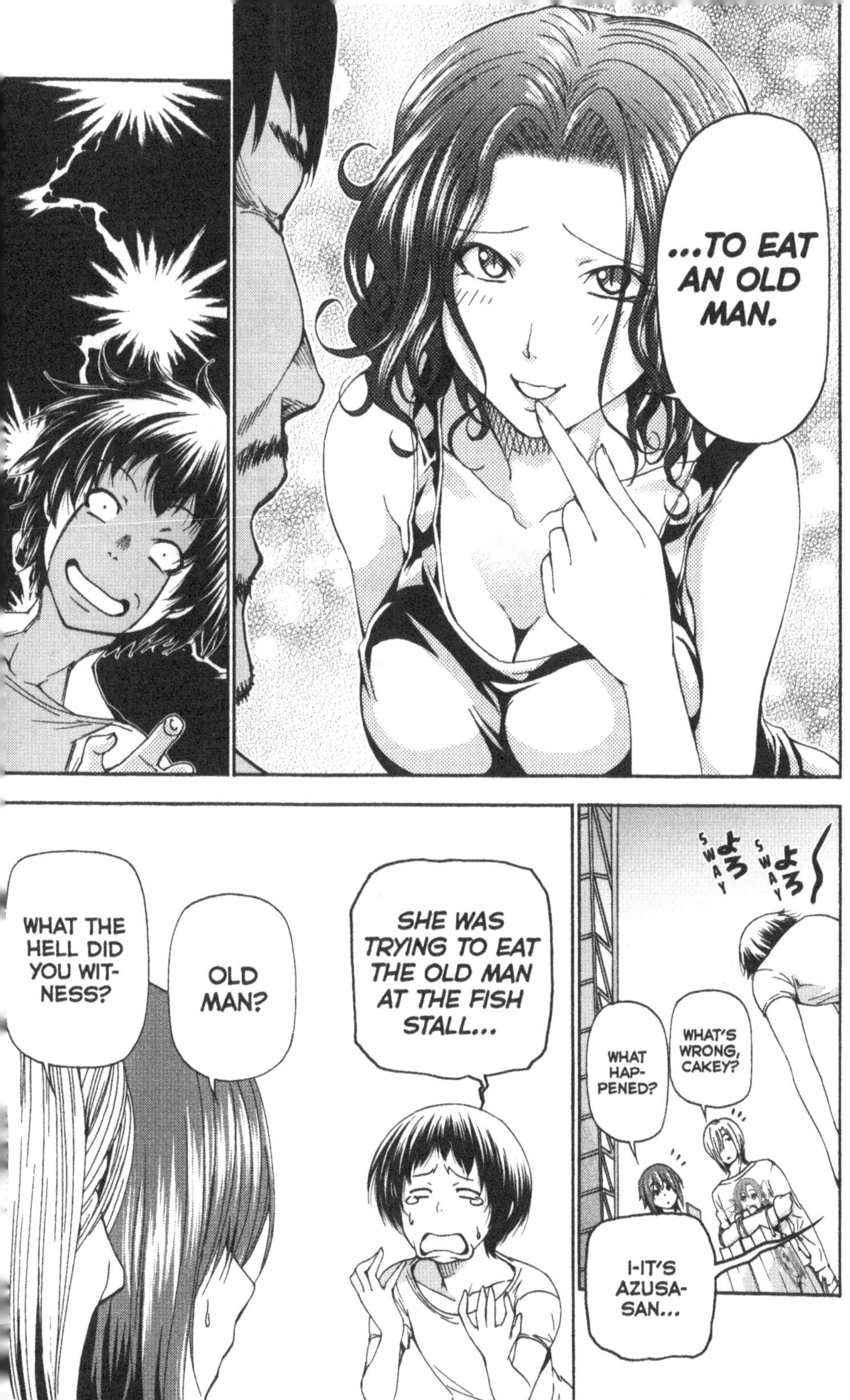
...TO EAT AN OLD MAN.
よろ SWAY よろ SWAY
WHAT'S WRONG, CAKEY?
WHAT HAPPENED?
I-IT'S AZUSA-SAN...
SHE WAS TRYING TO EAT THE OLD MAN AT THE FISH STALL...
OLD MAN?
WHAT THE HELL DID YOU WITNESS?

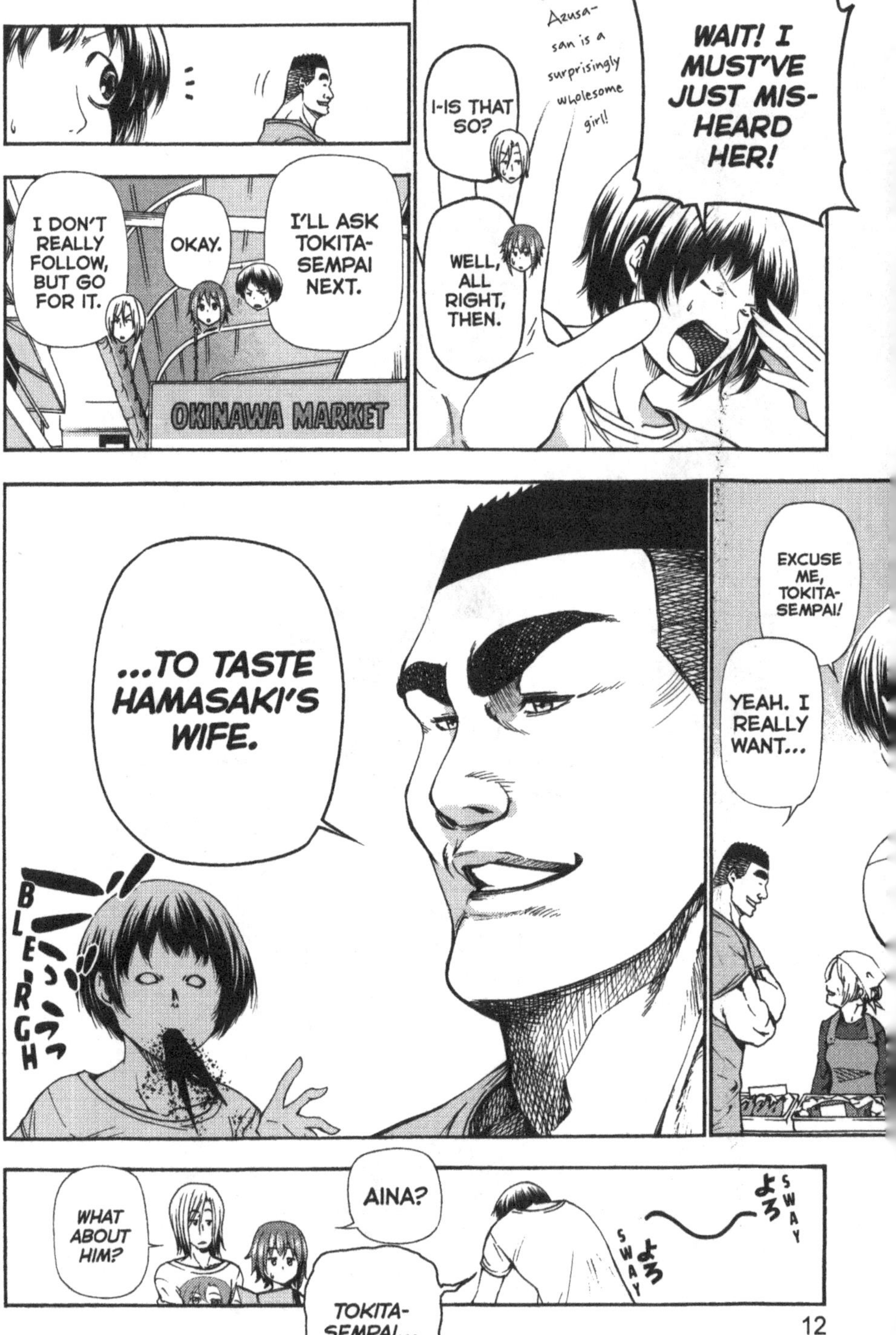

WAIT! I MUST'VE JUST MIS-HEARD HER!
I'm sure Azusa-san is a surprisingly wholesome girl!
I-IS THAT SO?
WELL, ALL RIGHT, THEN.
I'LL ASK TOKITA-SEMPAI NEXT.
OKAY.
I DON'T REALLY FOLLOW, BUT GO FOR IT.
OKINAWA MARKET
EXCUSE ME, TOKITA-SEMPAI!
YEAH. I REALLY WANT...
...TO TASTE HAMASAKI'S WIFE.
BLEERGH
よろ SWAY
よろ SWAY
TOKITA-SEMPAI...
AINA?
WHAT ABOUT HIM?

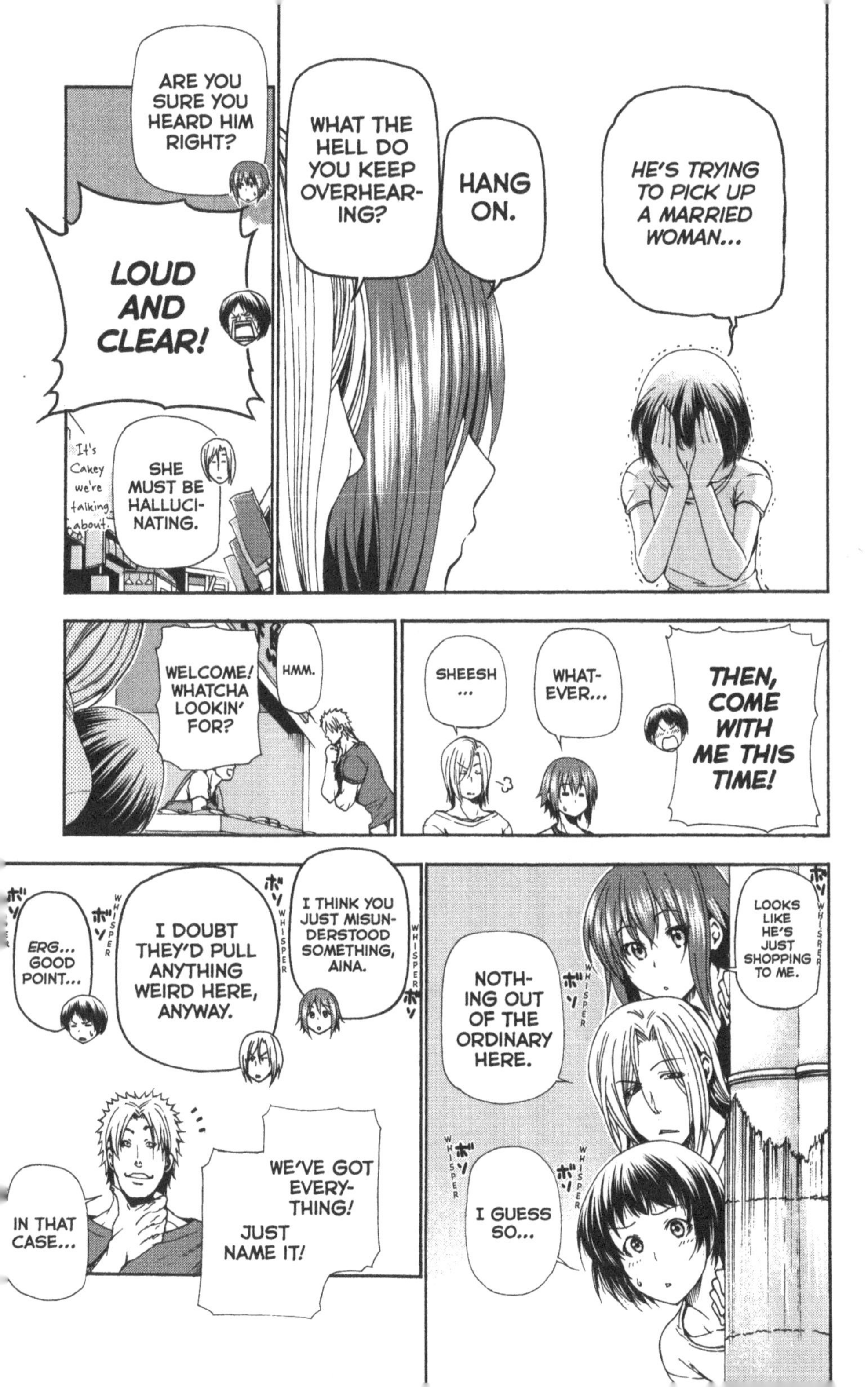
HE'S TRYING TO PICK UP A MARRIED WOMAN...
HANG ON.
WHAT THE HELL DO YOU KEEP OVERHEARING?
ARE YOU SURE YOU HEARD HIM RIGHT?
LOUD AND CLEAR!
SHE MUST BE HALLUCINATING.
It's Cakey we're talking about.
THEN, COME WITH ME THIS TIME!
WHATEVER...
SHEESH...
HMM.
WELCOME! WHATCHA LOOKIN' FOR?
ボソ WHISPER
LOOKS LIKE HE'S JUST SHOPPING TO ME.
ボソ WHISPER
NOTHING OUT OF THE ORDINARY HERE.
ボソ WHISPER
ボソ WHISPER
I GUESS SO...
ボソ WHISPER
I THINK YOU JUST MISUNDERSTOOD SOMETHING, AINA.
ボソ WHISPER
I DOUBT THEY'D PULL ANYTHING WEIRD HERE, ANYWAY.
ボソ WHISPER
ERG... GOOD POINT...
WE'VE GOT EVERYTHING!
JUST NAME IT!
IN THAT CASE...

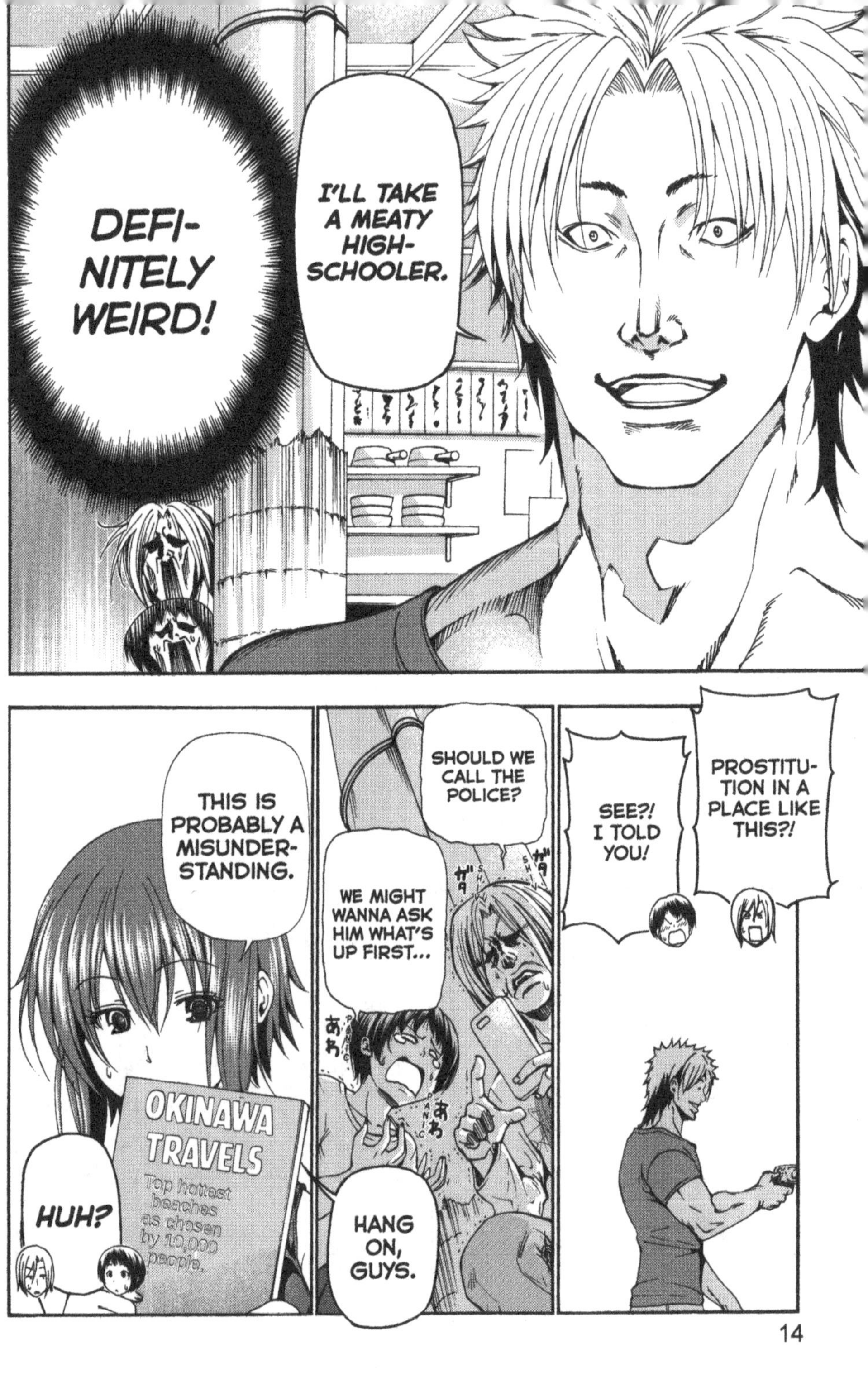
I'LL TAKE A MEATY HIGH-SCHOOLER.
DEFI-NITELY WEIRD!
PROSTITU-TION IN A PLACE LIKE THIS?!
SEE?! I TOLD YOU!
SHOULD WE CALL THE POLICE?
WE MIGHT WANNA ASK HIM WHAT'S UP FIRST...
HANG ON, GUYS.
THIS IS PROBABLY A MISUNDER-STANDING.
OKINAWA TRAVELS
Top hottest beaches as chosen by 10,000 people.
HUH?

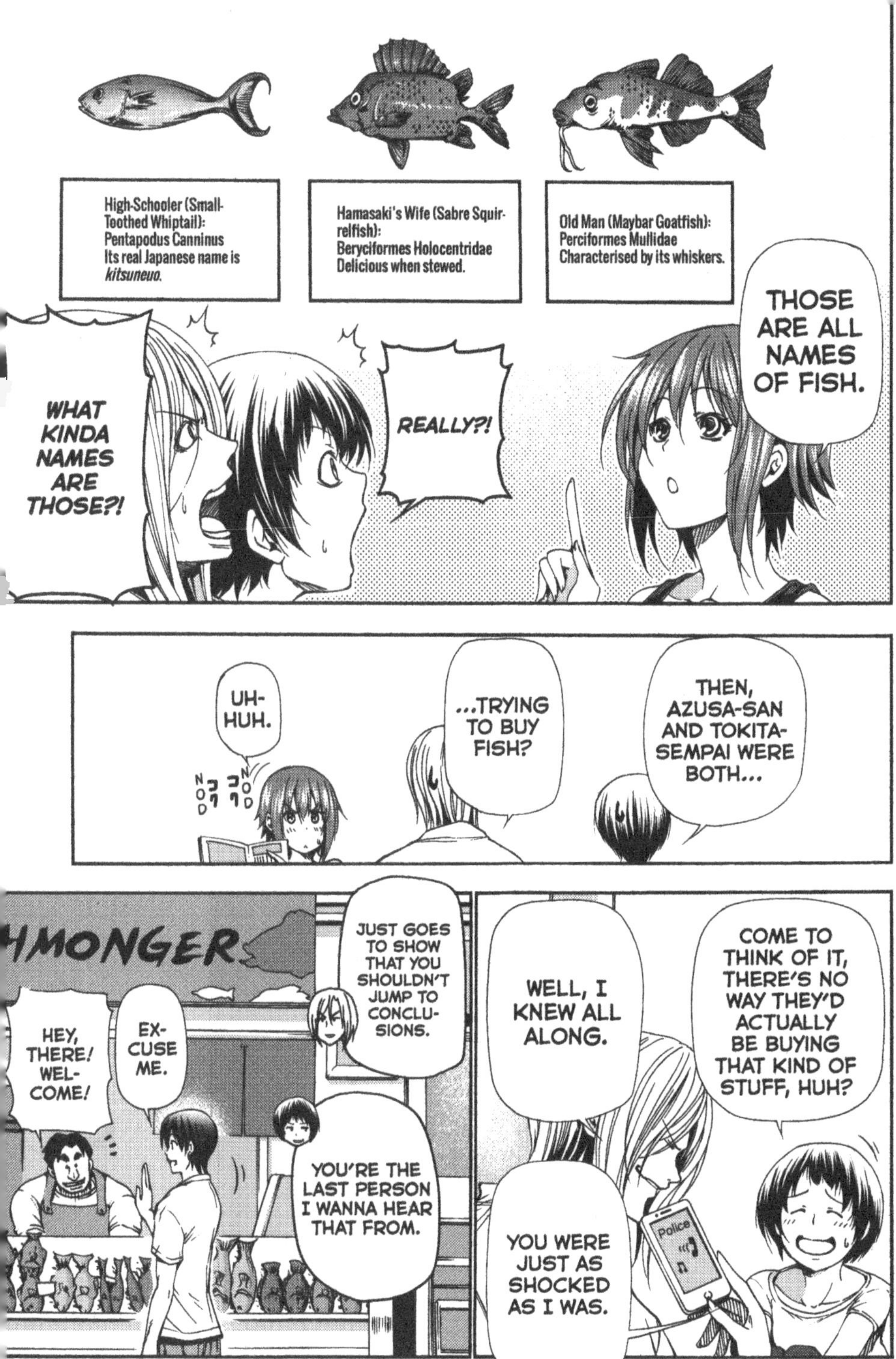
Old Man (Maybar Goatfish): Perciformes Mullidae Characterised by its whiskers.
Hamasaki's Wife (Sabre Squirrelfish): Beryciformes Holocentridae Delicious when stewed.
High-Schooler (Small-Toothed Whiptail): Pentapodus Canninus Its real Japanese name is *kitsuneuo*.
THOSE ARE ALL NAMES OF FISH.
REALLY?!
WHAT KINDA NAMES ARE THOSE?!
THEN, AZUSA-SAN AND TOKITA-SEMPAI WERE BOTH...
...TRYING TO BUY FISH?
UH-HUH.
NOD NOD
COME TO THINK OF IT, THERE'S NO WAY THEY'D ACTUALLY BE BUYING THAT KIND OF STUFF, HUH?
WELL, I KNEW ALL ALONG.
Police
YOU WERE JUST AS SHOCKED AS I WAS.
HMONGER
JUST GOES TO SHOW THAT YOU SHOULDN'T JUMP TO CONCLUSIONS.
YOU'RE THE LAST PERSON I WANNA HEAR THAT FROM.
EX-CUSE ME.
HEY, THERE! WELCOME!

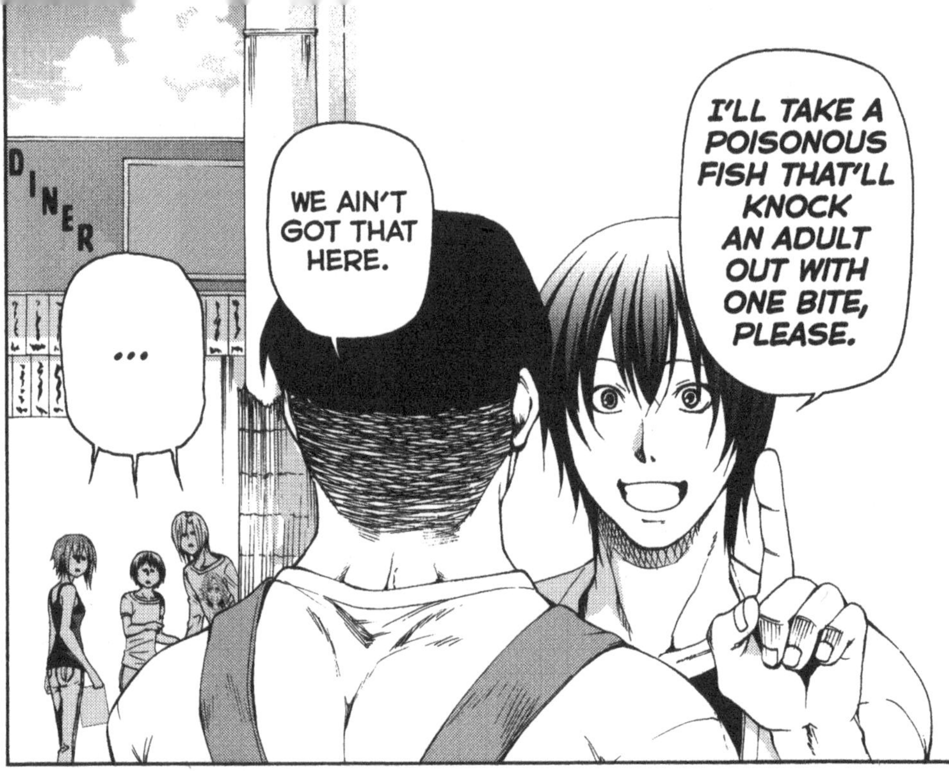
I'LL TAKE A POISONOUS FISH THAT'LL KNOCK AN ADULT OUT WITH ONE BITE, PLEASE.
WE AIN'T GOT THAT HERE.
DINER
...

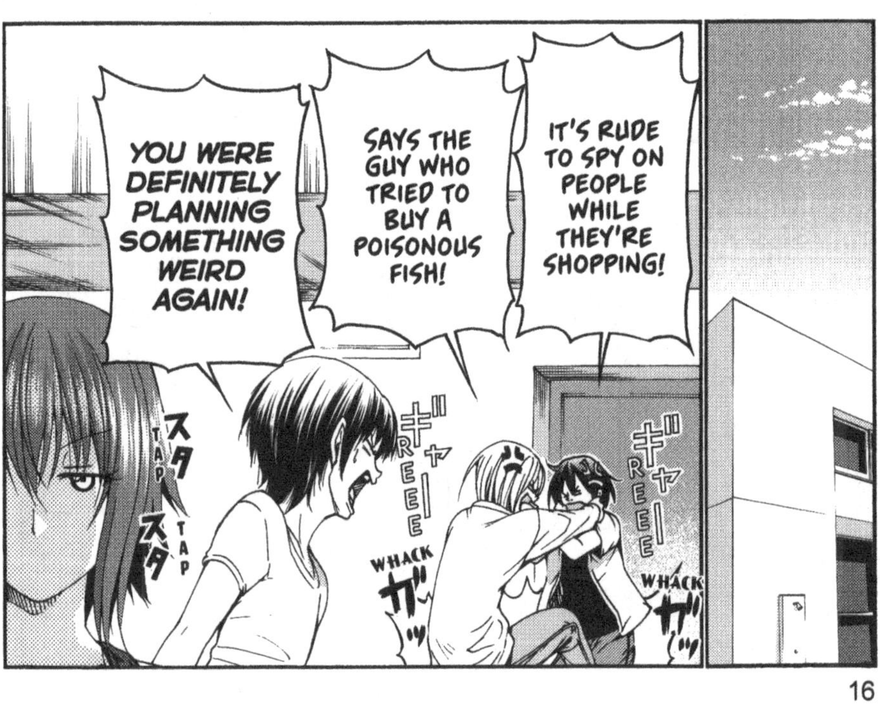
IT'S RUDE TO SPY ON PEOPLE WHILE THEY'RE SHOPPING!
SAYS THE GUY WHO TRIED TO BUY A POISONOUS FISH!
YOU WERE DEFINITELY PLANNING SOMETHING WEIRD AGAIN!
ギャー REEE
WHACK ガッ
ギャー REEE
WHACK ガッ
スタ TAP
スタ TAP

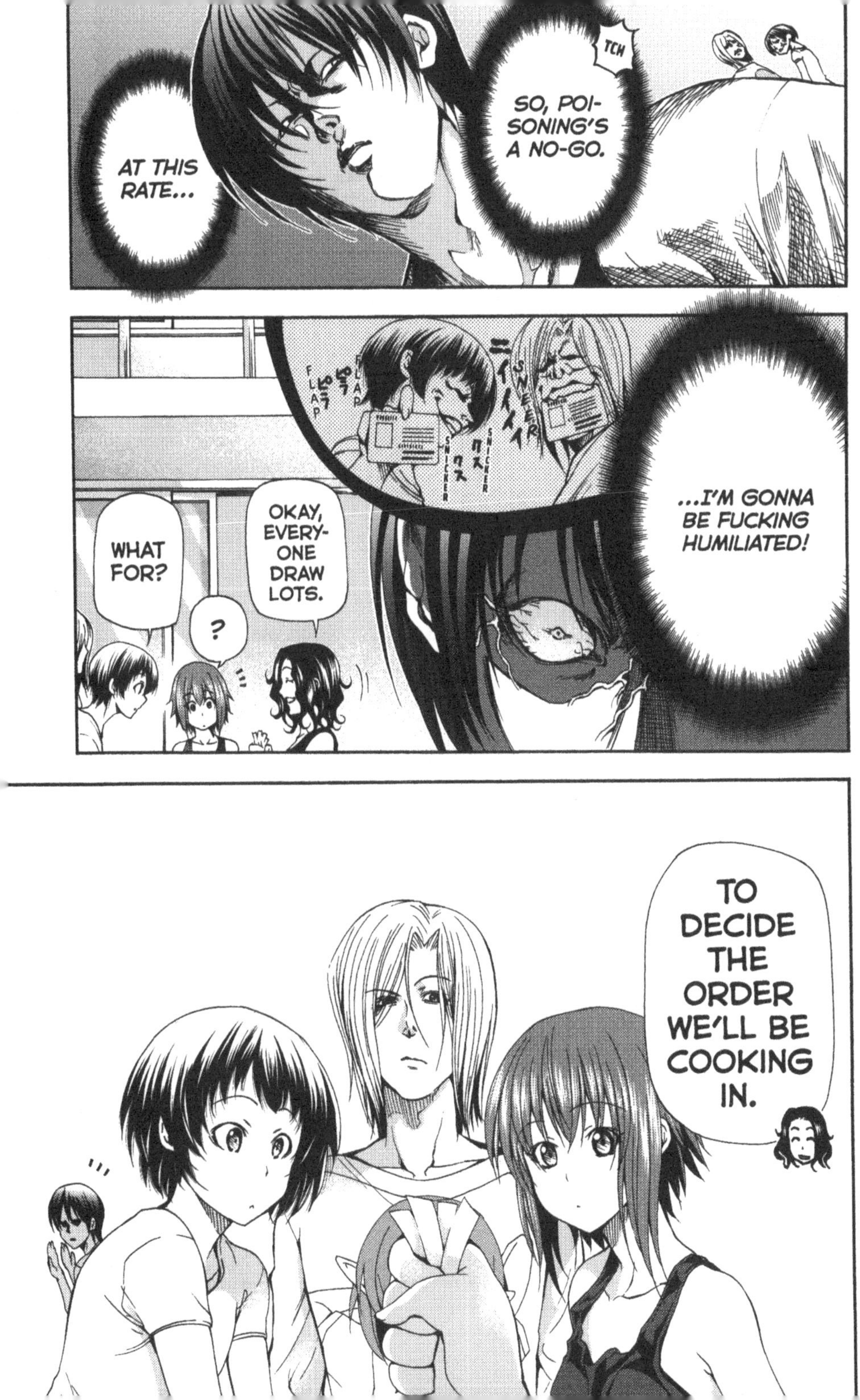
TCH
SO, POI-SONING'S A NO-GO.
AT THIS RATE...
...I'M GONNA BE FUCKING HUMILIATED!
SNEER
SNICKER
SNICKER
FLAP
FLAP
OKAY, EVERY-ONE DRAW LOTS.
?
WHAT FOR?
TO DECIDE THE ORDER WE'LL BE COOKING IN.

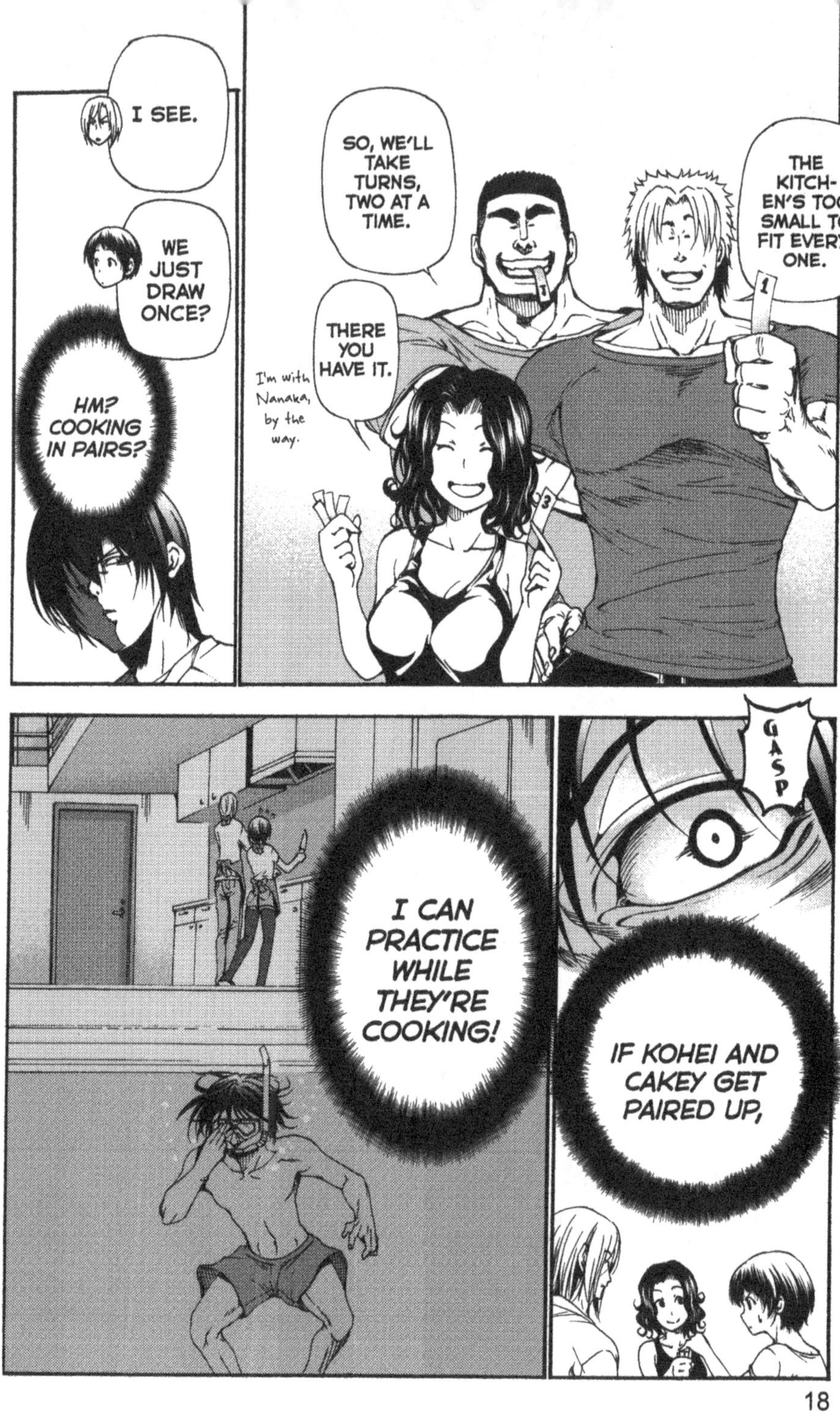
THE KITCHEN'S TOO SMALL TO FIT EVERYONE.
SO, WE'LL TAKE TURNS, TWO AT A TIME.
THERE YOU HAVE IT.
I'm with Nanaka, by the way.
I SEE.
WE JUST DRAW ONCE?
HM? COOKING IN PAIRS?
GASP
IF KOHEI AND CAKEY GET PAIRED UP,
I CAN PRACTICE WHILE THEY'RE COOKING!

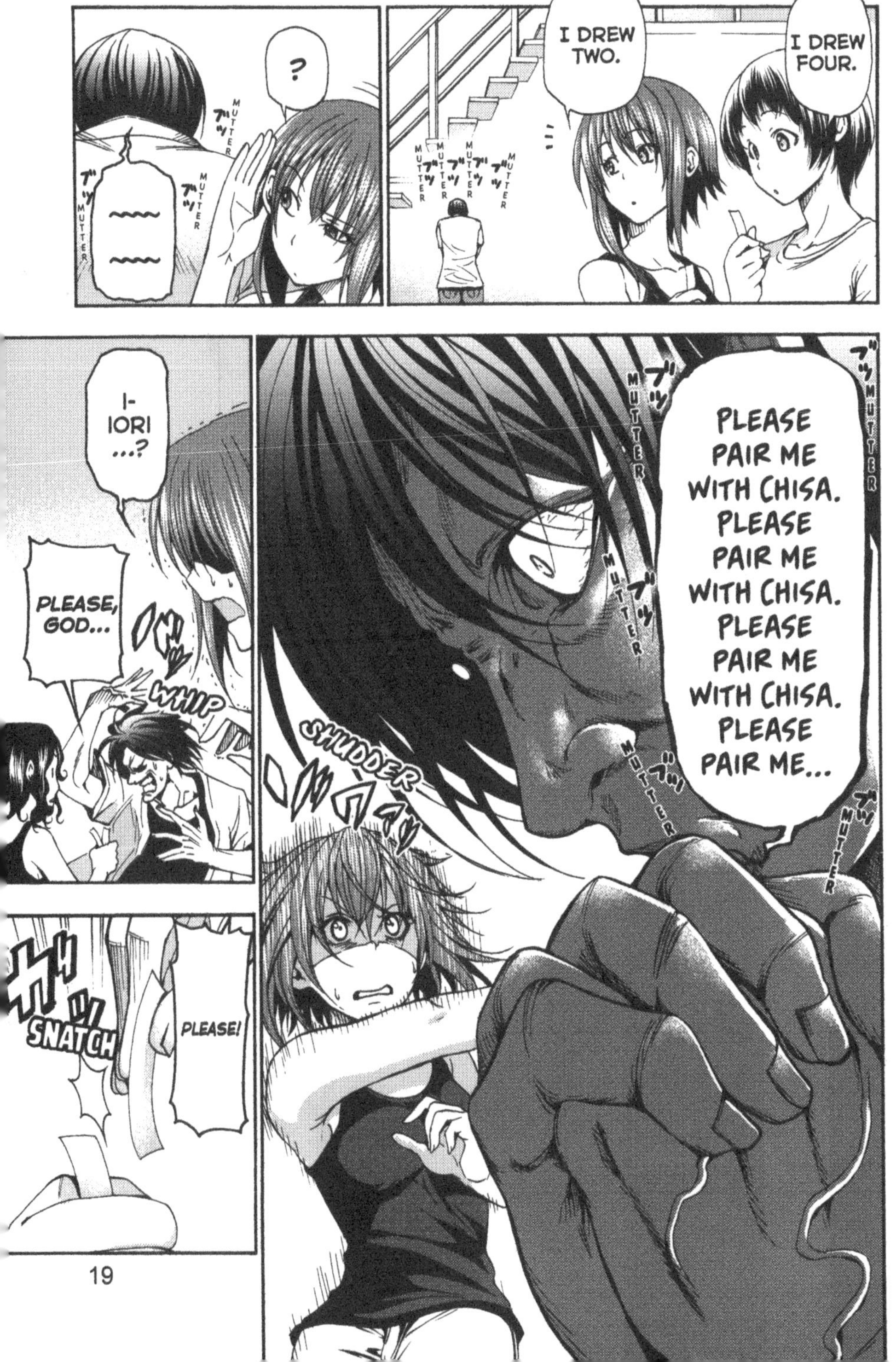
I DREW FOUR.
I DREW TWO.
MUTTER MUTTER MUTTER MUTTER
?
~~~
~~~
MUTTER MUTTER MUTTER
PLEASE PAIR ME WITH CHISA. PLEASE PAIR ME WITH CHISA. PLEASE PAIR ME WITH CHISA. PLEASE PAIR ME...
MUTTER MUTTER MUTTER MUTTER MUTTER
SHUDDER
I- IORI ...?
PLEASE, GOD...
WHIP
PLEASE!
SNATCH

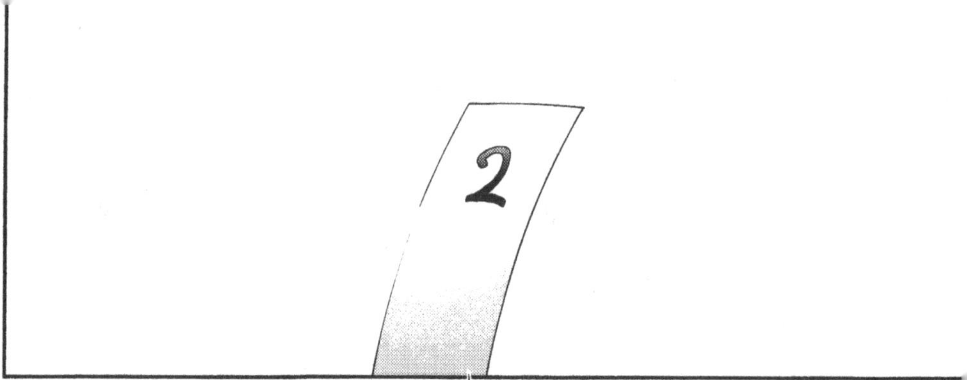
2
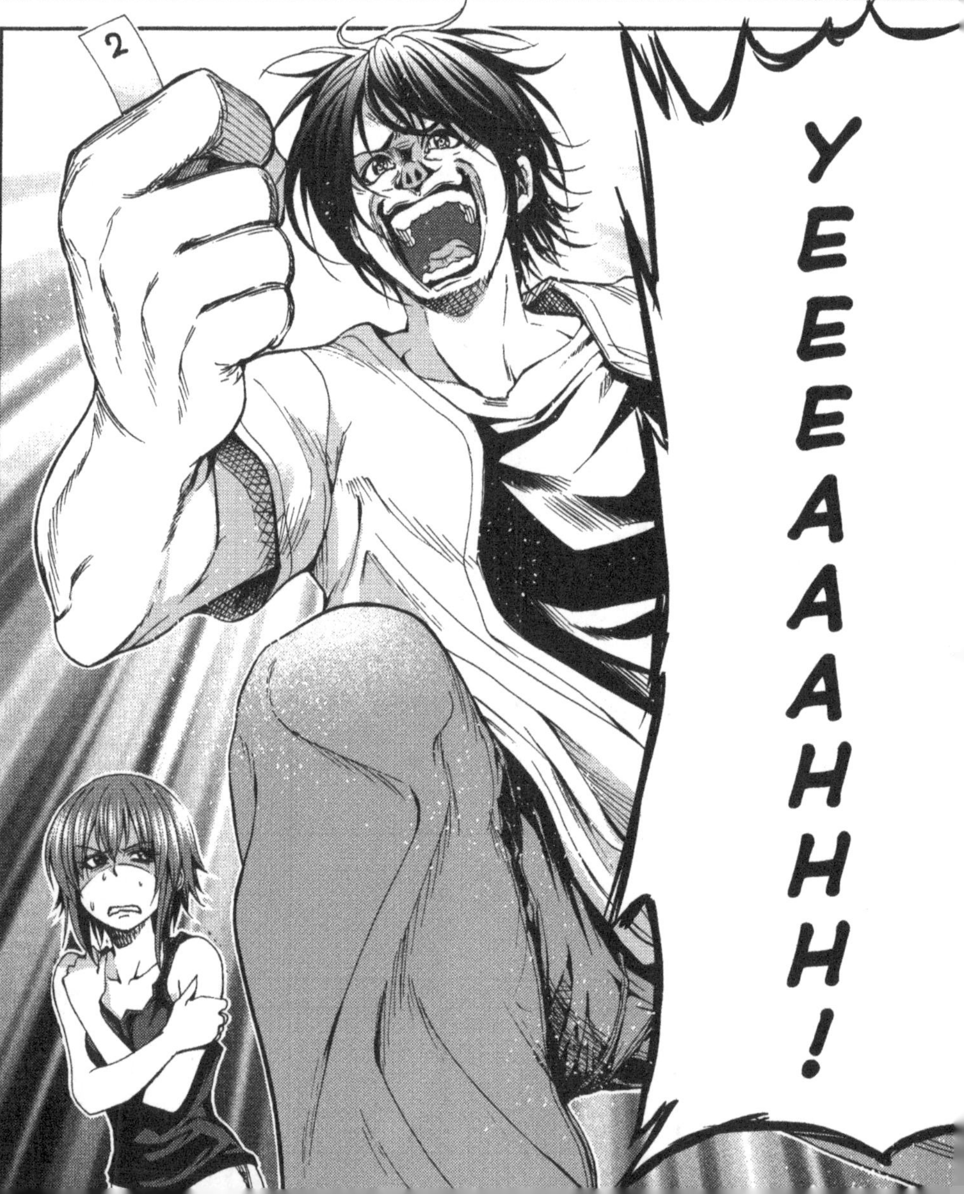
2
YEEEAAAAHHHH!

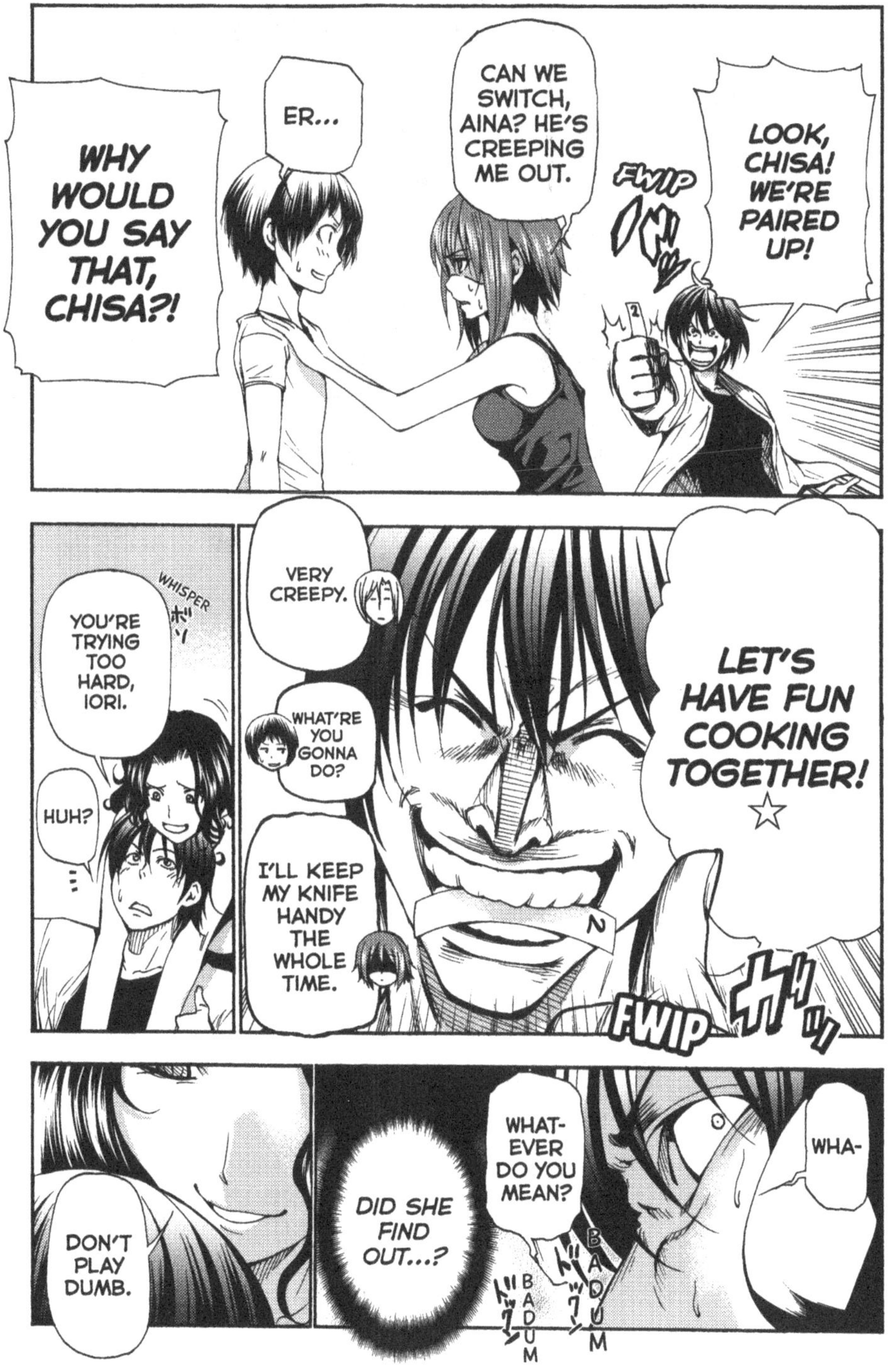
LOOK, CHISA! WE'RE PAIRED UP!
FWIP
CAN WE SWITCH, AINA? HE'S CREEPING ME OUT.
ER...
WHY WOULD YOU SAY THAT, CHISA?!
LET'S HAVE FUN COOKING TOGETHER! ☆
FWIP
VERY CREEPY.
WHAT'RE YOU GONNA DO?
I'LL KEEP MY KNIFE HANDY THE WHOLE TIME.
WHISPER
YOU'RE TRYING TOO HARD, IORI.
HUH?
...
WHA-
WHAT-EVER DO YOU MEAN?
BADUM
DID SHE FIND OUT...?
BADUM
DON'T PLAY DUMB.

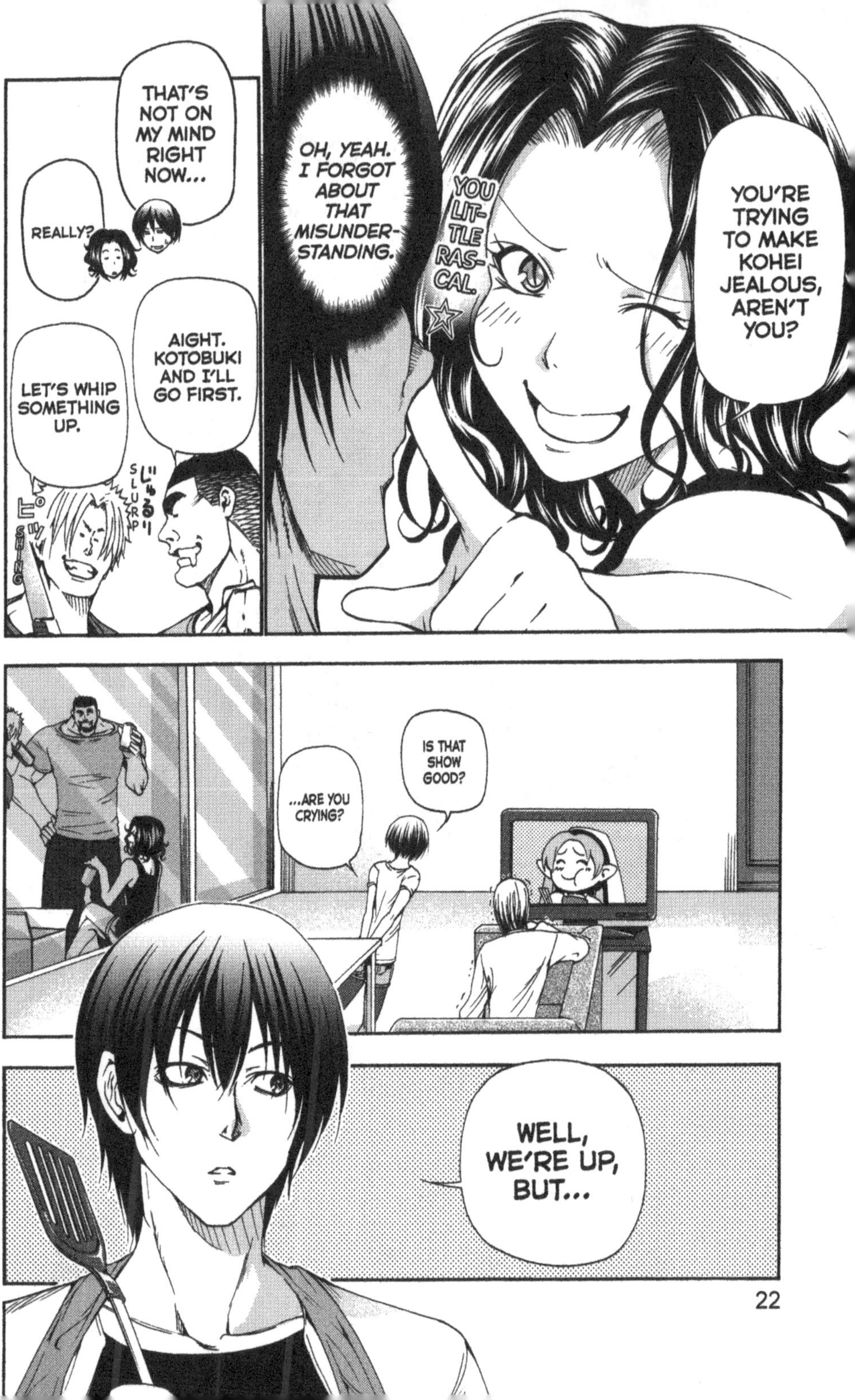
YOU'RE TRYING TO MAKE KOHEI JEALOUS, AREN'T YOU?
YOU LITTLE RASCAL. ☆
OH, YEAH. I FORGOT ABOUT THAT MISUNDERSTANDING.
THAT'S NOT ON MY MIND RIGHT NOW...
REALLY?
AIGHT. KOTOBUKI AND I'LL GO FIRST.
LET'S WHIP SOMETHING UP.
SLURP
SHING
IS THAT SHOW GOOD?
...ARE YOU CRYING?
WELL, WE'RE UP, BUT...

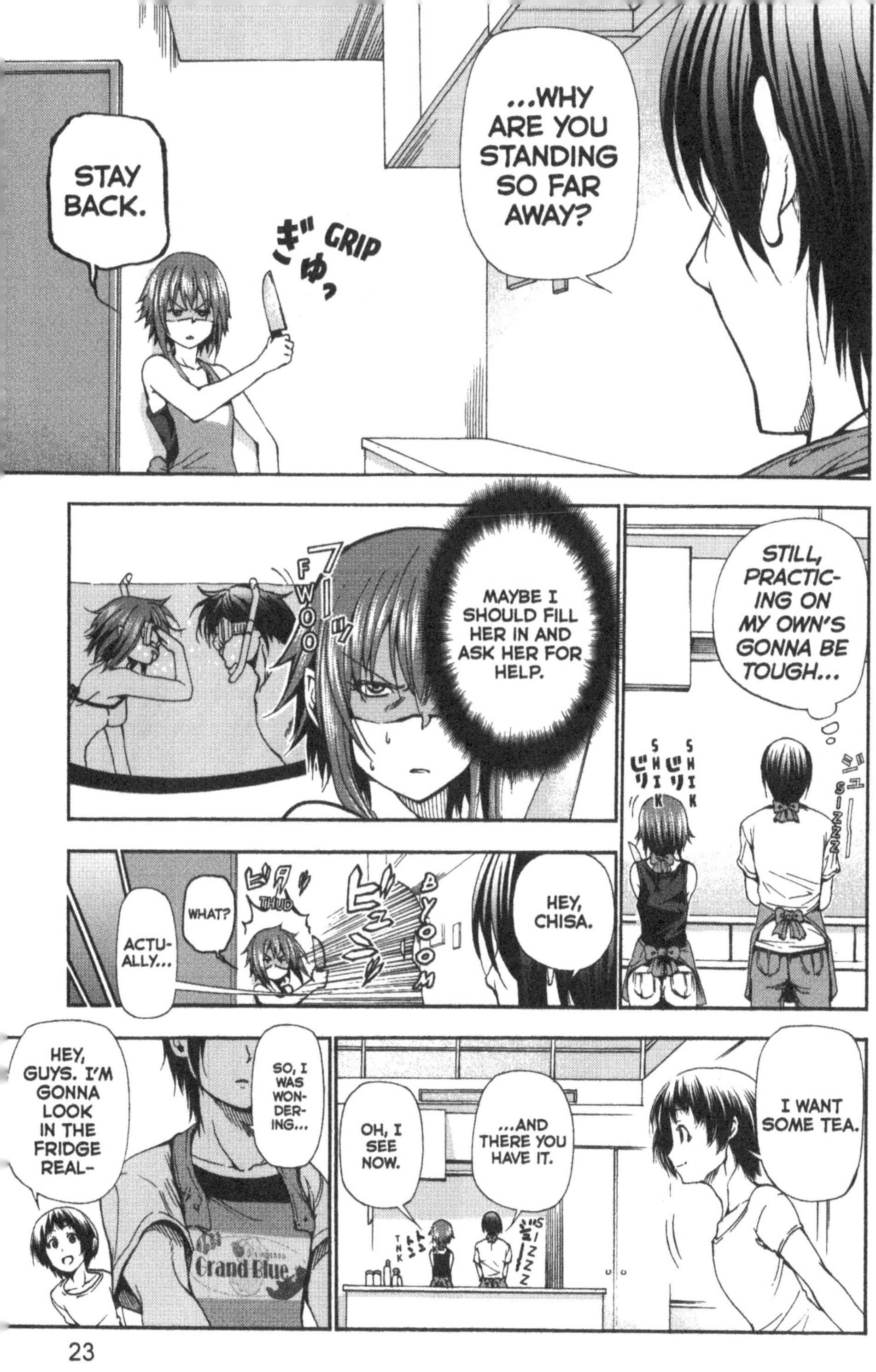
...WHY ARE YOU STANDING SO FAR AWAY?
STAY BACK.
GRIP
STILL, PRACTICING ON MY OWN'S GONNA BE TOUGH...
SHIK SHIK
SIZZZ
MAYBE I SHOULD FILL HER IN AND ASK HER FOR HELP.
FWOO
HEY, CHISA.
BYOOOM
THUD
WHAT?
ACTU-ALLY...
I WANT SOME TEA.
...AND THERE YOU HAVE IT.
SIZZZ
TNK
OH, I SEE NOW.
SO, I WAS WONDER-ING...
Grand Blue
HEY, GUYS. I'M GONNA LOOK IN THE FRIDGE REAL-

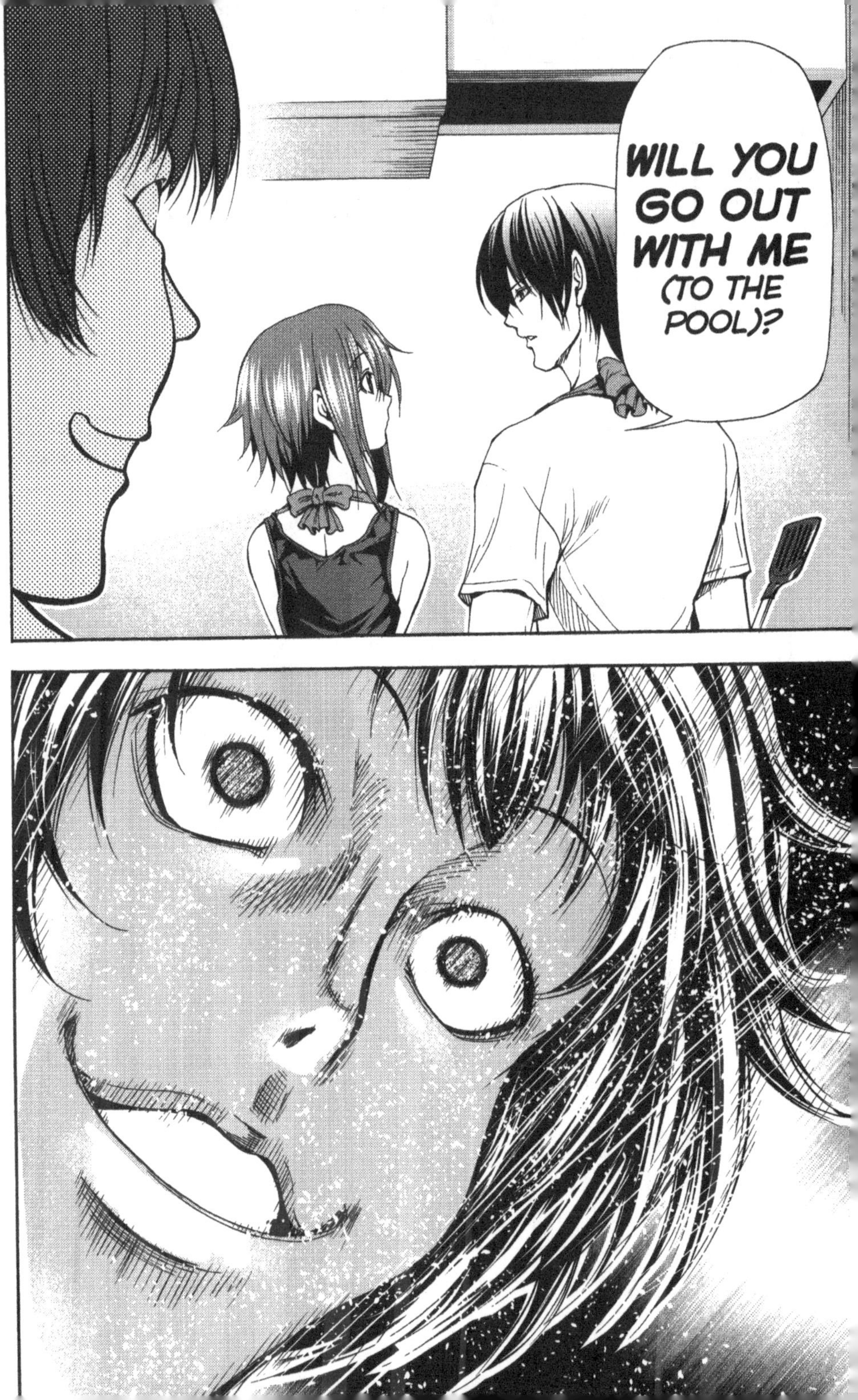
WILL YOU GO OUT WITH ME (TO THE POOL)?

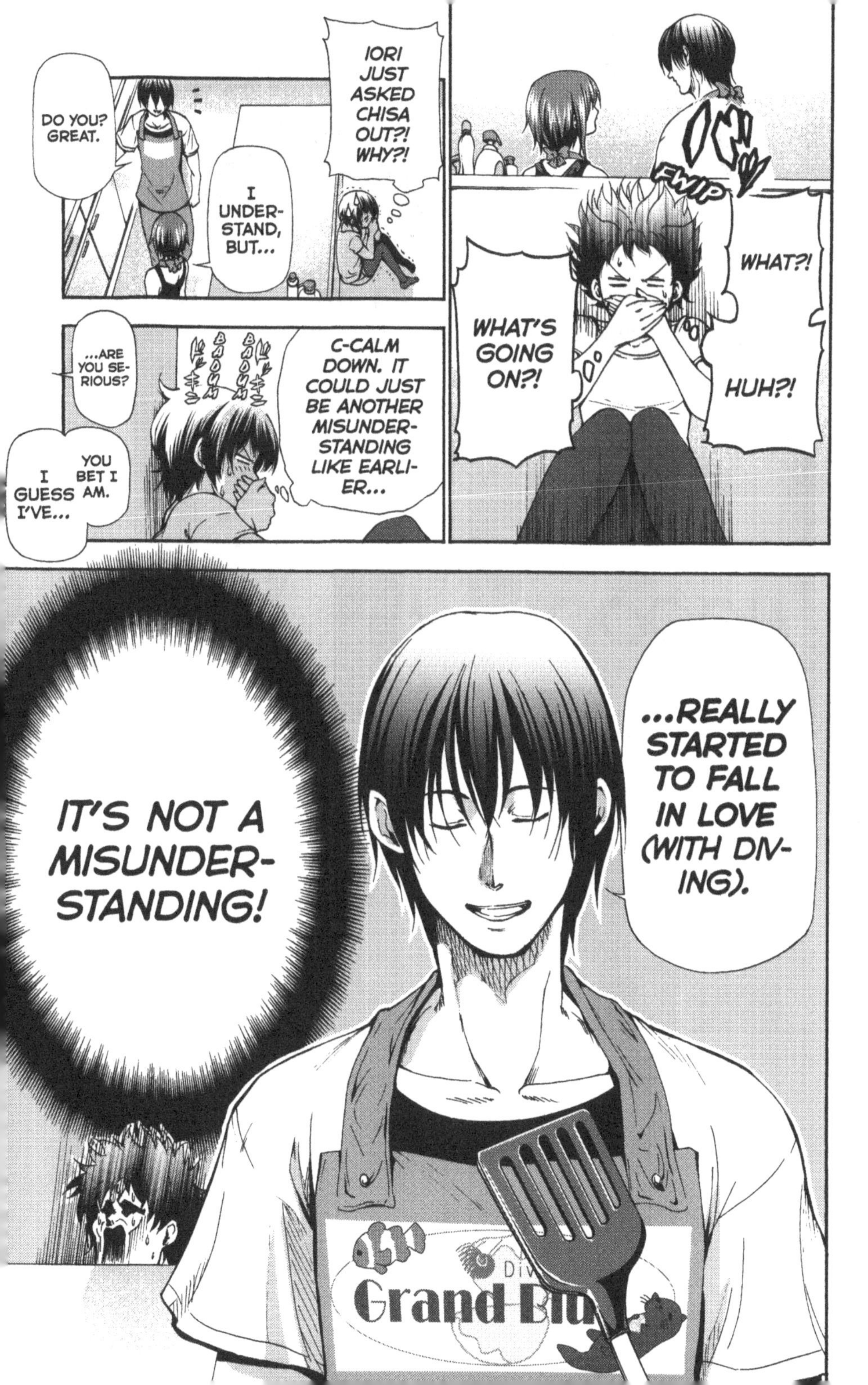
FWIP
WHAT?!
HUH?!
WHAT'S GOING ON?!
IORI JUST ASKED CHISA OUT?! WHY?!
I UNDERSTAND, BUT...
DO YOU? GREAT.
C-CALM DOWN. IT COULD JUST BE ANOTHER MISUNDERSTANDING LIKE EARLIER...
BADUM
BADUM
...ARE YOU SERIOUS?
YOU BET I AM.
I GUESS I'VE...
...REALLY STARTED TO FALL IN LOVE (WITH DIVING).
IT'S NOT A MISUNDERSTANDING!
Grand Blu

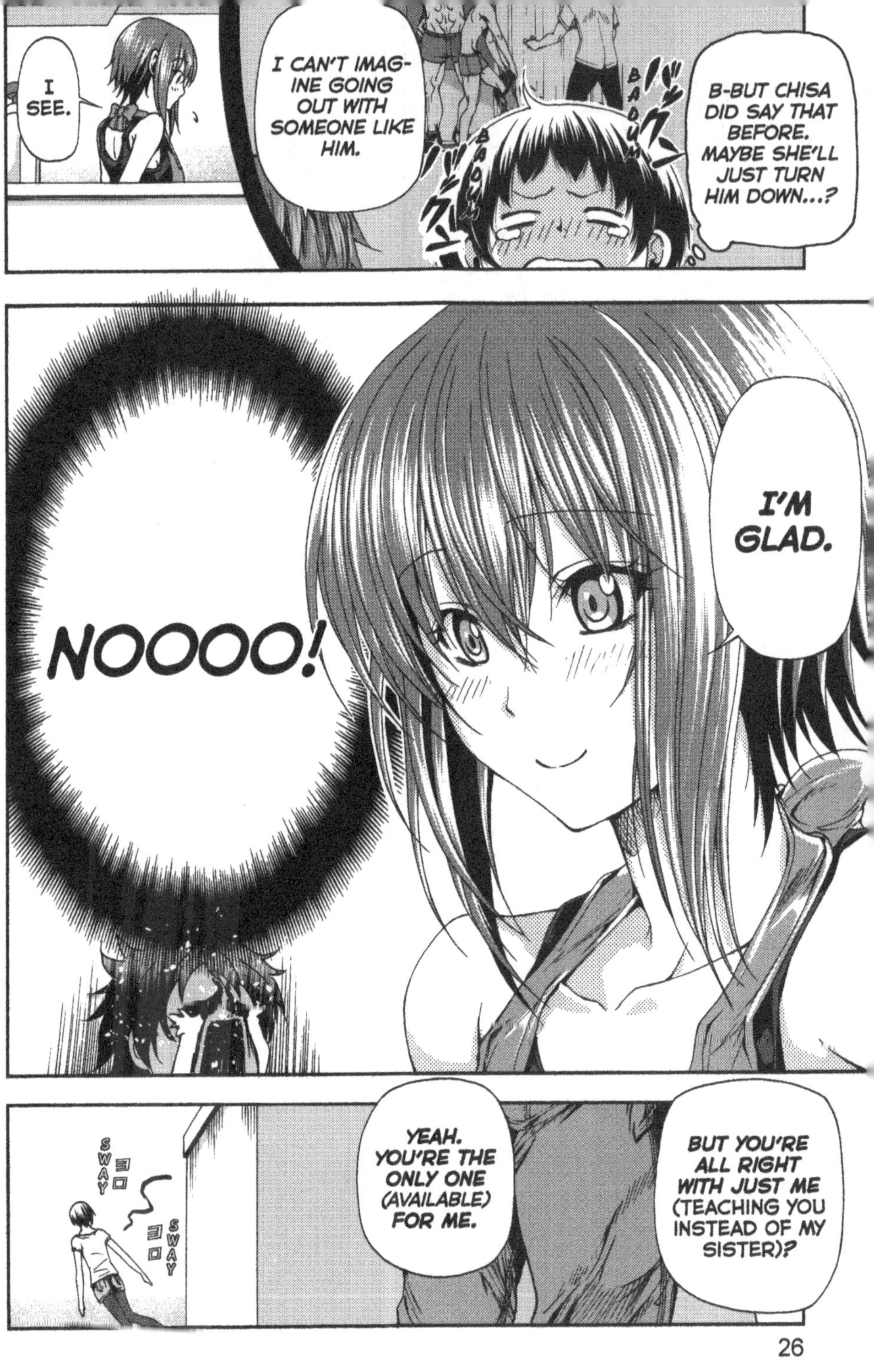
B-BUT CHISA DID SAY THAT BEFORE. MAYBE SHE'LL JUST TURN HIM DOWN...?
BADUM
BADUM
I CAN'T IMAG-INE GOING OUT WITH SOMEONE LIKE HIM.
I SEE.
I'M GLAD.
NOOOO!
BUT YOU'RE ALL RIGHT WITH JUST ME (TEACHING YOU INSTEAD OF MY SISTER)?
YEAH. YOU'RE THE ONLY ONE (AVAILABLE) FOR ME.
SWAY
SWAY

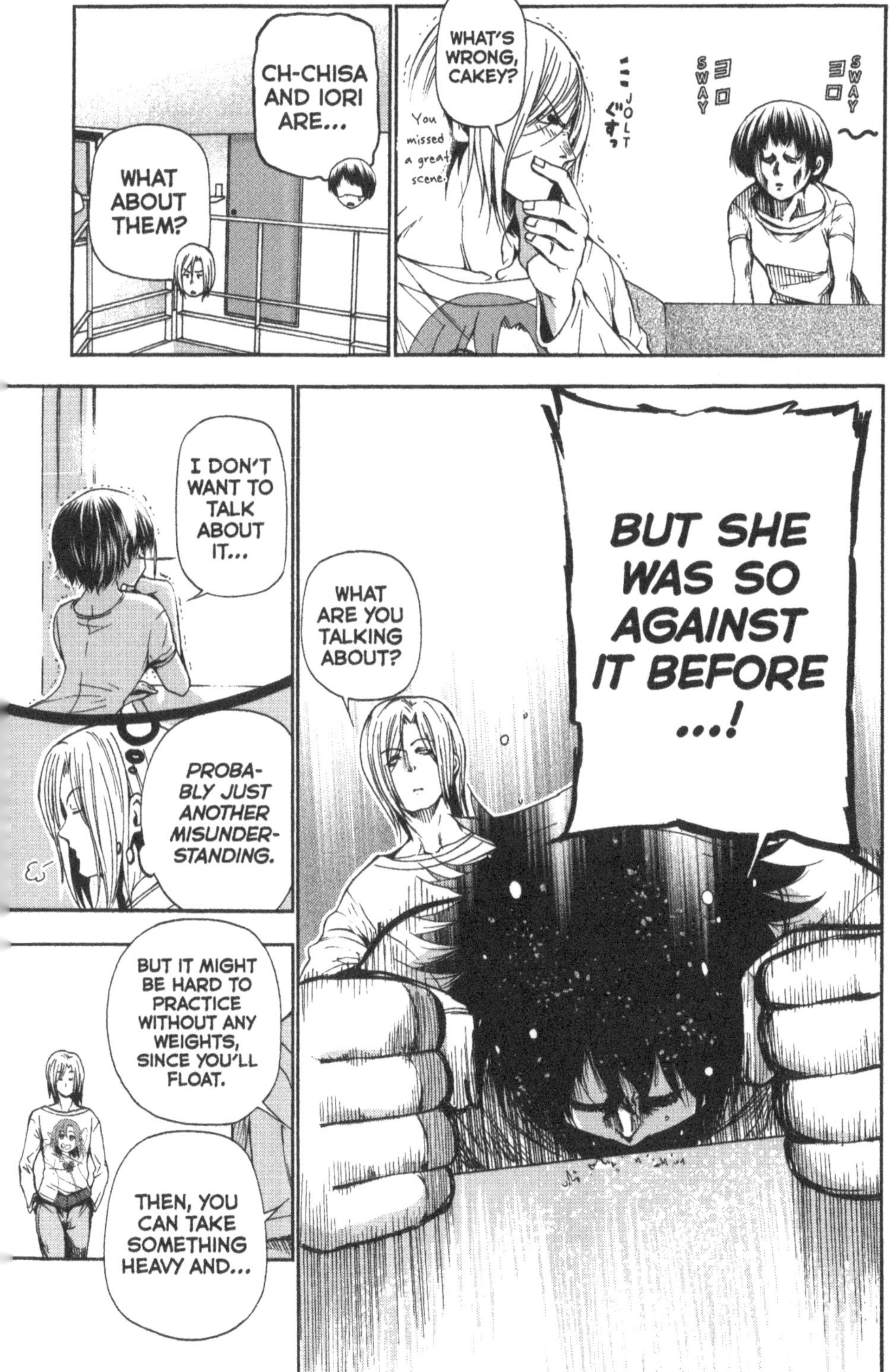
SWAY ヨロ
ヨロ SWAY
JOLT ぐすっ
WHAT'S WRONG, CAKEY?
You missed a great scene.
CH-CHISA AND IORI ARE...
WHAT ABOUT THEM?
BUT SHE WAS SO AGAINST IT BEFORE ...!
WHAT ARE YOU TALKING ABOUT?
I DON'T WANT TO TALK ABOUT IT...
PROBA-BLY JUST ANOTHER MISUNDER-STANDING.
BUT IT MIGHT BE HARD TO PRACTICE WITHOUT ANY WEIGHTS, SINCE YOU'LL FLOAT.
THEN, YOU CAN TAKE SOMETHING HEAVY AND...

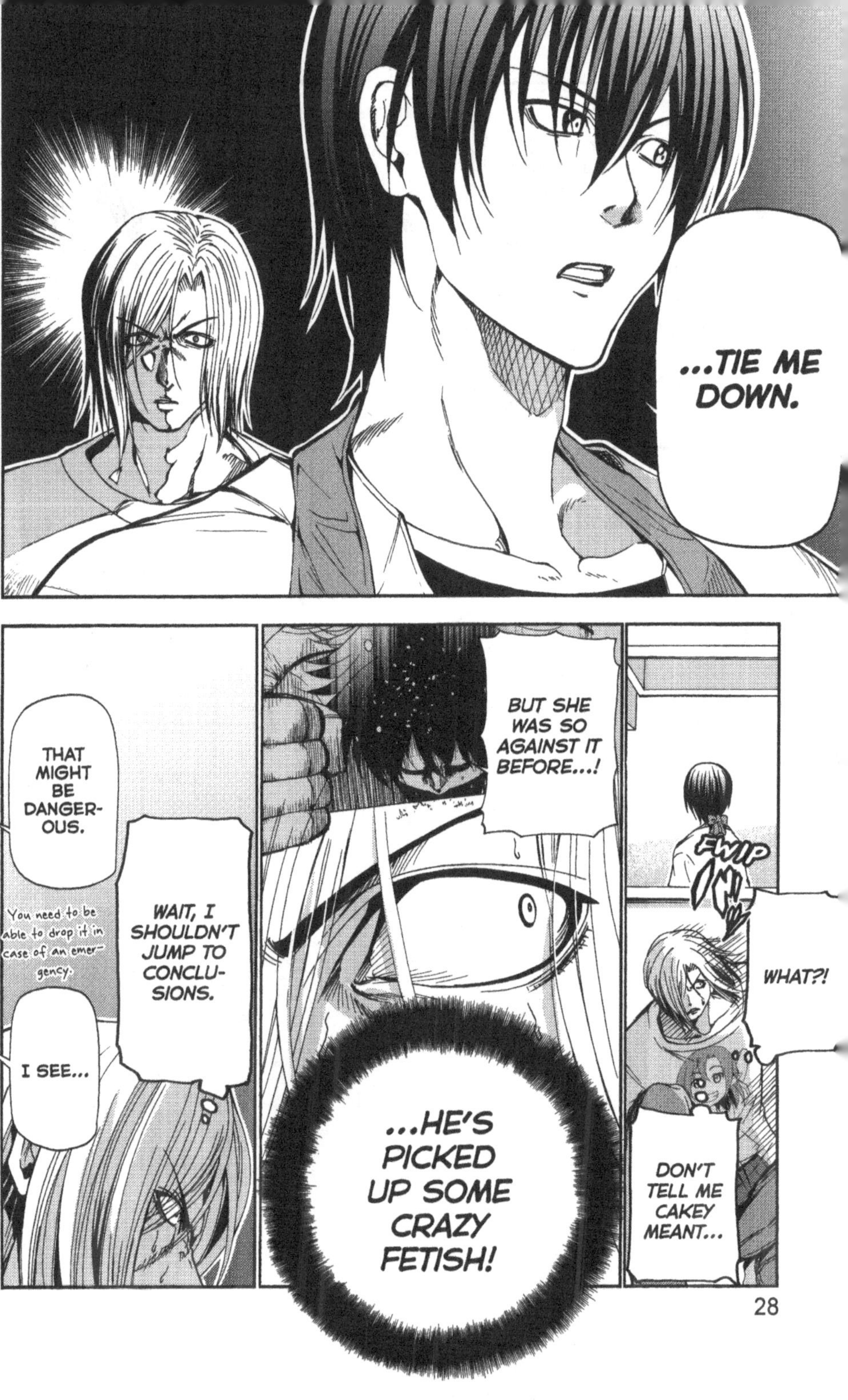
...TIE ME DOWN.
FWIP
WHAT?!
DON'T TELL ME CAKEY MEANT...
BUT SHE WAS SO AGAINST IT BEFORE...!
...HE'S PICKED UP SOME CRAZY FETISH!
THAT MIGHT BE DANGER-OUS.
WAIT, I SHOULDN'T JUMP TO CONCLU-SIONS.
You need to be able to drop it in case of an emer-gency.
I SEE...

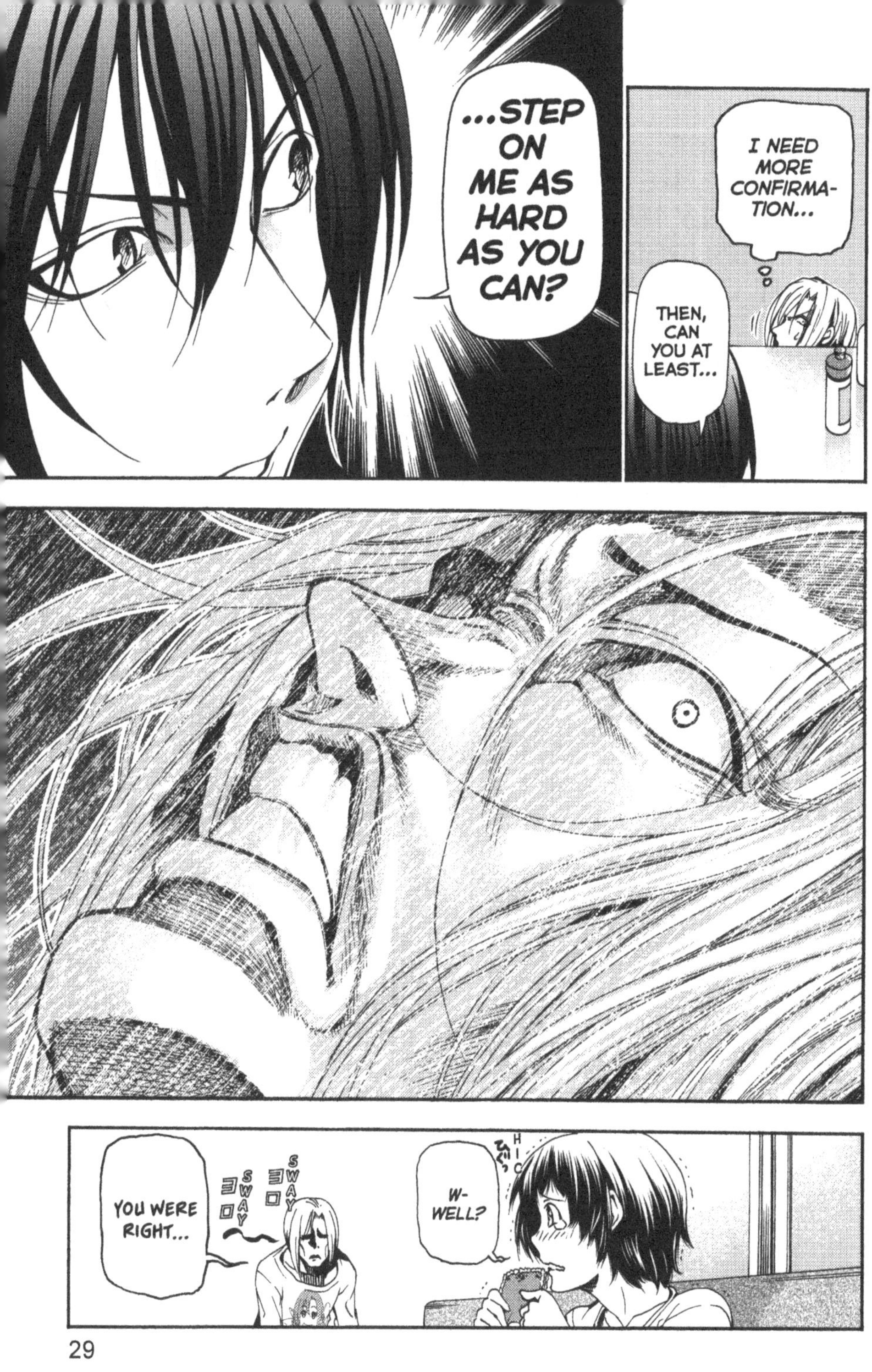
I NEED MORE CONFIRMATION...
THEN, CAN YOU AT LEAST...
...STEP ON ME AS HARD AS YOU CAN?
HIC
W-WELL?
SWAY
SWAY
YOU WERE RIGHT...

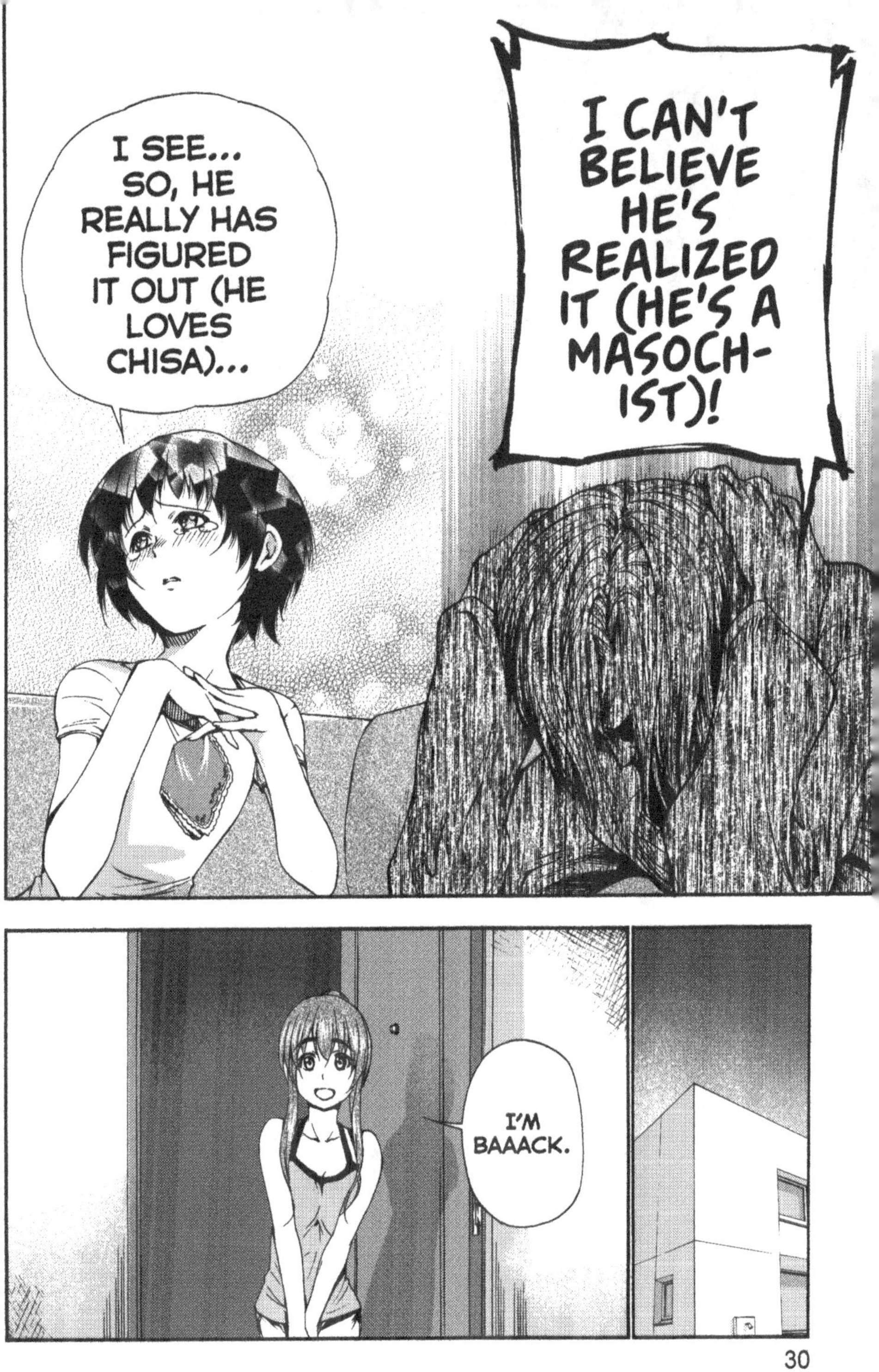
I CAN'T BELIEVE HE'S REALIZED IT (HE'S A MASOCH-IST)!
I SEE... SO, HE REALLY HAS FIGURED IT OUT (HE LOVES CHISA)...
I'M BAAACK.

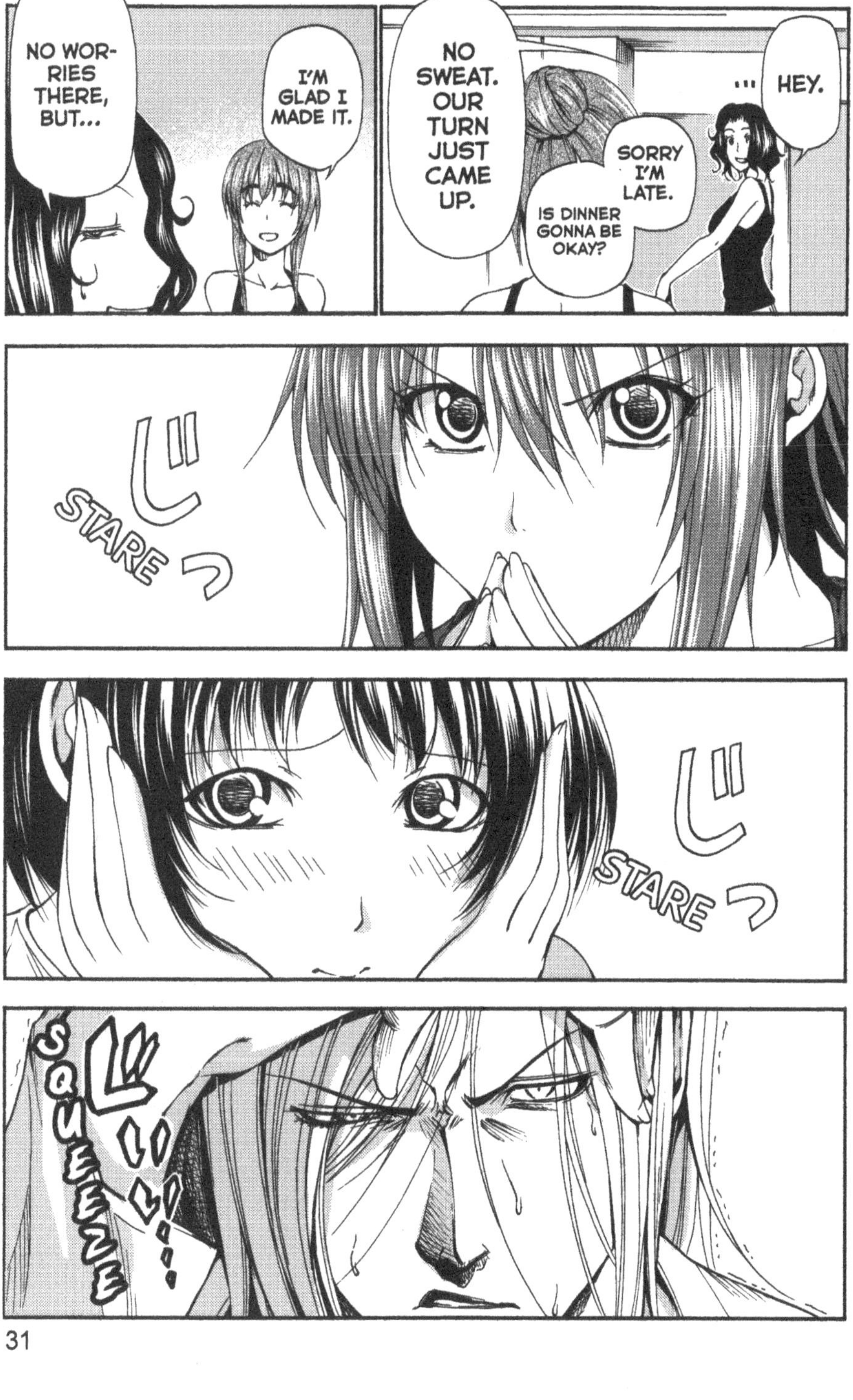
... HEY.
SORRY I'M LATE.
IS DINNER GONNA BE OKAY?
NO SWEAT. OUR TURN JUST CAME UP.
I'M GLAD I MADE IT.
NO WORRIES THERE, BUT...
じっ
STARE
じっ
STARE
SQUEEZE

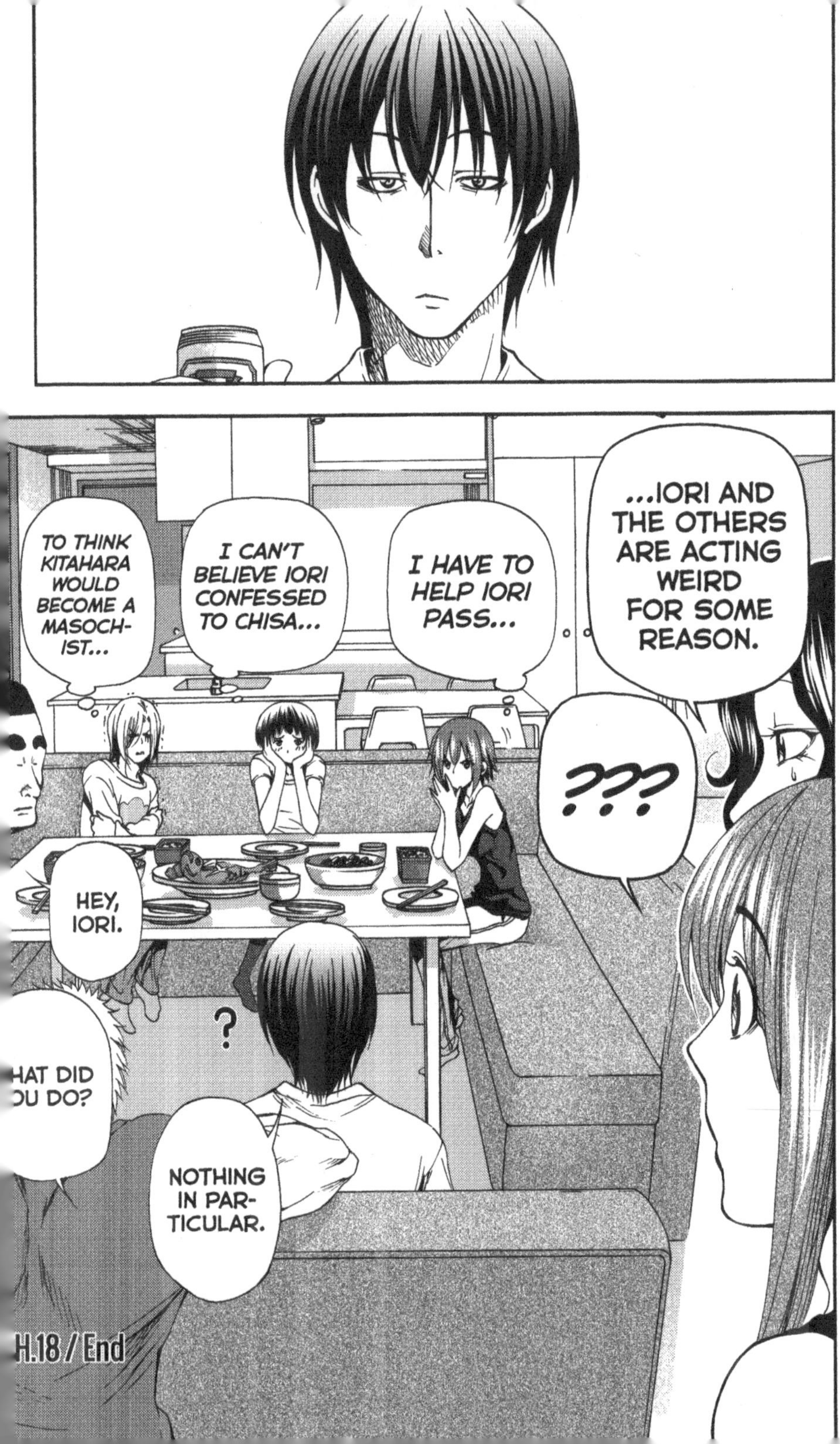
...IORI AND THE OTHERS ARE ACTING WEIRD FOR SOME REASON.
???
I HAVE TO HELP IORI PASS...
I CAN'T BELIEVE IORI CONFESSED TO CHISA...
TO THINK KITAHARA WOULD BECOME A MASOCH-IST...
HEY, IORI.
?
HAT DID OU DO?
NOTHING IN PAR-TICULAR.
H.18 / End

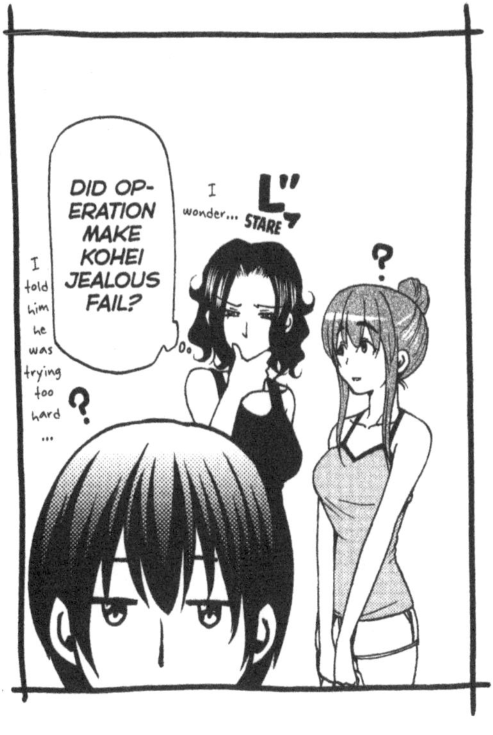
I wonder...
STARE
DID OPERATION MAKE KOHEI JEALOUS FAIL?
I told him he was trying too hard...
?
?

Grand Blue Dreaming

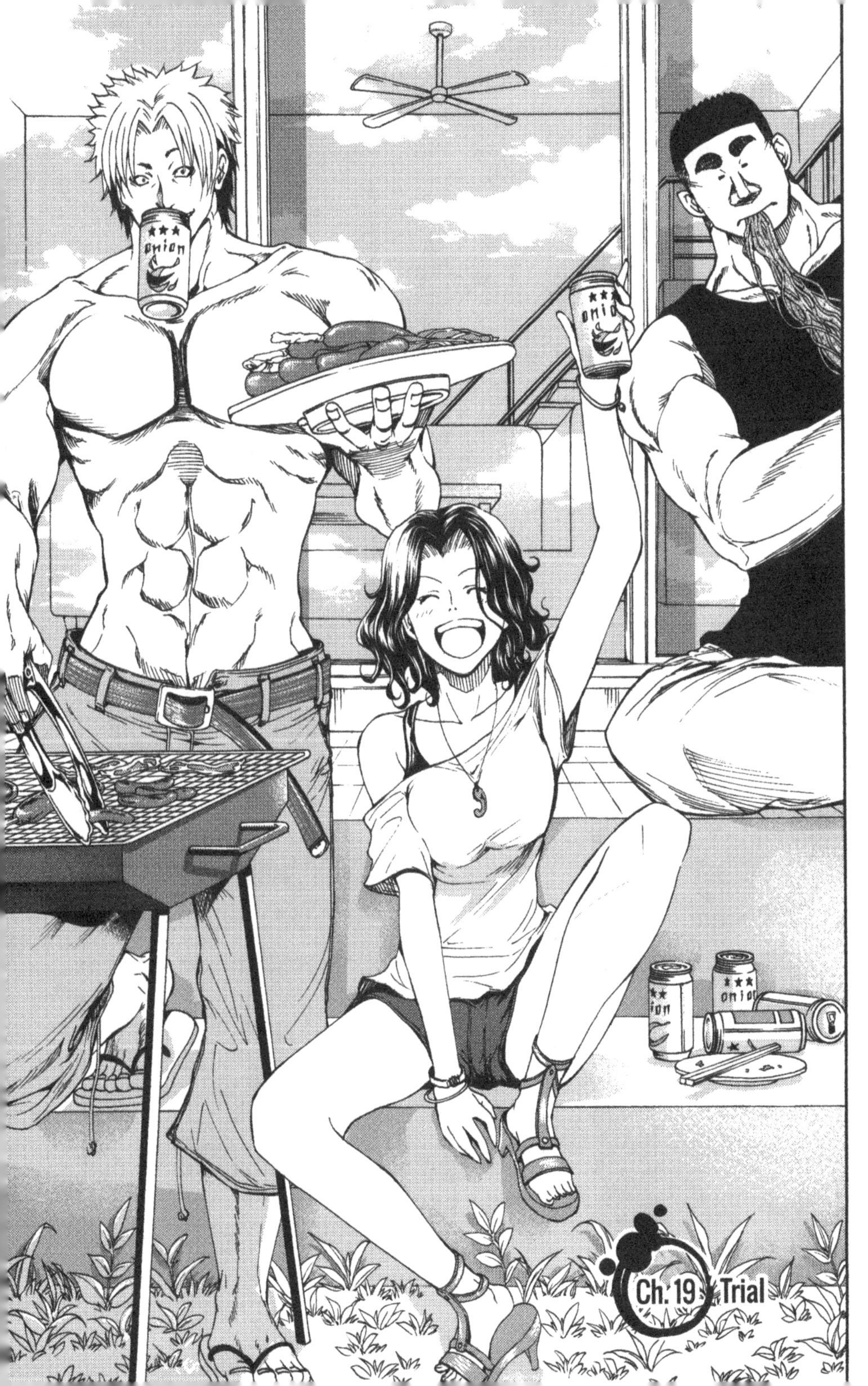
Ch. 19 Trial
onion

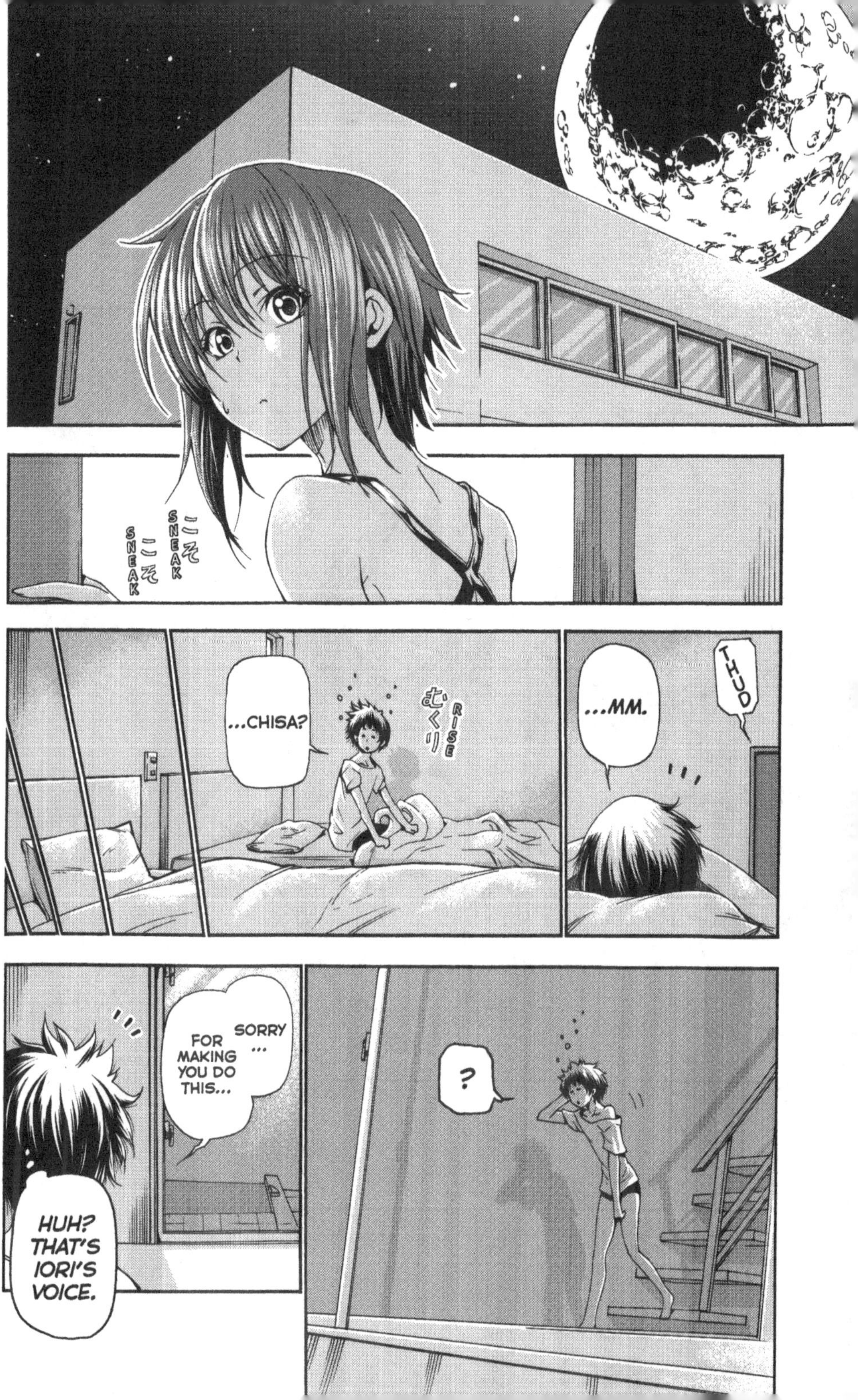
こそ SNEAK
こそ SNEAK
THUD
...MM.
むくり RISE
...CHISA?
?
SORRY... FOR MAKING YOU DO THIS...
HUH? THAT'S IORI'S VOICE.

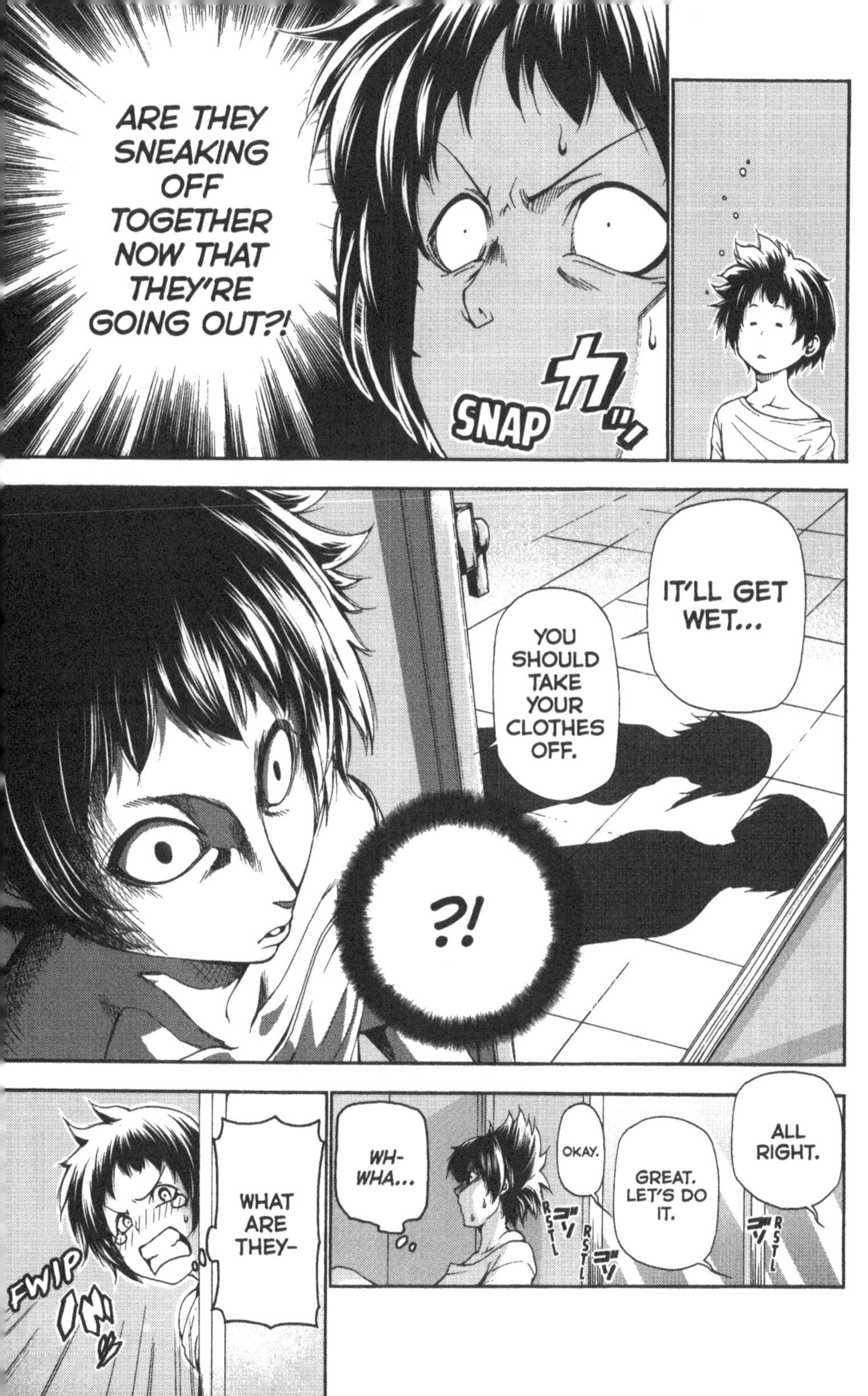
ARE THEY SNEAKING OFF TOGETHER NOW THAT THEY'RE GOING OUT?!
SNAP
カッ
IT'LL GET WET...
YOU SHOULD TAKE YOUR CLOTHES OFF.
?!
ALL RIGHT.
RSTL
ゴソ
GREAT. LET'S DO IT.
RSTL
ゴソ
OKAY.
RSTL
ゴソ
WH- WHA...
WHAT ARE THEY-
FWIP

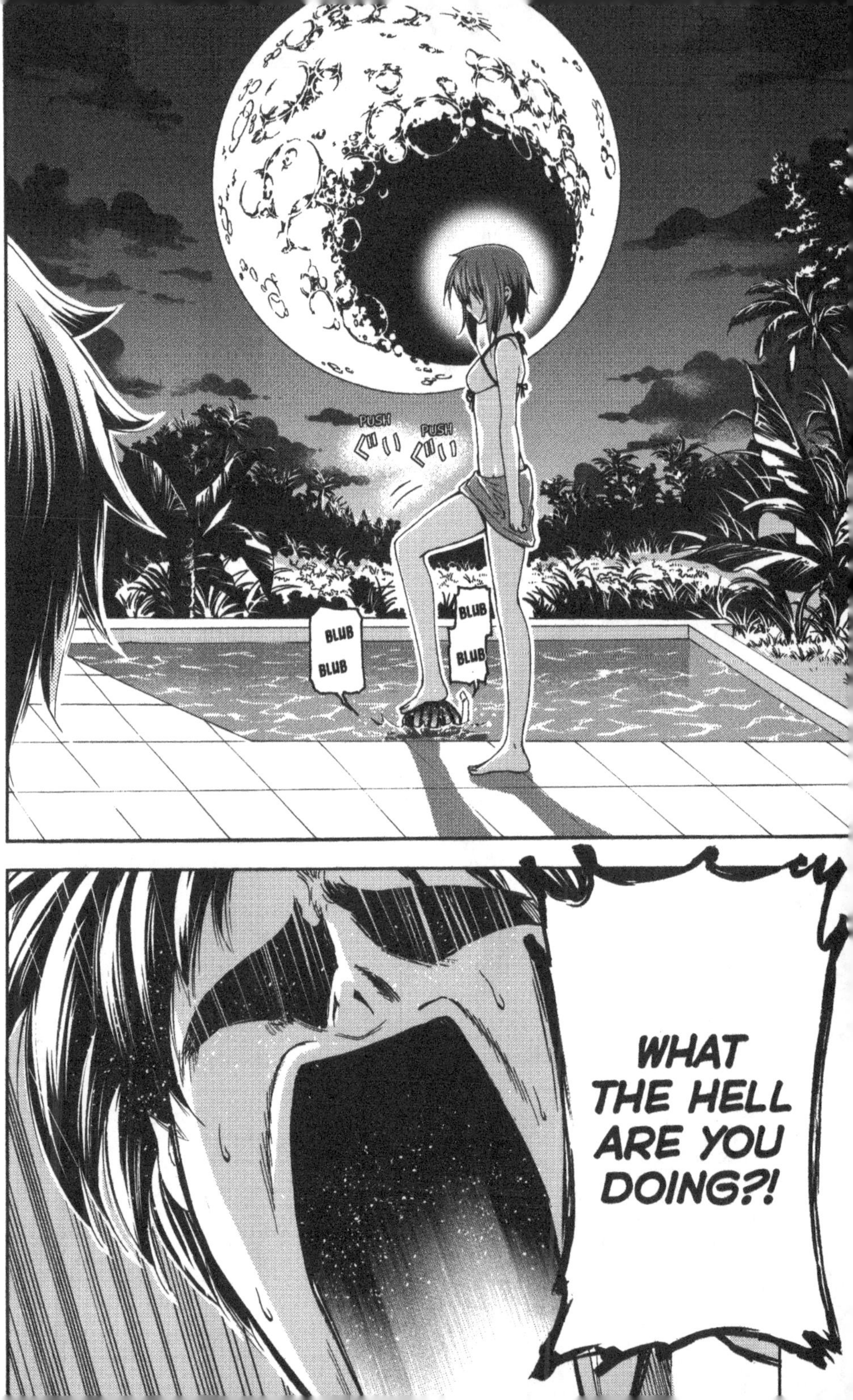
PUSH
PUSH
BLUB BLUB
BLUB BLUB
WHAT THE HELL ARE YOU DOING?!

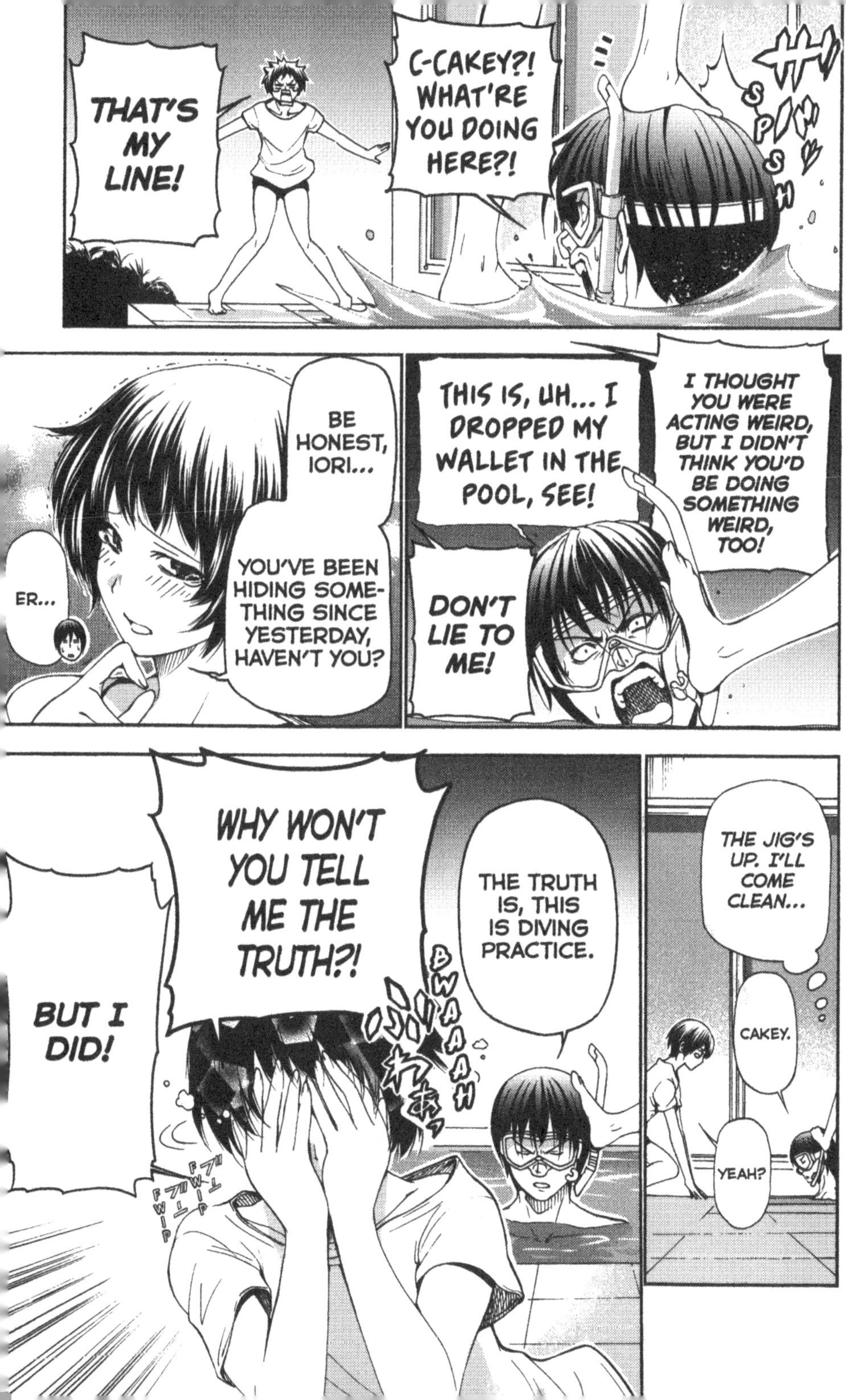
SPSH
C-CAKEY?! WHAT'RE YOU DOING HERE?!
THAT'S MY LINE!
I THOUGHT YOU WERE ACTING WEIRD, BUT I DIDN'T THINK YOU'D BE DOING SOMETHING WEIRD, TOO!
THIS IS, UH... I DROPPED MY WALLET IN THE POOL, SEE!
DON'T LIE TO ME!
BE HONEST, IORI...
YOU'VE BEEN HIDING SOMETHING SINCE YESTERDAY, HAVEN'T YOU?
ER...
THE JIG'S UP. I'LL COME CLEAN...
CAKEY.
YEAH?
THE TRUTH IS, THIS IS DIVING PRACTICE.
BWAAAAH
WHY WON'T YOU TELL ME THE TRUTH?!
BUT I DID!
FWIP
FWIP

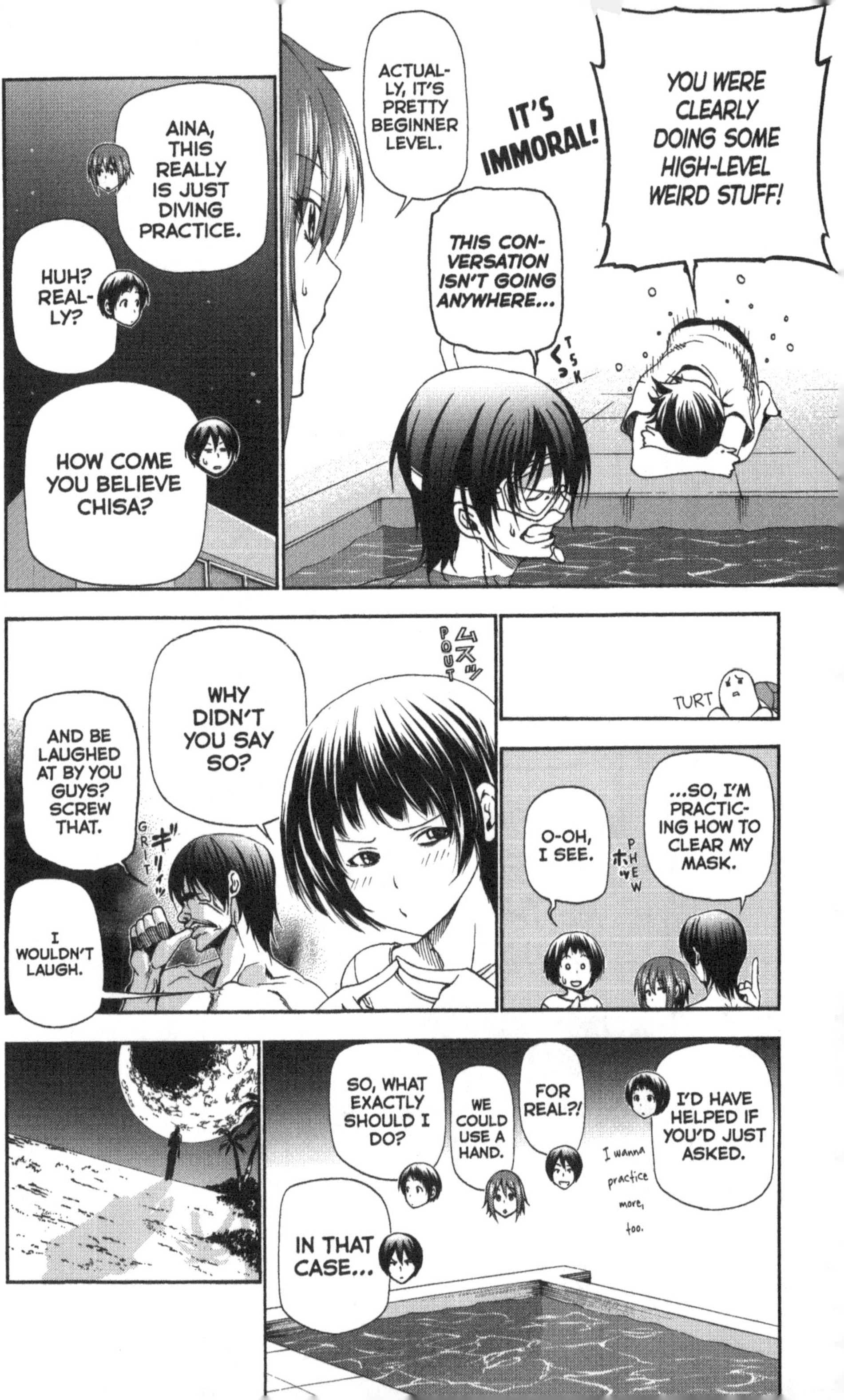
YOU WERE CLEARLY DOING SOME HIGH-LEVEL WEIRD STUFF!
IT'S IMMORAL!
ACTUALLY, IT'S PRETTY BEGINNER LEVEL.
THIS CONVERSATION ISN'T GOING ANYWHERE...
TSK
AINA, THIS REALLY IS JUST DIVING PRACTICE.
HUH? REALLY?
HOW COME YOU BELIEVE CHISA?
TURT
...SO, I'M PRACTICING HOW TO CLEAR MY MASK.
PHEW
O-OH, I SEE.
POUT
WHY DIDN'T YOU SAY SO?
AND BE LAUGHED AT BY YOU GUYS? SCREW THAT.
GRIT
I WOULDN'T LAUGH.
I'D HAVE HELPED IF YOU'D JUST ASKED.
I wanna practice more, too.
FOR REAL?!
WE COULD USE A HAND.
SO, WHAT EXACTLY SHOULD I DO?
IN THAT CASE...

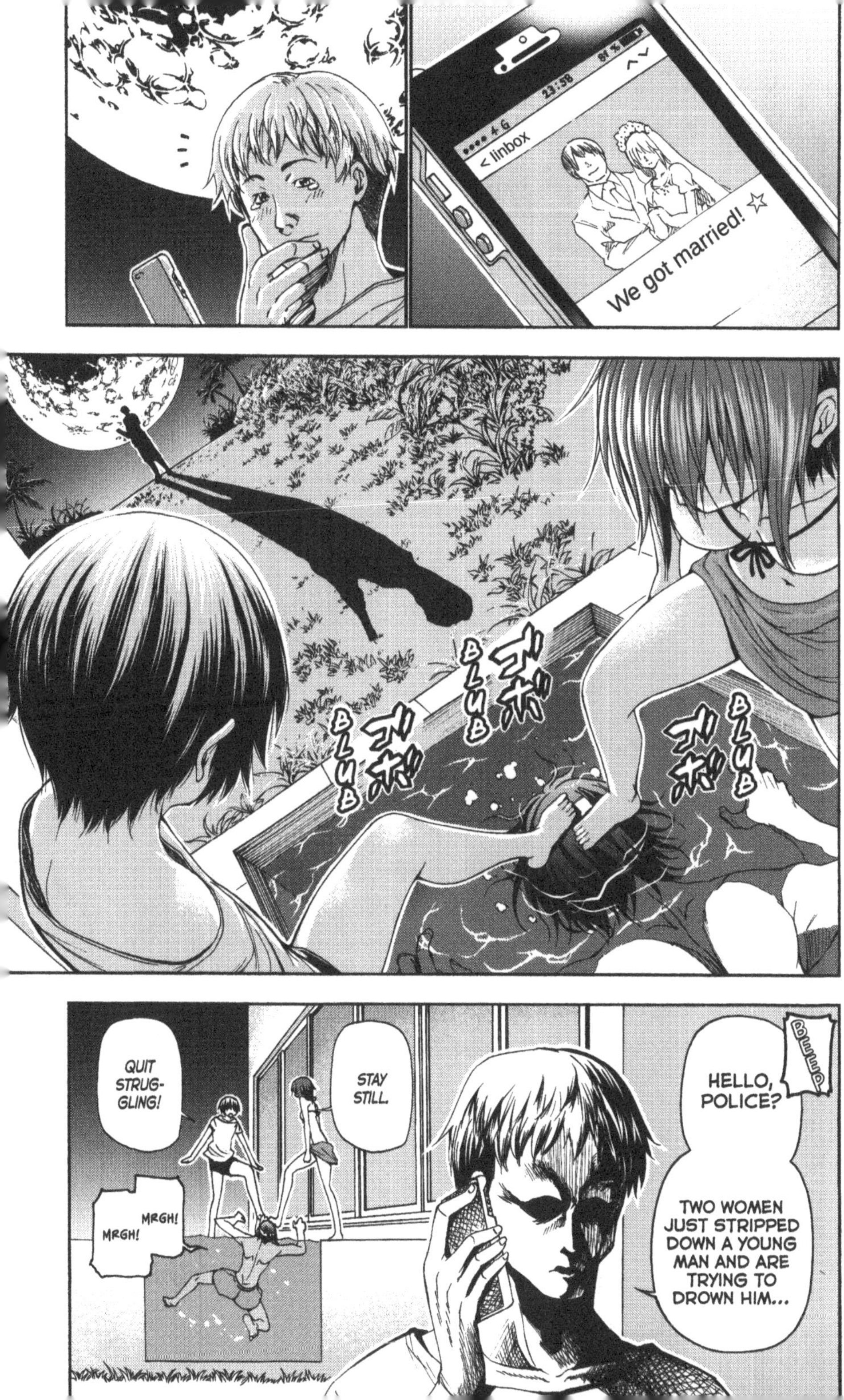

23:58
81%
4G
< linbox
We got married! ☆
ゴボ BLUB
ゴボ BLUB
ゴボ BLUB
BEEP
HELLO, POLICE?
TWO WOMEN JUST STRIPPED DOWN A YOUNG MAN AND ARE TRYING TO DROWN HIM...
STAY STILL.
QUIT STRUG-GLING!
MRGH! MRGH!

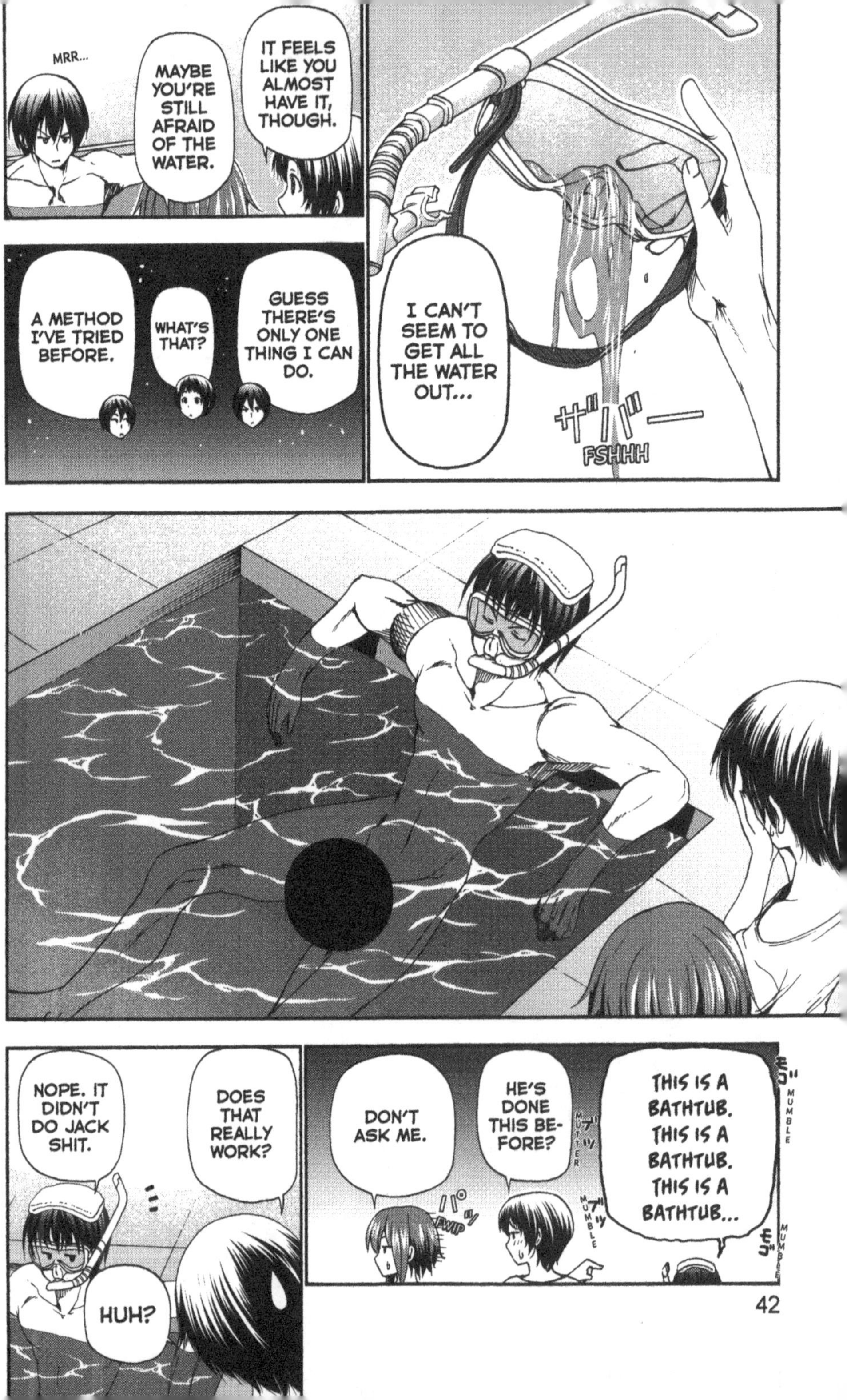

I CAN'T SEEM TO GET ALL THE WATER OUT...
FSHHH
IT FEELS LIKE YOU ALMOST HAVE IT, THOUGH.
MAYBE YOU'RE STILL AFRAID OF THE WATER.
MRR...
GUESS THERE'S ONLY ONE THING I CAN DO.
WHAT'S THAT?
A METHOD I'VE TRIED BEFORE.
MUMBLE
THIS IS A BATHTUB. THIS IS A BATHTUB. THIS IS A BATHTUB...
MUMBLE
HE'S DONE THIS BE-FORE?
MUTTER
MUMBLE
DON'T ASK ME.
FWIP
DOES THAT REALLY WORK?
NOPE. IT DIDN'T DO JACK SHIT.
HUH?

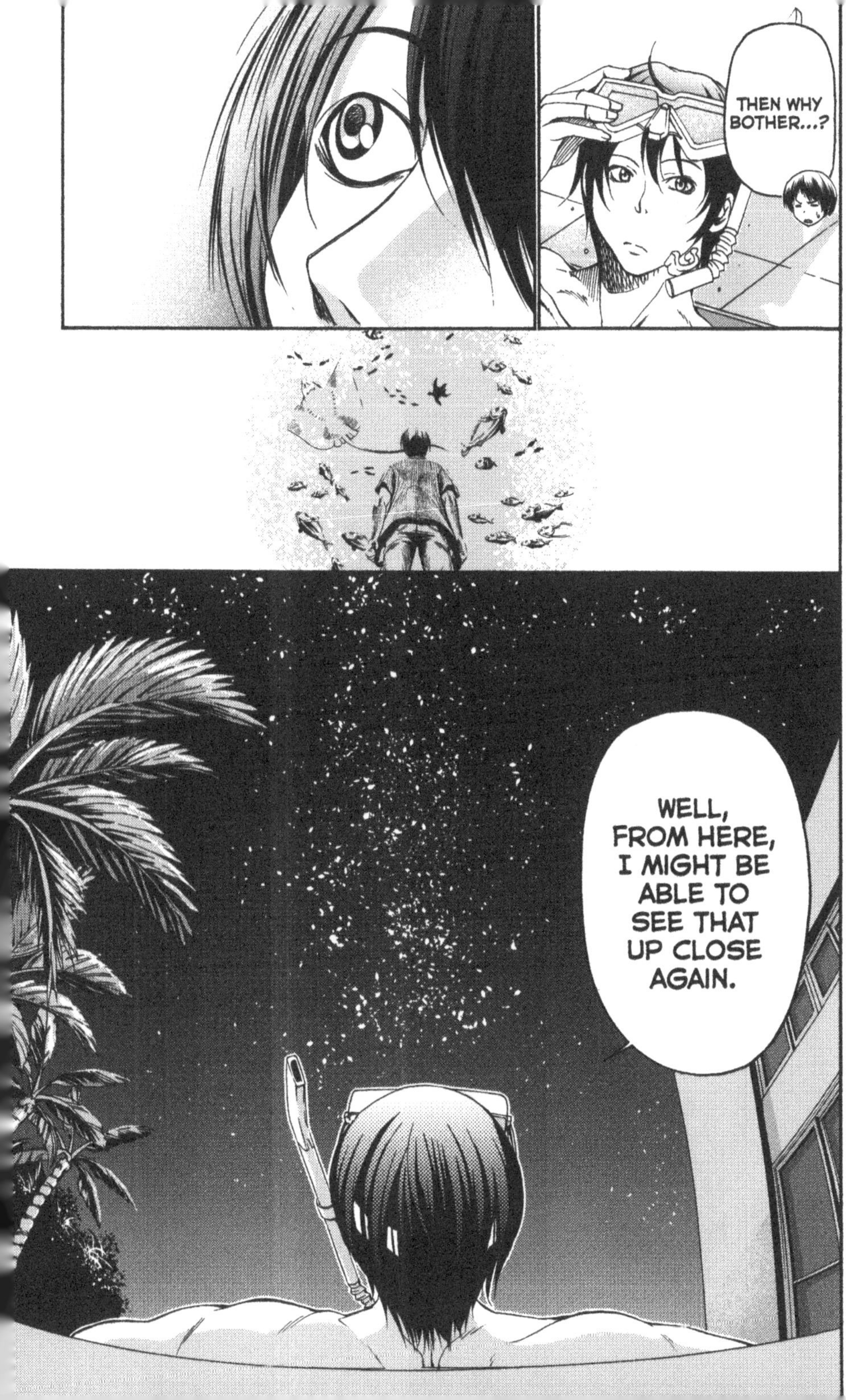
THEN WHY BOTHER...?
WELL, FROM HERE, I MIGHT BE ABLE TO SEE THAT UP CLOSE AGAIN.

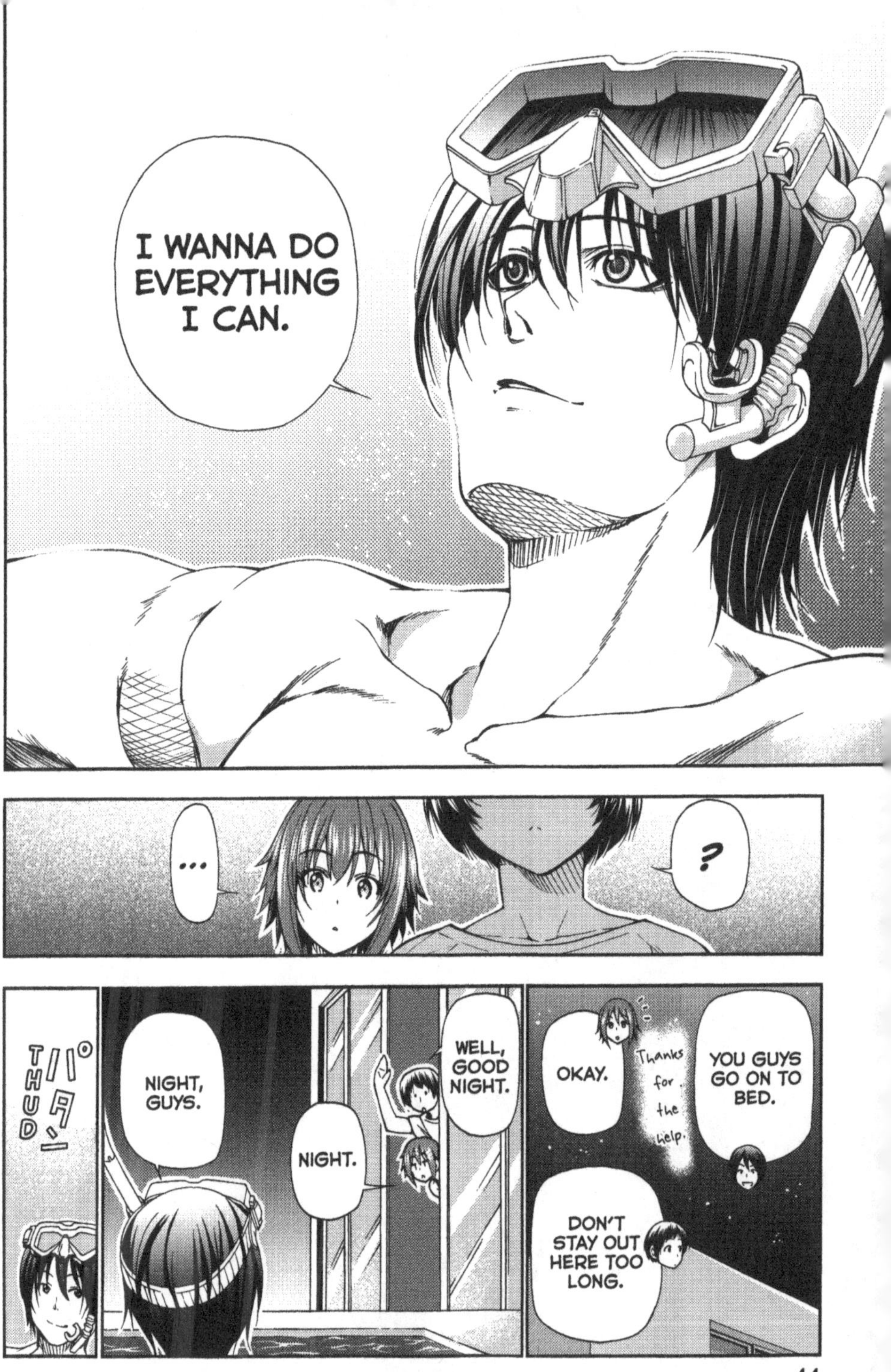
I WANNA DO EVERYTHING I CAN.
?
...
YOU GUYS GO ON TO BED.
Thanks for the help.
OKAY.
DON'T STAY OUT HERE TOO LONG.
WELL, GOOD NIGHT.
NIGHT.
NIGHT, GUYS.
THUD

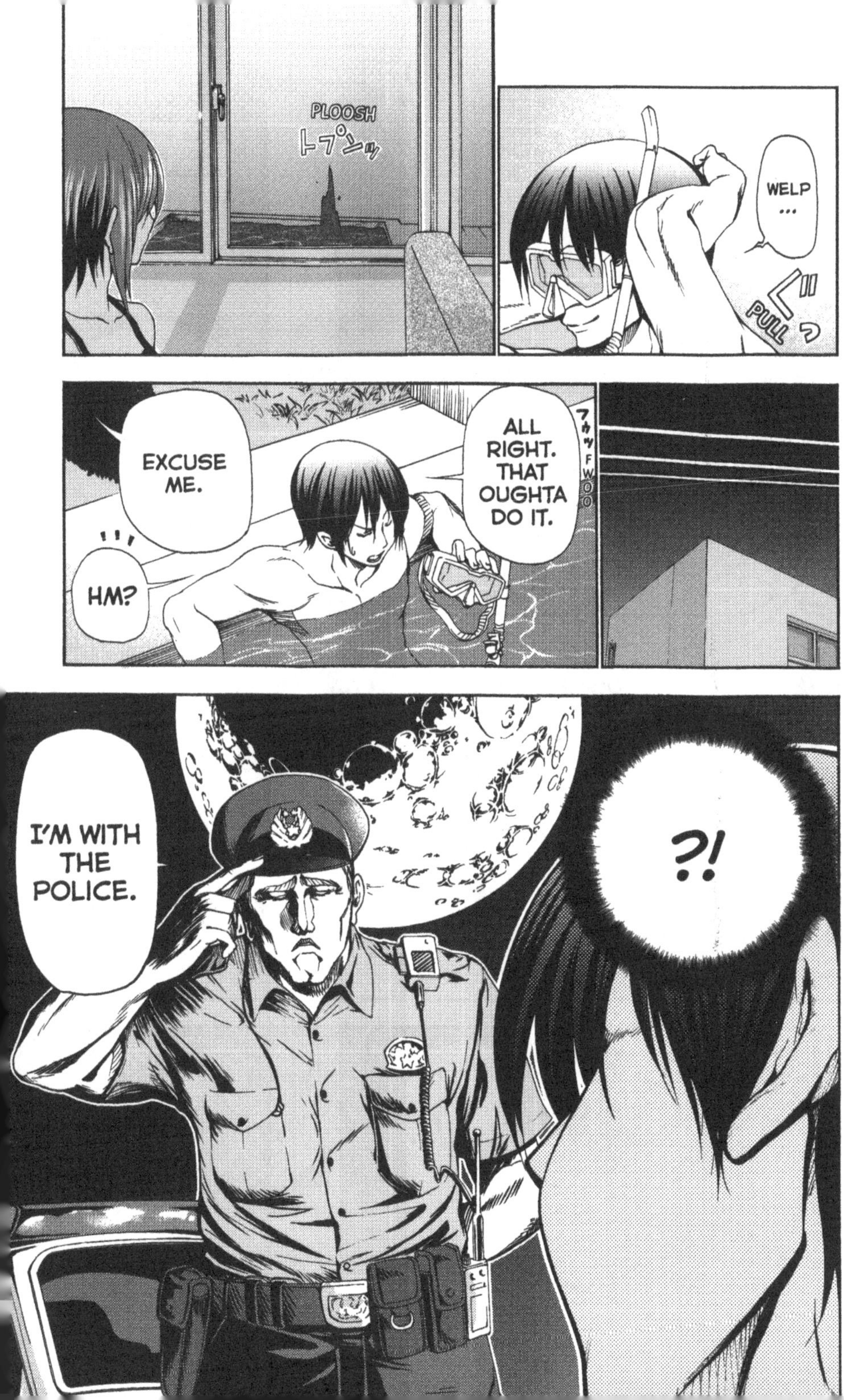
WELP ...
ぐぃっ
PULL
PLOOSH
トプンッ
フゥッ
FWOO
ALL RIGHT. THAT OUGHTA DO IT.
EXCUSE ME.
!!!
HM?
?!
I'M WITH THE POLICE.

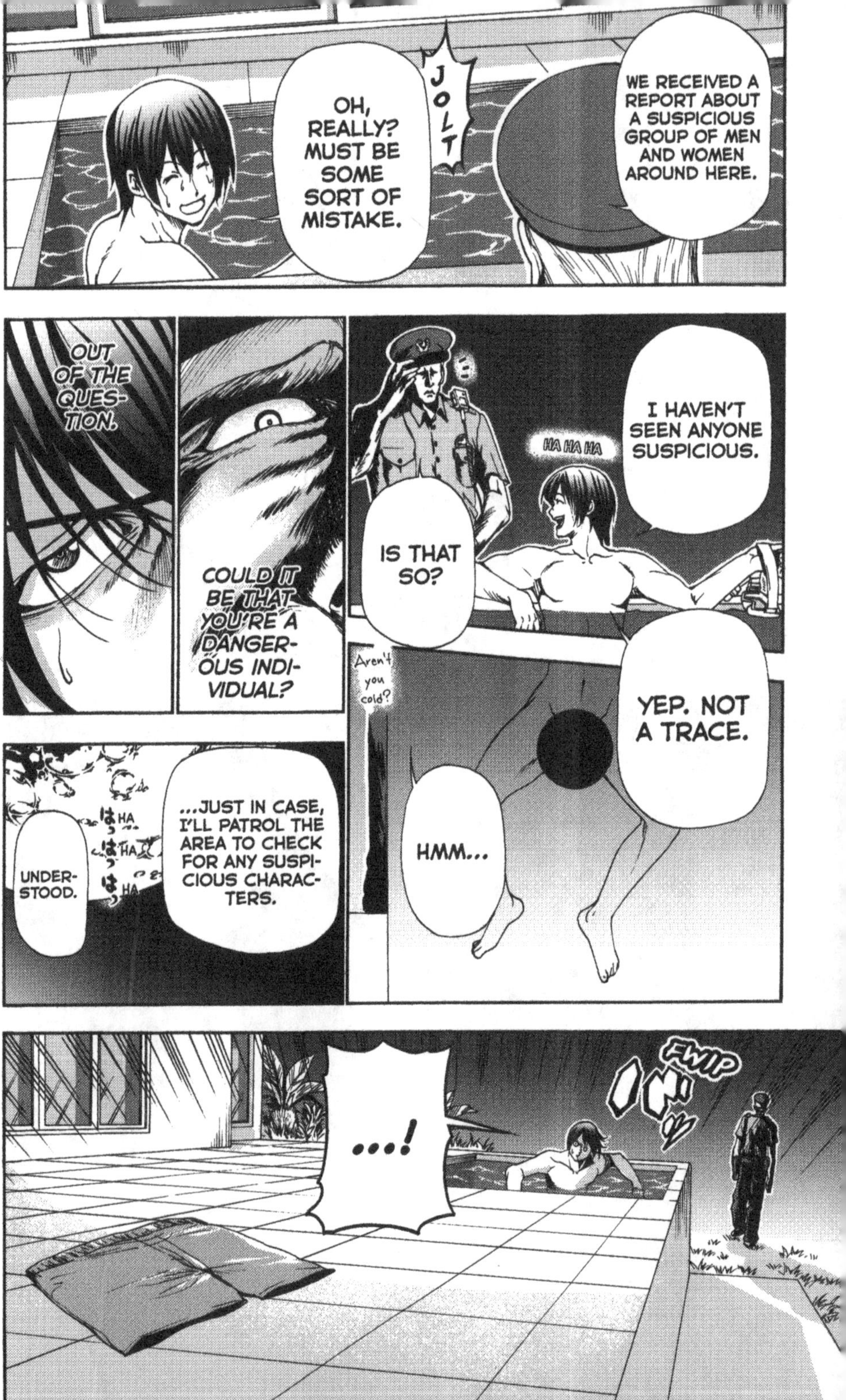

WE RECEIVED A REPORT ABOUT A SUSPICIOUS GROUP OF MEN AND WOMEN AROUND HERE.
JOLT
OH, REALLY? MUST BE SOME SORT OF MISTAKE.
I HAVEN'T SEEN ANYONE SUSPICIOUS.
HA HA HA
IS THAT SO?
YEP. NOT A TRACE.
HMM...
Aren't you cold?
COULD IT BE THAT YOU'RE A DANGER-OUS INDI-VIDUAL?
OUT OF THE QUES-TION.
...JUST IN CASE, I'LL PATROL THE AREA TO CHECK FOR ANY SUSPI-CIOUS CHARAC-TERS.
はっ HA
はっ HA
はっ HA
UNDER-STOOD.
FWIP
...!

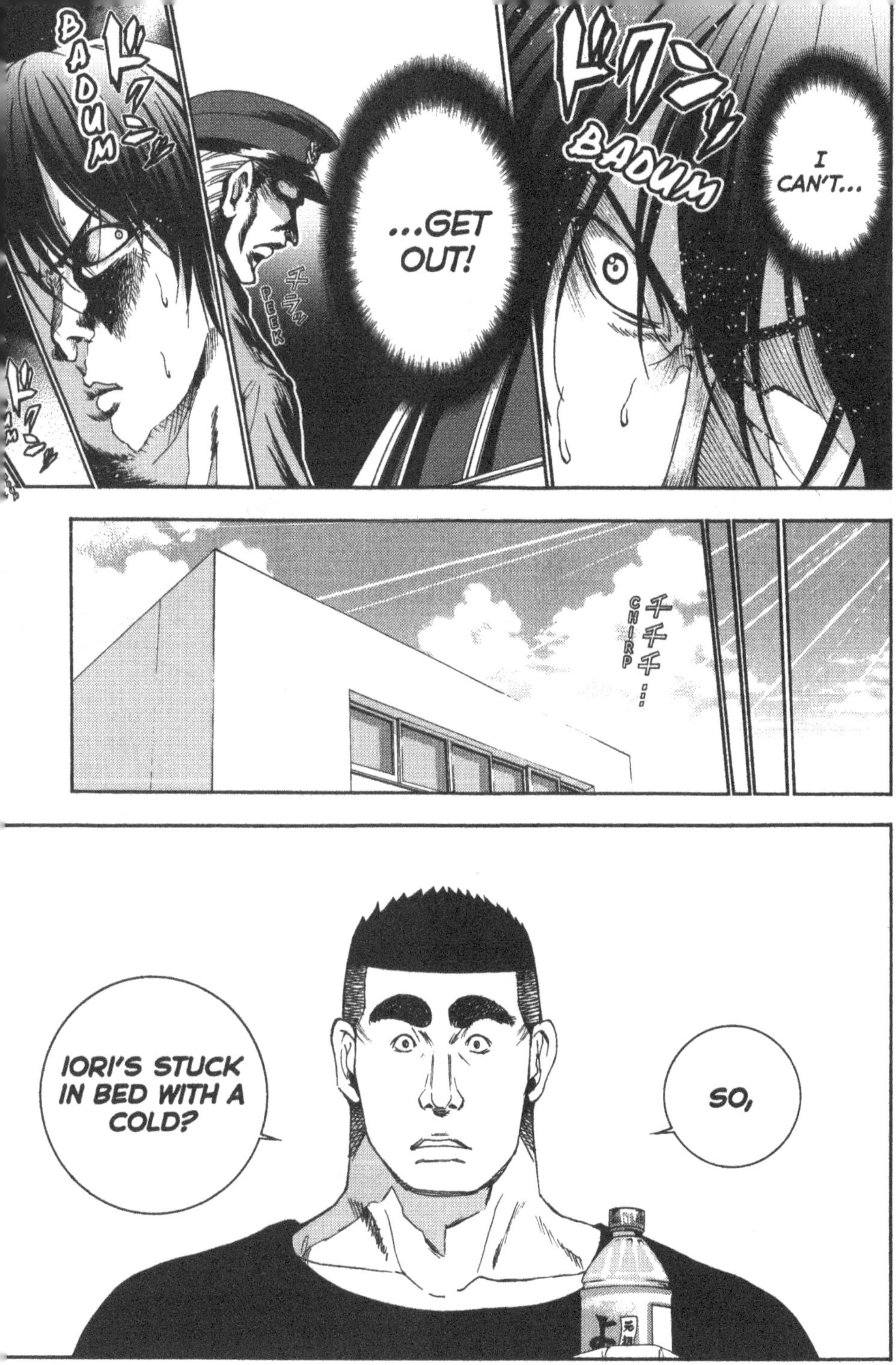
BADUM
I CAN'T...
...GET OUT!
PEEK
BADUM
CHIRP...
SO,
IORI'S STUCK IN BED WITH A COLD?

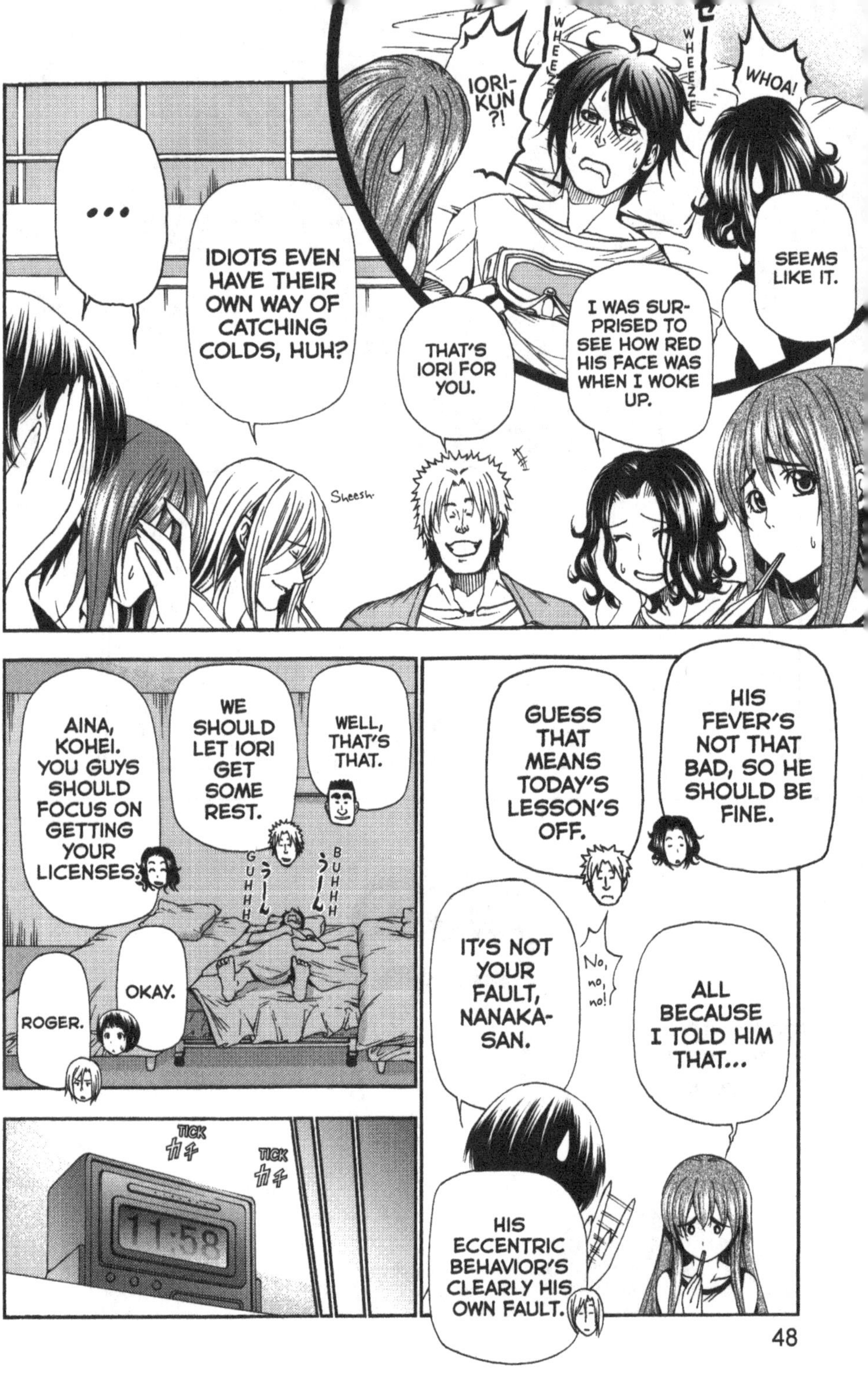
WHOA!
WHEEZE
WHEEZE
IORI-KUN?!
SEEMS LIKE IT.
I WAS SURPRISED TO SEE HOW RED HIS FACE WAS WHEN I WOKE UP.
THAT'S IORI FOR YOU.
IDIOTS EVEN HAVE THEIR OWN WAY OF CATCHING COLDS, HUH?
Sheesh.
...
HIS FEVER'S NOT THAT BAD, SO HE SHOULD BE FINE.
GUESS THAT MEANS TODAY'S LESSON'S OFF.
ALL BECAUSE I TOLD HIM THAT...
No, no, no!
IT'S NOT YOUR FAULT, NANAKA-SAN.
HIS ECCENTRIC BEHAVIOR'S CLEARLY HIS OWN FAULT.
WELL, THAT'S THAT.
WE SHOULD LET IORI GET SOME REST.
AINA, KOHEI. YOU GUYS SHOULD FOCUS ON GETTING YOUR LICENSES.
BUHHH
GUHHH
OKAY.
ROGER.
TICK
TICK
11:58

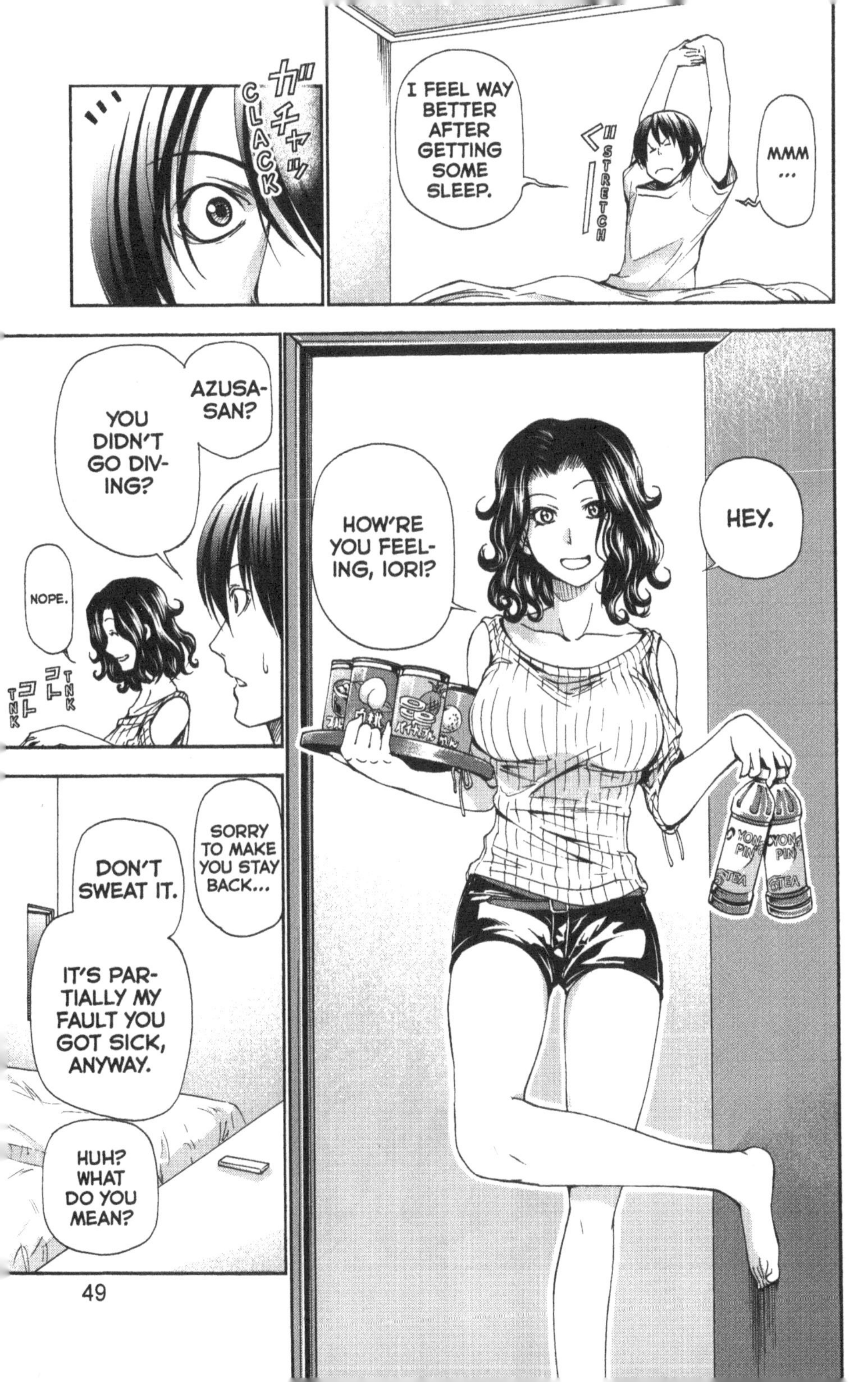
MMM...
ぐー
STRETCH
I FEEL WAY BETTER AFTER GETTING SOME SLEEP.
ガチャッ
CLACK
...
HEY.
HOW'RE YOU FEELING, IORI?
YON-PIN TEA
AZUSA-SAN?
YOU DIDN'T GO DIVING?
NOPE.
コトコト
TNK TNK
SORRY TO MAKE YOU STAY BACK...
DON'T SWEAT IT.
IT'S PARTIALLY MY FAULT YOU GOT SICK, ANYWAY.
HUH? WHAT DO YOU MEAN?

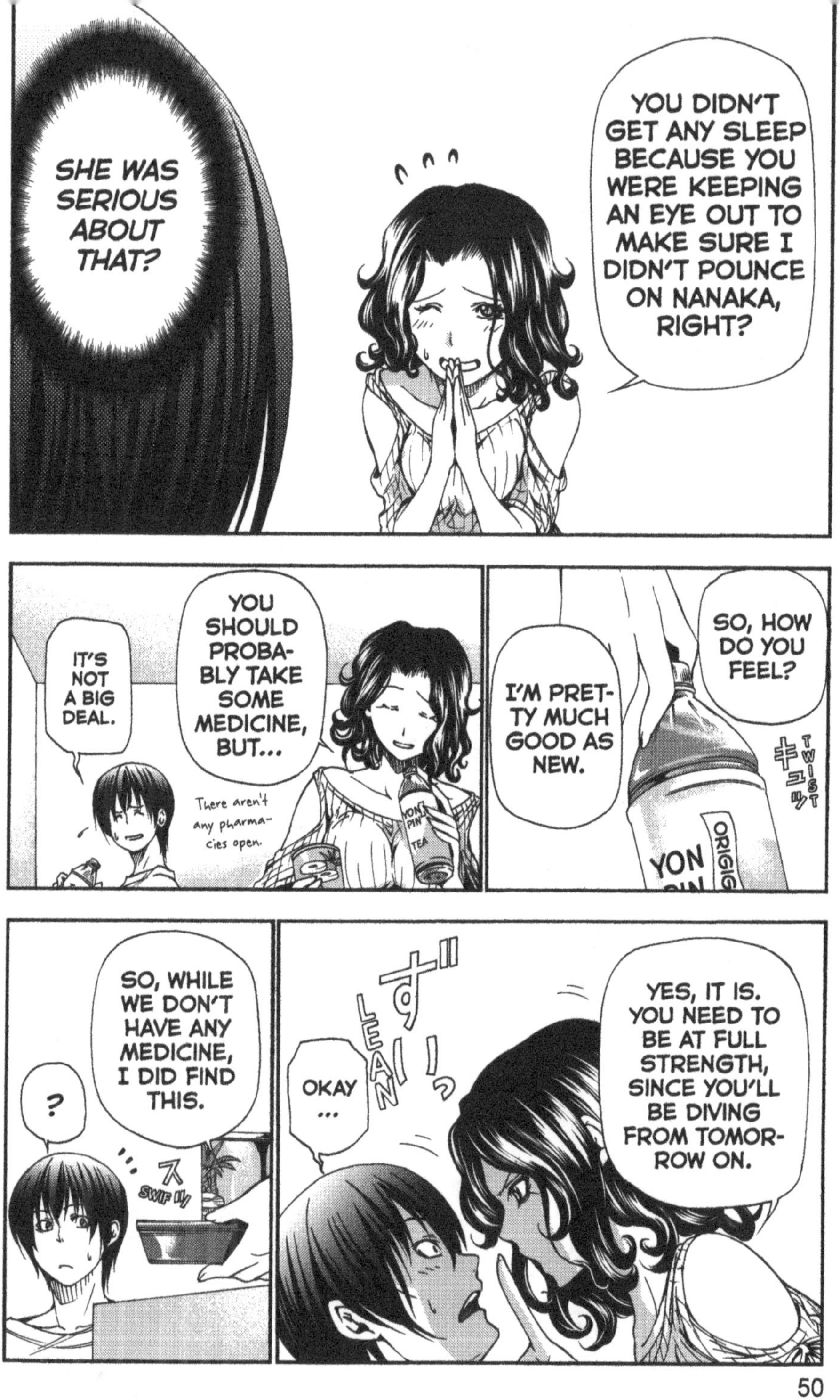
YOU DIDN'T GET ANY SLEEP BECAUSE YOU WERE KEEPING AN EYE OUT TO MAKE SURE I DIDN'T POUNCE ON NANAKA, RIGHT?
SHE WAS SERIOUS ABOUT THAT?
SO, HOW DO YOU FEEL?
I'M PRETTY MUCH GOOD AS NEW.
TWIST
YON
YOU SHOULD PROBABLY TAKE SOME MEDICINE, BUT...
IT'S NOT A BIG DEAL.
There aren't any pharmacies open.
YES, IT IS. YOU NEED TO BE AT FULL STRENGTH, SINCE YOU'LL BE DIVING FROM TOMORROW ON.
LEAN
OKAY...
SO, WHILE WE DON'T HAVE ANY MEDICINE, I DID FIND THIS.
?
SWIP

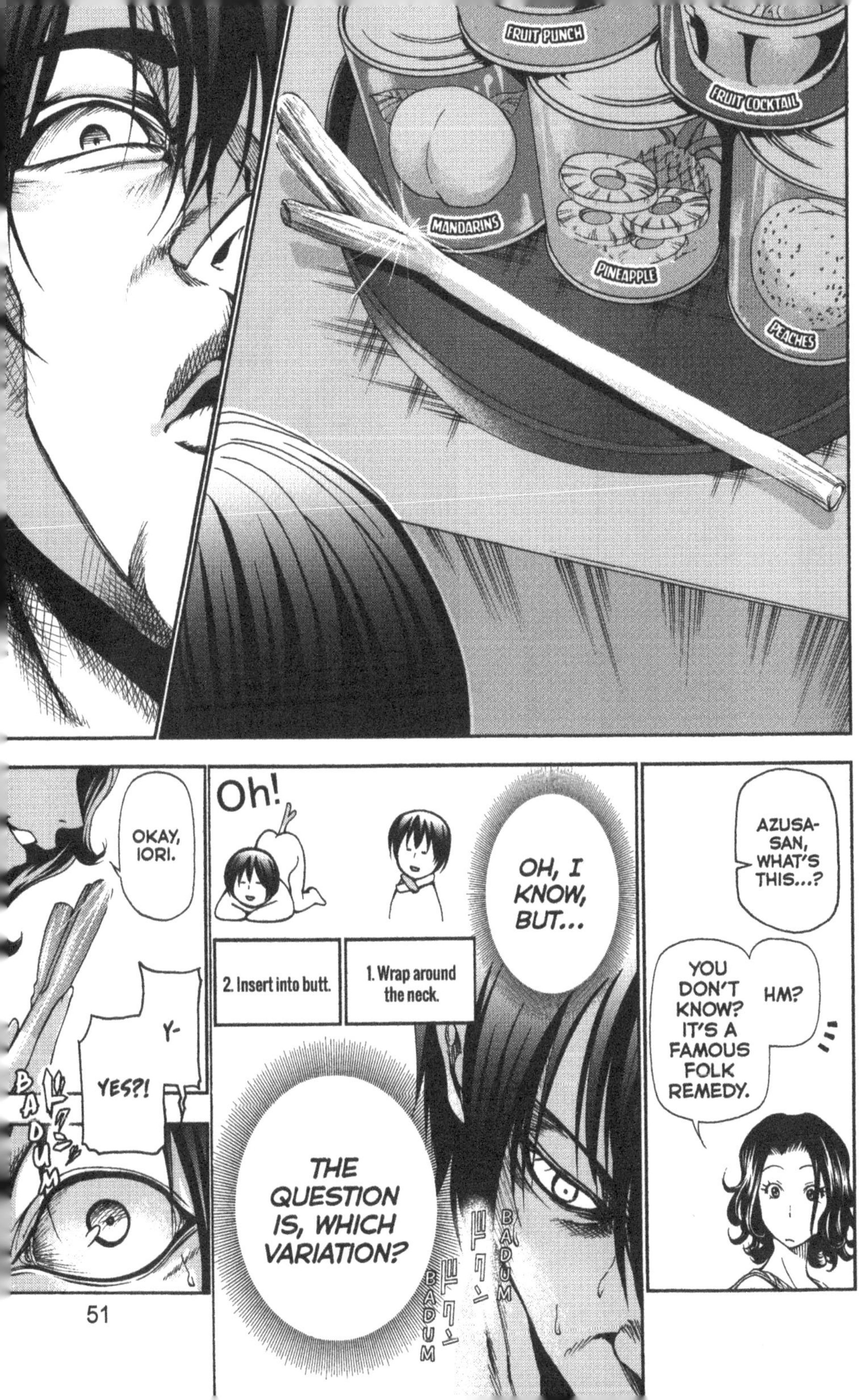
FRUIT COCKTAIL
FRUIT PUNCH
PEACHES
PINEAPPLE
MANDARINS
AZUSA-SAN, WHAT'S THIS...?
HM?
YOU DON'T KNOW? IT'S A FAMOUS FOLK REMEDY.
OH, I KNOW, BUT...
Oh!
1. Wrap around the neck.
2. Insert into butt.
BADUM
BADUM
THE QUESTION IS, WHICH VARIATION?
OKAY, IORI.
Y- YES?!
BADUM

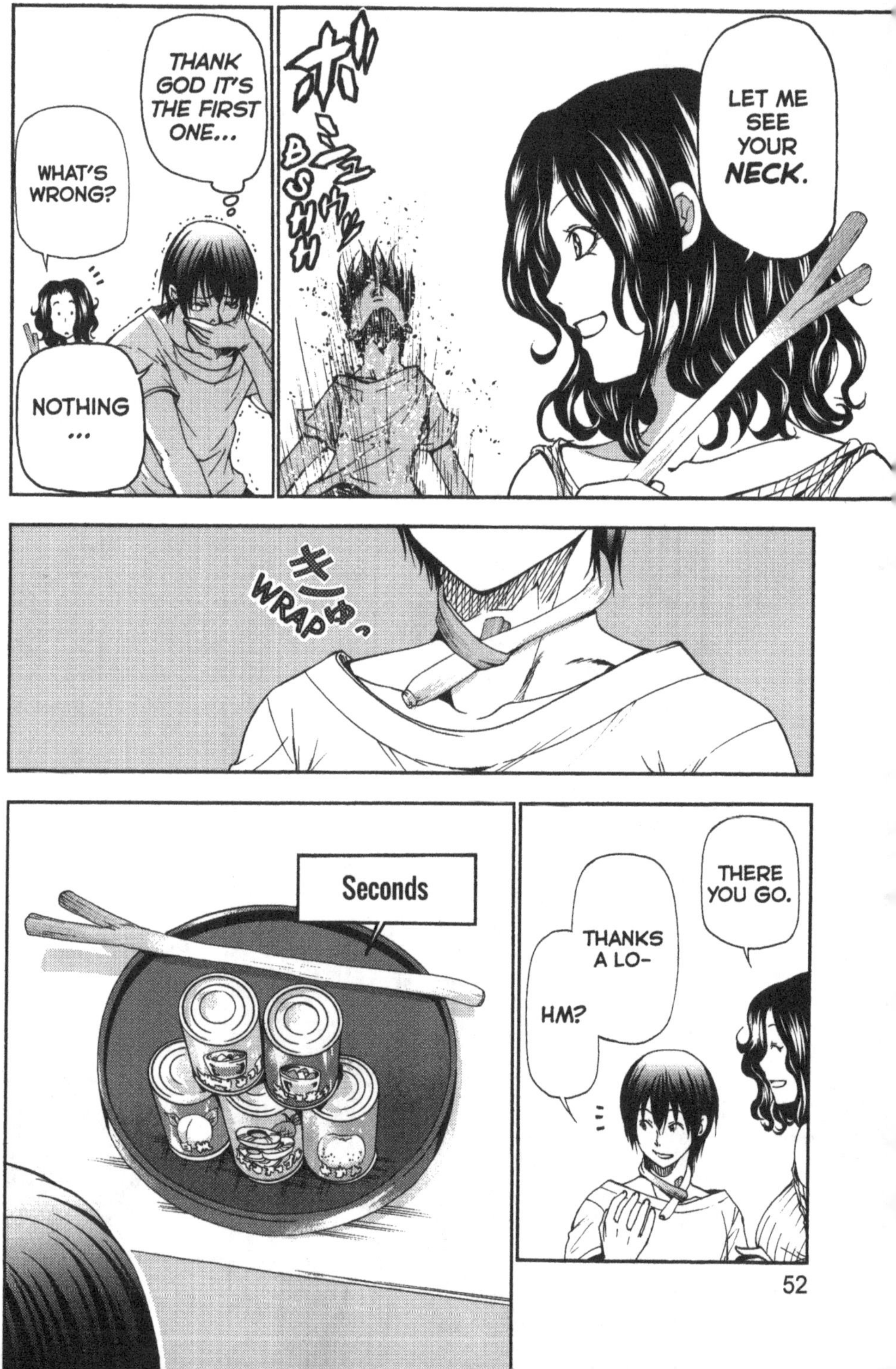
LET ME SEE YOUR NECK.
BSHHH
THANK GOD IT'S THE FIRST ONE...
WHAT'S WRONG?
NOTHING...
WRAP
THERE YOU GO.
THANKS A LO-
HM?
Seconds

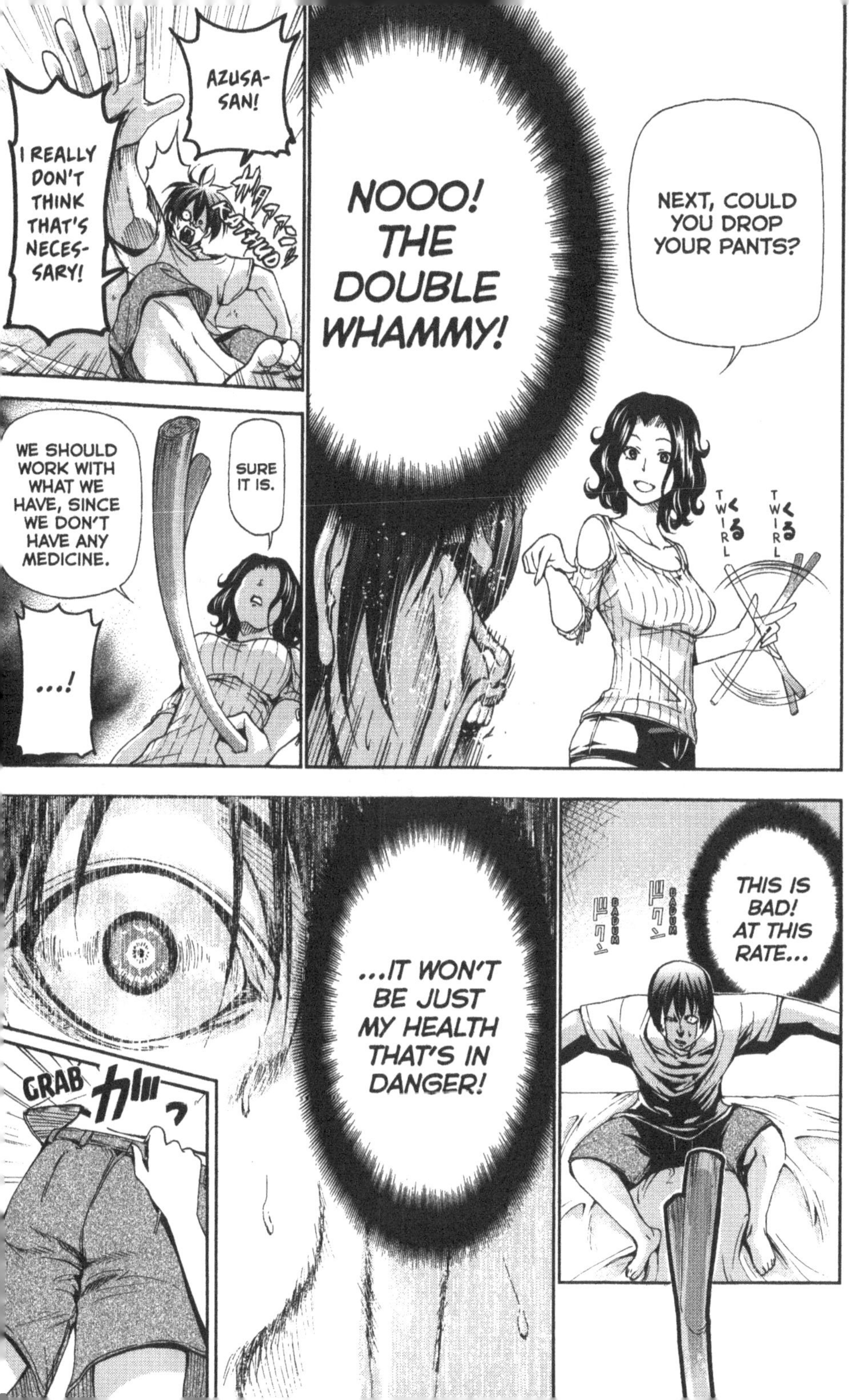
NEXT, COULD YOU DROP YOUR PANTS?
TWIRL くる
TWIRL くる
NOOO! THE DOUBLE WHAMMY!
AZUSA-SAN!
I REALLY DON'T THINK THAT'S NECES-SARY!
KATATHUD
SURE IT IS.
WE SHOULD WORK WITH WHAT WE HAVE, SINCE WE DON'T HAVE ANY MEDICINE.
...!
THIS IS BAD! AT THIS RATE...
BADUM
BADUM
...IT WON'T BE JUST MY HEALTH THAT'S IN DANGER!
GRAB

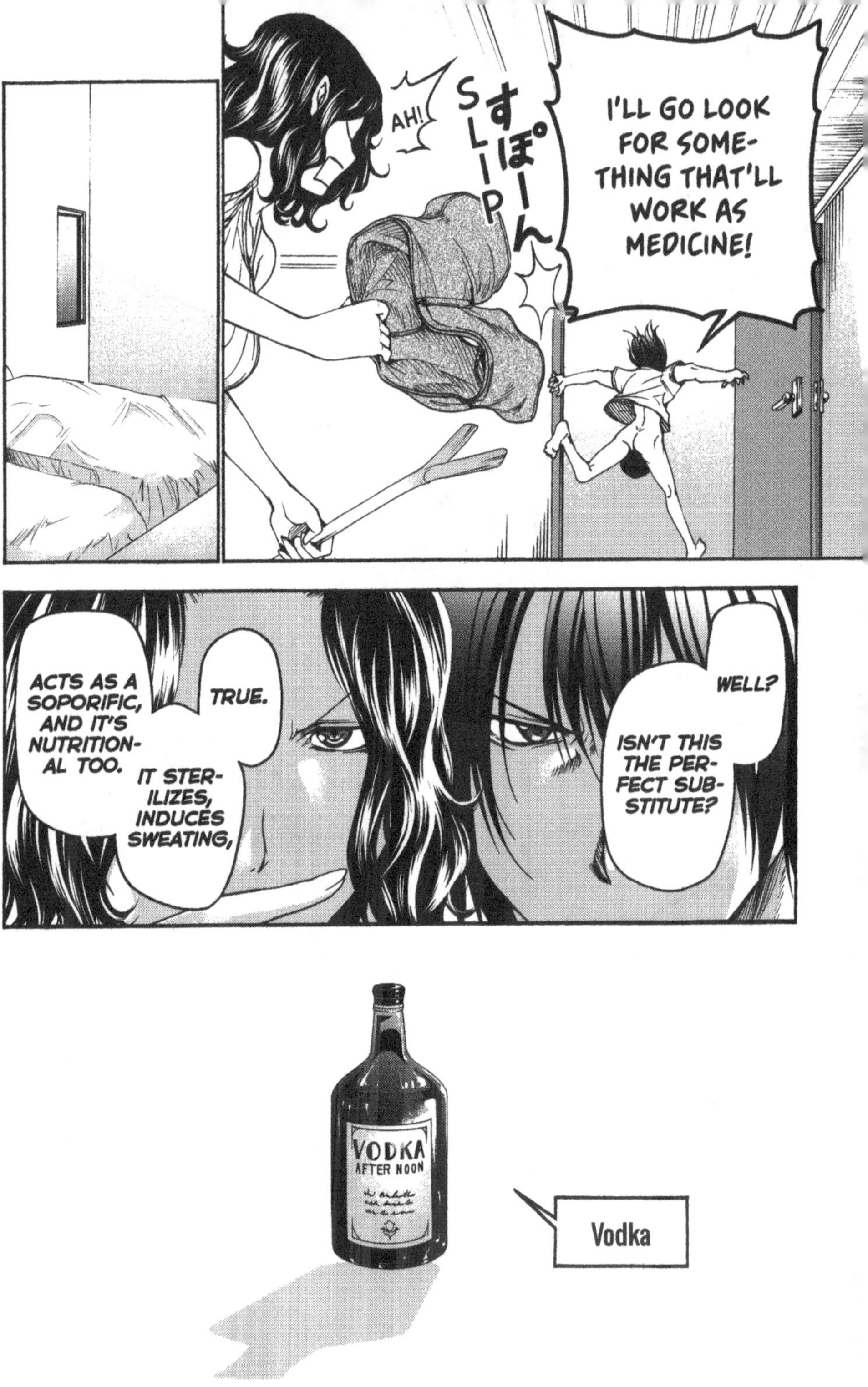
I'LL GO LOOK FOR SOME-THING THAT'LL WORK AS MEDICINE!
すぽーん
SLIP
AH!
WELL?
ISN'T THIS THE PER-FECT SUB-STITUTE?
TRUE.
IT STER-ILIZES, INDUCES SWEATING,
ACTS AS A SOPORIFIC, AND IT'S NUTRITION-AL TOO.
VODKA
AFTER NOON
Vodka

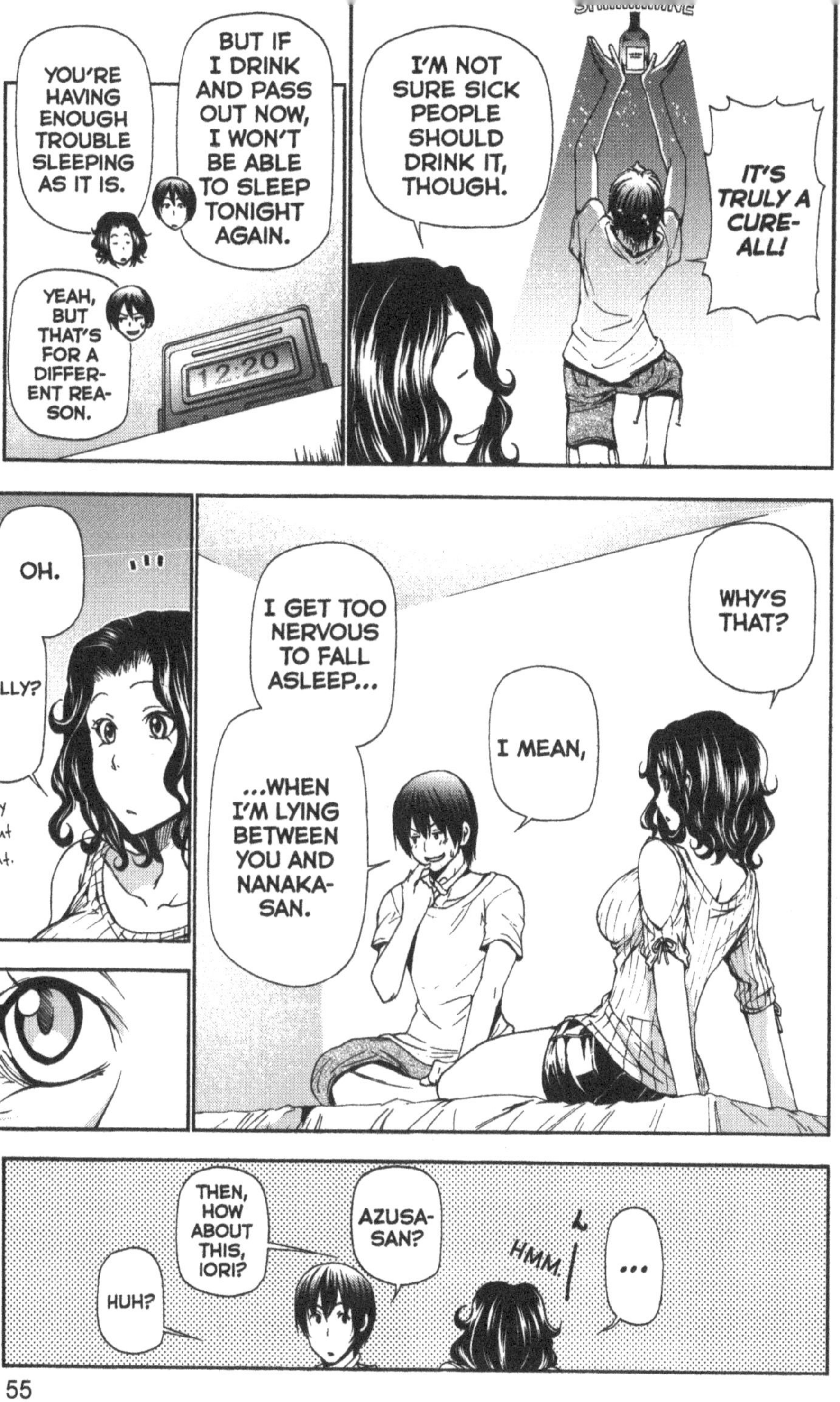
IT'S TRULY A CURE-ALL!
I'M NOT SURE SICK PEOPLE SHOULD DRINK IT, THOUGH.
BUT IF I DRINK AND PASS OUT NOW, I WON'T BE ABLE TO SLEEP TONIGHT AGAIN.
YOU'RE HAVING ENOUGH TROUBLE SLEEPING AS IT IS.
YEAH, BUT THAT'S FOR A DIFFER-ENT REA-SON.
12:20
WHY'S THAT?
I MEAN,
I GET TOO NERVOUS TO FALL ASLEEP...
...WHEN I'M LYING BETWEEN YOU AND NANAKA-SAN.
...
OH.
REALLY?
Sorry about that.
...
HMM.
AZUSA-SAN?
THEN, HOW ABOUT THIS, IORI?
HUH?

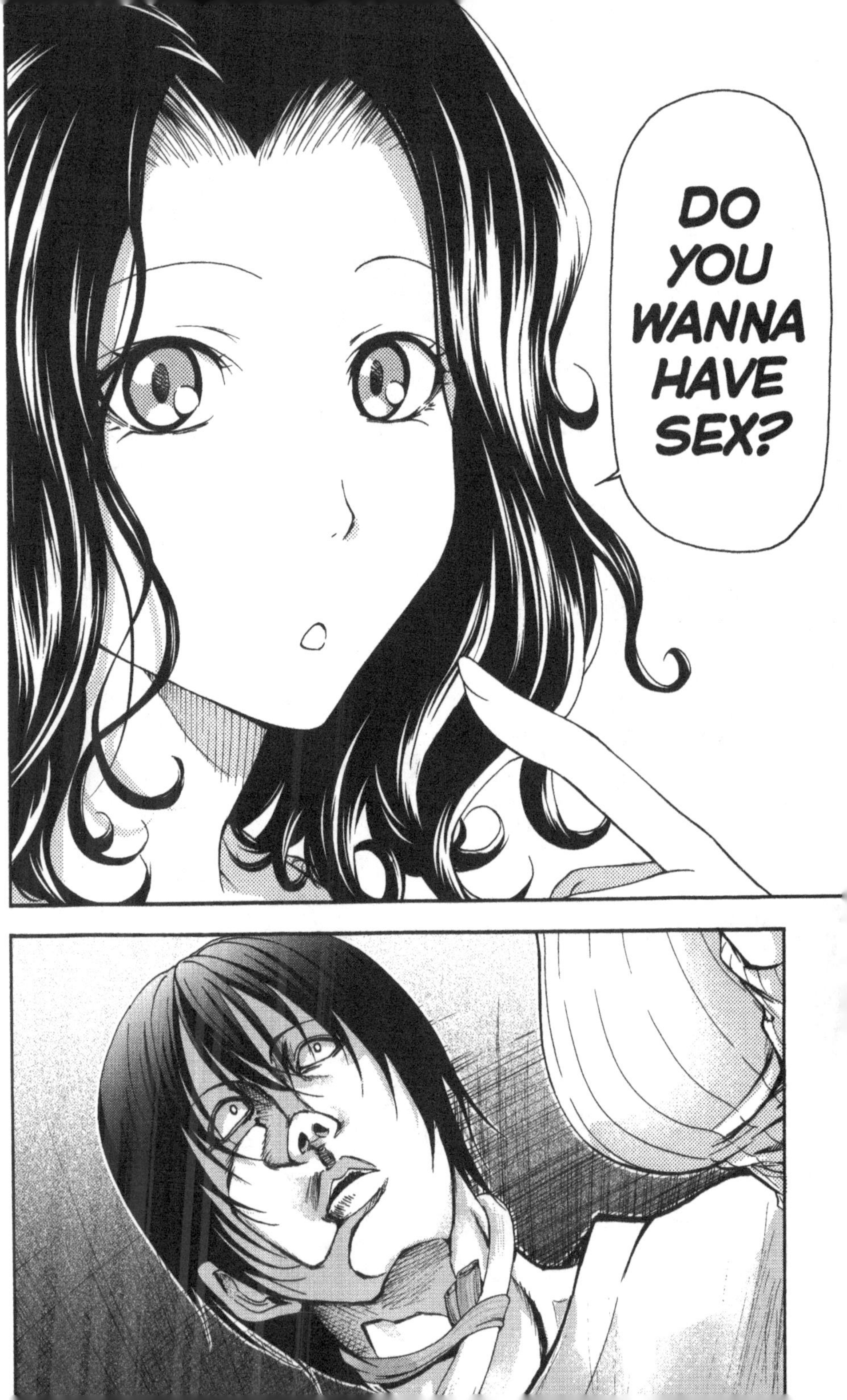
DO YOU WANNA HAVE SEX?

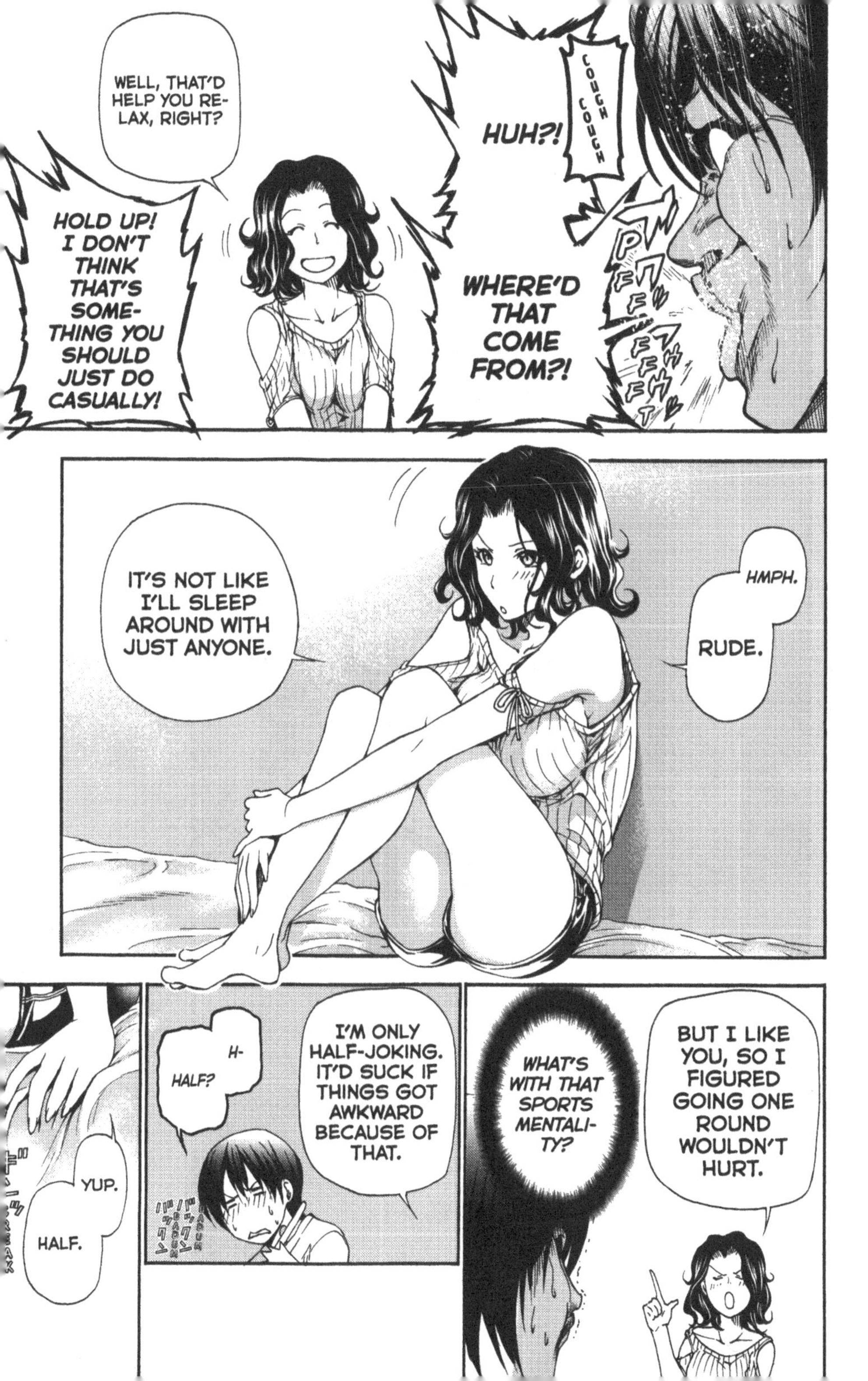
COUGH COUGH
HUH?!
PFFFFFT
WHERE'D THAT COME FROM?!
WELL, THAT'D HELP YOU RE-LAX, RIGHT?
HOLD UP! I DON'T THINK THAT'S SOME-THING YOU SHOULD JUST DO CASUALLY!
HMPH.
RUDE.
IT'S NOT LIKE I'LL SLEEP AROUND WITH JUST ANYONE.
BUT I LIKE YOU, SO I FIGURED GOING ONE ROUND WOULDN'T HURT.
WHAT'S WITH THAT SPORTS MENTALI-TY?
I'M ONLY HALF-JOKING. IT'D SUCK IF THINGS GOT AWKWARD BECAUSE OF THAT.
H- HALF?
BADUM BADUM
YUP.
HALF.

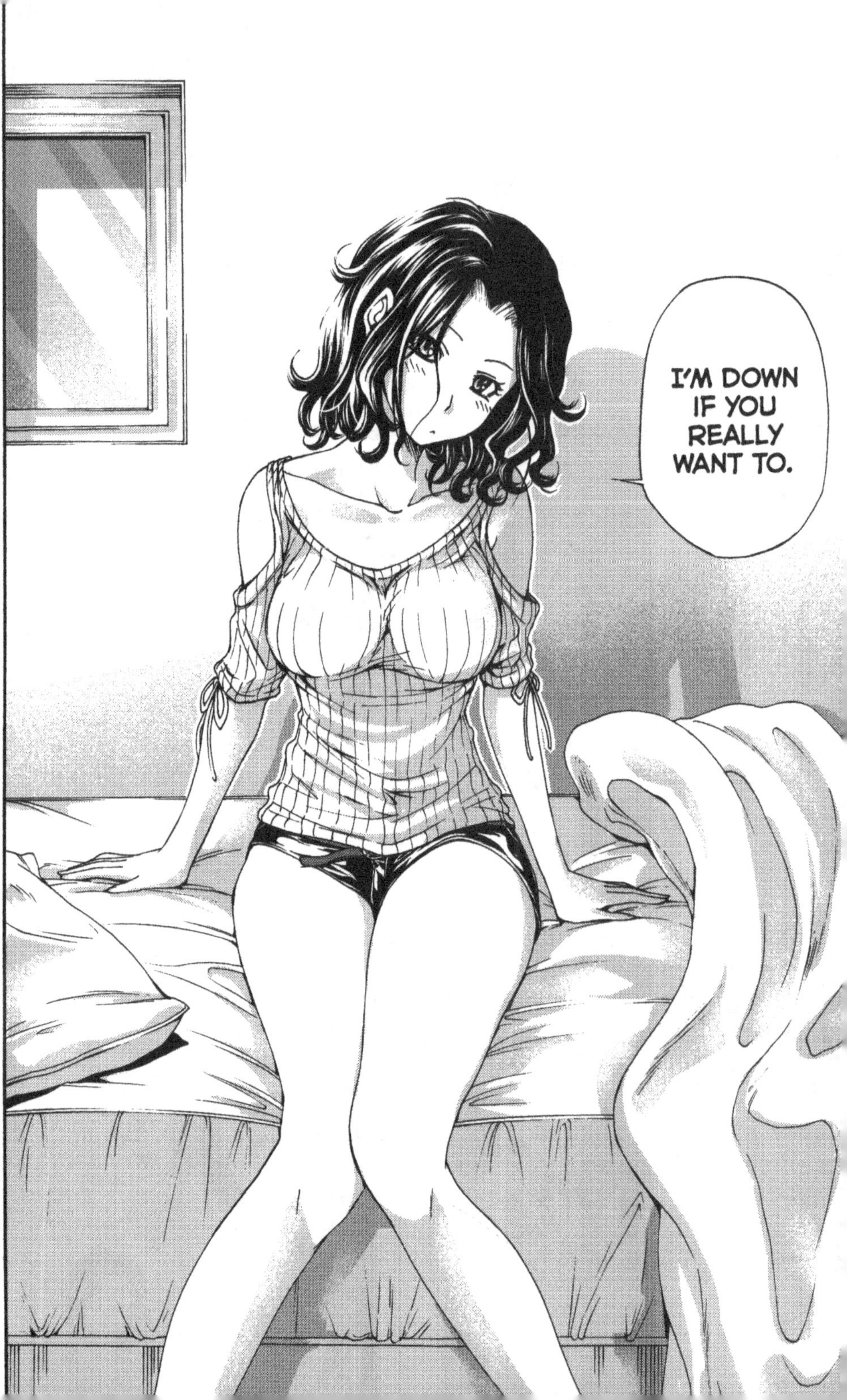
I'M DOWN IF YOU REALLY WANT TO.

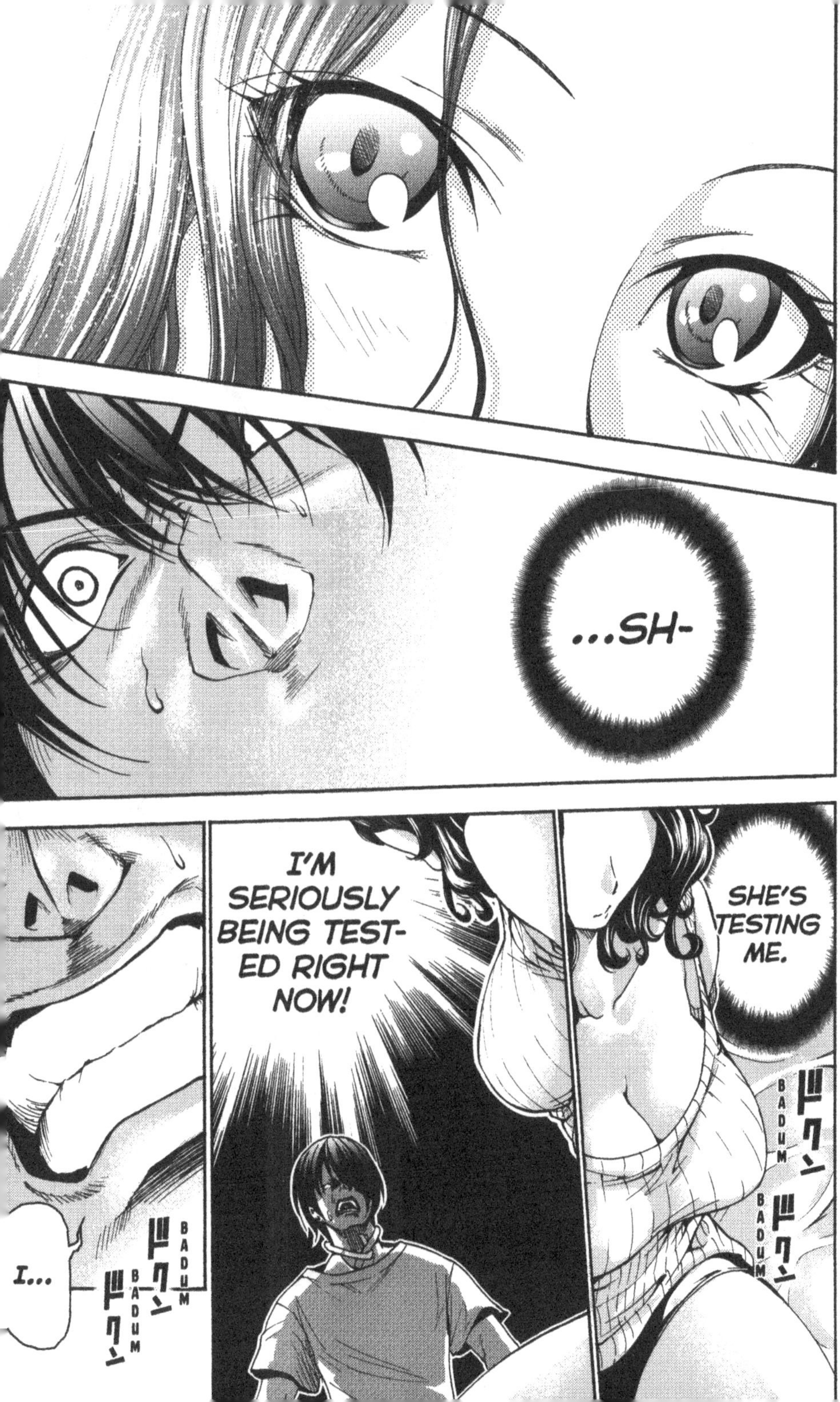
...SH-
SHE'S TESTING ME.
ドクン BADUM
ドクン BADUM
I'M SERIOUSLY BEING TEST-ED RIGHT NOW!
I...
ドクン BADUM
ドクン BADUM

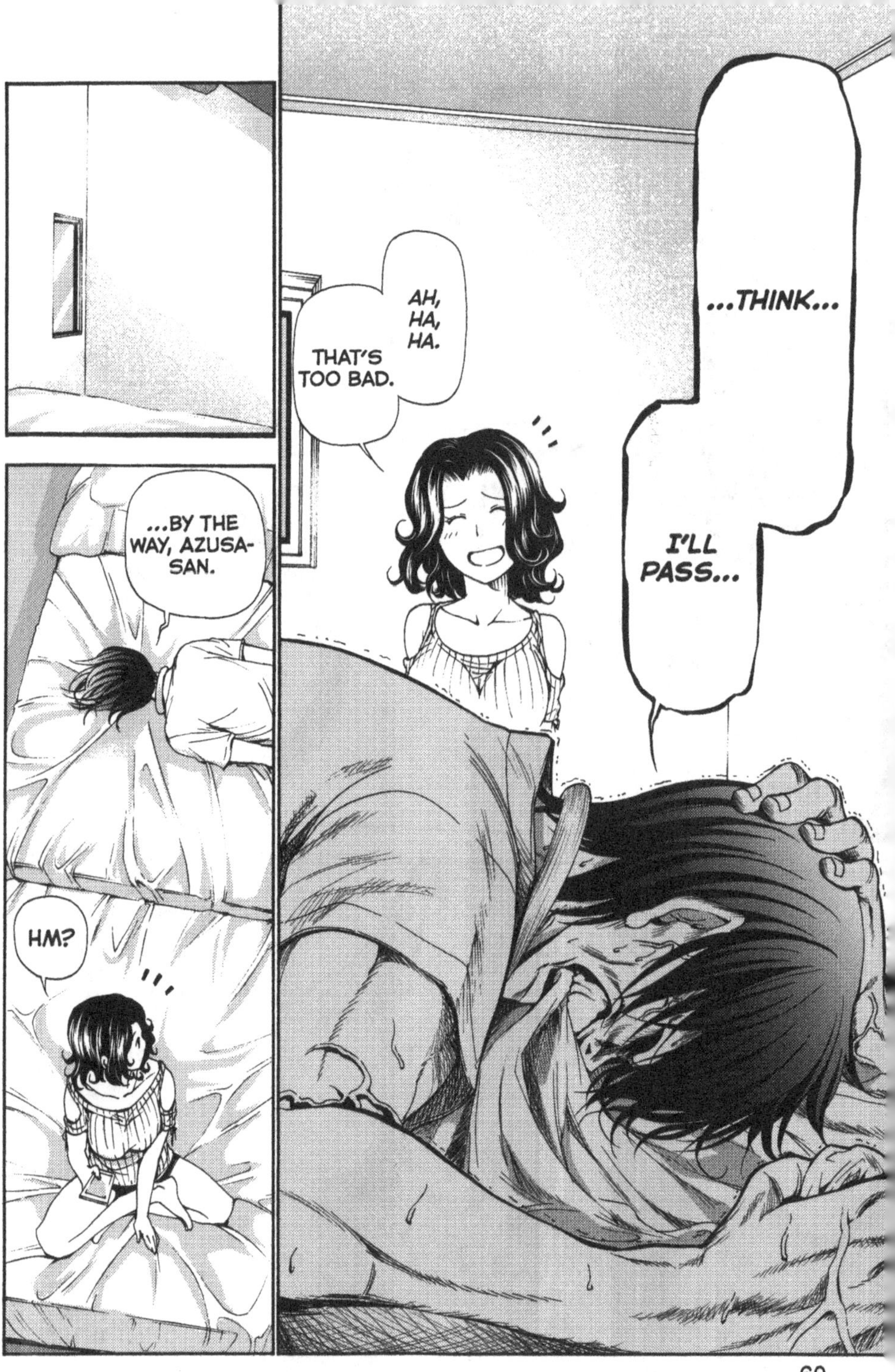
...THINK...
I'LL PASS...
AH, HA, HA.
THAT'S TOO BAD.
...BY THE WAY, AZUSA-SAN.
HM?

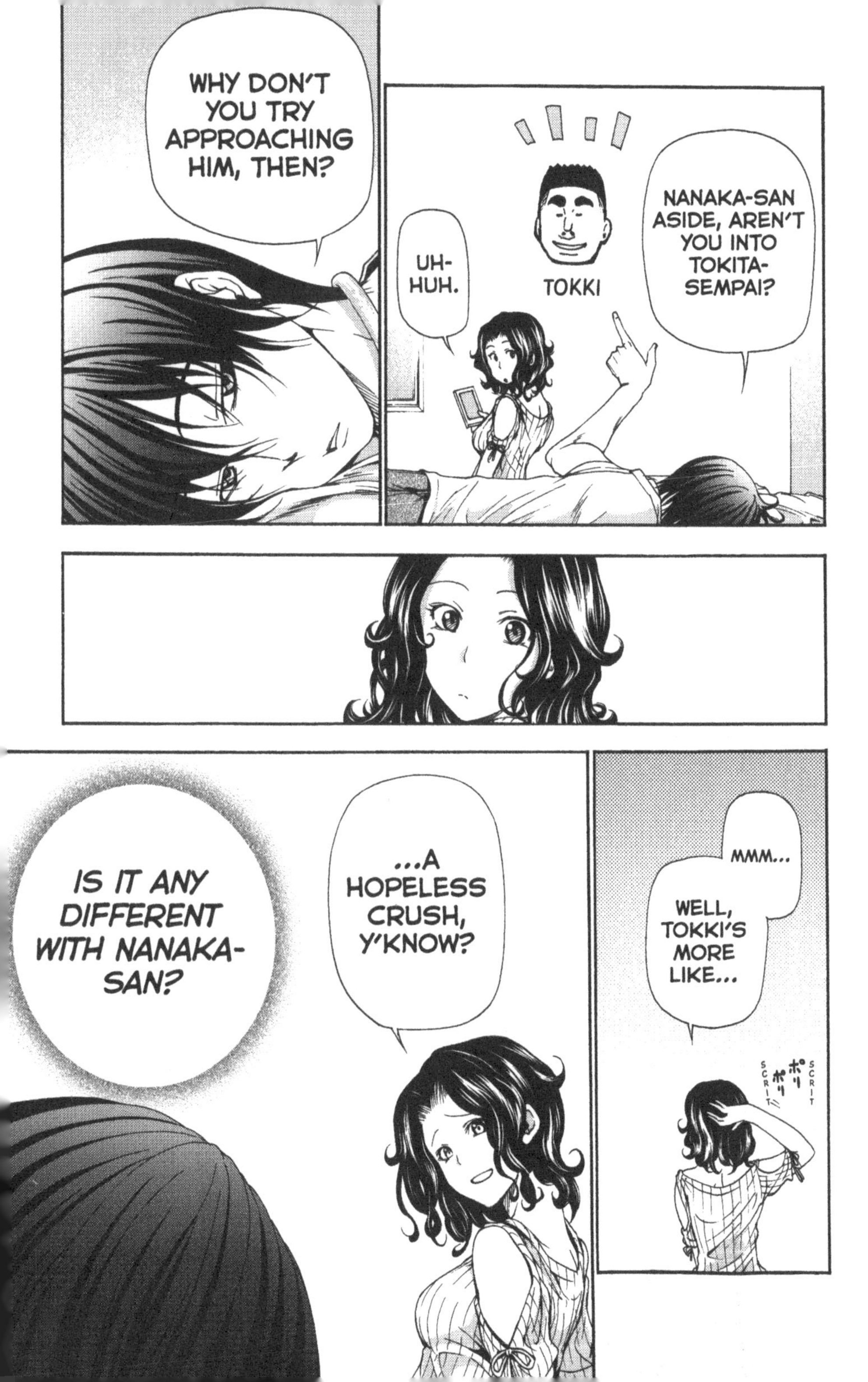
NANAKA-SAN ASIDE, AREN'T YOU INTO TOKITA-SEMPAI?
TOKKI
UH-HUH.
WHY DON'T YOU TRY APPROACHING HIM, THEN?
MMM...
WELL, TOKKI'S MORE LIKE...
ポリ ポリ
SCRIT SCRIT
...A HOPELESS CRUSH, Y'KNOW?
IS IT ANY DIFFERENT WITH NANAKA-SAN?

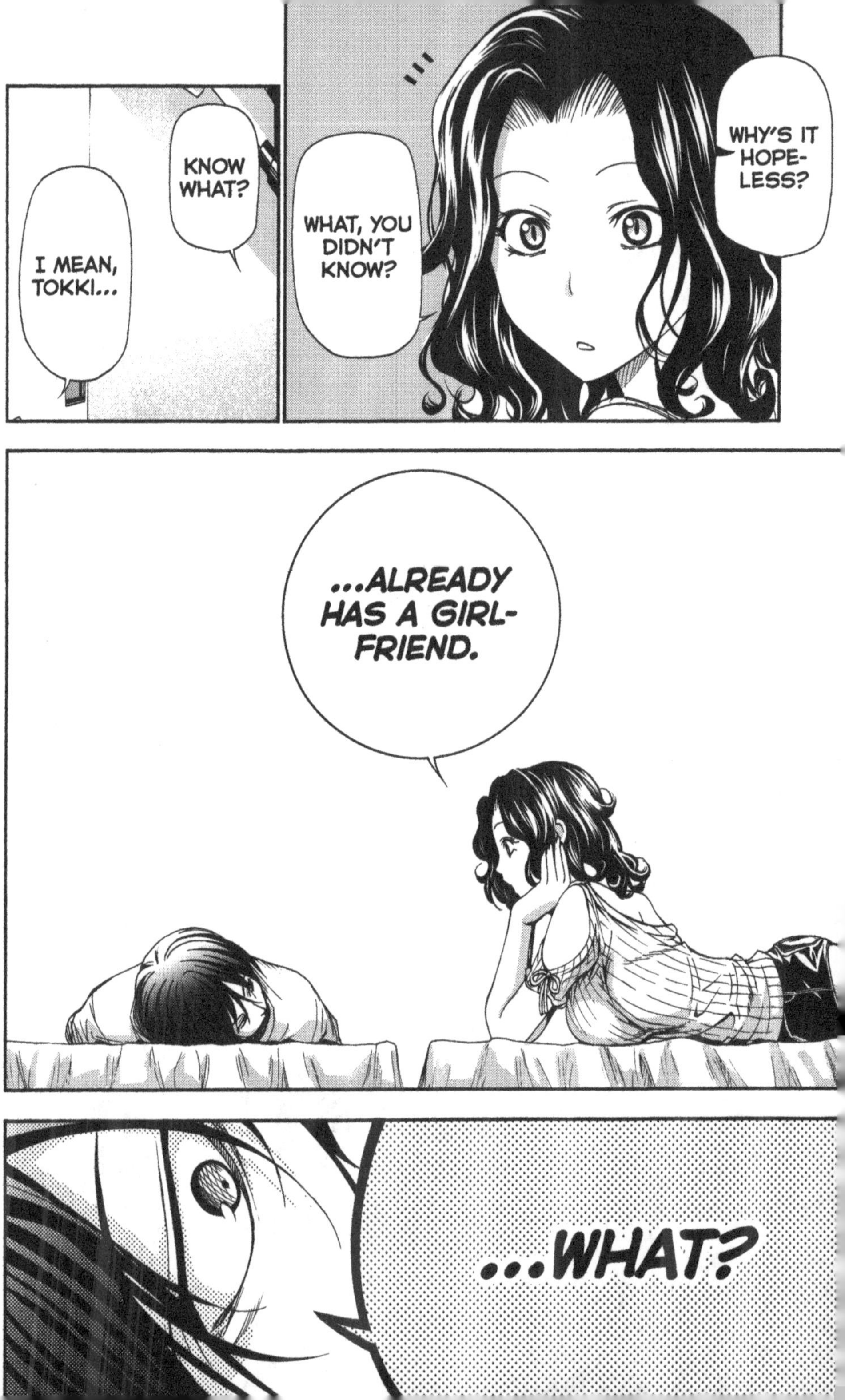
WHY'S IT HOPE-LESS?
WHAT, YOU DIDN'T KNOW?
KNOW WHAT?
I MEAN, TOKKI...
...ALREADY HAS A GIRL-FRIEND.
...WHAT?

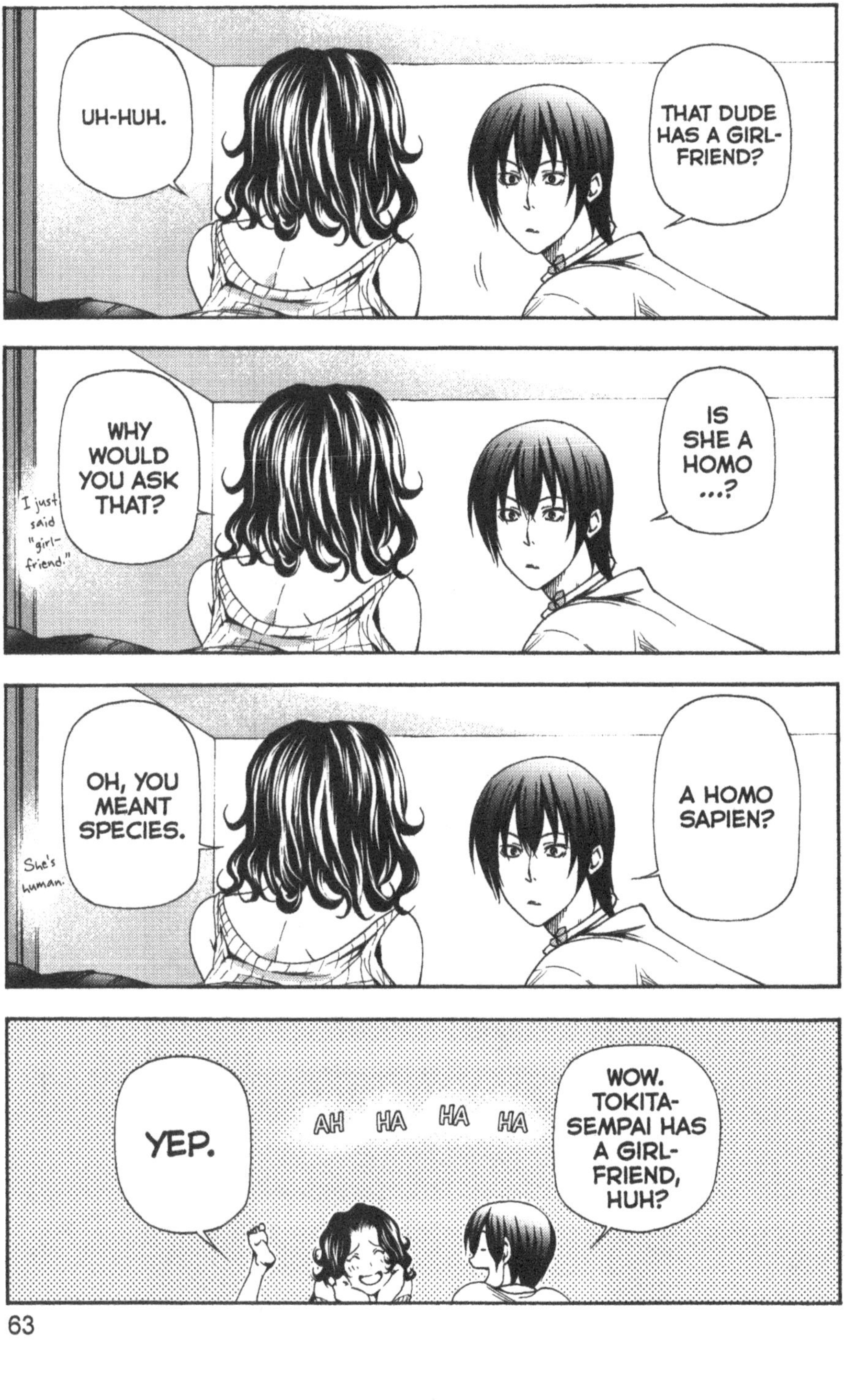
THAT DUDE HAS A GIRL-FRIEND?
UH-HUH.
IS SHE A HOMO ...?
WHY WOULD YOU ASK THAT?
I just said "girl-friend."
A HOMO SAPIEN?
OH, YOU MEANT SPECIES.
She's human.
WOW. TOKITA-SEMPAI HAS A GIRL-FRIEND, HUH?
AH HA HA HA
YEP.

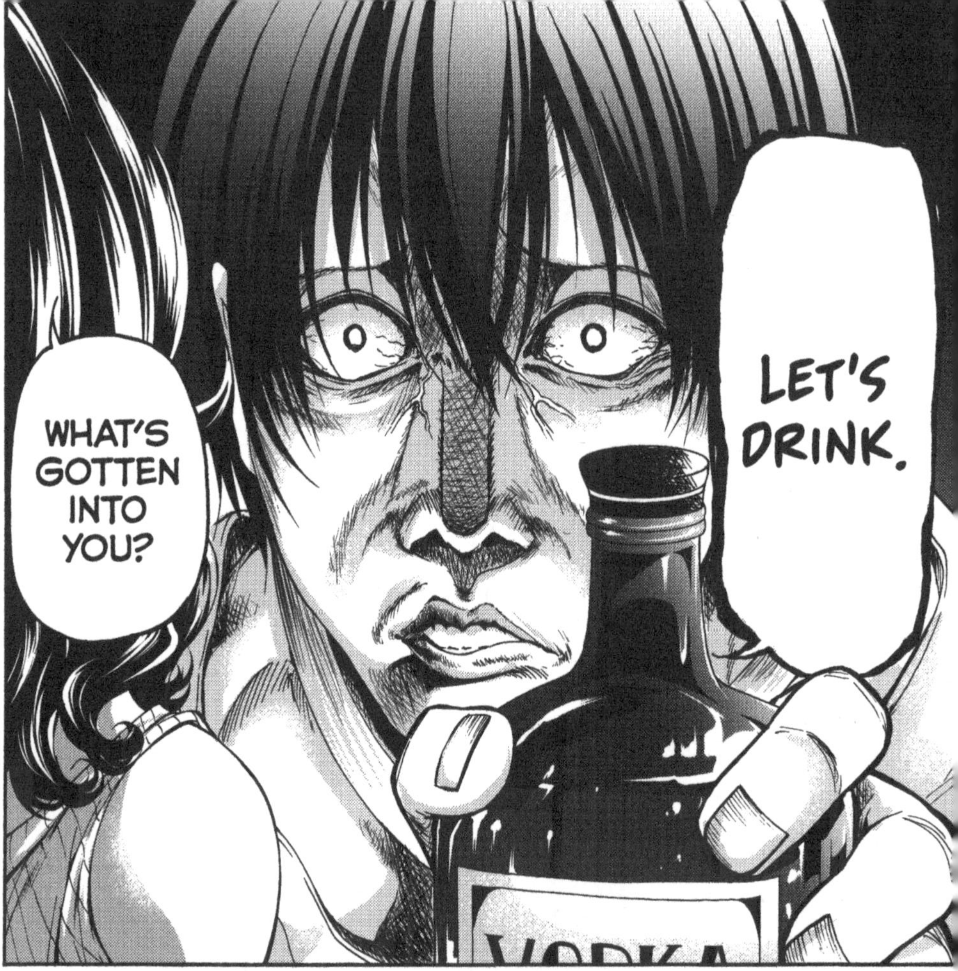
LET'S DRINK.
WHAT'S GOTTEN INTO YOU?
VODKA

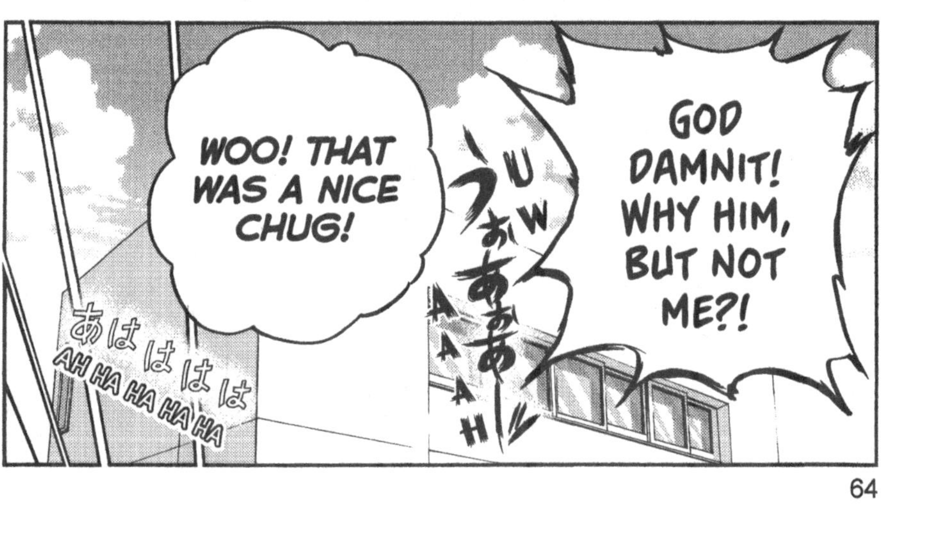
GOD DAMNIT! WHY HIM, BUT NOT ME?!
うぉあぁあ
UWAAAAH
WOO! THAT WAS A NICE CHUG!
あははははは
AH HA HA HA HA

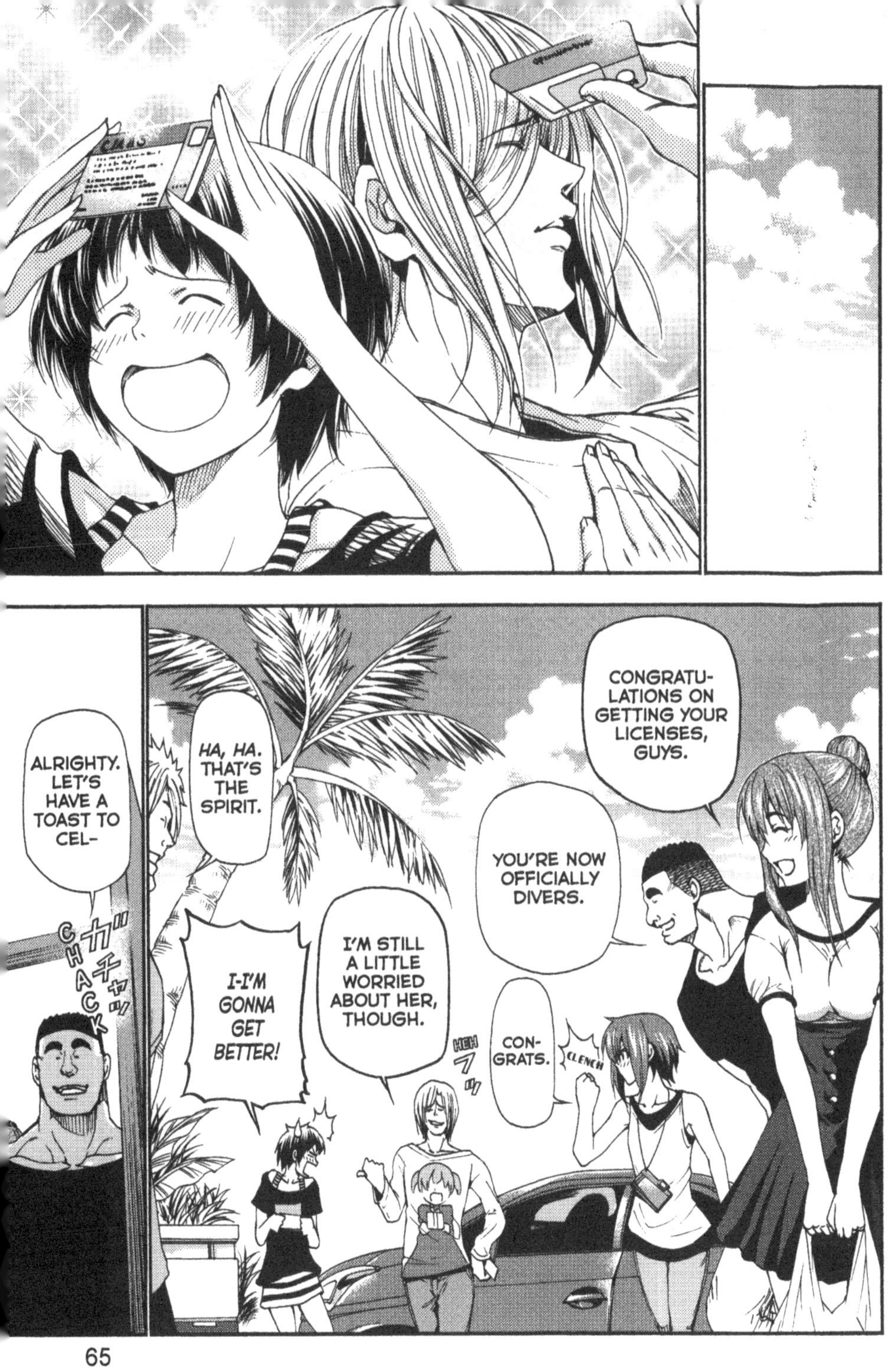
CONGRATU-LATIONS ON GETTING YOUR LICENSES, GUYS.
YOU'RE NOW OFFICIALLY DIVERS.
CON-GRATS.
CLENCH
HEH
I'M STILL A LITTLE WORRIED ABOUT HER, THOUGH.
I-I'M GONNA GET BETTER!
HA, HA. THAT'S THE SPIRIT.
ALRIGHTY. LET'S HAVE A TOAST TO CEL-
CHACK

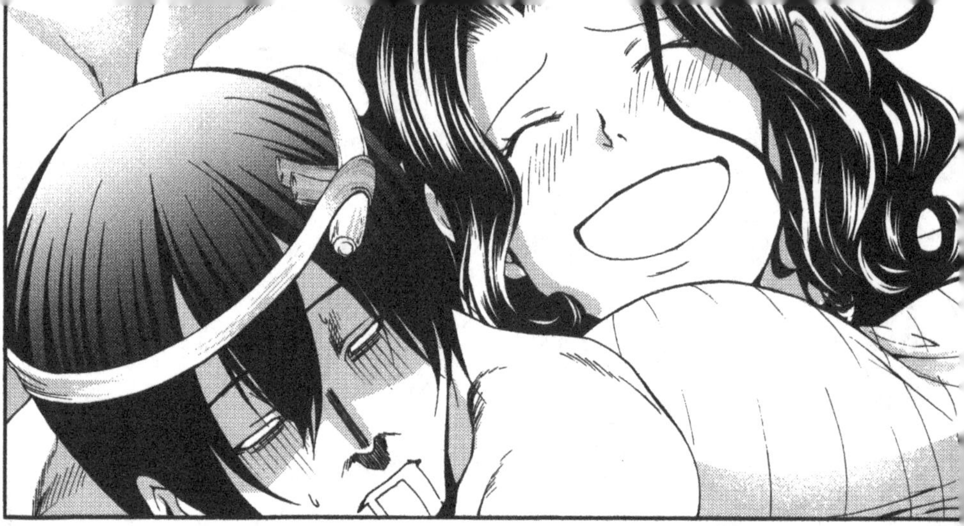

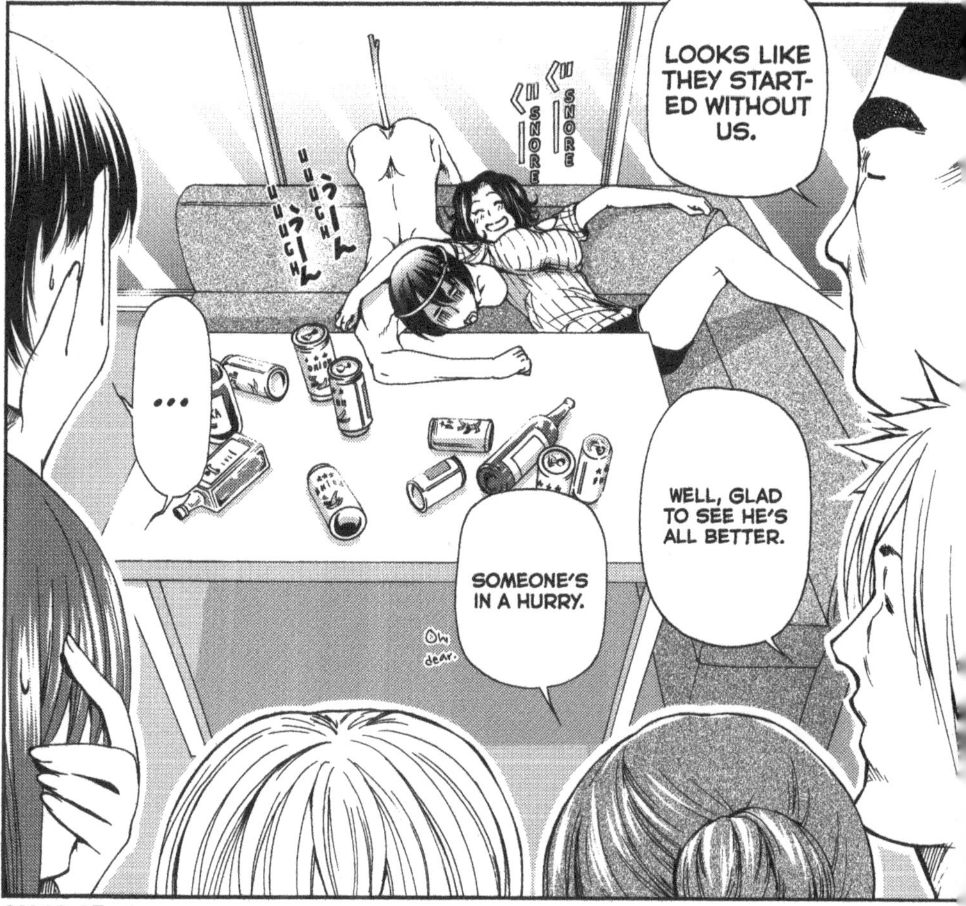
LOOKS LIKE THEY STARTED WITHOUT US.
SNORE
SNORE
UUUGH
UUUGH
...
WELL, GLAD TO SEE HE'S ALL BETTER.
SOMEONE'S IN A HURRY.
Oh dear.

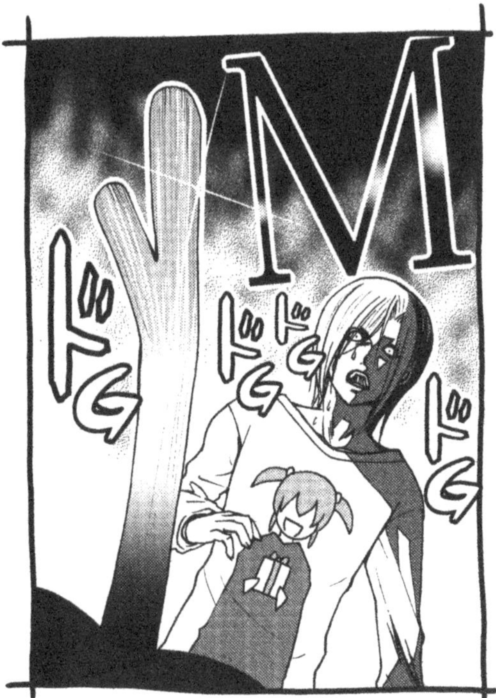
M
ドG
ドG
ドG
ドG

Grand Blue Dreaming

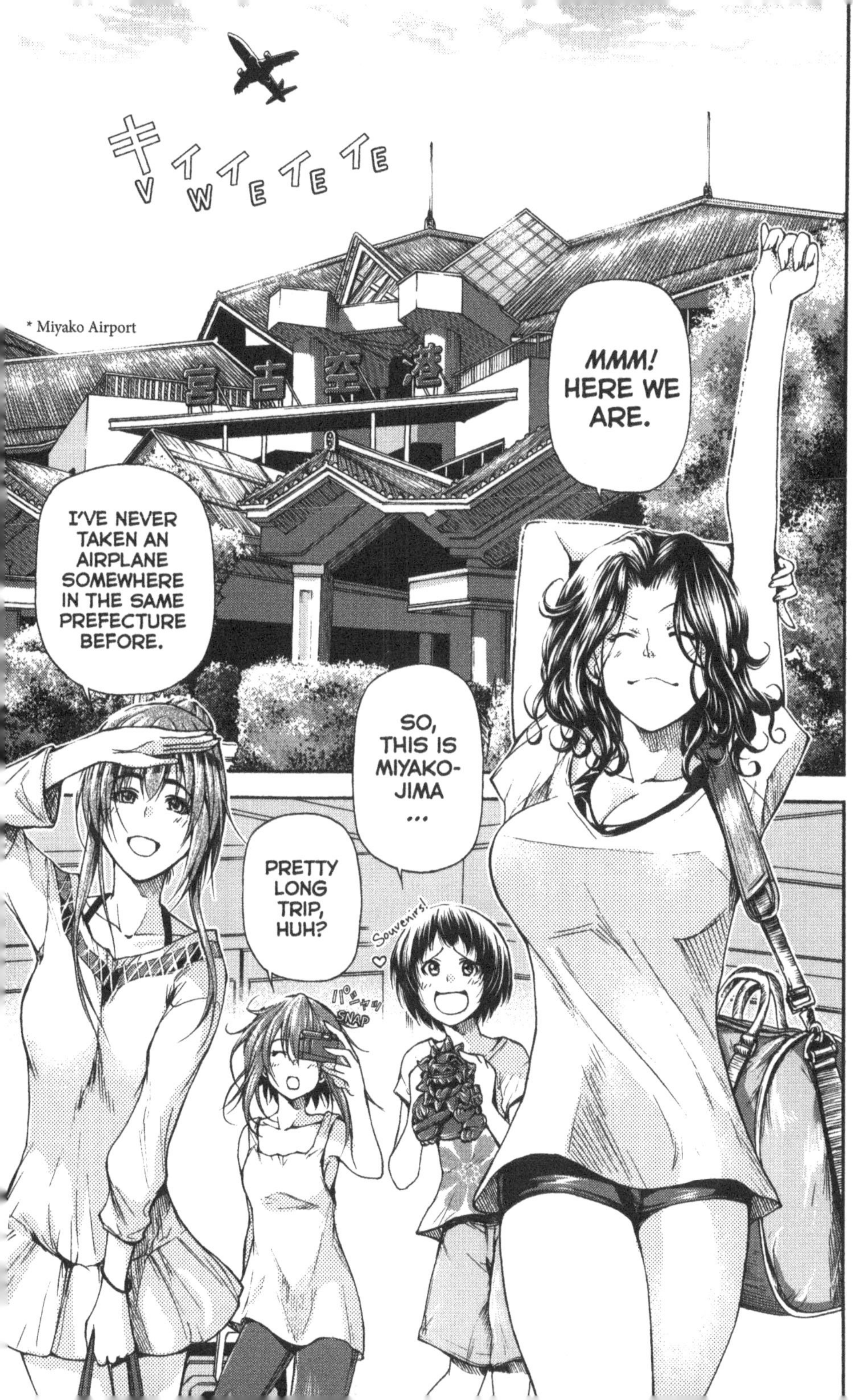
VWEEE
* Miyako Airport
MMM! HERE WE ARE.
I'VE NEVER TAKEN AN AIRPLANE SOMEWHERE IN THE SAME PREFECTURE BEFORE.
SO, THIS IS MIYAKO-JIMA ...
PRETTY LONG TRIP, HUH?
Souvenirs!
SNAP

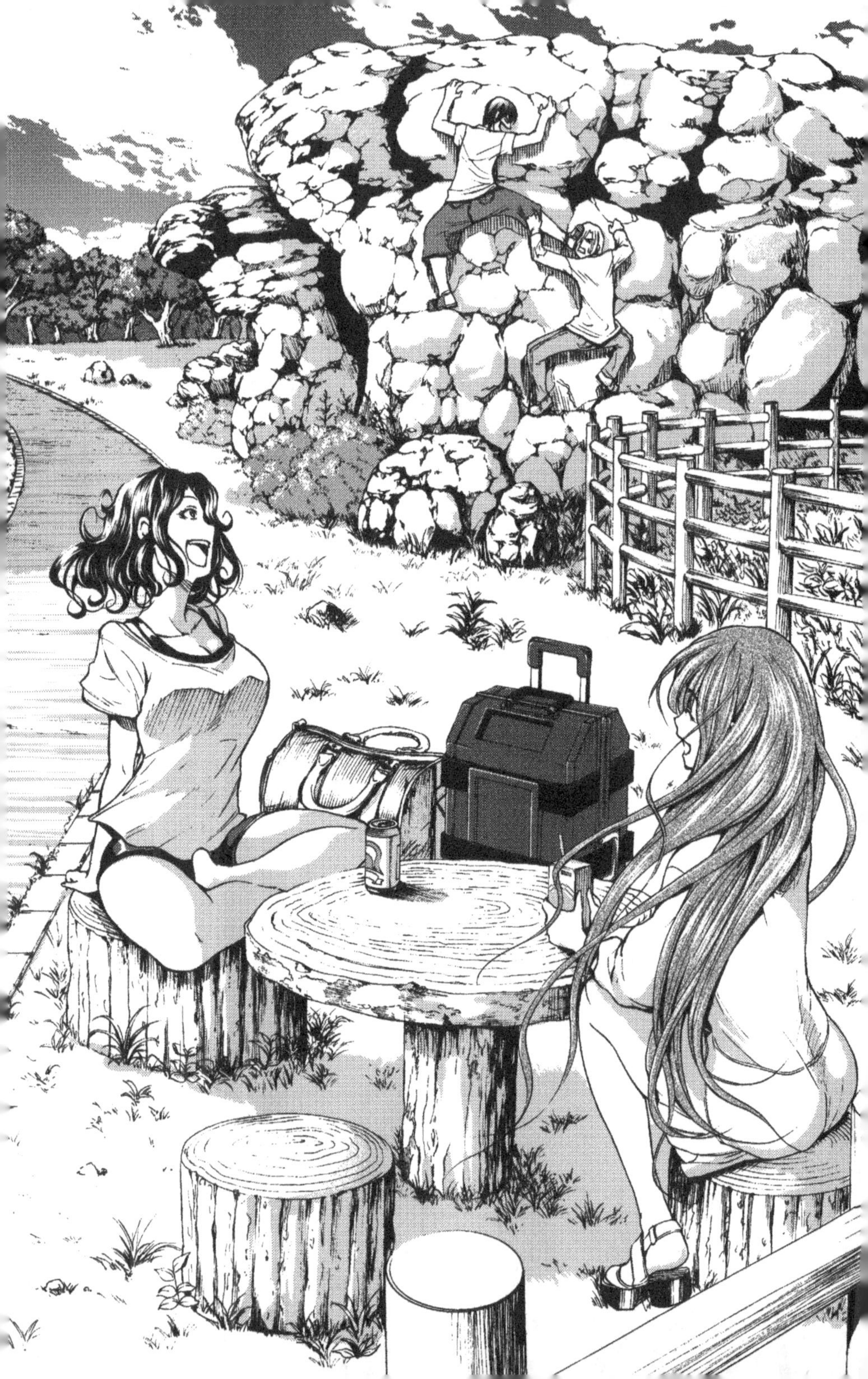

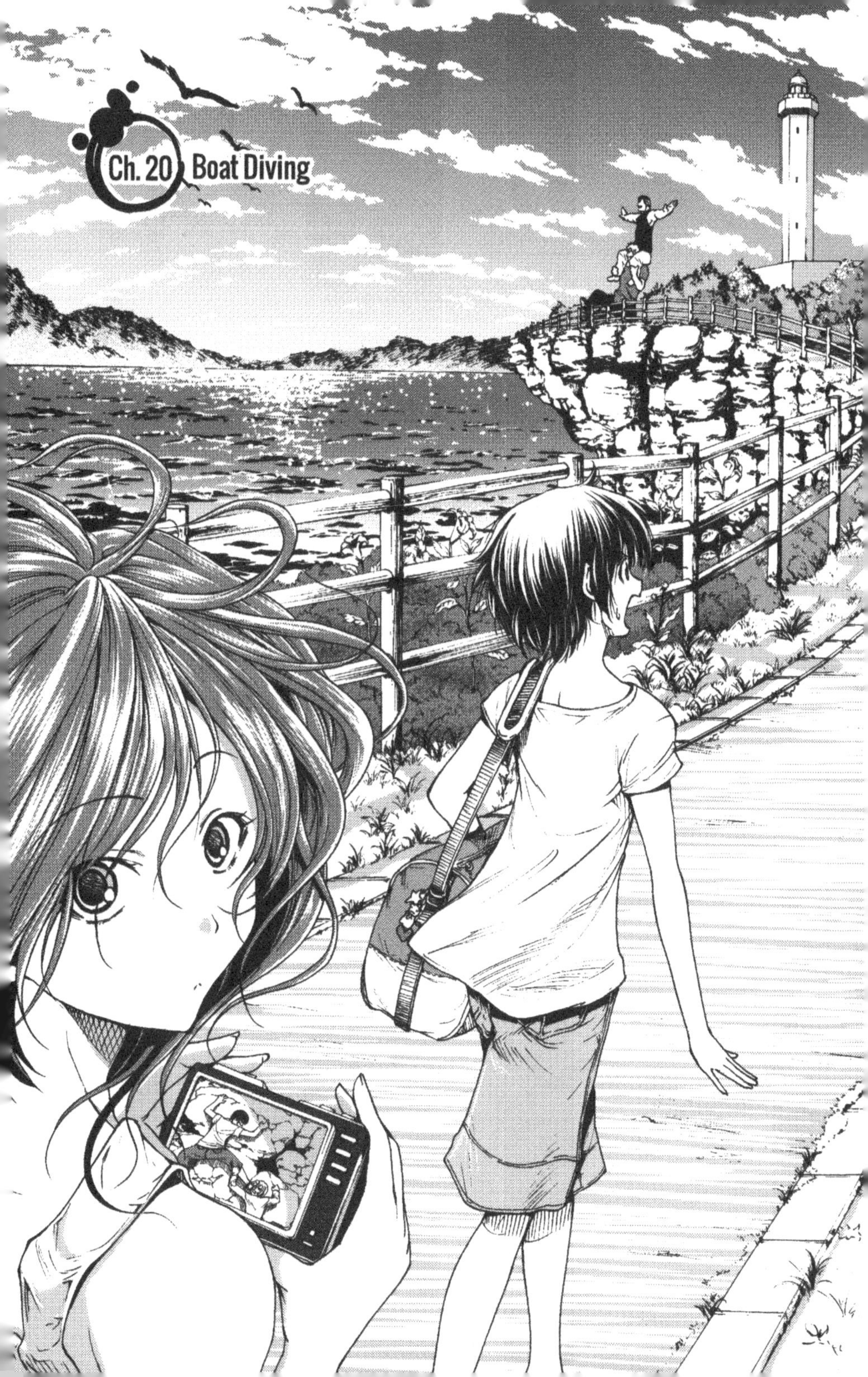
Ch. 20 Boat Diving

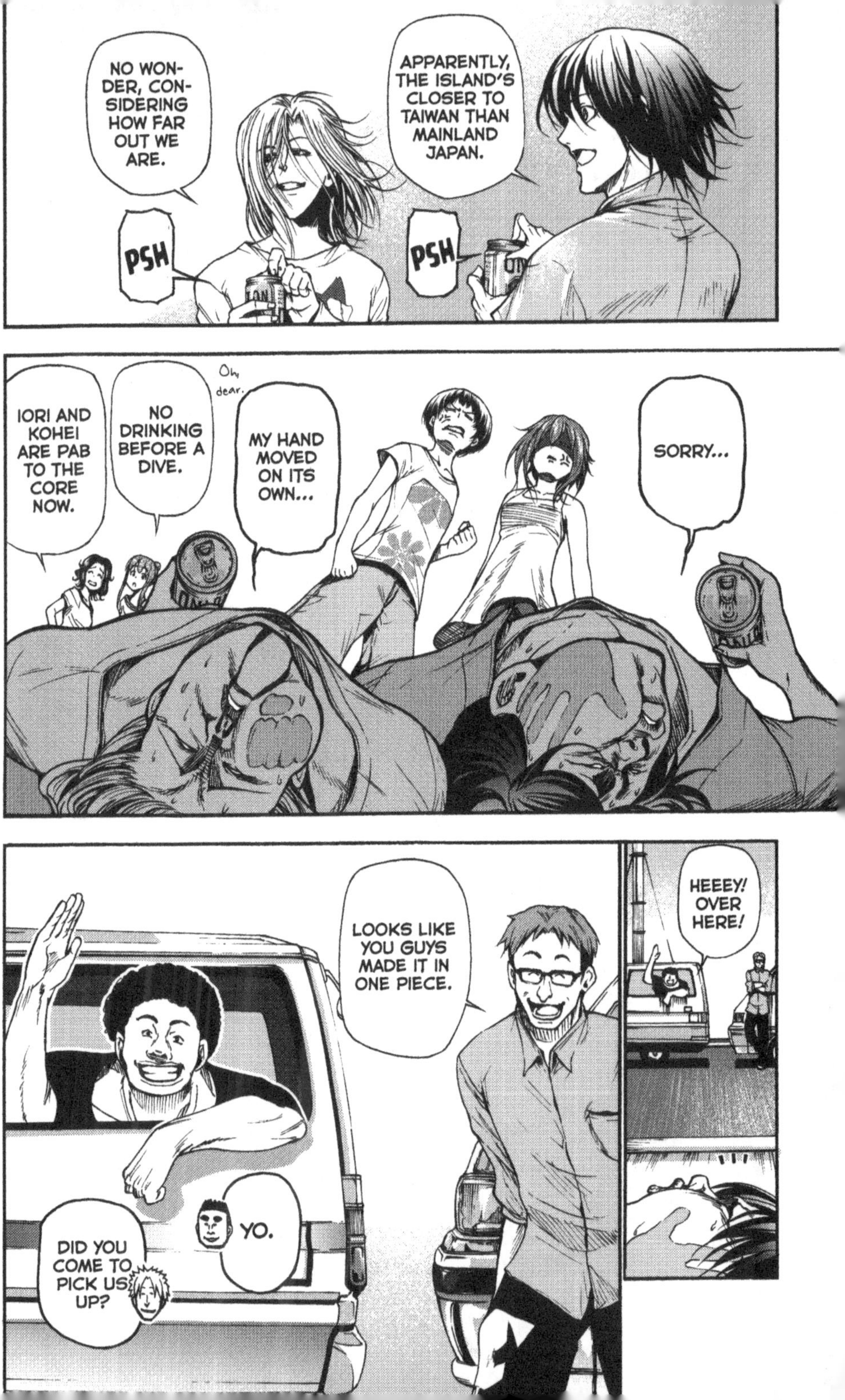
APPARENTLY, THE ISLAND'S CLOSER TO TAIWAN THAN MAINLAND JAPAN.
PSH
NO WONDER, CONSIDERING HOW FAR OUT WE ARE.
PSH
SORRY...
MY HAND MOVED ON ITS OWN...
Oh dear.
NO DRINKING BEFORE A DIVE.
IORI AND KOHEI ARE PAB TO THE CORE NOW.
HEEEY! OVER HERE!
LOOKS LIKE YOU GUYS MADE IT IN ONE PIECE.
YO.
DID YOU COME TO PICK US UP?

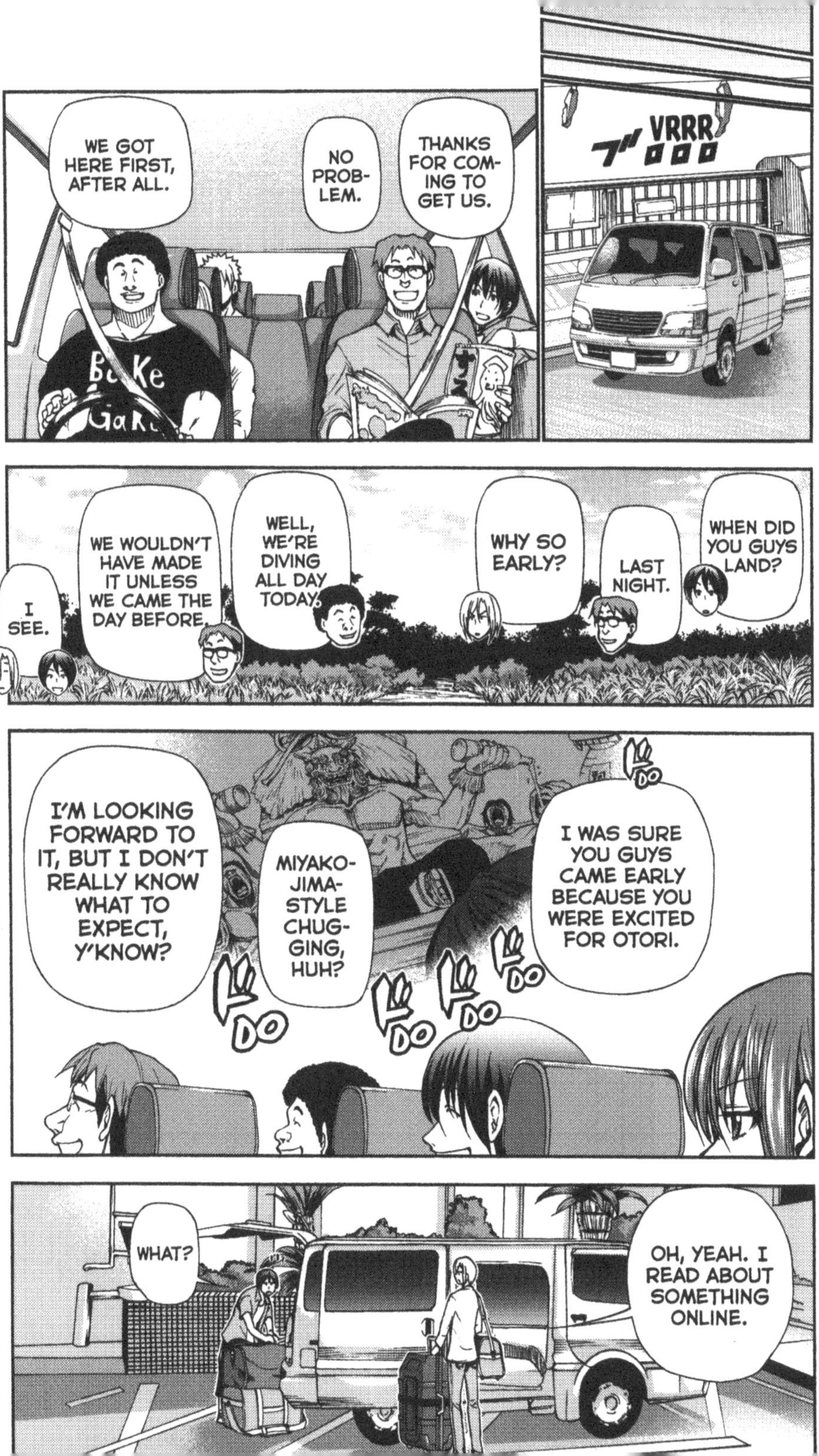

ブロロロ VRRR
THANKS FOR COMING TO GET US.
NO PROBLEM.
WE GOT HERE FIRST, AFTER ALL.
WHEN DID YOU GUYS LAND?
LAST NIGHT.
WHY SO EARLY?
WELL, WE'RE DIVING ALL DAY TODAY.
WE WOULDN'T HAVE MADE IT UNLESS WE CAME THE DAY BEFORE.
I SEE.
ド DO
I WAS SURE YOU GUYS CAME EARLY BECAUSE YOU WERE EXCITED FOR OTORI.
MIYAKOJIMA-STYLE CHUGGING, HUH?
I'M LOOKING FORWARD TO IT, BUT I DON'T REALLY KNOW WHAT TO EXPECT, Y'KNOW?
ド DO
ド DO
ド DO
ド DO
OH, YEAH. I READ ABOUT SOMETHING ONLINE.
WHAT?

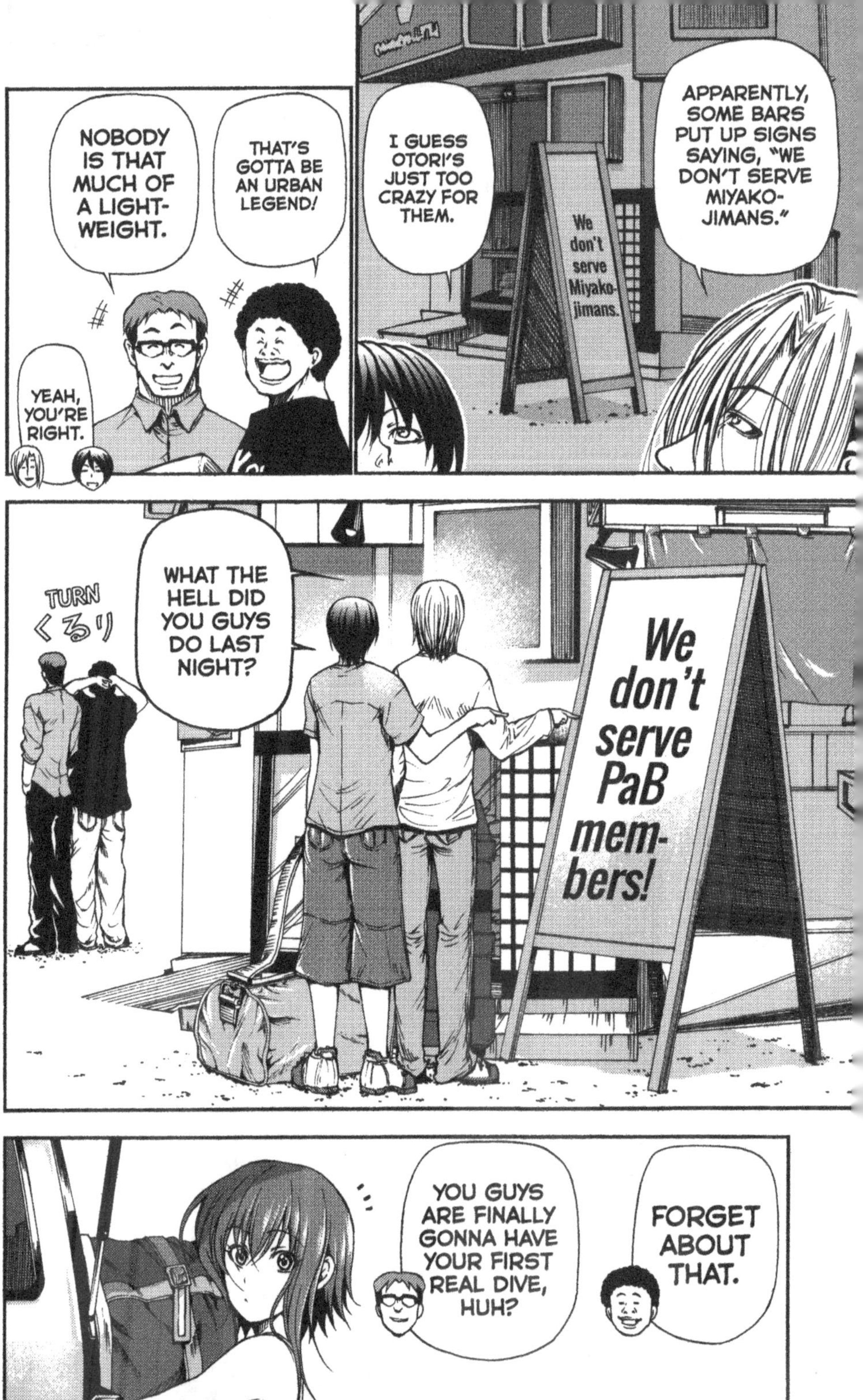
APPARENTLY, SOME BARS PUT UP SIGNS SAYING, "WE DON'T SERVE MIYAKO-JIMANS."
I GUESS OTORI'S JUST TOO CRAZY FOR THEM.
We don't serve Miyako-jimans.
THAT'S GOTTA BE AN URBAN LEGEND!
NOBODY IS THAT MUCH OF A LIGHT-WEIGHT.
YEAH, YOU'RE RIGHT.
We don't serve PaB mem-bers!
WHAT THE HELL DID YOU GUYS DO LAST NIGHT?
TURN
くるり
FORGET ABOUT THAT.
YOU GUYS ARE FINALLY GONNA HAVE YOUR FIRST REAL DIVE, HUH?

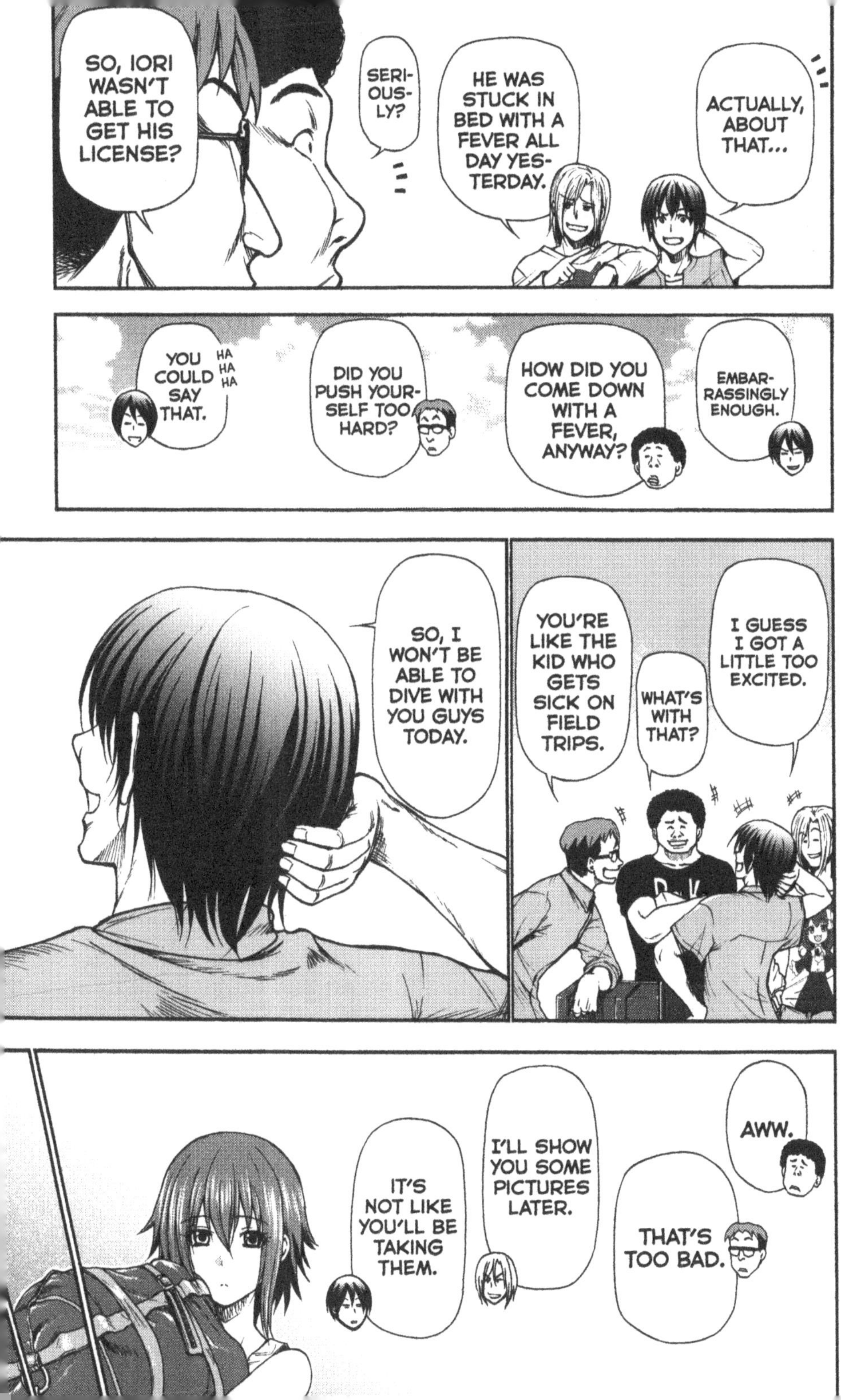
ACTUALLY, ABOUT THAT...
HE WAS STUCK IN BED WITH A FEVER ALL DAY YESTERDAY.
SERIOUSLY?
SO, IORI WASN'T ABLE TO GET HIS LICENSE?
EMBARRASSINGLY ENOUGH.
HOW DID YOU COME DOWN WITH A FEVER, ANYWAY?
DID YOU PUSH YOURSELF TOO HARD?
YOU COULD SAY THAT.
HA HA HA
I GUESS I GOT A LITTLE TOO EXCITED.
WHAT'S WITH THAT?
YOU'RE LIKE THE KID WHO GETS SICK ON FIELD TRIPS.
SO, I WON'T BE ABLE TO DIVE WITH YOU GUYS TODAY.
AWW.
THAT'S TOO BAD.
I'LL SHOW YOU SOME PICTURES LATER.
IT'S NOT LIKE YOU'LL BE TAKING THEM.

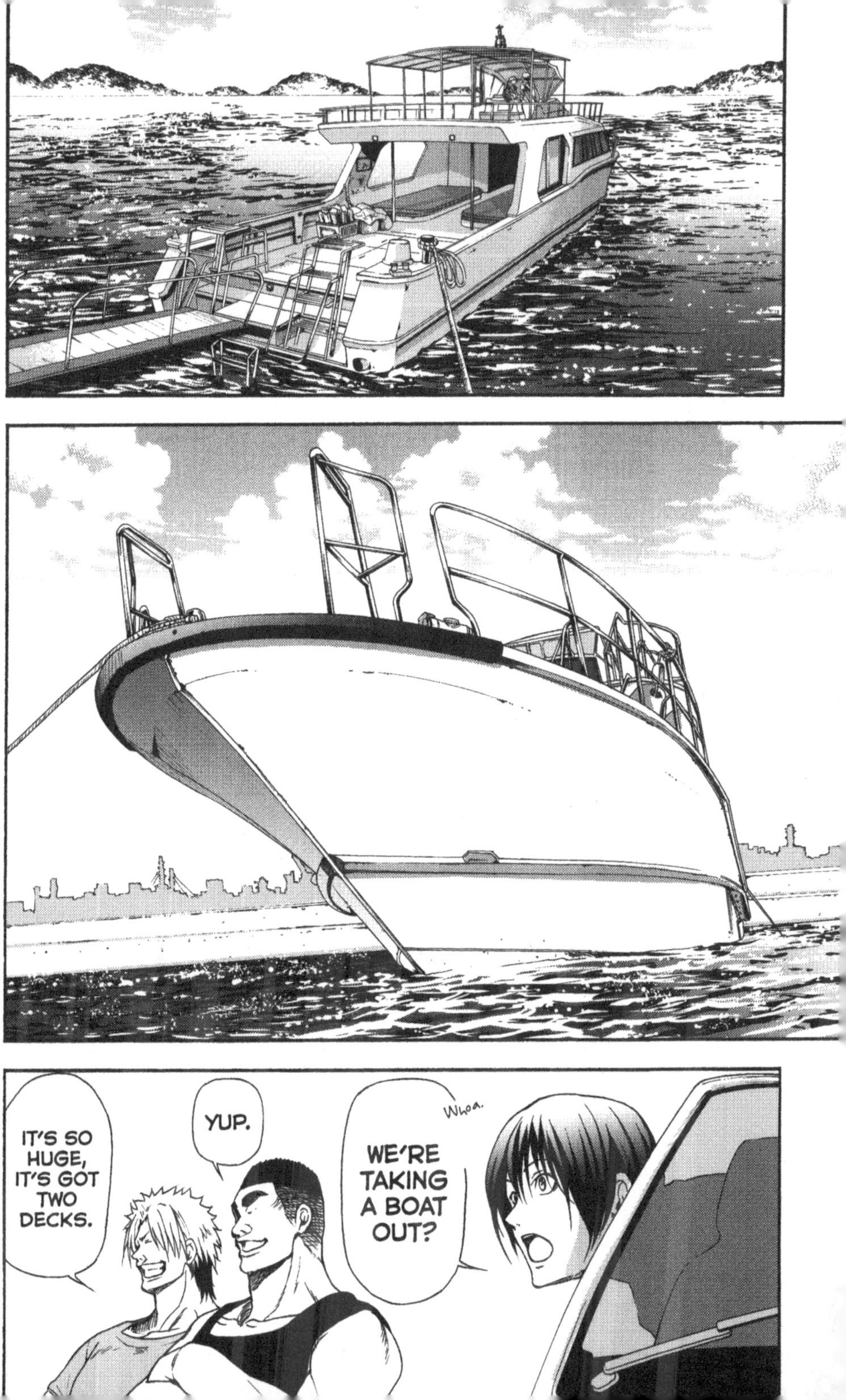
Whoa.
WE'RE TAKING A BOAT OUT?
YUP.
IT'S SO HUGE, IT'S GOT TWO DECKS.

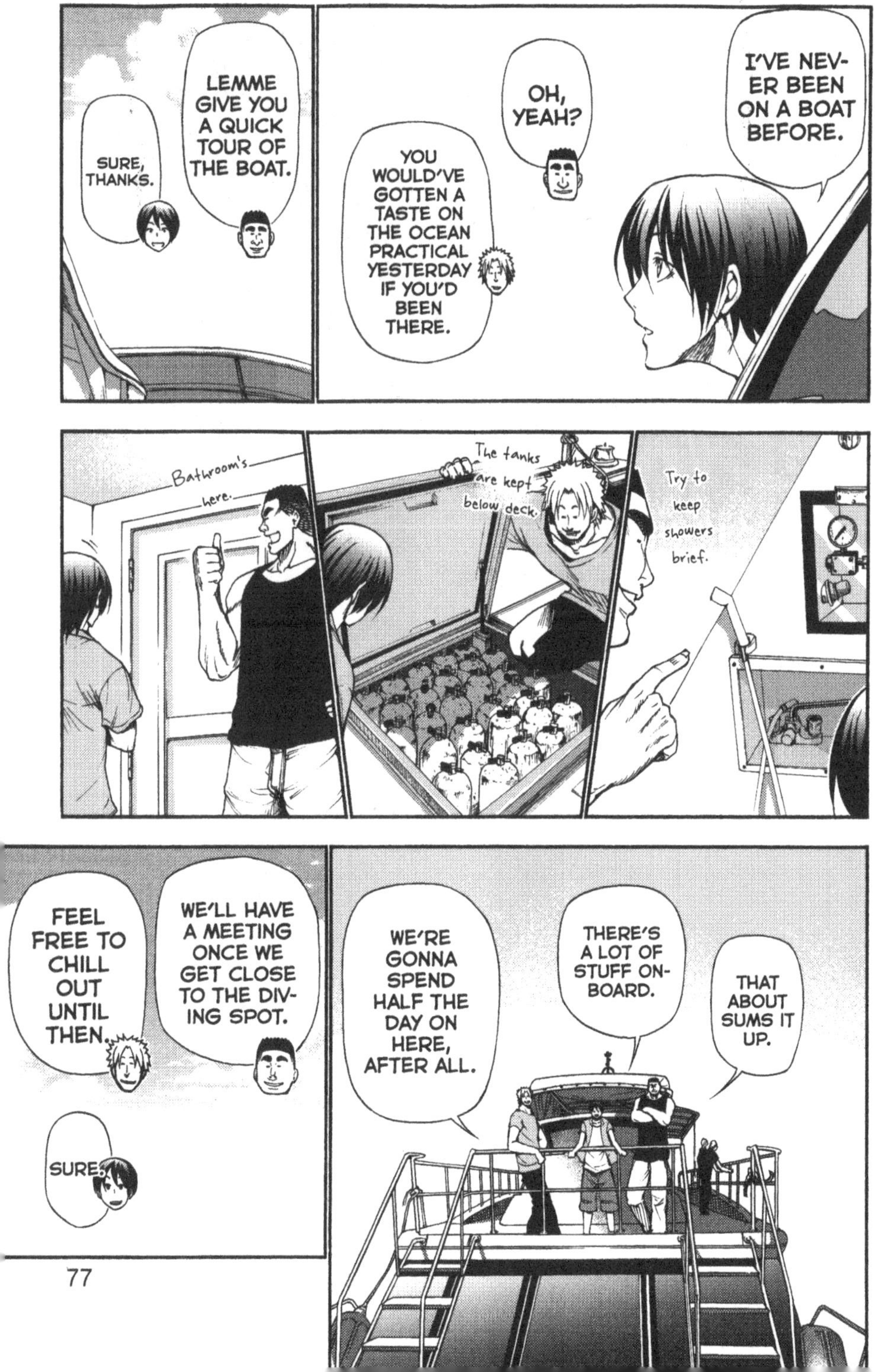
I'VE NEVER BEEN ON A BOAT BEFORE.
OH, YEAH?
YOU WOULD'VE GOTTEN A TASTE ON THE OCEAN PRACTICAL YESTERDAY IF YOU'D BEEN THERE.
LEMME GIVE YOU A QUICK TOUR OF THE BOAT.
SURE, THANKS.
Try to keep showers brief.
The tanks are kept below deck.
Bathroom's here.
THAT ABOUT SUMS IT UP.
THERE'S A LOT OF STUFF ONBOARD.
WE'RE GONNA SPEND HALF THE DAY ON HERE, AFTER ALL.
WE'LL HAVE A MEETING ONCE WE GET CLOSE TO THE DIVING SPOT.
FEEL FREE TO CHILL OUT UNTIL THEN.
SURE.

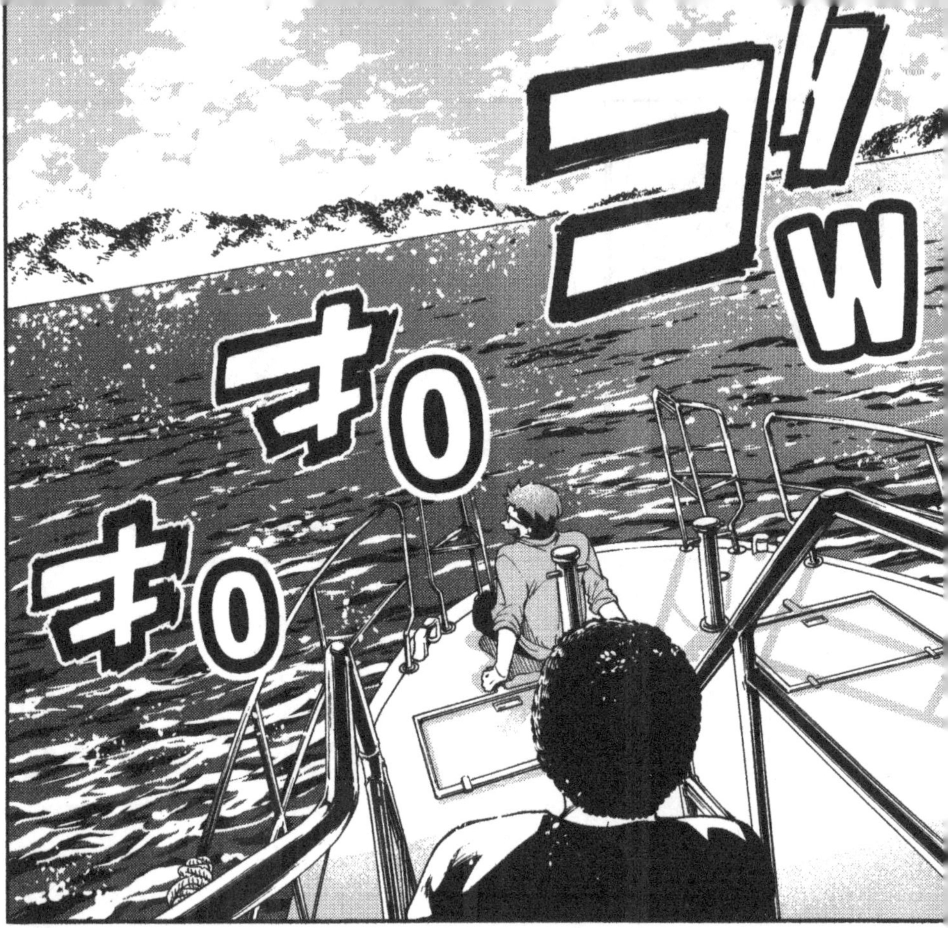

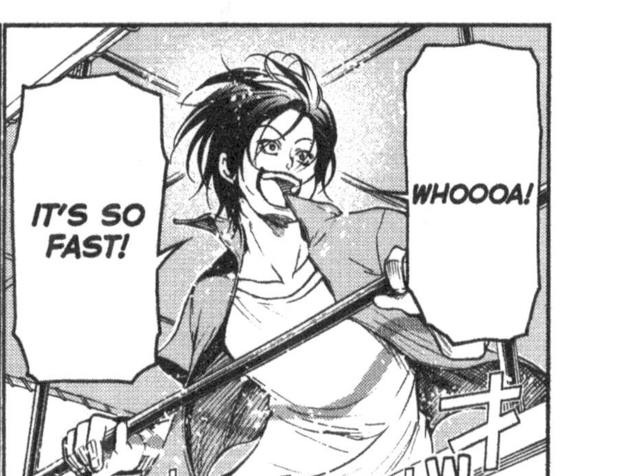
WHOOOA!
IT'S SO FAST!

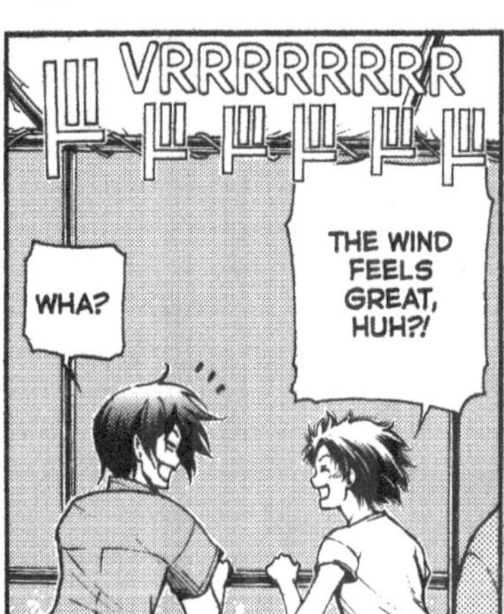
VRRRRRRRR
THE WIND FEELS GREAT, HUH?!
WHA?

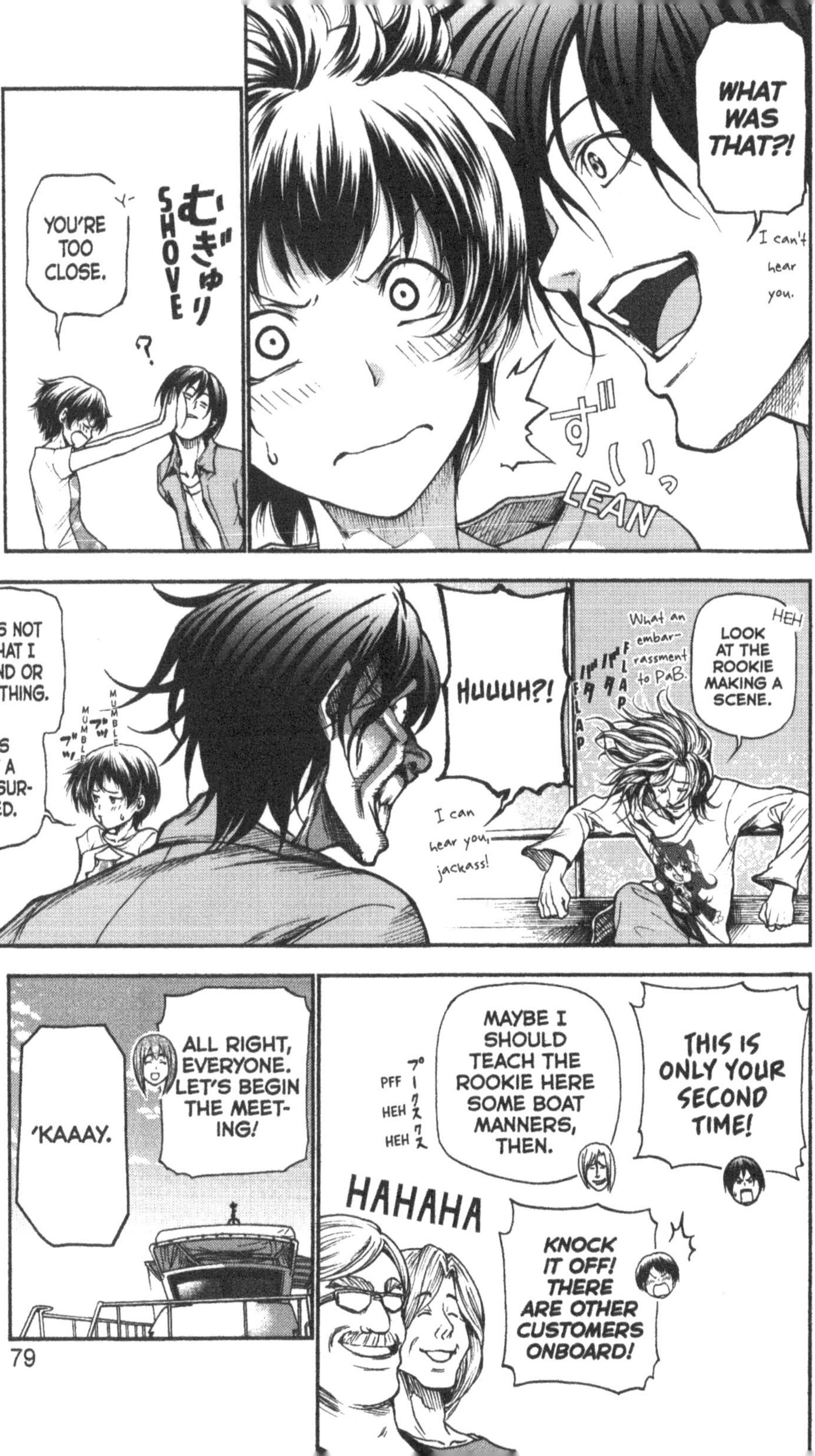
WHAT WAS THAT?!
I can't hear you.
ずいっ
LEAN
むぎゅり
SHOVE
YOU'RE TOO CLOSE.
?
HEH
LOOK AT THE ROOKIE MAKING A SCENE.
What an embarrassment to PaB.
バタバタ
FLAP FLAP
HUUUH?!
I can hear you, jackass!
IT'S NOT THAT I MIND OR ANYTHING.
I WAS JUST A LITTLE SURPRISED.
ブツブツ
MUMBLE MUMBLE
THIS IS ONLY YOUR SECOND TIME!
MAYBE I SHOULD TEACH THE ROOKIE HERE SOME BOAT MANNERS, THEN.
プークスクス
PFF HEH HEH
HAHAHA
KNOCK IT OFF! THERE ARE OTHER CUSTOMERS ONBOARD!
ALL RIGHT, EVERYONE. LET'S BEGIN THE MEETING!
'KAAAY.

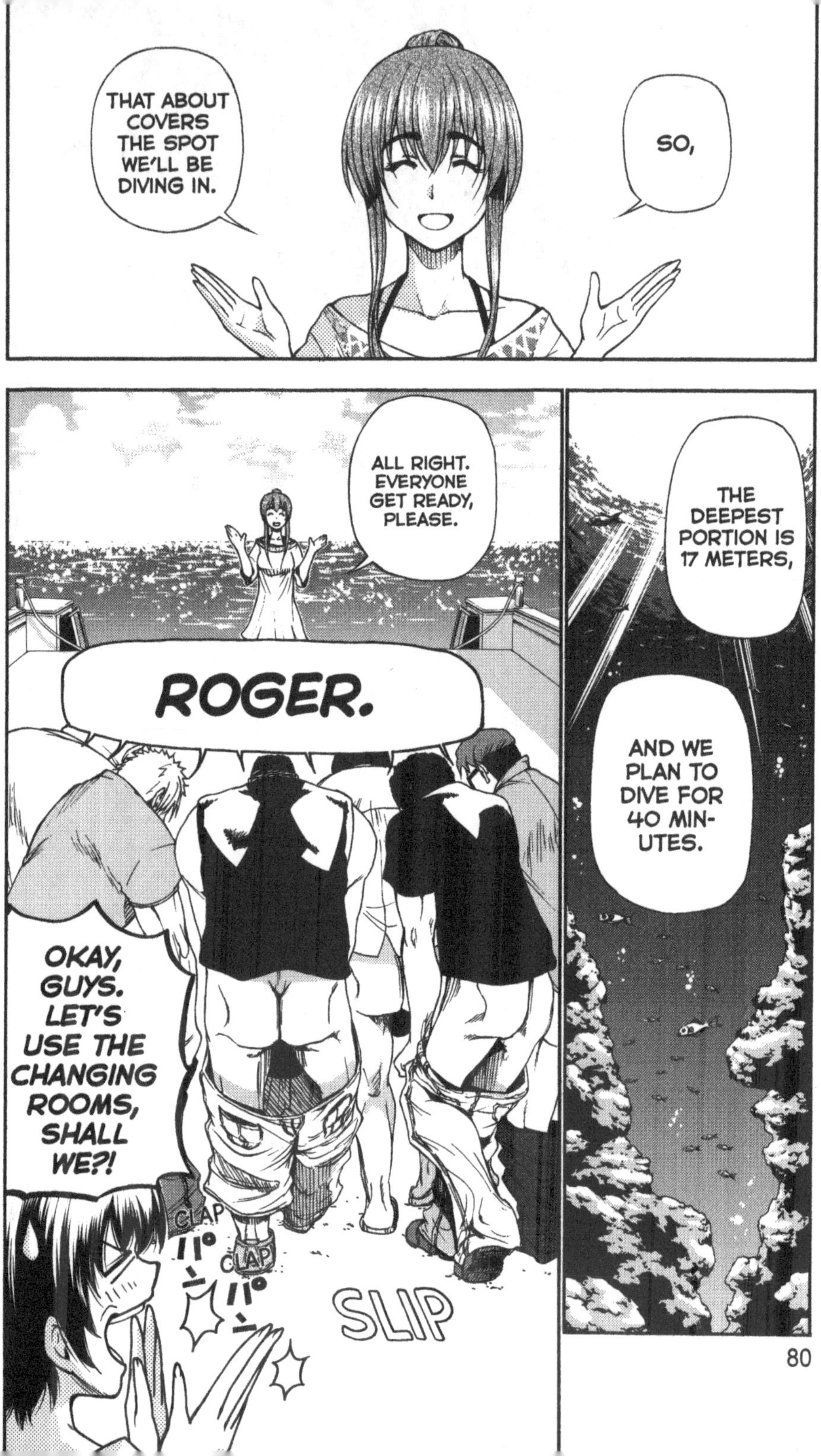
SO,
THAT ABOUT COVERS THE SPOT WE'LL BE DIVING IN.
THE DEEPEST PORTION IS 17 METERS,
AND WE PLAN TO DIVE FOR 40 MIN-UTES.
ALL RIGHT. EVERYONE GET READY, PLEASE.
ROGER.
OKAY, GUYS. LET'S USE THE CHANGING ROOMS, SHALL WE?!
CLAP
CLAP
SLIP

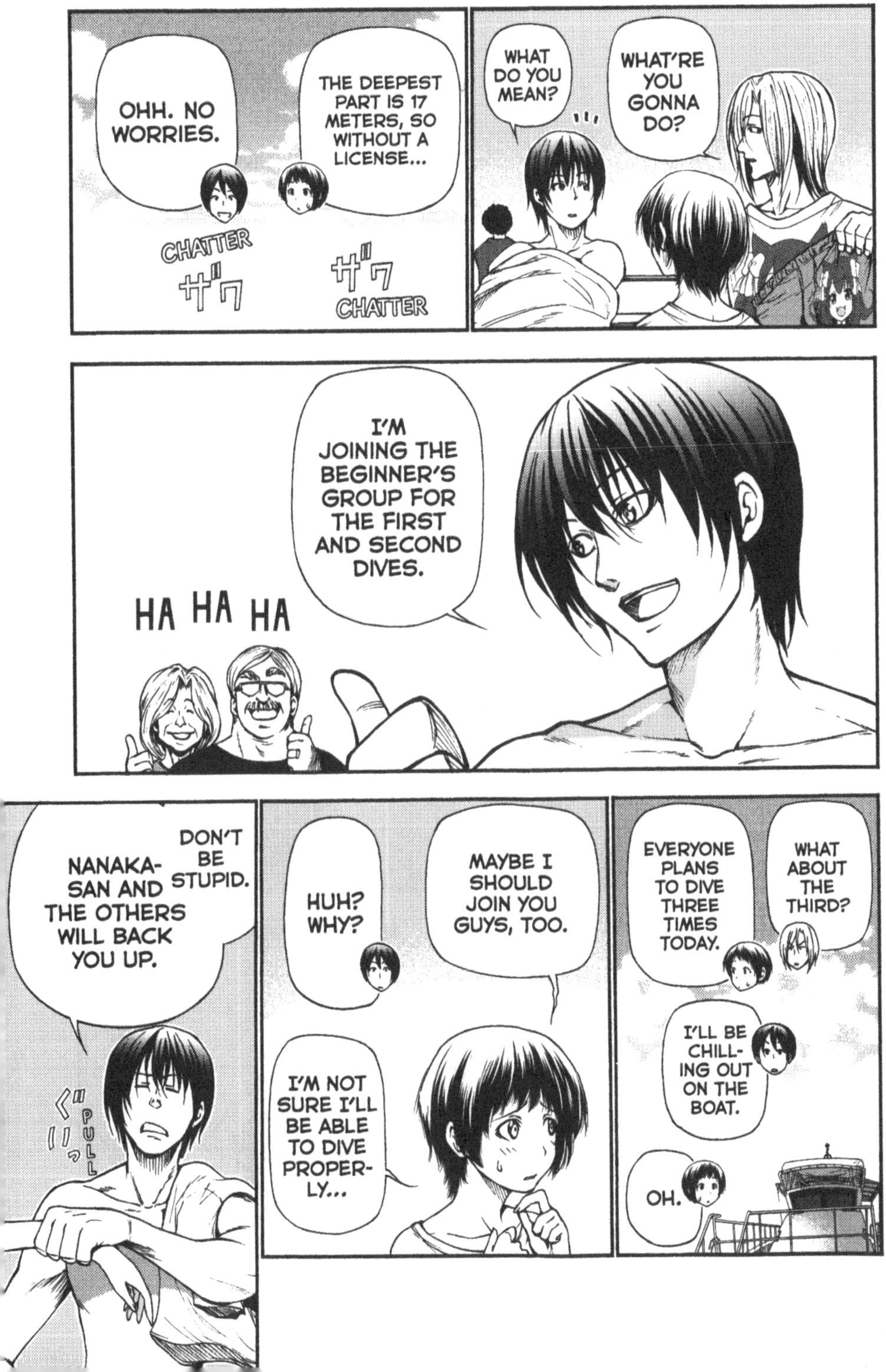
WHAT'RE YOU GONNA DO?
WHAT DO YOU MEAN?
THE DEEPEST PART IS 17 METERS, SO WITHOUT A LICENSE...
OHH. NO WORRIES.
ザワ
CHATTER
ザワ
CHATTER
I'M JOINING THE BEGINNER'S GROUP FOR THE FIRST AND SECOND DIVES.
HA HA HA
WHAT ABOUT THE THIRD?
EVERYONE PLANS TO DIVE THREE TIMES TODAY.
I'LL BE CHILLING OUT ON THE BOAT.
OH.
MAYBE I SHOULD JOIN YOU GUYS, TOO.
HUH? WHY?
I'M NOT SURE I'LL BE ABLE TO DIVE PROPERLY...
DON'T BE STUPID.
NANAKA-SAN AND THE OTHERS WILL BACK YOU UP.
ぐいっ
PULL

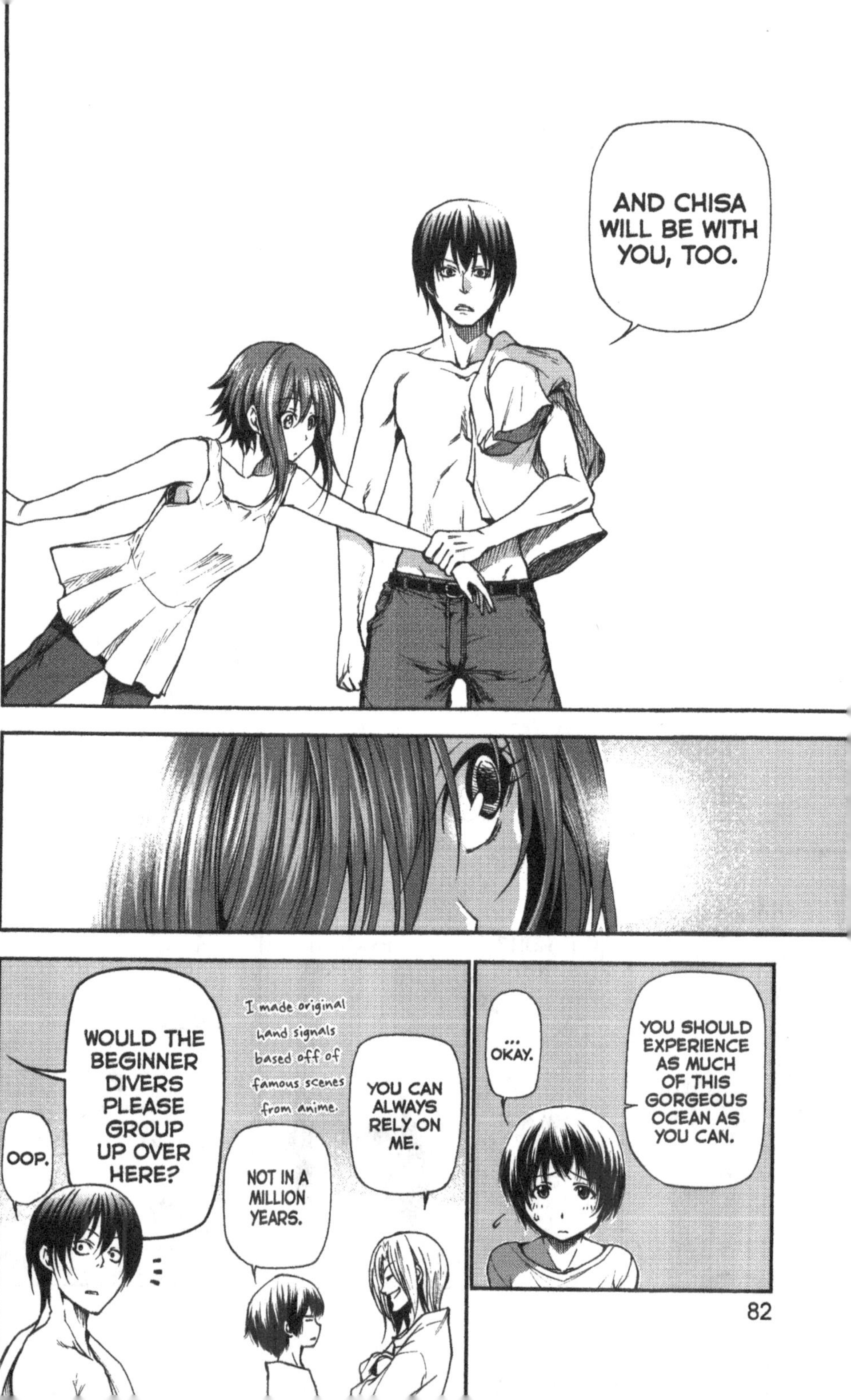
AND CHISA WILL BE WITH YOU, TOO.
YOU SHOULD EXPERIENCE AS MUCH OF THIS GORGEOUS OCEAN AS YOU CAN.
...OKAY.
I made original hand signals based off of famous scenes from anime.
YOU CAN ALWAYS RELY ON ME.
NOT IN A MILLION YEARS.
WOULD THE BEGINNER DIVERS PLEASE GROUP UP OVER HERE?
OOP.

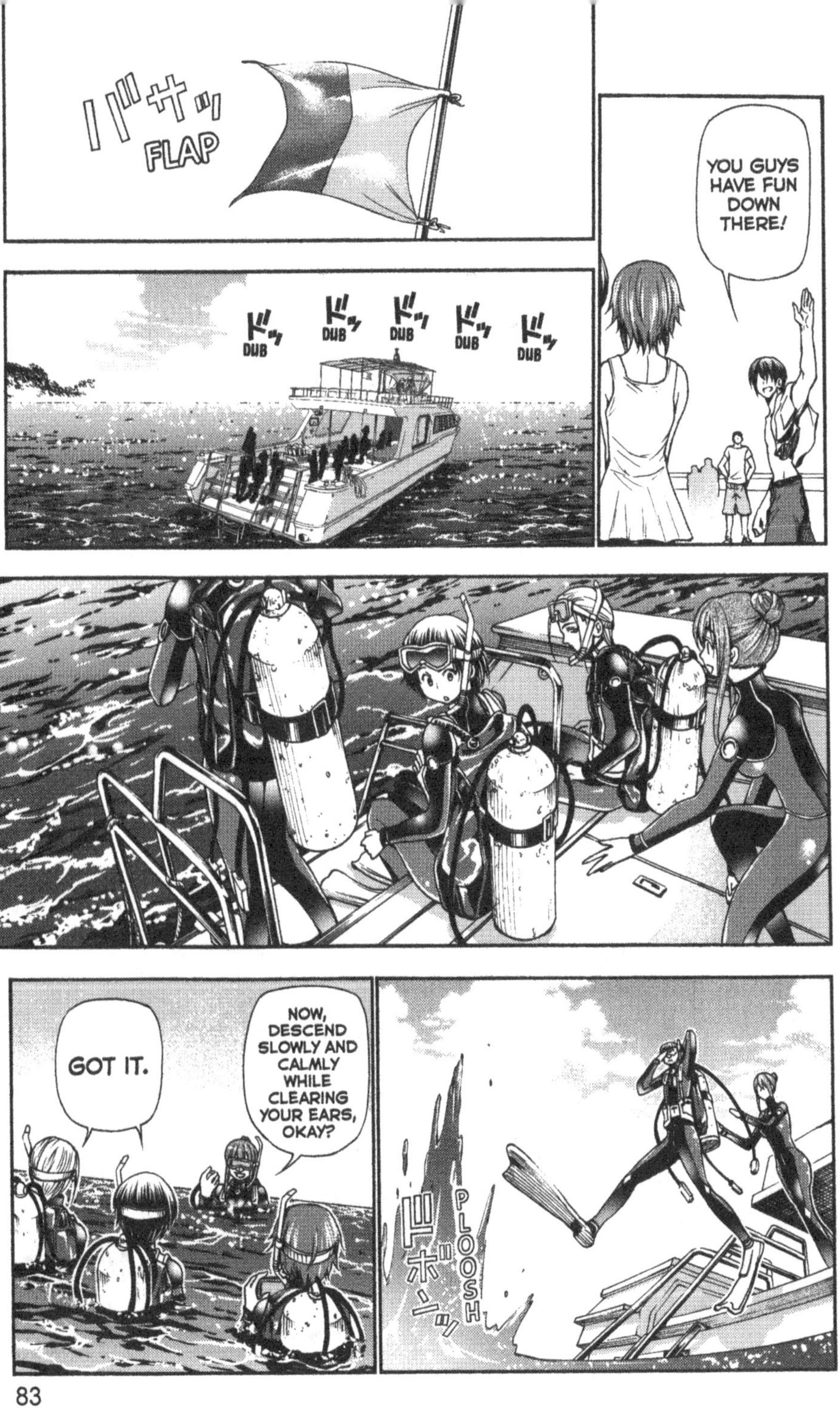
YOU GUYS HAVE FUN DOWN THERE!
バサッ
FLAP
ドッ DUB
ドッ DUB
ドッ DUB
ドッ DUB
ドッ DUB
ドボーンッ
PLOOSH
NOW, DESCEND SLOWLY AND CALMLY WHILE CLEARING YOUR EARS, OKAY?
GOT IT.

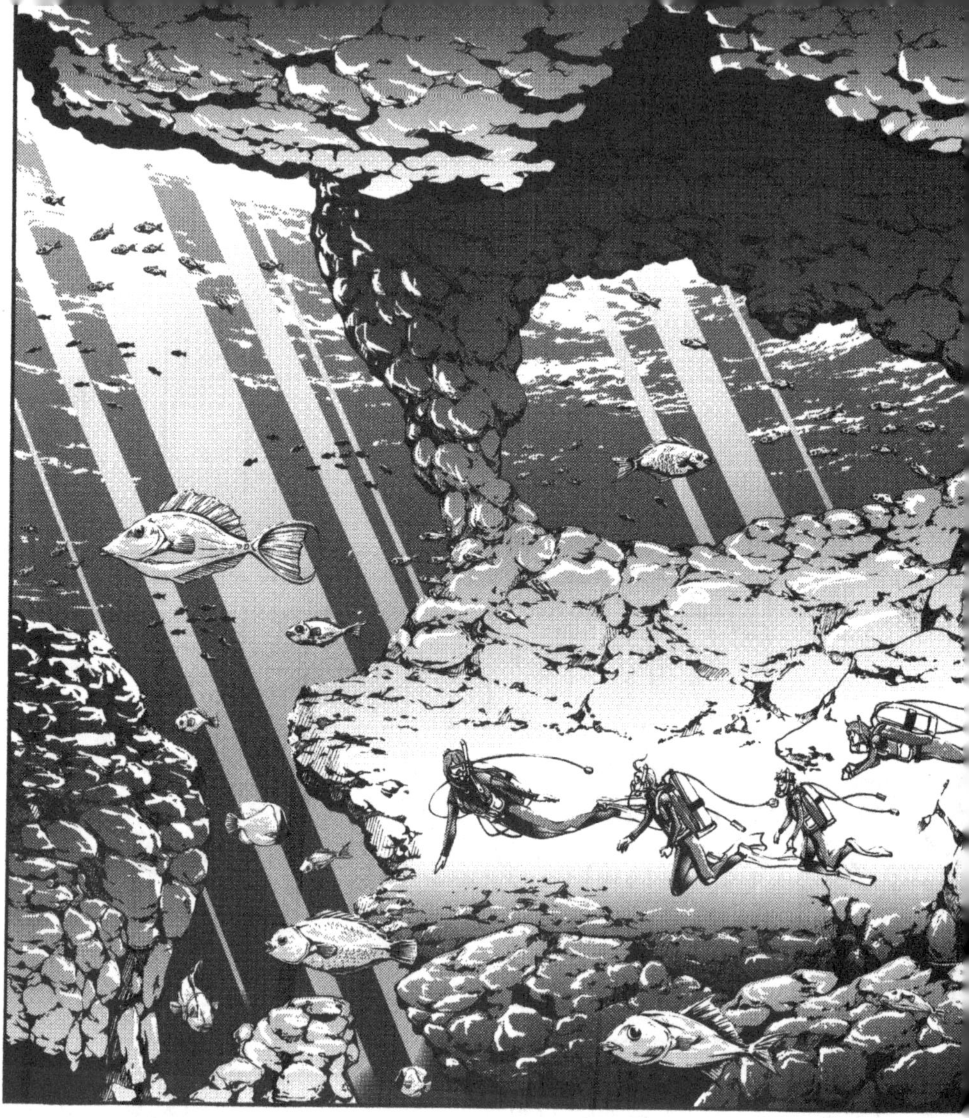

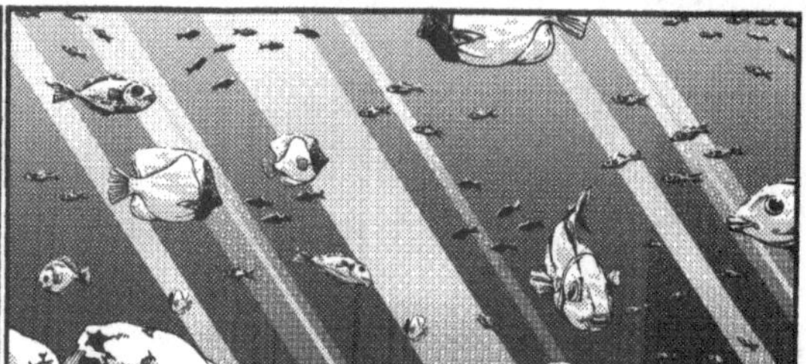

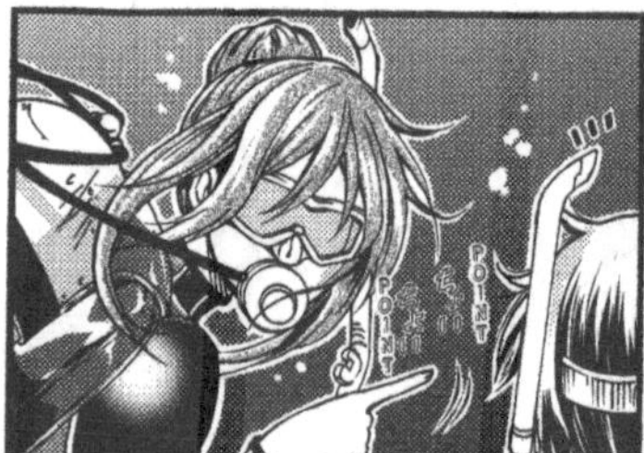
POINT
POINT

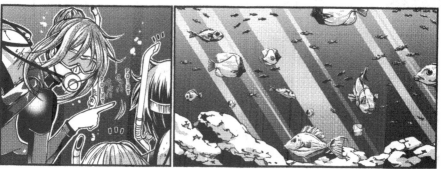

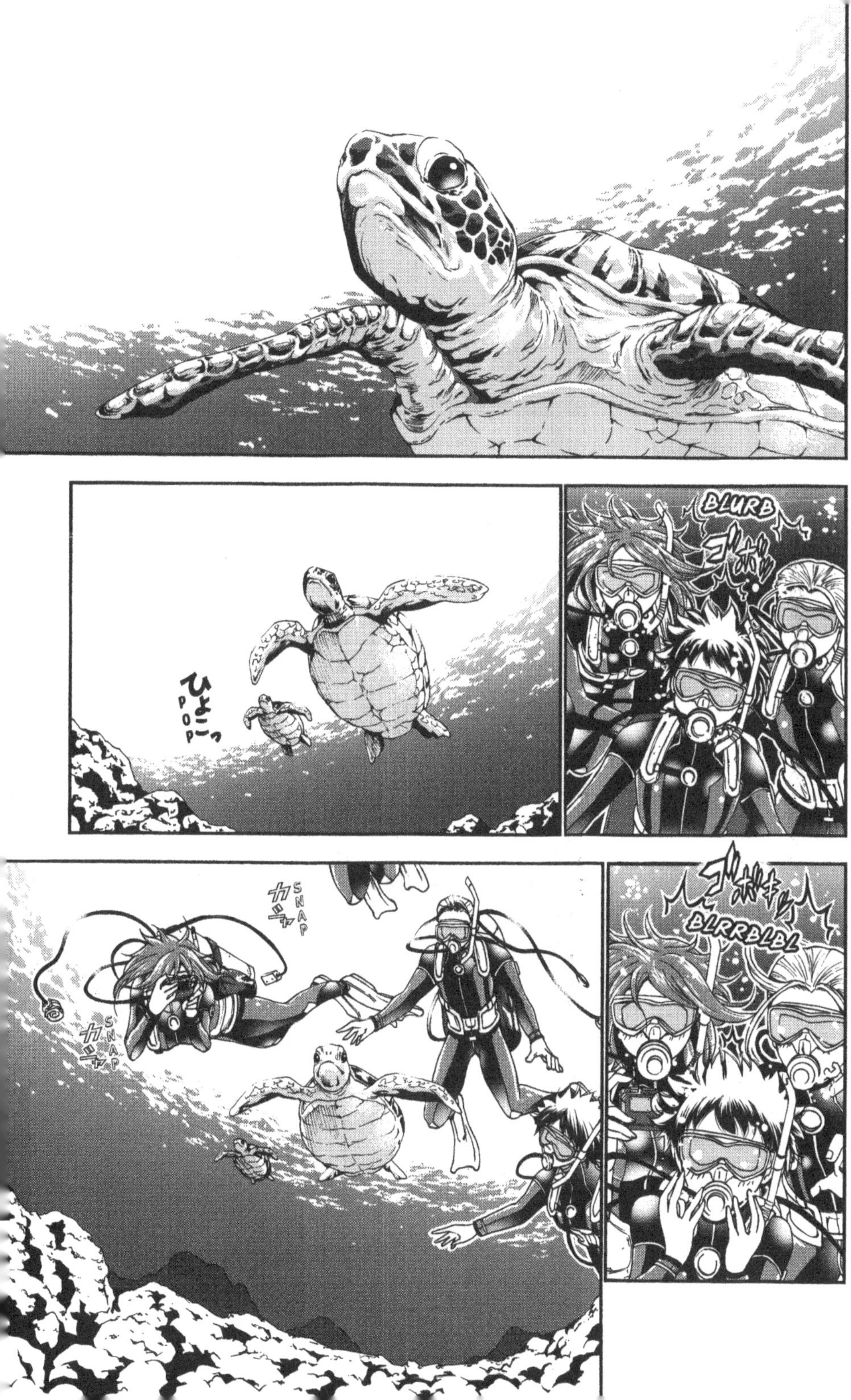
BLURB
ひよこっ
POP
BLRRBLBL
カシャ
SNAP
カシャ
SNAP

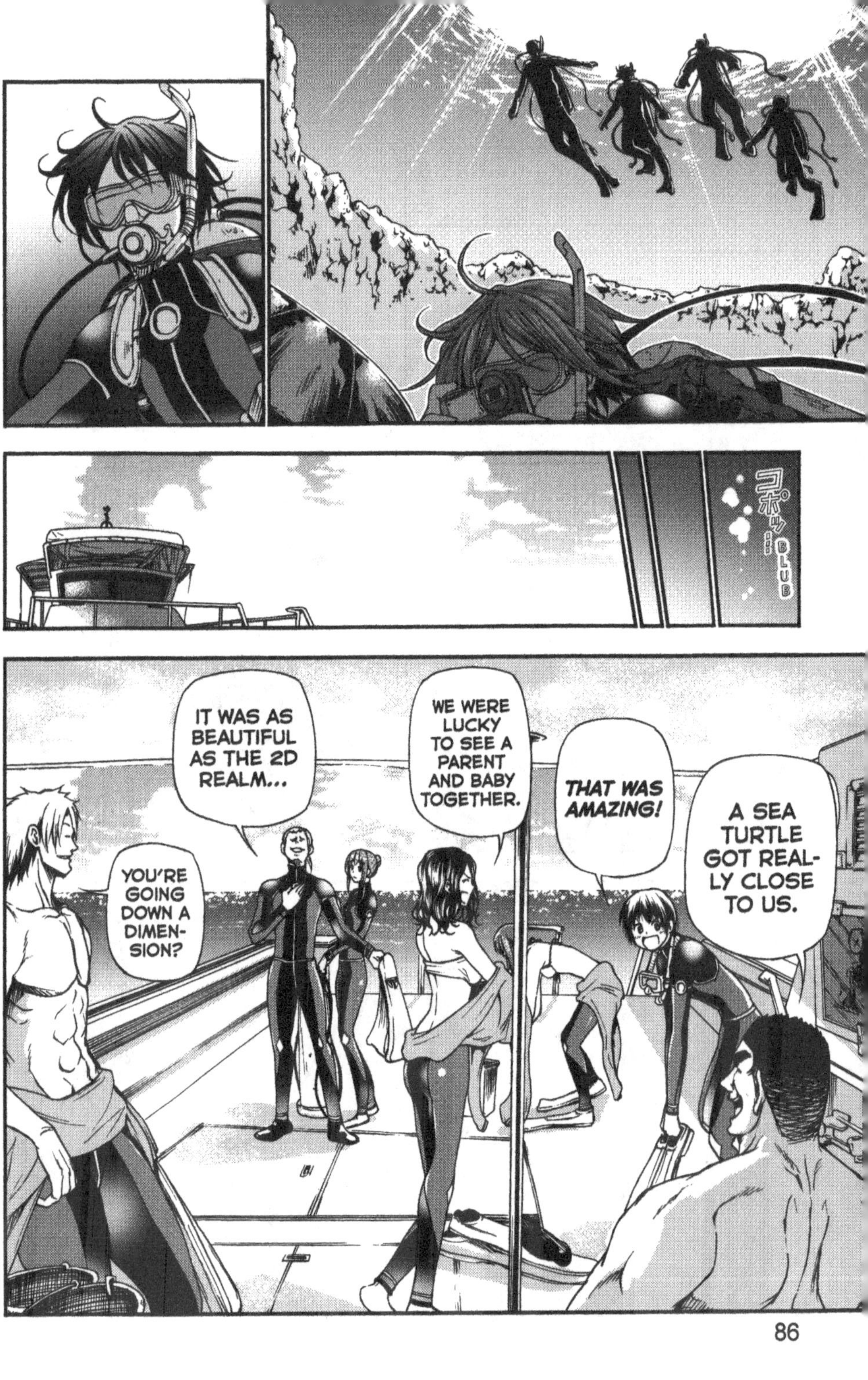

コポッ
BLUB
A SEA TURTLE GOT REALLY CLOSE TO US.
THAT WAS AMAZING!
WE WERE LUCKY TO SEE A PARENT AND BABY TOGETHER.
IT WAS AS BEAUTIFUL AS THE 2D REALM...
YOU'RE GOING DOWN A DIMENSION?

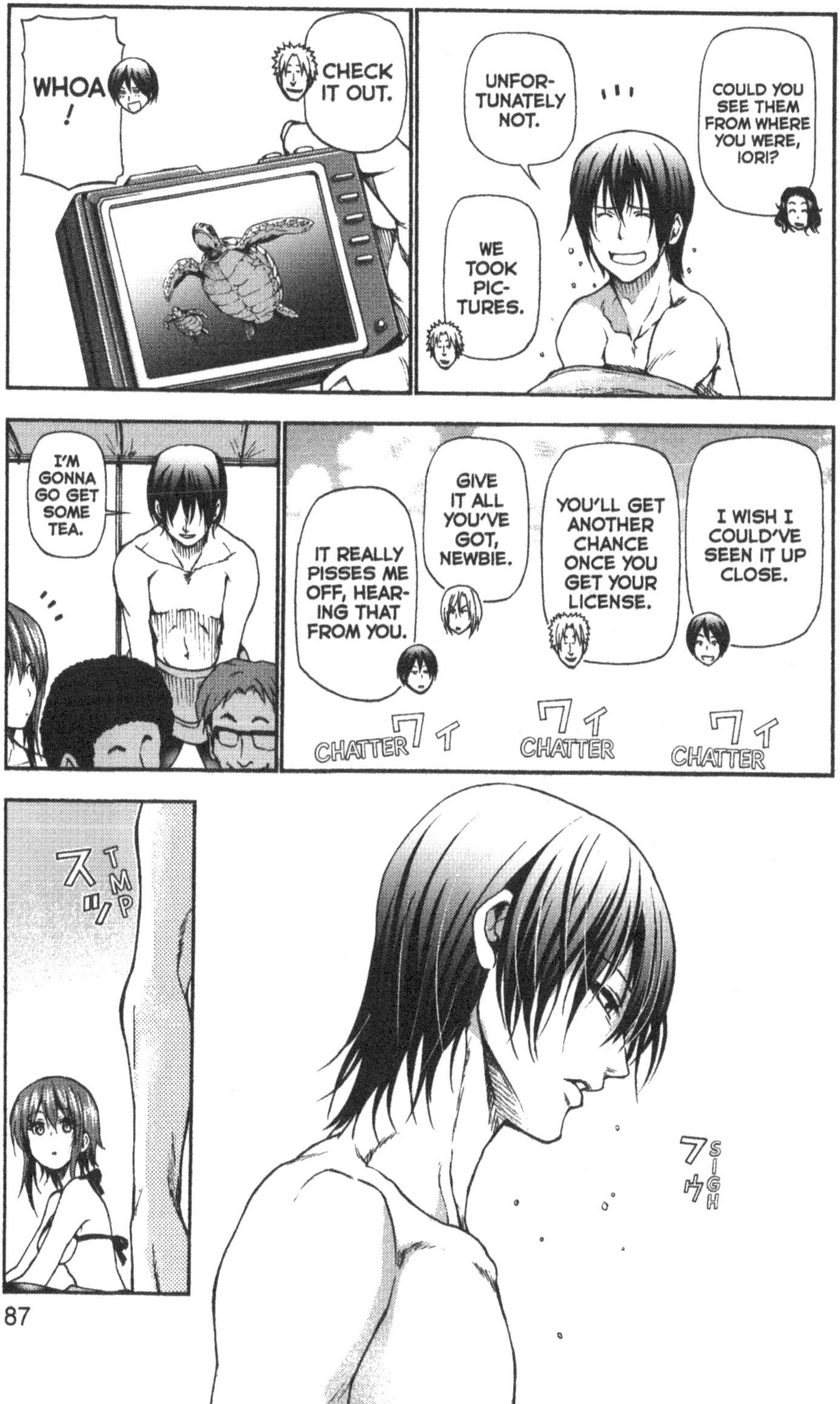
COULD YOU SEE THEM FROM WHERE YOU WERE, IORI?
...
UNFORTUNATELY NOT.
WE TOOK PICTURES.
CHECK IT OUT.
WHOA!
I WISH I COULD'VE SEEN IT UP CLOSE.
YOU'LL GET ANOTHER CHANCE ONCE YOU GET YOUR LICENSE.
GIVE IT ALL YOU'VE GOT, NEWBIE.
IT REALLY PISSES ME OFF, HEARING THAT FROM YOU.
ワイ CHATTER
ワイ CHATTER
ワイ CHATTER
I'M GONNA GO GET SOME TEA.
...
フゥ SIGH
スッ TMP

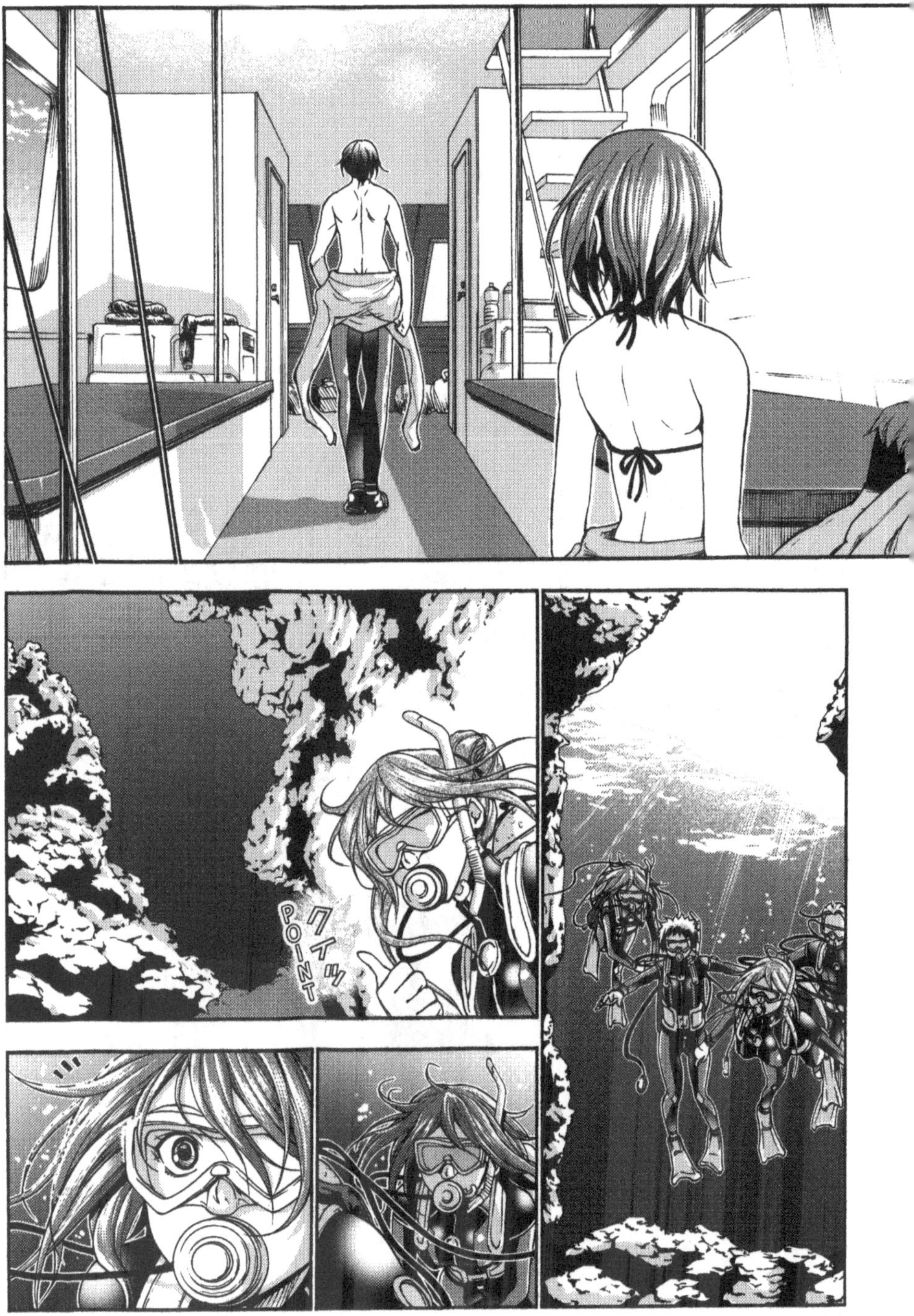
クイッ
POINT

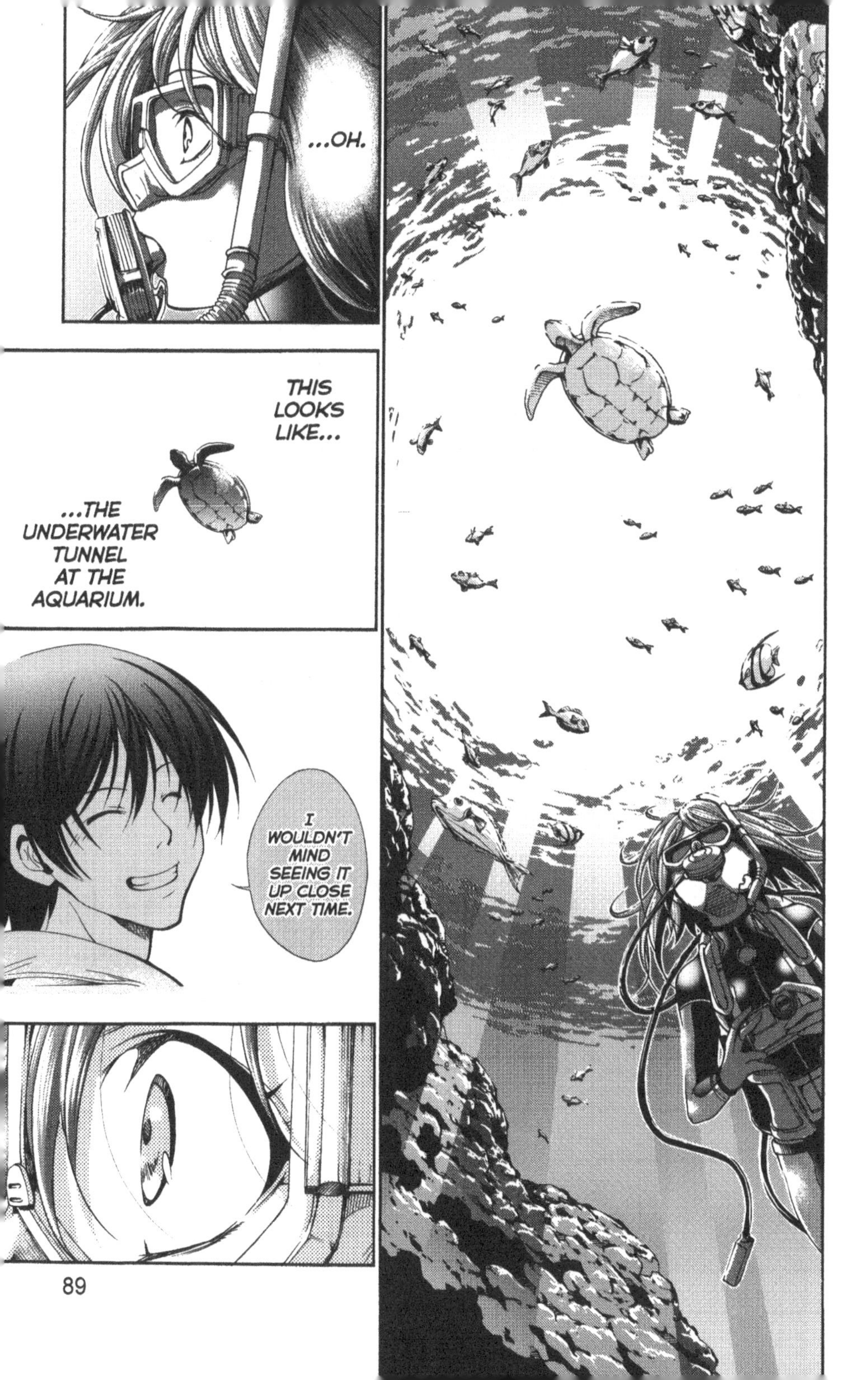
...OH.
THIS LOOKS LIKE...
...THE UNDERWATER TUNNEL AT THE AQUARIUM.
I WOULDN'T MIND SEEING IT UP CLOSE NEXT TIME.

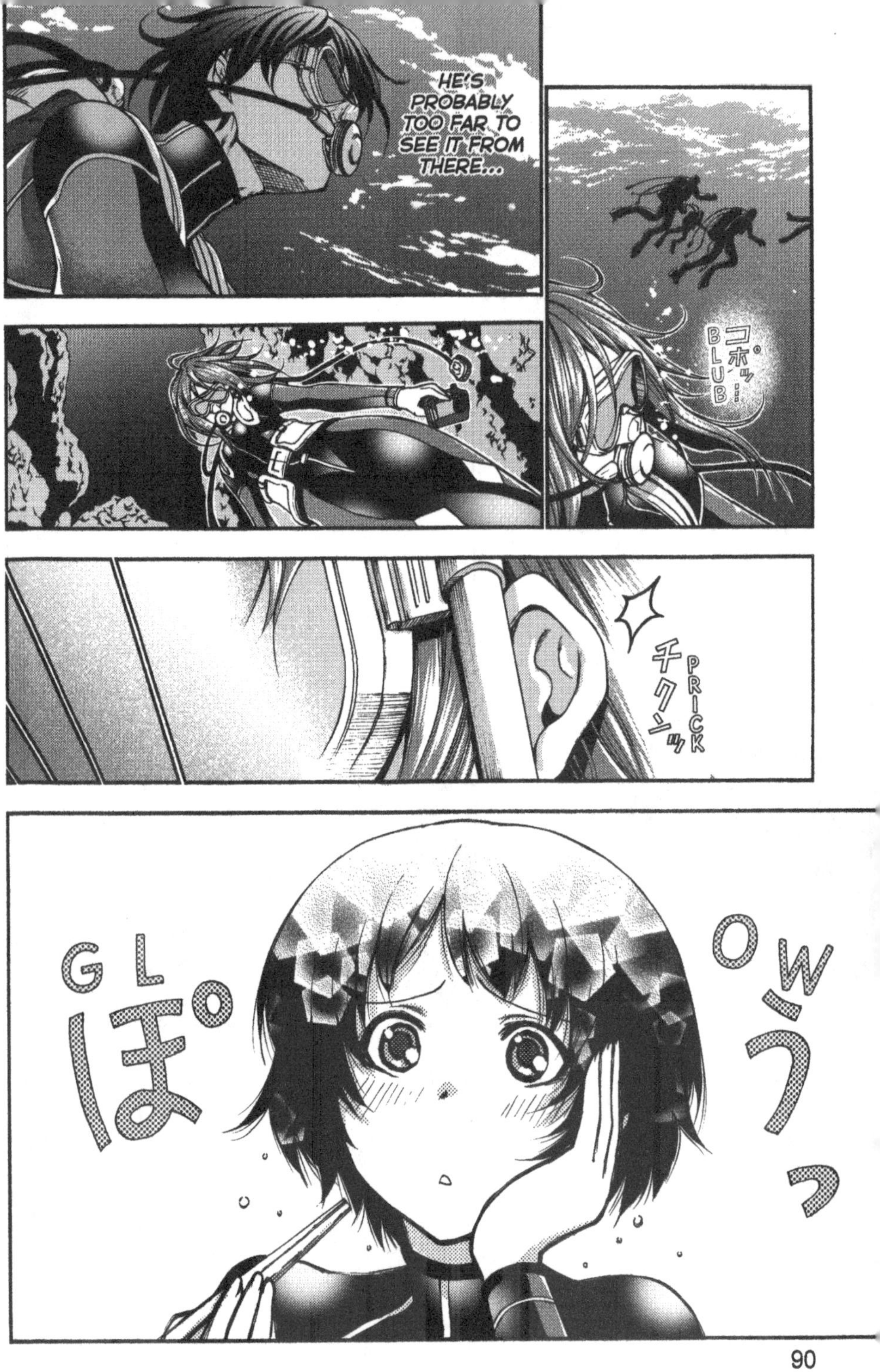
コポッ!!
BLUB
HE'S PROBABLY TOO FAR TO SEE IT FROM THERE...
チクンッ
PRICK
ぽうっ
GLOW

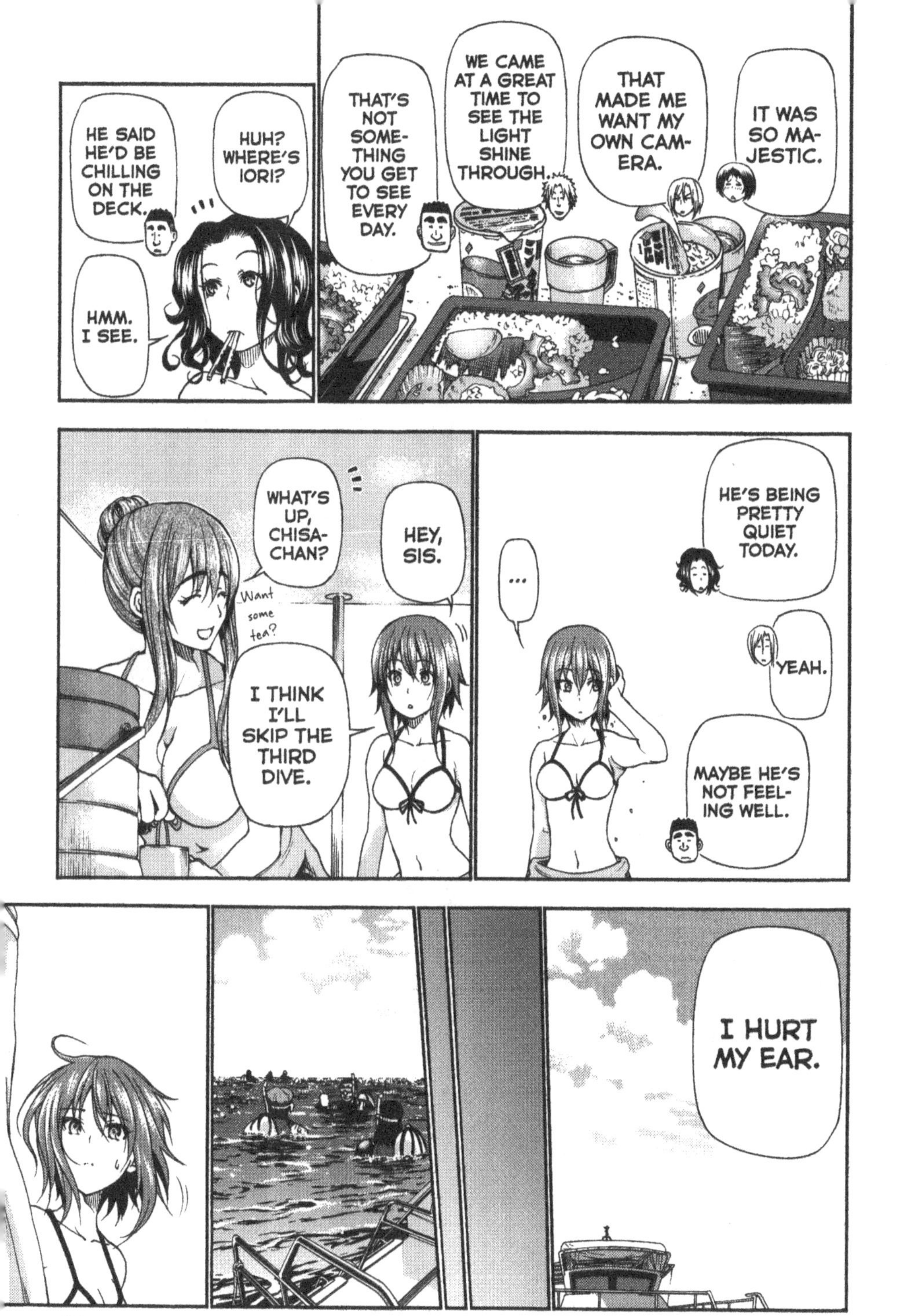
IT WAS SO MAJESTIC.
THAT MADE ME WANT MY OWN CAMERA.
WE CAME AT A GREAT TIME TO SEE THE LIGHT SHINE THROUGH.
THAT'S NOT SOMETHING YOU GET TO SEE EVERY DAY.
HUH? WHERE'S IORI?
HE SAID HE'D BE CHILLING ON THE DECK.
HMM. I SEE.
HE'S BEING PRETTY QUIET TODAY.
...
YEAH.
MAYBE HE'S NOT FEELING WELL.
HEY, SIS.
WHAT'S UP, CHISA-CHAN?
Want some tea?
I THINK I'LL SKIP THE THIRD DIVE.
I HURT MY EAR.

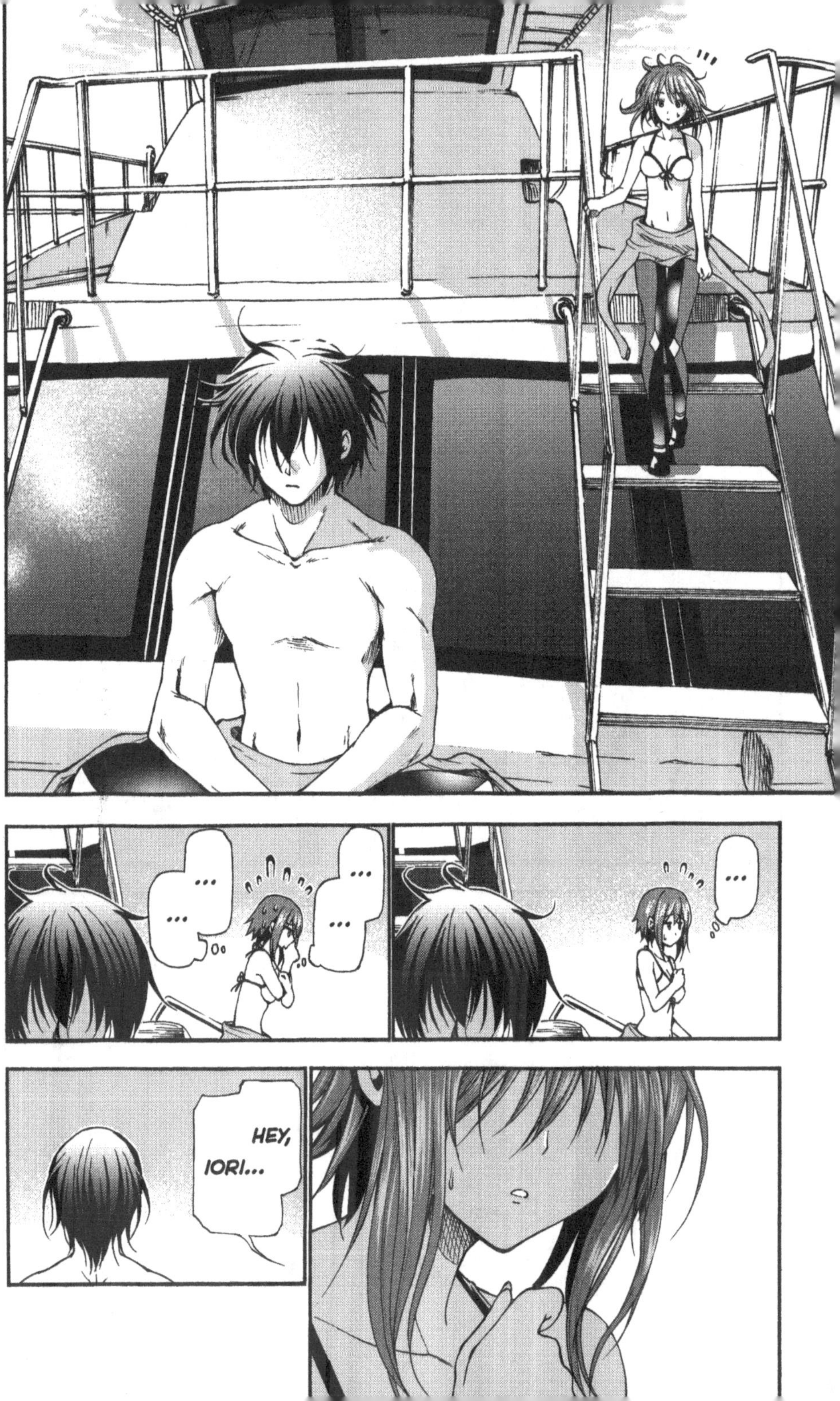
...
... ...
... ...
HEY, IORI...

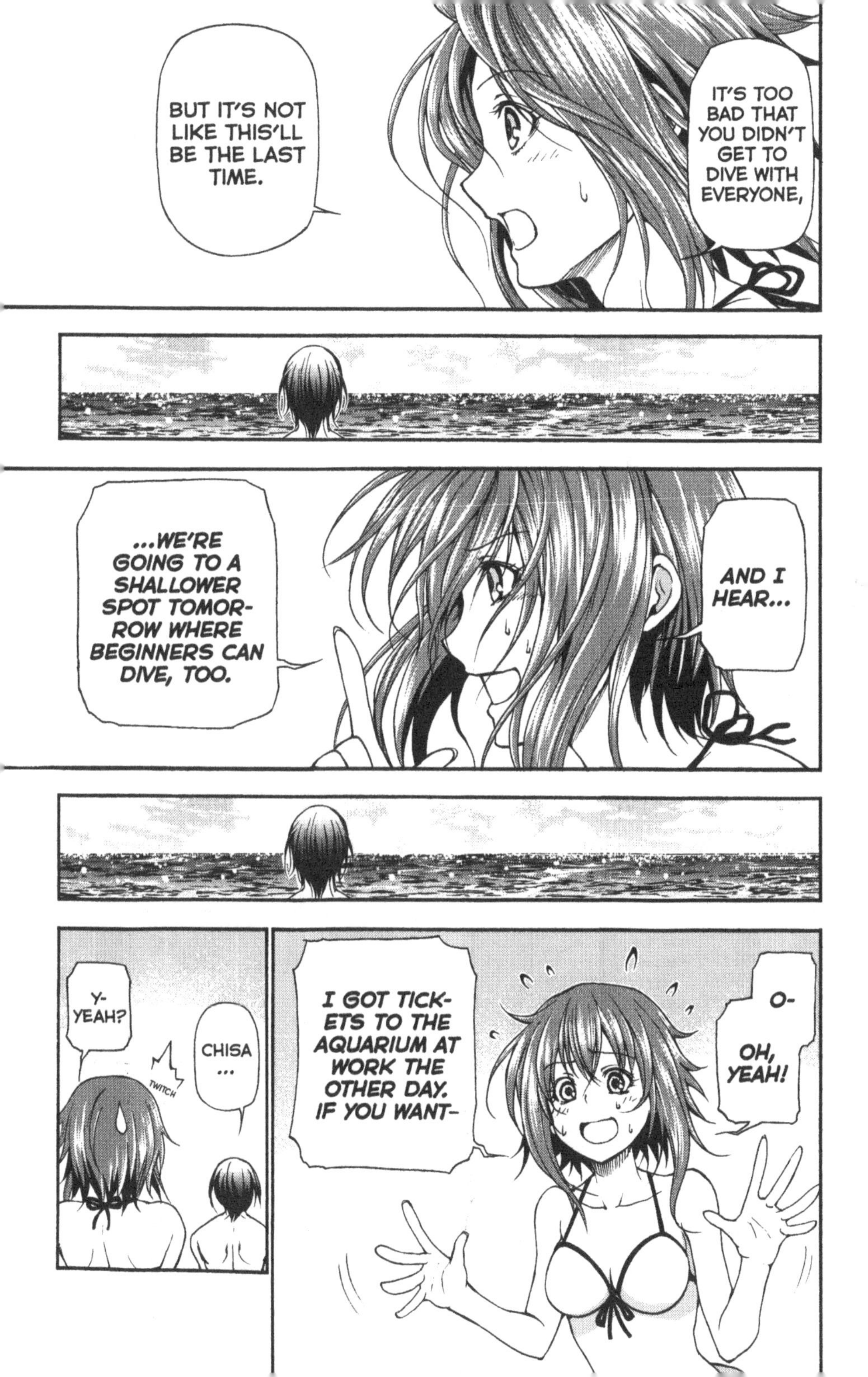
IT'S TOO BAD THAT YOU DIDN'T GET TO DIVE WITH EVERYONE,
BUT IT'S NOT LIKE THIS'LL BE THE LAST TIME.
AND I HEAR...
...WE'RE GOING TO A SHALLOWER SPOT TOMORROW WHERE BEGINNERS CAN DIVE, TOO.
O- OH, YEAH!
I GOT TICKETS TO THE AQUARIUM AT WORK THE OTHER DAY. IF YOU WANT-
CHISA ...
TWITCH
Y-YEAH?

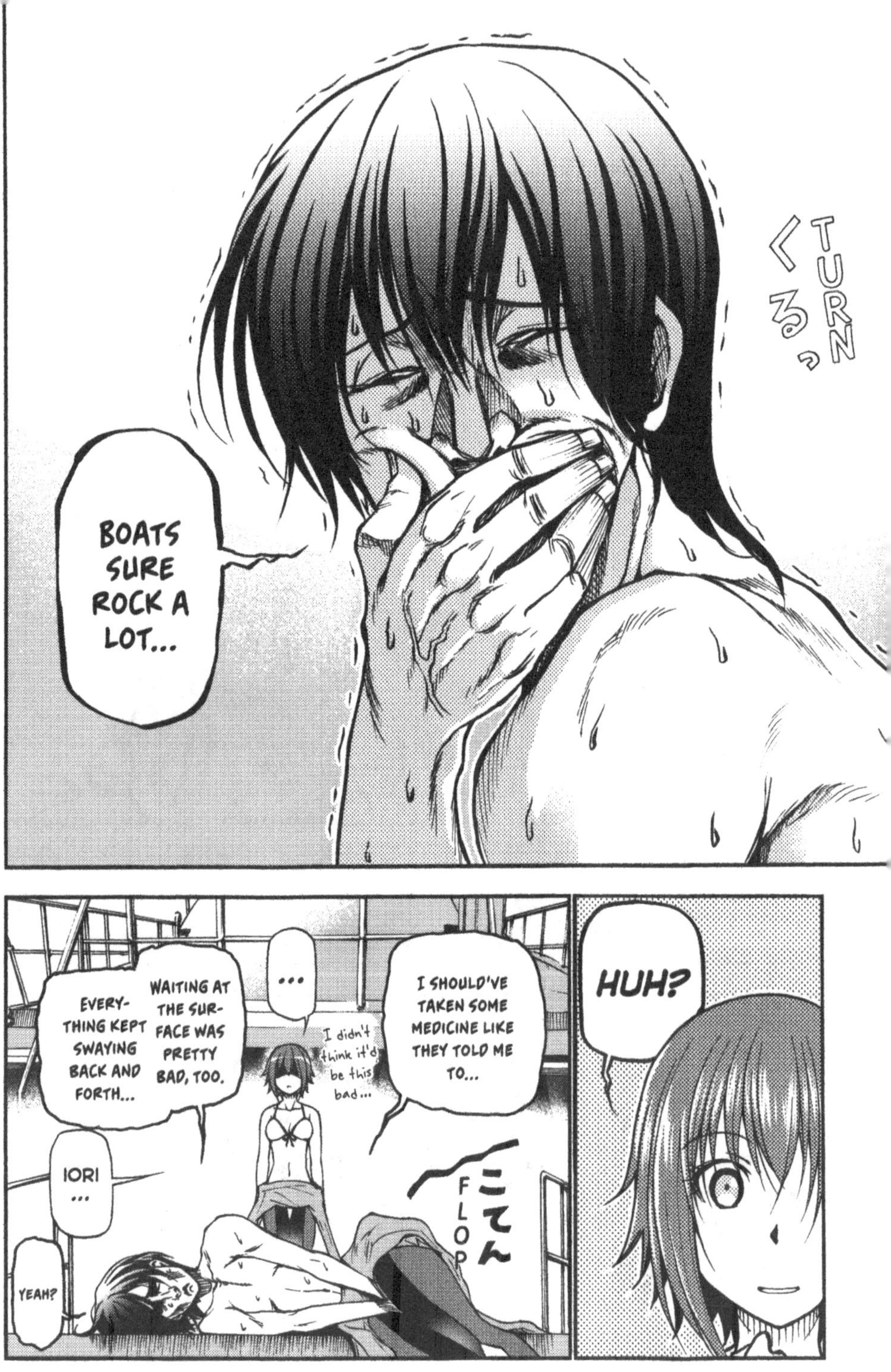
くるっ TURN
BOATS SURE ROCK A LOT...
HUH?
I SHOULD'VE TAKEN SOME MEDICINE LIKE THEY TOLD ME TO...
I didn't think it'd be this bad...
...
WAITING AT THE SURFACE WAS PRETTY BAD, TOO.
EVERYTHING KEPT SWAYING BACK AND FORTH...
こてん FLOP
IORI...
YEAH?

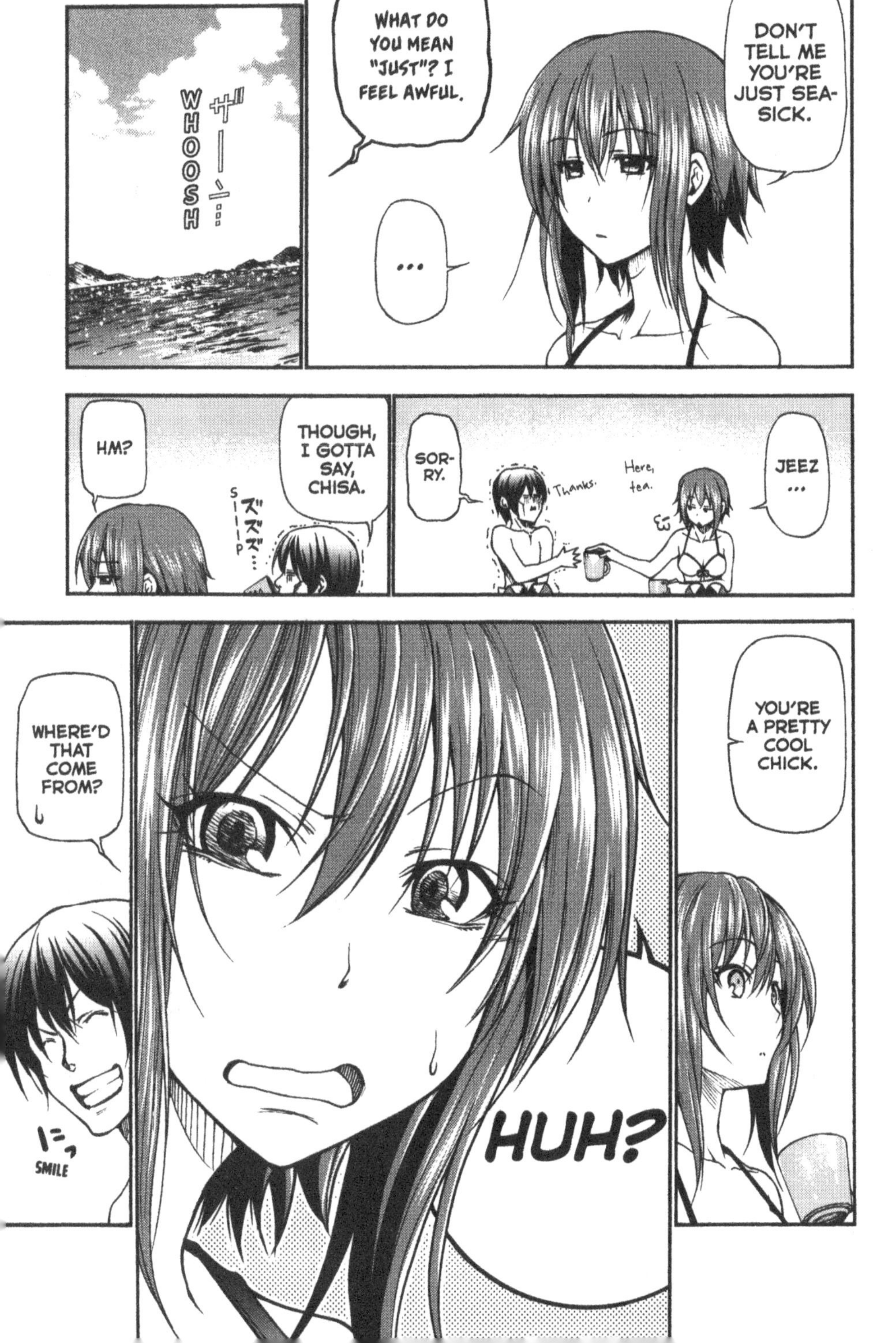
DON'T TELL ME YOU'RE JUST SEA-SICK.
WHAT DO YOU MEAN "JUST"? I FEEL AWFUL.
...
ザーー…
WHOOSH
JEEZ...
Here, tea.
Thanks.
SOR-RY.
THOUGH, I GOTTA SAY, CHISA.
ズズズ…
SIIIP
HM?
YOU'RE A PRETTY COOL CHICK.
HUH?
WHERE'D THAT COME FROM?
にっ
SMILE

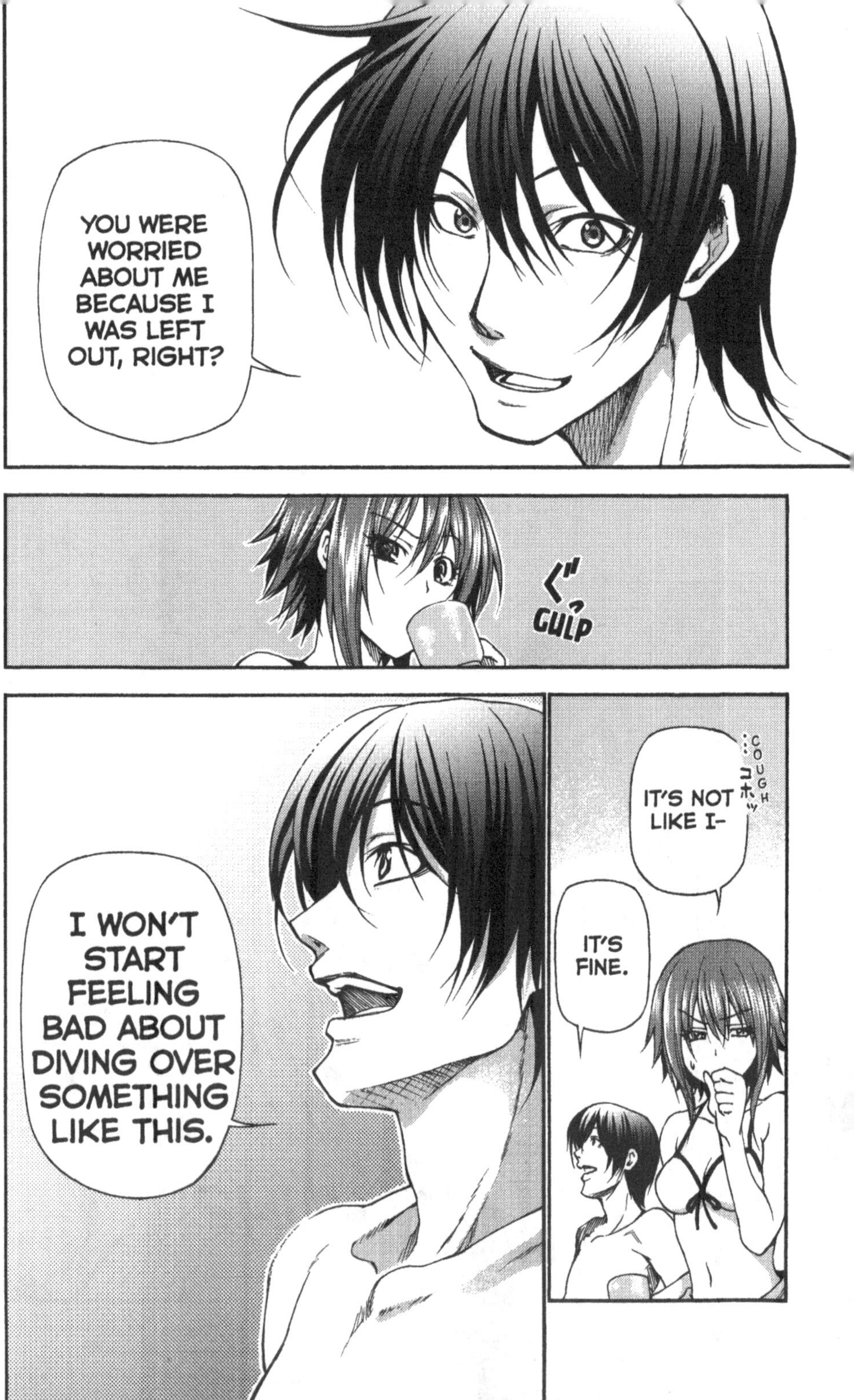
YOU WERE WORRIED ABOUT ME BECAUSE I WAS LEFT OUT, RIGHT?
ぐっ
GULP
コホッ
COUGH
IT'S NOT LIKE I-
IT'S FINE.
I WON'T START FEELING BAD ABOUT DIVING OVER SOMETHING LIKE THIS.

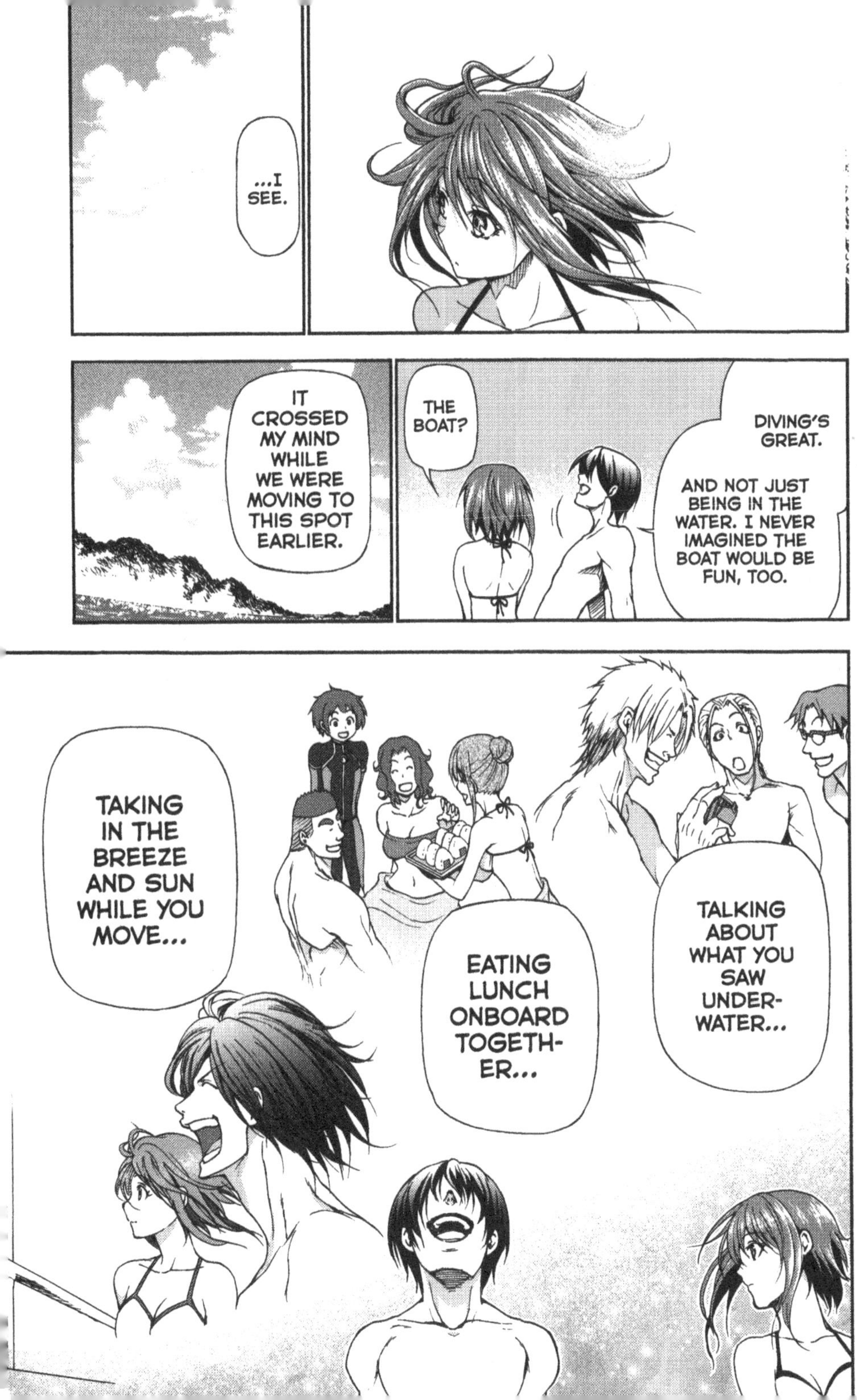
...I SEE.
DIVING'S GREAT.
AND NOT JUST BEING IN THE WATER. I NEVER IMAGINED THE BOAT WOULD BE FUN, TOO.
THE BOAT?
IT CROSSED MY MIND WHILE WE WERE MOVING TO THIS SPOT EARLIER.
TALKING ABOUT WHAT YOU SAW UNDER-WATER...
EATING LUNCH ONBOARD TOGETH-ER...
TAKING IN THE BREEZE AND SUN WHILE YOU MOVE...

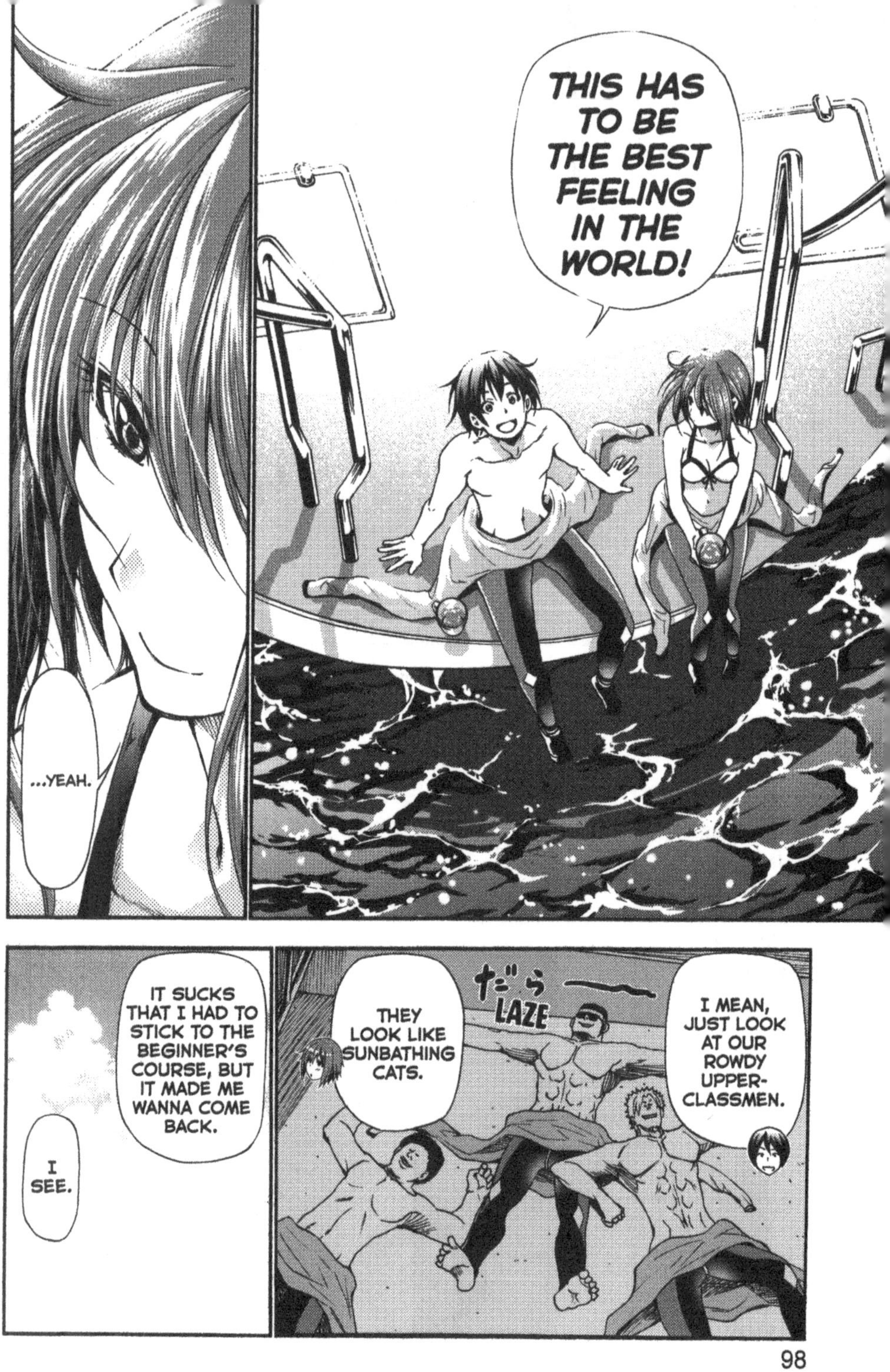
THIS HAS TO BE THE BEST FEELING IN THE WORLD!
...YEAH.
I MEAN, JUST LOOK AT OUR ROWDY UPPER-CLASSMEN.
だら
LAZE
THEY LOOK LIKE SUNBATHING CATS.
IT SUCKS THAT I HAD TO STICK TO THE BEGINNER'S COURSE, BUT IT MADE ME WANNA COME BACK.
I SEE.

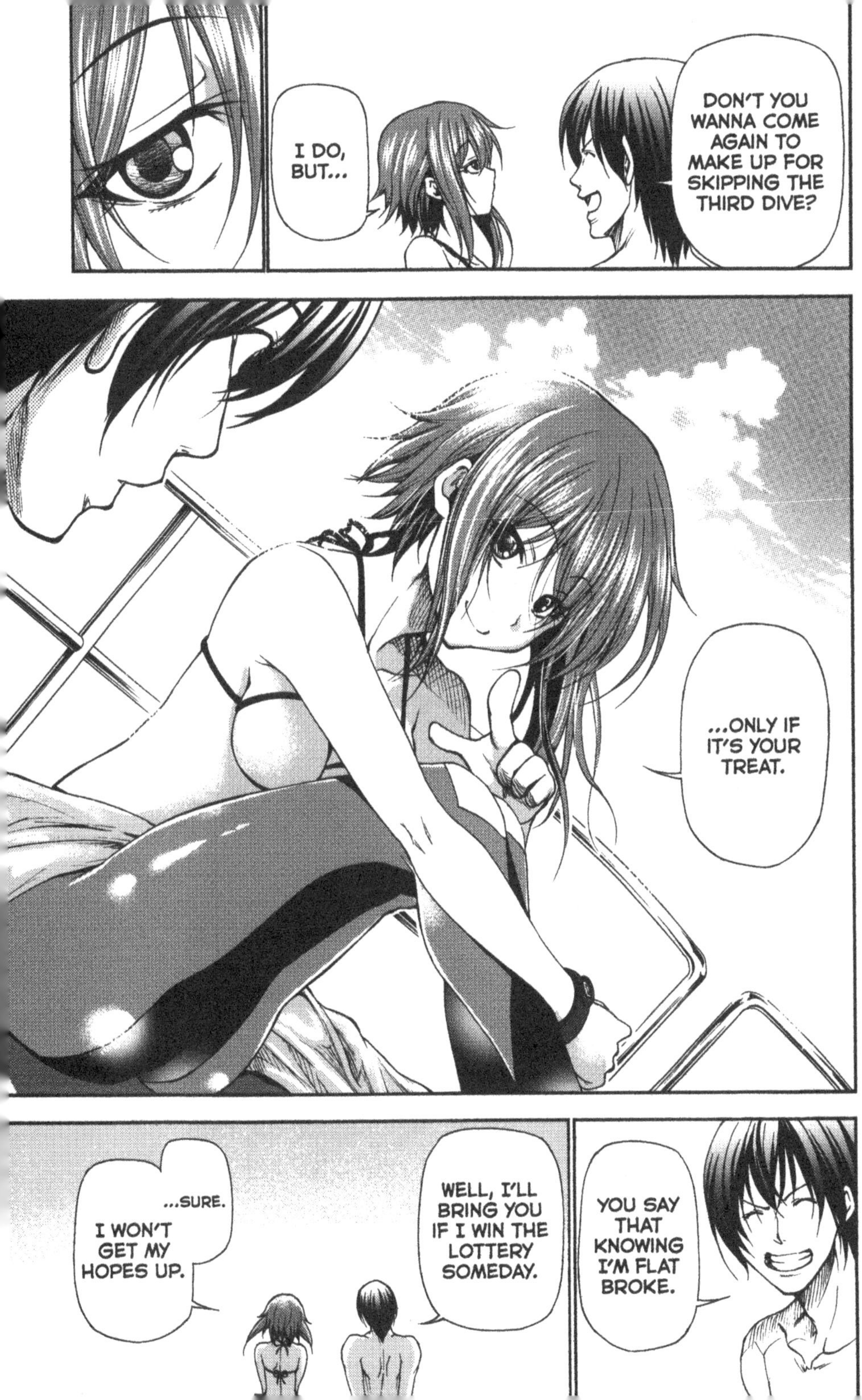
DON'T YOU WANNA COME AGAIN TO MAKE UP FOR SKIPPING THE THIRD DIVE?
I DO, BUT...
...ONLY IF IT'S YOUR TREAT.
YOU SAY THAT KNOWING I'M FLAT BROKE.
WELL, I'LL BRING YOU IF I WIN THE LOTTERY SOMEDAY.
...SURE. I WON'T GET MY HOPES UP.

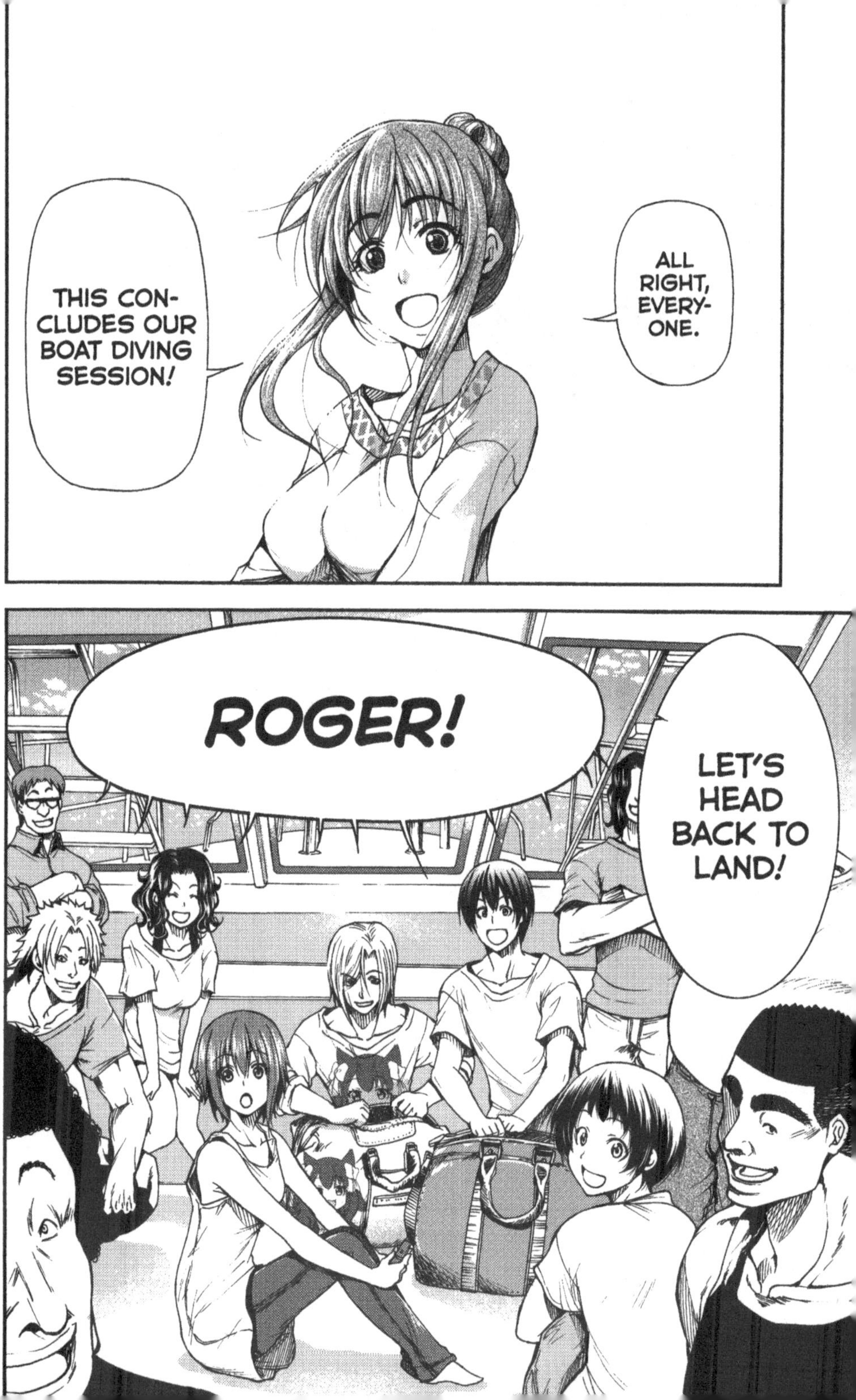
ALL RIGHT, EVERY-ONE.
THIS CON-CLUDES OUR BOAT DIVING SESSION!
LET'S HEAD BACK TO LAND!
ROGER!

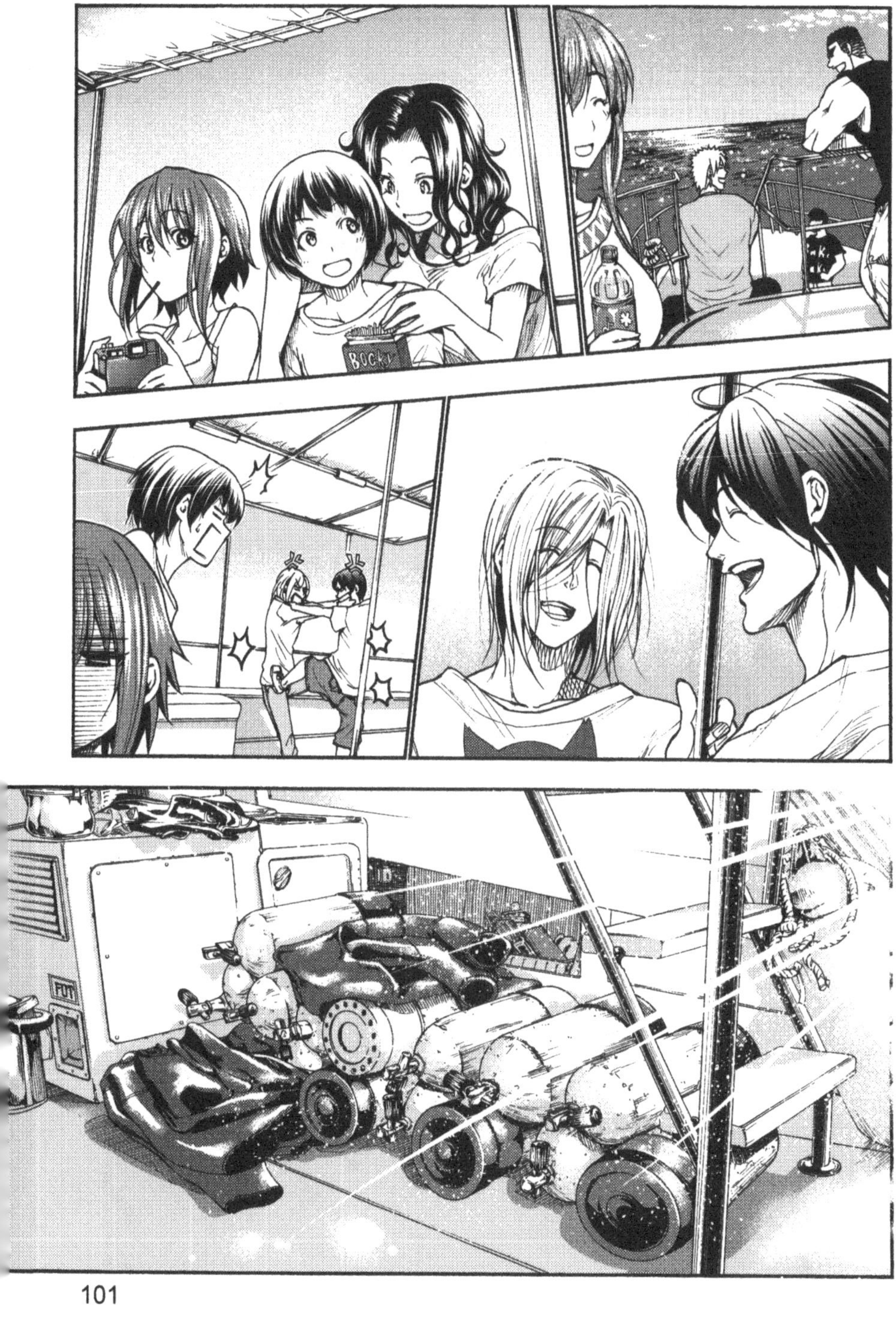
BOCKY

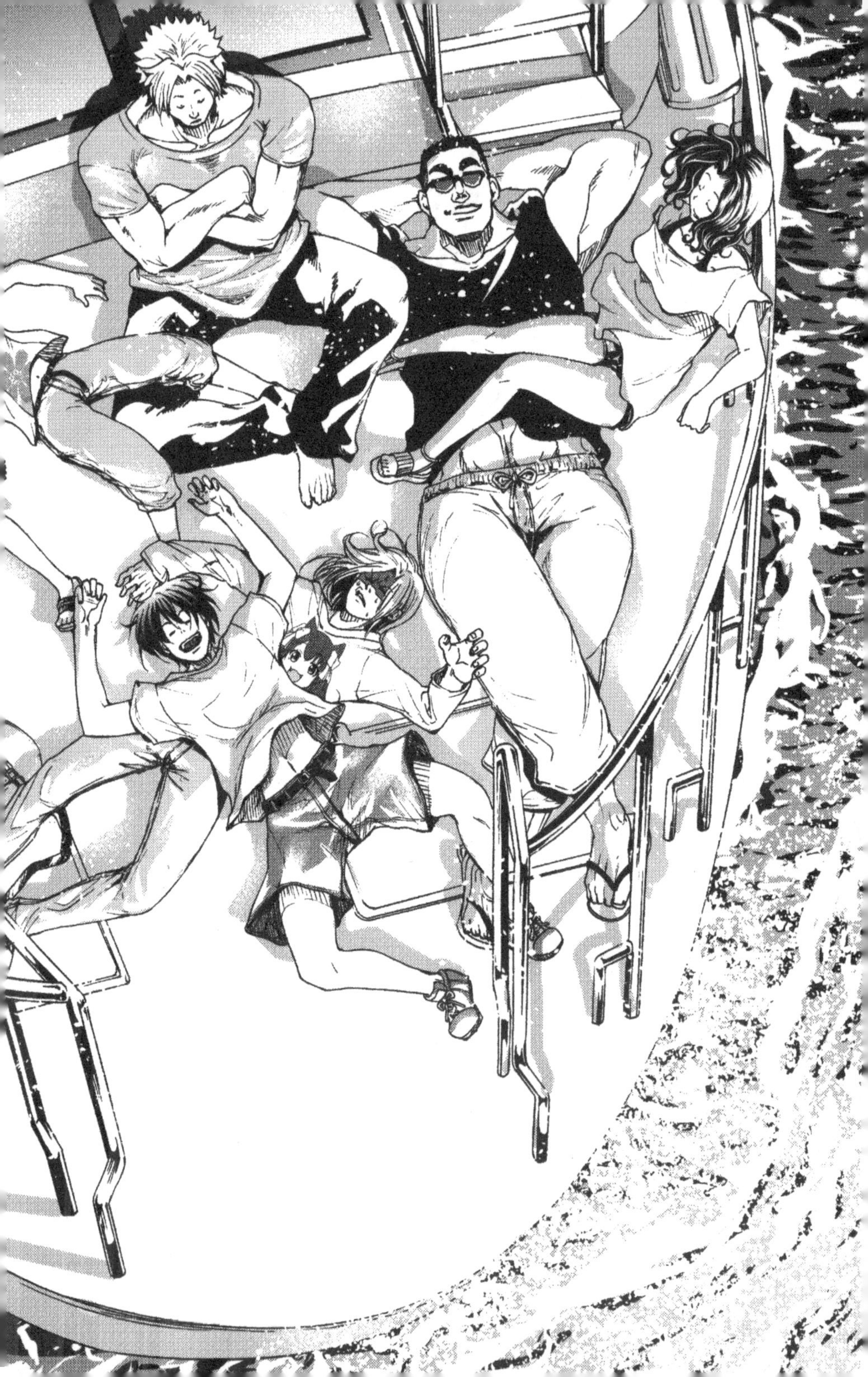

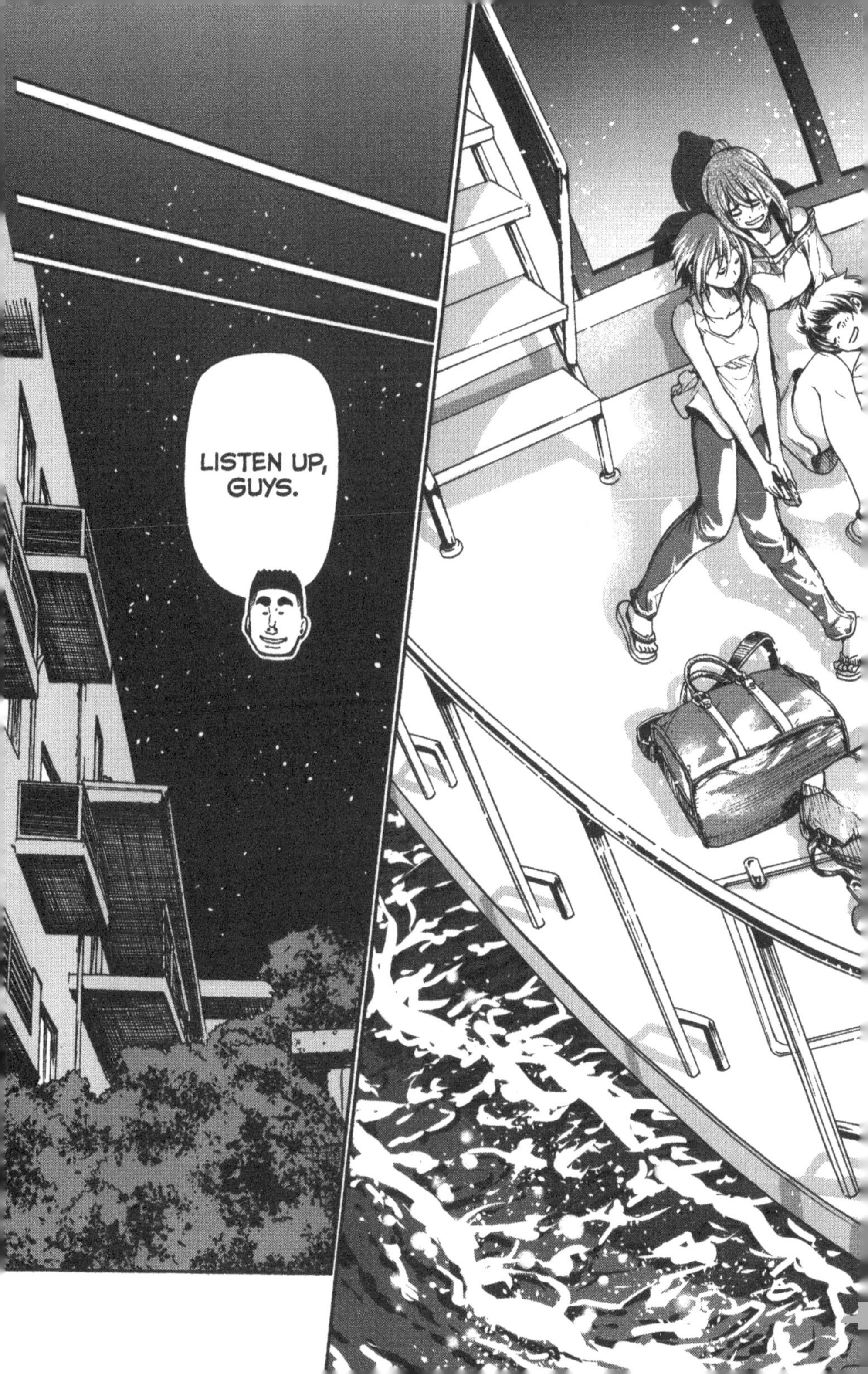
LISTEN UP, GUYS.

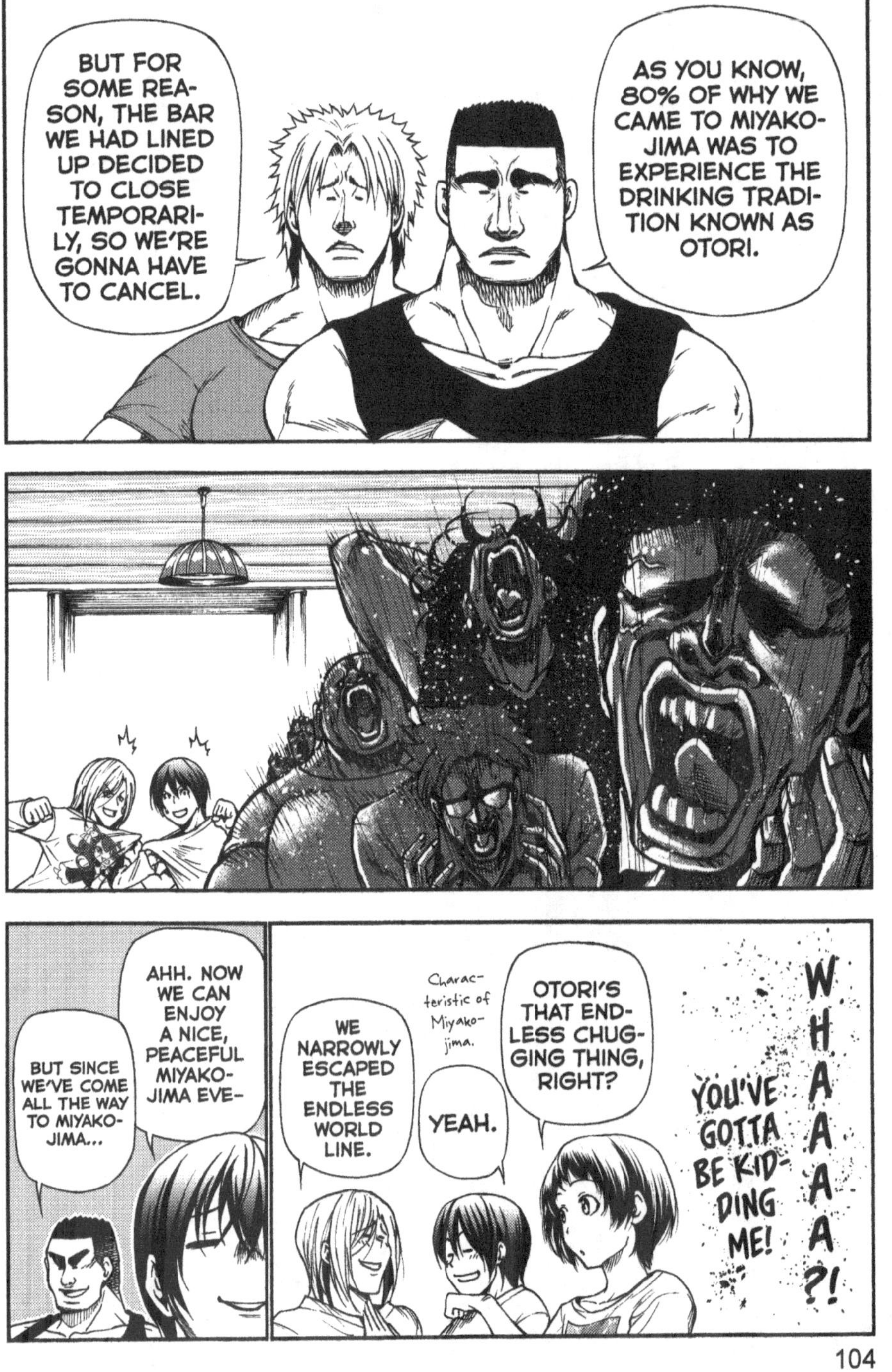
AS YOU KNOW, 80% OF WHY WE CAME TO MIYAKOJIMA WAS TO EXPERIENCE THE DRINKING TRADITION KNOWN AS OTORI.
BUT FOR SOME REASON, THE BAR WE HAD LINED UP DECIDED TO CLOSE TEMPORARILY, SO WE'RE GONNA HAVE TO CANCEL.
WHAAAAA?!
YOU'VE GOTTA BE KIDDING ME!
OTORI'S THAT ENDLESS CHUGGING THING, RIGHT?
Characteristic of Miyakojima.
YEAH.
WE NARROWLY ESCAPED THE ENDLESS WORLD LINE.
AHH. NOW WE CAN ENJOY A NICE, PEACEFUL MIYAKOJIMA EVE-
BUT SINCE WE'VE COME ALL THE WAY TO MIYAKOJIMA...

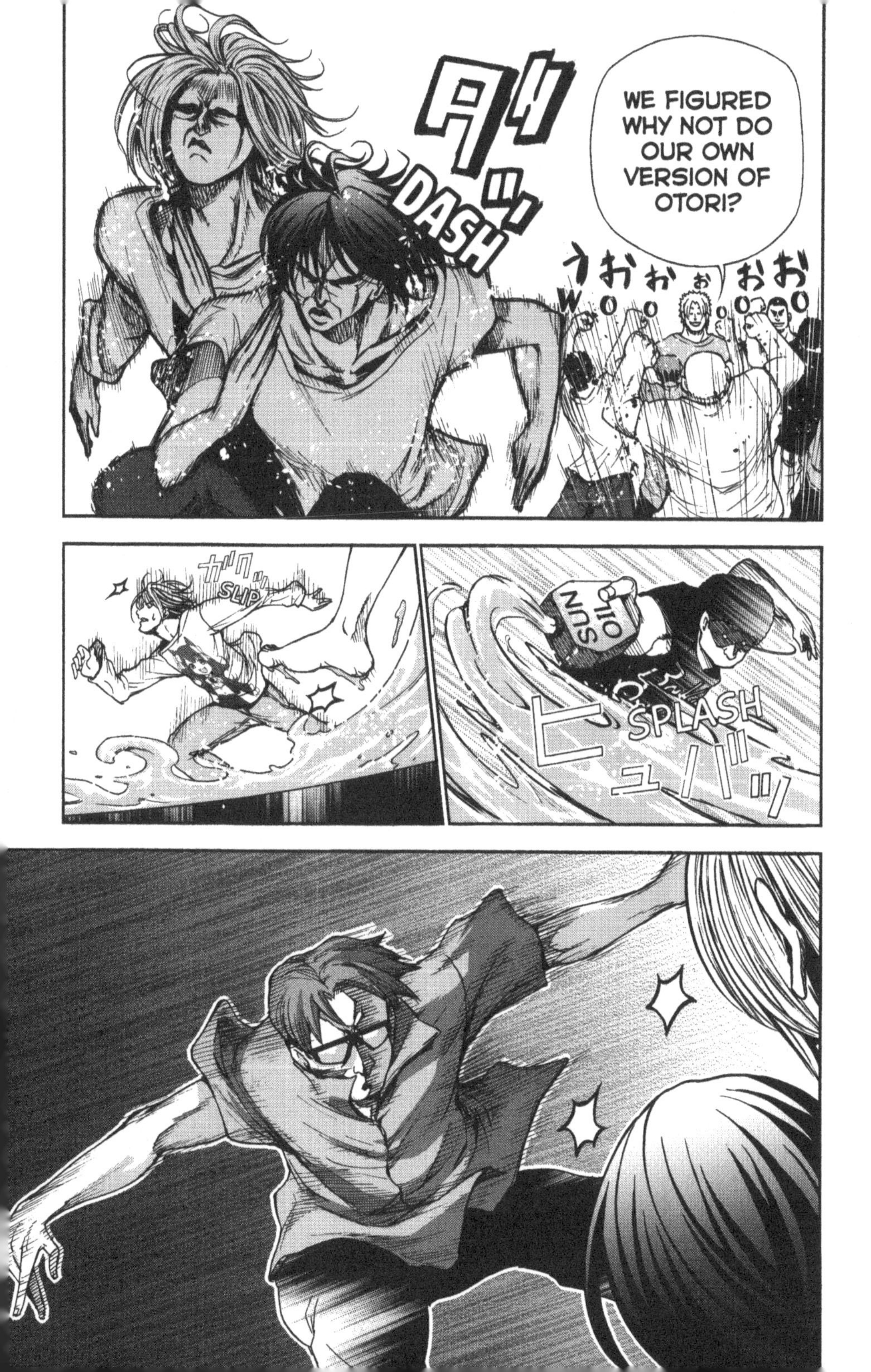
WE FIGURED WHY NOT DO OUR OWN VERSION OF OTORI?
うおぉぉおお
WOOOOOO
タタッ
DASH
ヒュバッ
SPLASH
ガクッ
SLIP

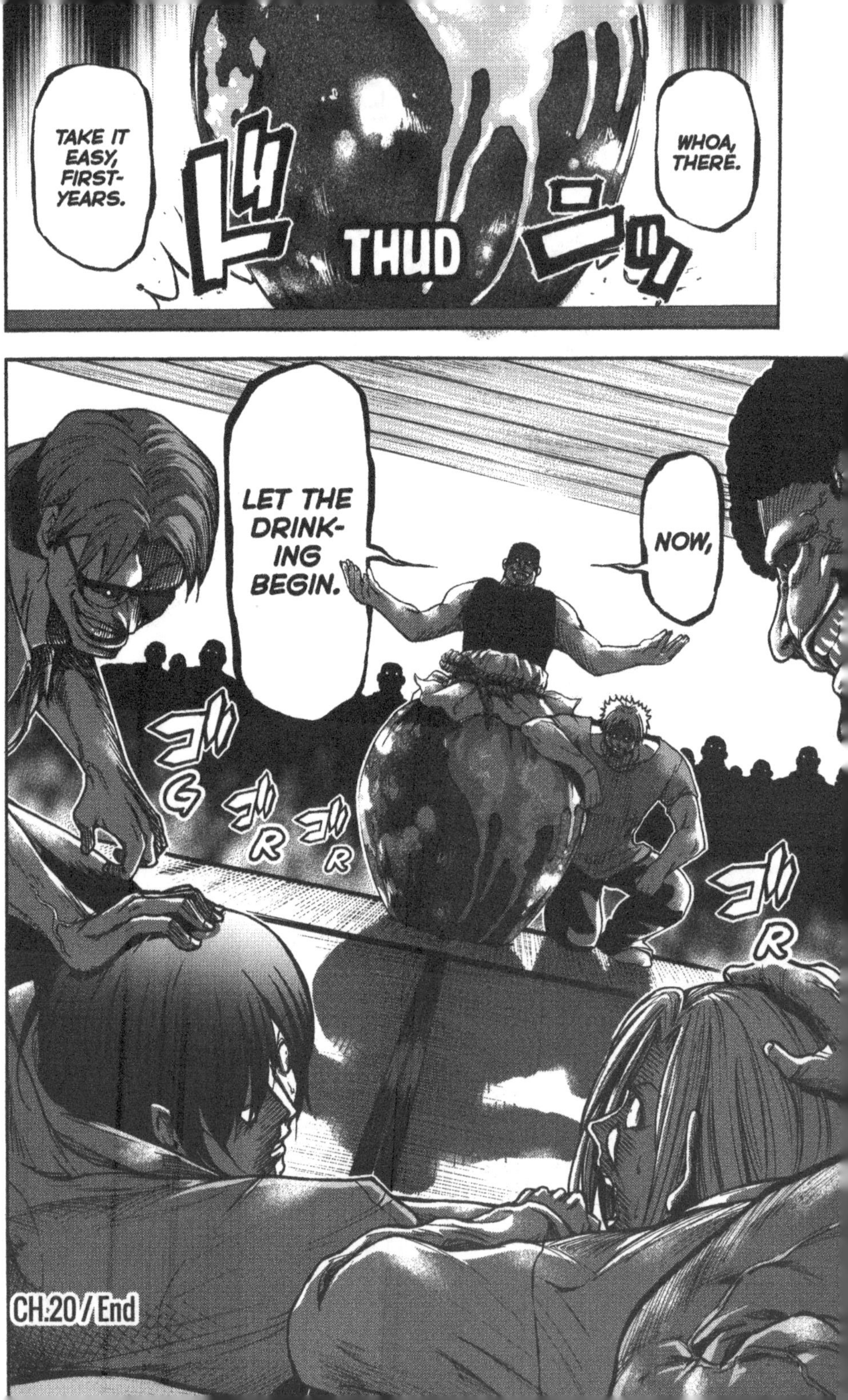
WHOA, THERE.
THUD
TAKE IT EASY, FIRST-YEARS.
NOW,
LET THE DRINK-ING BEGIN.
R
G
R
R
CH.20 / End

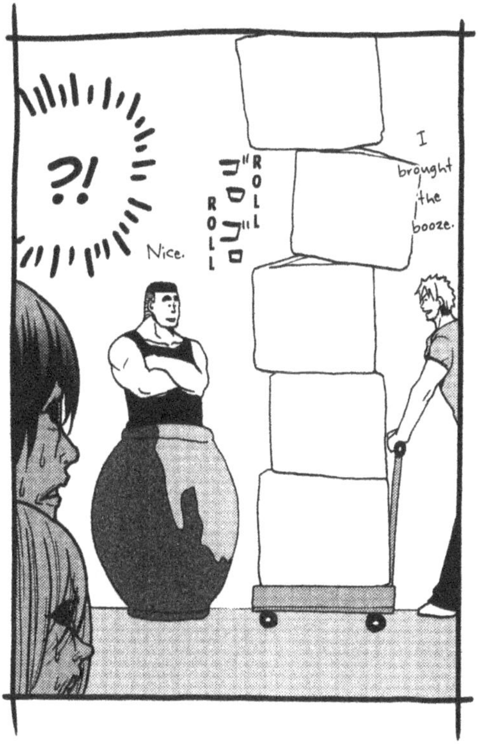
I brought the booze.
ゴロゴロ
ROLL ROLL
Nice.
?!

Grand Blue Dreaming

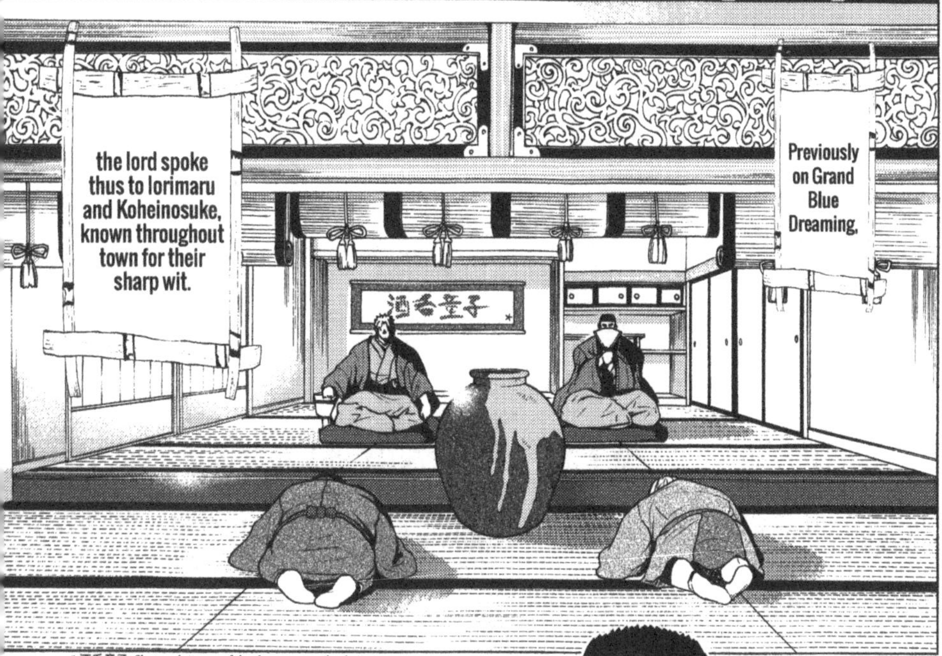
Previously on Grand Blue Dreaming,
the lord spoke thus to Iorimaru and Koheinosuke, known throughout town for their sharp wit.
酒呑童子 *

* 酒呑童子: Shuten-doji, one of the three great evil yokai in Japanese mythology with an unquenchable thirst for sake

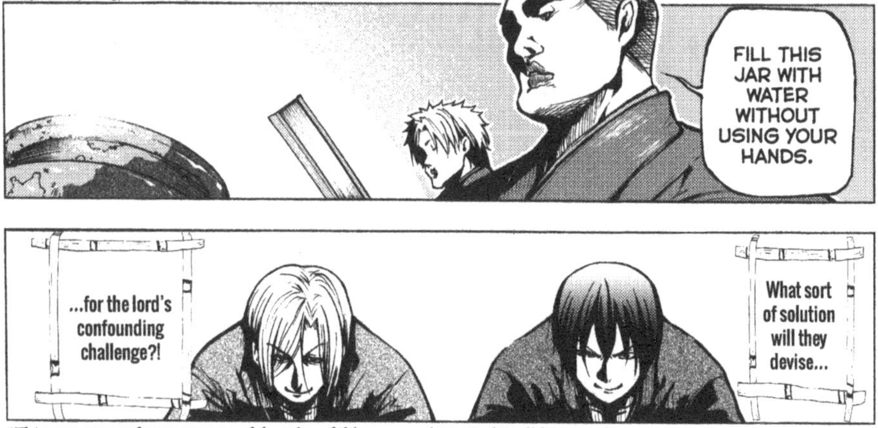
FILL THIS JAR WITH WATER WITHOUT USING YOUR HANDS.
What sort of solution will they devise...
...for the lord's confounding challenge?!

*This scene is a reference to one of the tales of Ikkyu-san, a historical Budhhist monk.

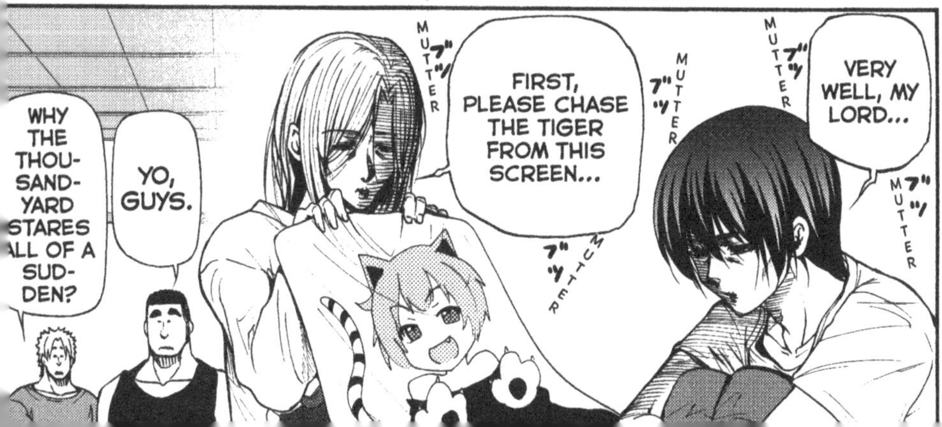
ブツ MUTTER
VERY WELL, MY LORD...
ブツ MUTTER
ブツ MUTTER
FIRST, PLEASE CHASE THE TIGER FROM THIS SCREEN...
ブツ MUTTER
ブツ MUTTER
YO, GUYS.
WHY THE THOUSAND-YARD STARES ALL OF A SUDDEN?

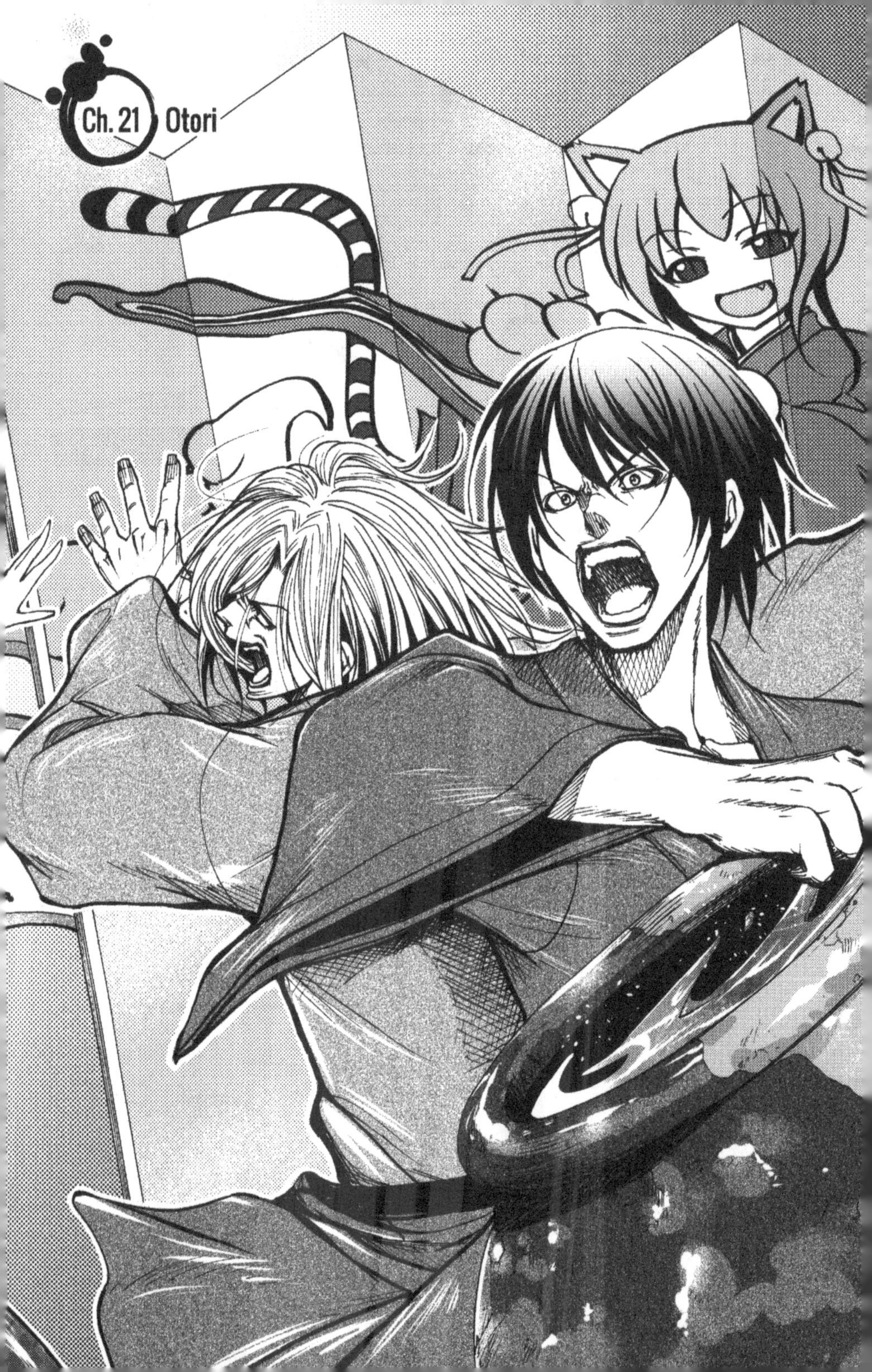
Ch. 21 Otori

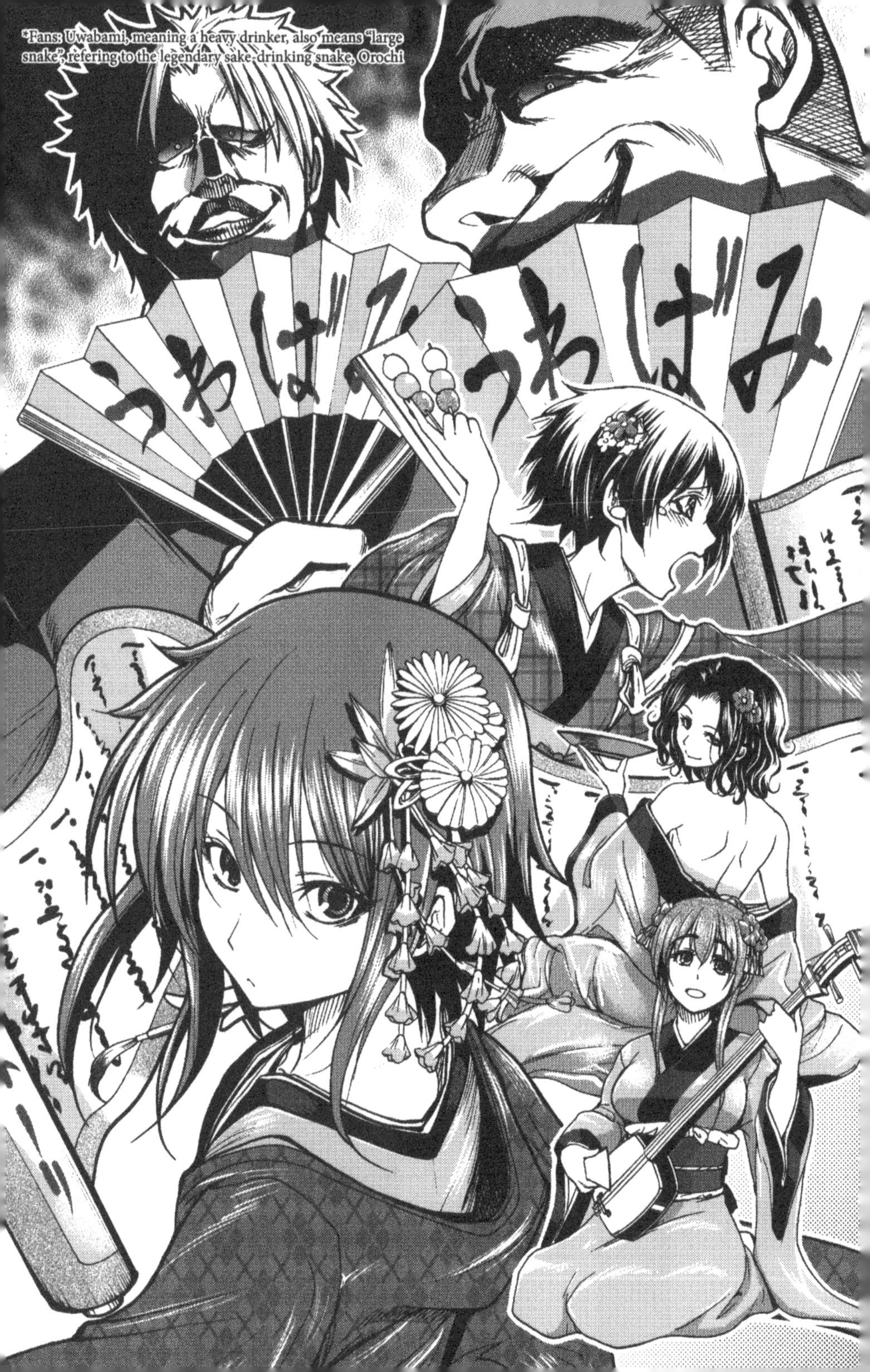
*Fans: Uwabami, meaning a heavy drinker, also means "large snake", refering to the legendary sake-drinking snake, Orochi
うわばみ
うわば

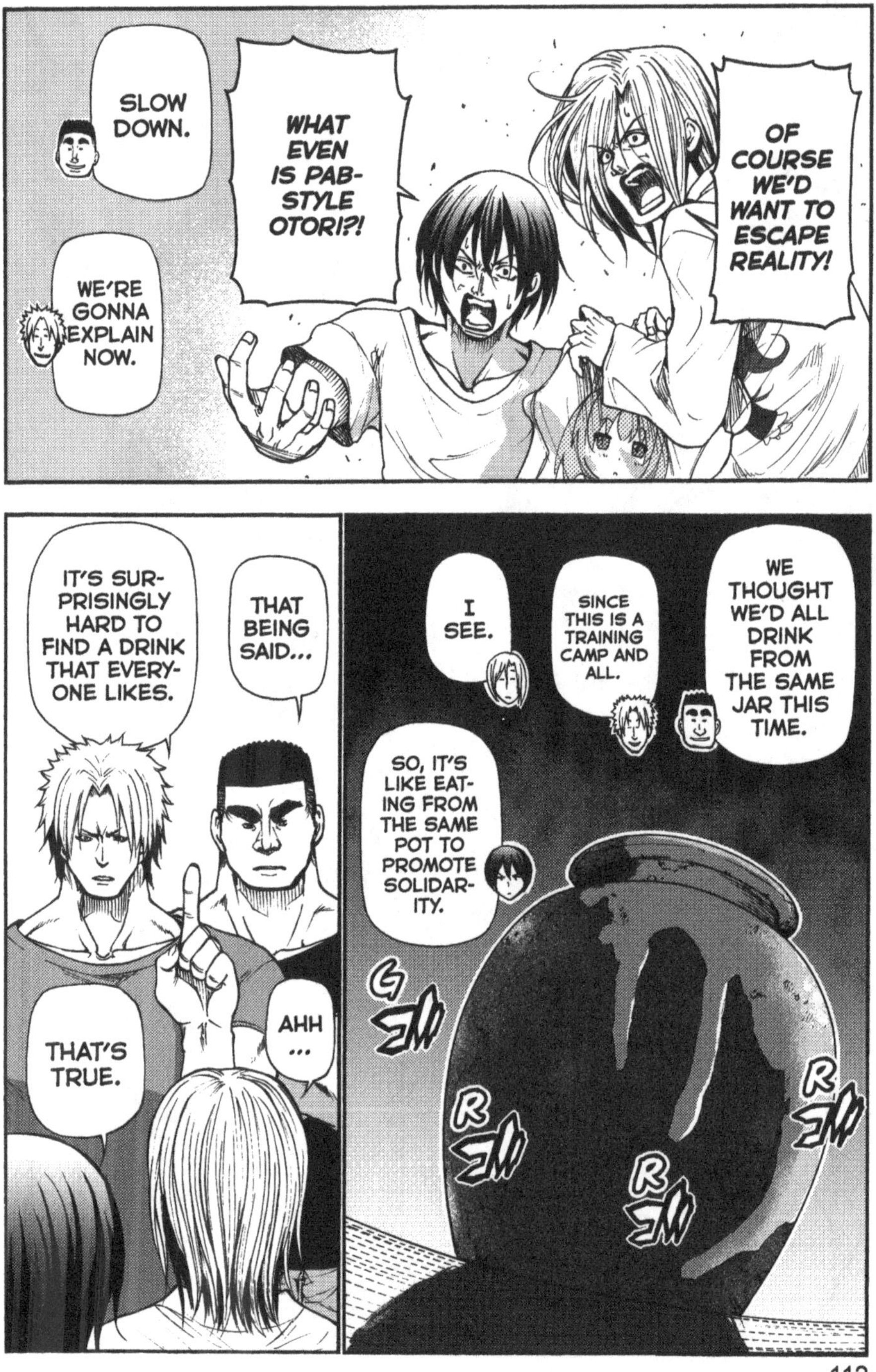
OF COURSE WE'D WANT TO ESCAPE REALITY!
WHAT EVEN IS PAB-STYLE OTORI?!
SLOW DOWN.
WE'RE GONNA EXPLAIN NOW.
WE THOUGHT WE'D ALL DRINK FROM THE SAME JAR THIS TIME.
SINCE THIS IS A TRAINING CAMP AND ALL.
I SEE.
SO, IT'S LIKE EATING FROM THE SAME POT TO PROMOTE SOLIDARITY.
G
R
R
R
THAT BEING SAID...
IT'S SURPRISINGLY HARD TO FIND A DRINK THAT EVERYONE LIKES.
AHH...
THAT'S TRUE.

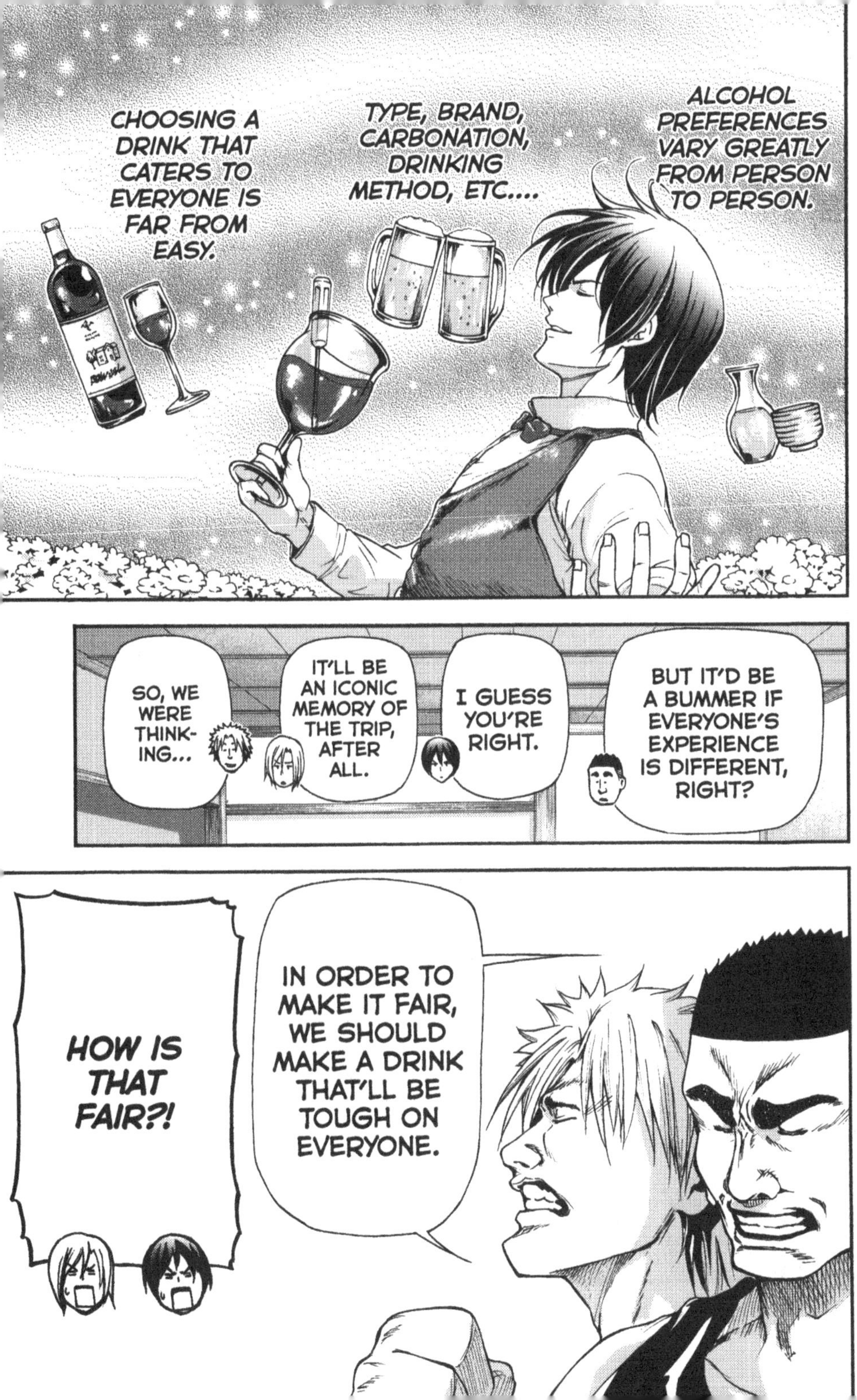
ALCOHOL PREFERENCES VARY GREATLY FROM PERSON TO PERSON.
TYPE, BRAND, CARBONATION, DRINKING METHOD, ETC....
CHOOSING A DRINK THAT CATERS TO EVERYONE IS FAR FROM EASY.
BUT IT'D BE A BUMMER IF EVERYONE'S EXPERIENCE IS DIFFERENT, RIGHT?
I GUESS YOU'RE RIGHT.
IT'LL BE AN ICONIC MEMORY OF THE TRIP, AFTER ALL.
SO, WE WERE THINKING...
IN ORDER TO MAKE IT FAIR, WE SHOULD MAKE A DRINK THAT'LL BE TOUGH ON EVERYONE.
HOW IS THAT FAIR?!

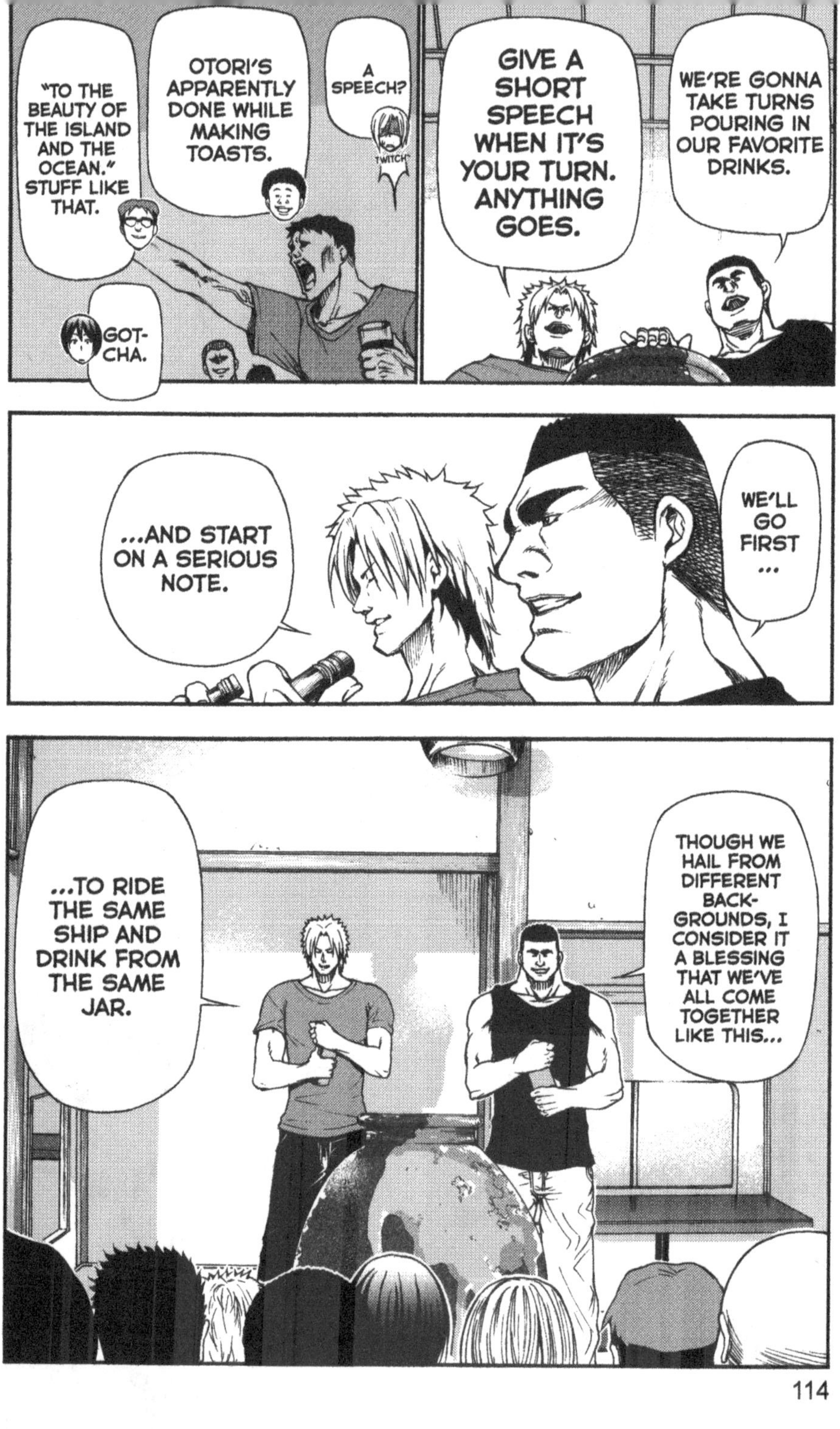
WE'RE GONNA TAKE TURNS POURING IN OUR FAVORITE DRINKS.
GIVE A SHORT SPEECH WHEN IT'S YOUR TURN. ANYTHING GOES.
A SPEECH?
TWITCH
OTORI'S APPARENTLY DONE WHILE MAKING TOASTS.
"TO THE BEAUTY OF THE ISLAND AND THE OCEAN." STUFF LIKE THAT.
GOT-CHA.
WE'LL GO FIRST ...
...AND START ON A SERIOUS NOTE.
THOUGH WE HAIL FROM DIFFERENT BACK-GROUNDS, I CONSIDER IT A BLESSING THAT WE'VE ALL COME TOGETHER LIKE THIS...
...TO RIDE THE SAME SHIP AND DRINK FROM THE SAME JAR.

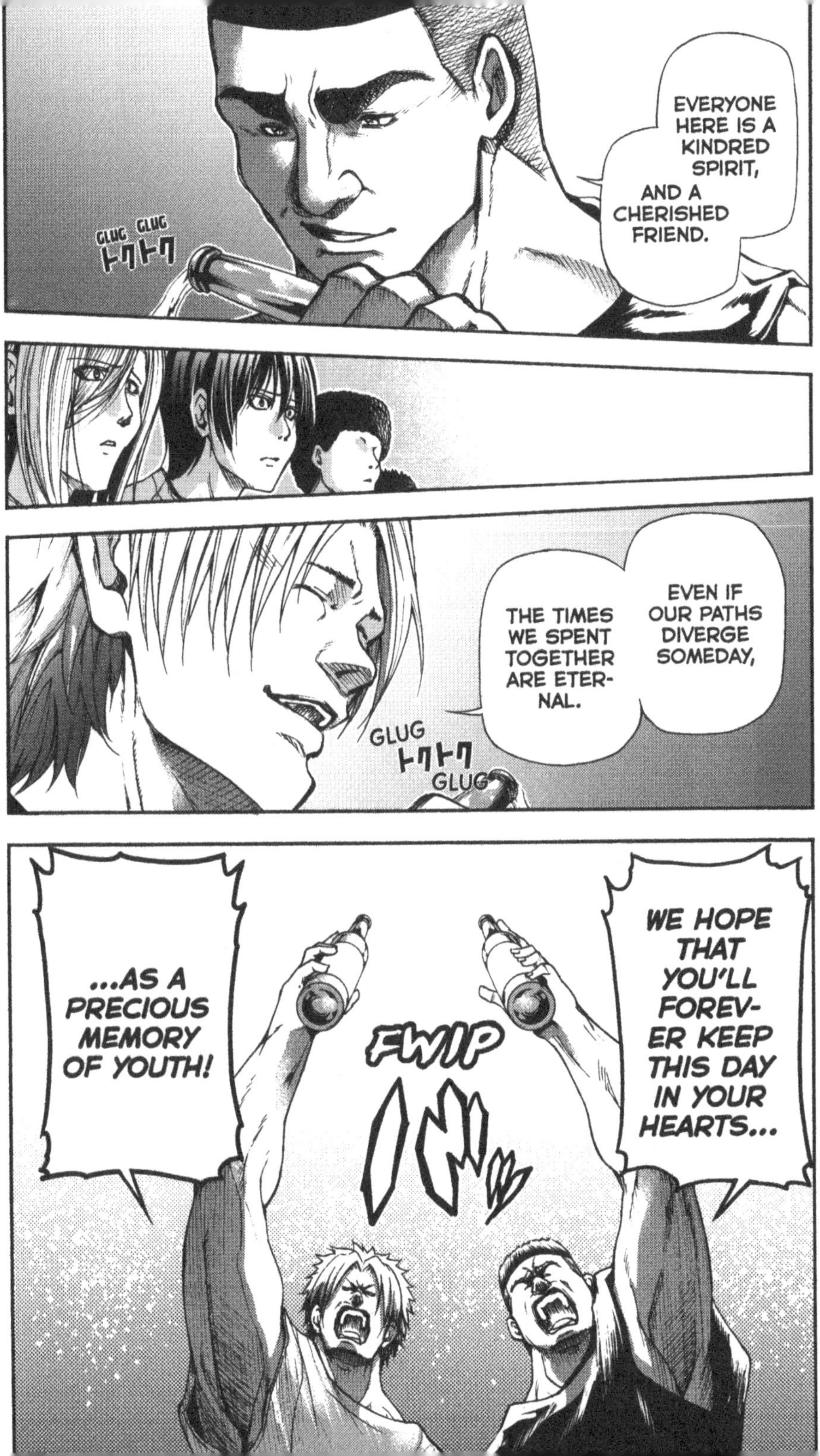
EVERYONE HERE IS A KINDRED SPIRIT,
AND A CHERISHED FRIEND.
GLUG GLUG
トクトク
EVEN IF OUR PATHS DIVERGE SOMEDAY,
THE TIMES WE SPENT TOGETHER ARE ETER-NAL.
GLUG
トクトク
GLUG
WE HOPE THAT YOU'LL FOREV-ER KEEP THIS DAY IN YOUR HEARTS...
FWIP
...AS A PRECIOUS MEMORY OF YOUTH!

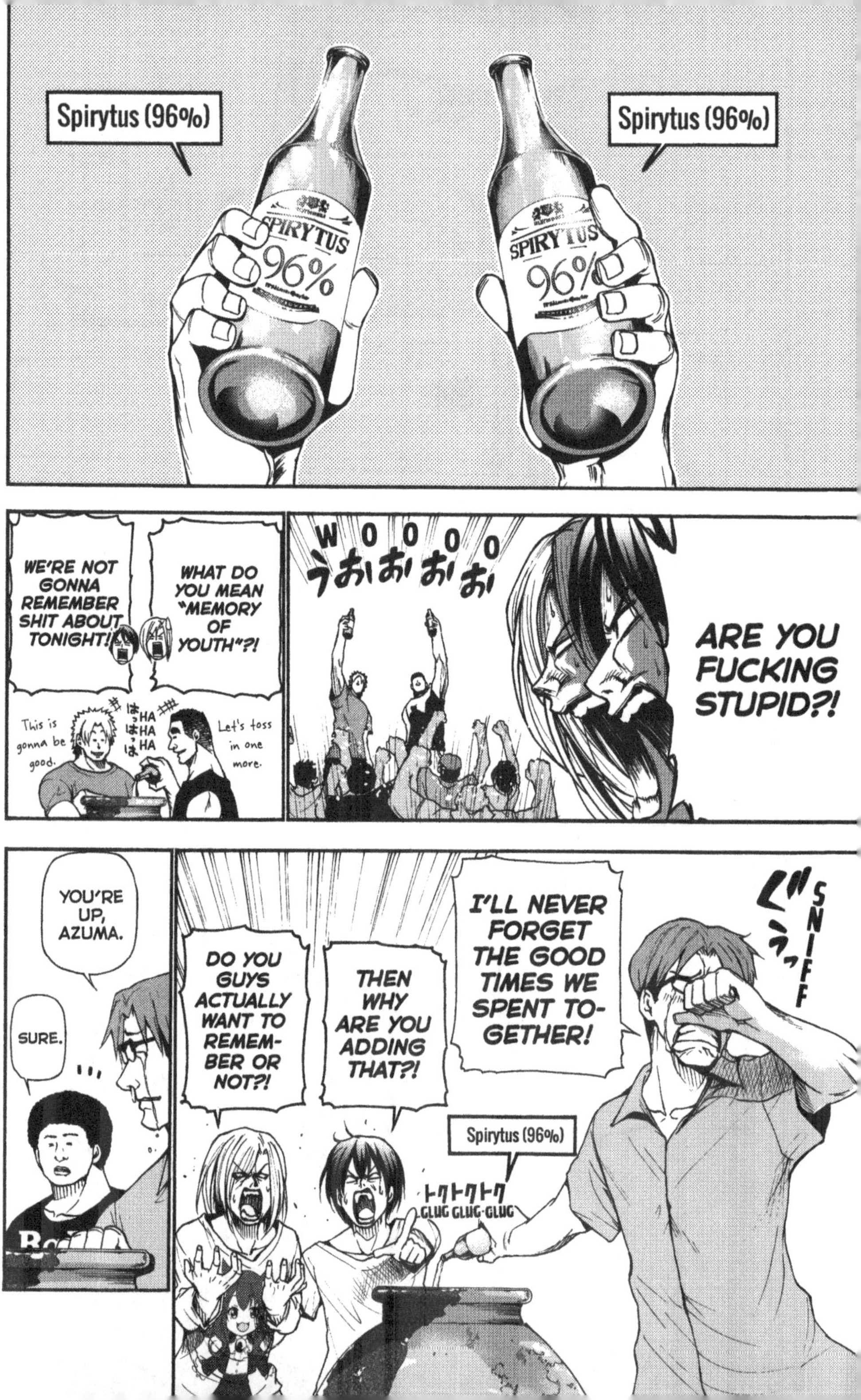
Spirytus (96%)
Spirytus (96%)
SPIRYTUS 96%
SPIRYTUS 96%
WOOOO
うおおおお
ARE YOU FUCKING STUPID?!
WHAT DO YOU MEAN "MEMORY OF YOUTH"?!
WE'RE NOT GONNA REMEMBER SHIT ABOUT TONIGHT!
Let's toss in one more.
はっはっは
HA HA HA
This is gonna be good.
ぐすっ
SNIFF
I'LL NEVER FORGET THE GOOD TIMES WE SPENT TO-GETHER!
THEN WHY ARE YOU ADDING THAT?!
DO YOU GUYS ACTUALLY WANT TO REMEM-BER OR NOT?!
Spirytus (96%)
トクトクトク
GLUG GLUG GLUG
YOU'RE UP, AZUMA.
SURE.

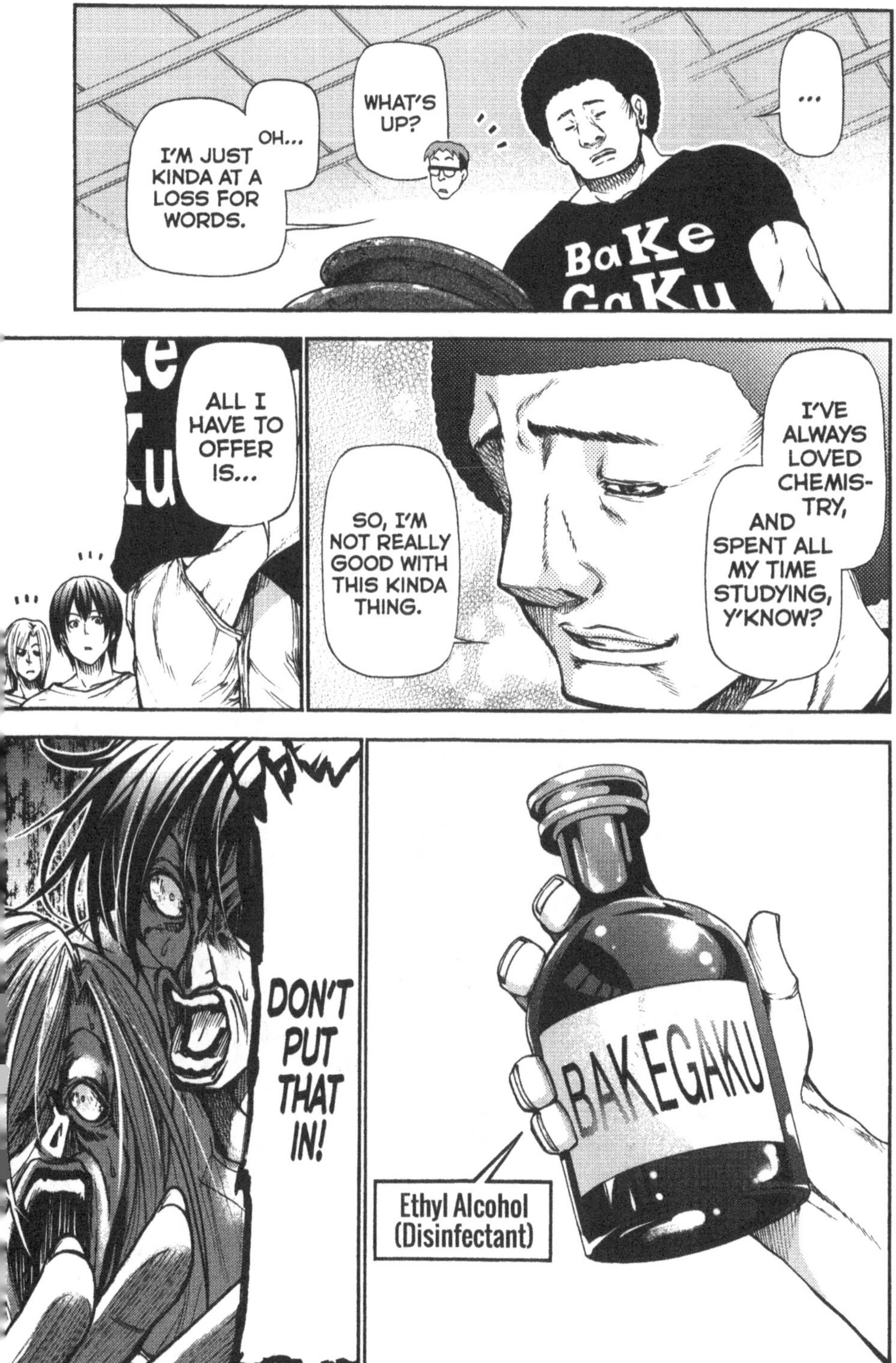
...
WHAT'S UP?
OH... I'M JUST KINDA AT A LOSS FOR WORDS.
BaKe
I'VE ALWAYS LOVED CHEMISTRY, AND SPENT ALL MY TIME STUDYING, Y'KNOW?
SO, I'M NOT REALLY GOOD WITH THIS KINDA THING.
ALL I HAVE TO OFFER IS...
BAKEGAKU
Ethyl Alcohol (Disinfectant)
DON'T PUT THAT IN!

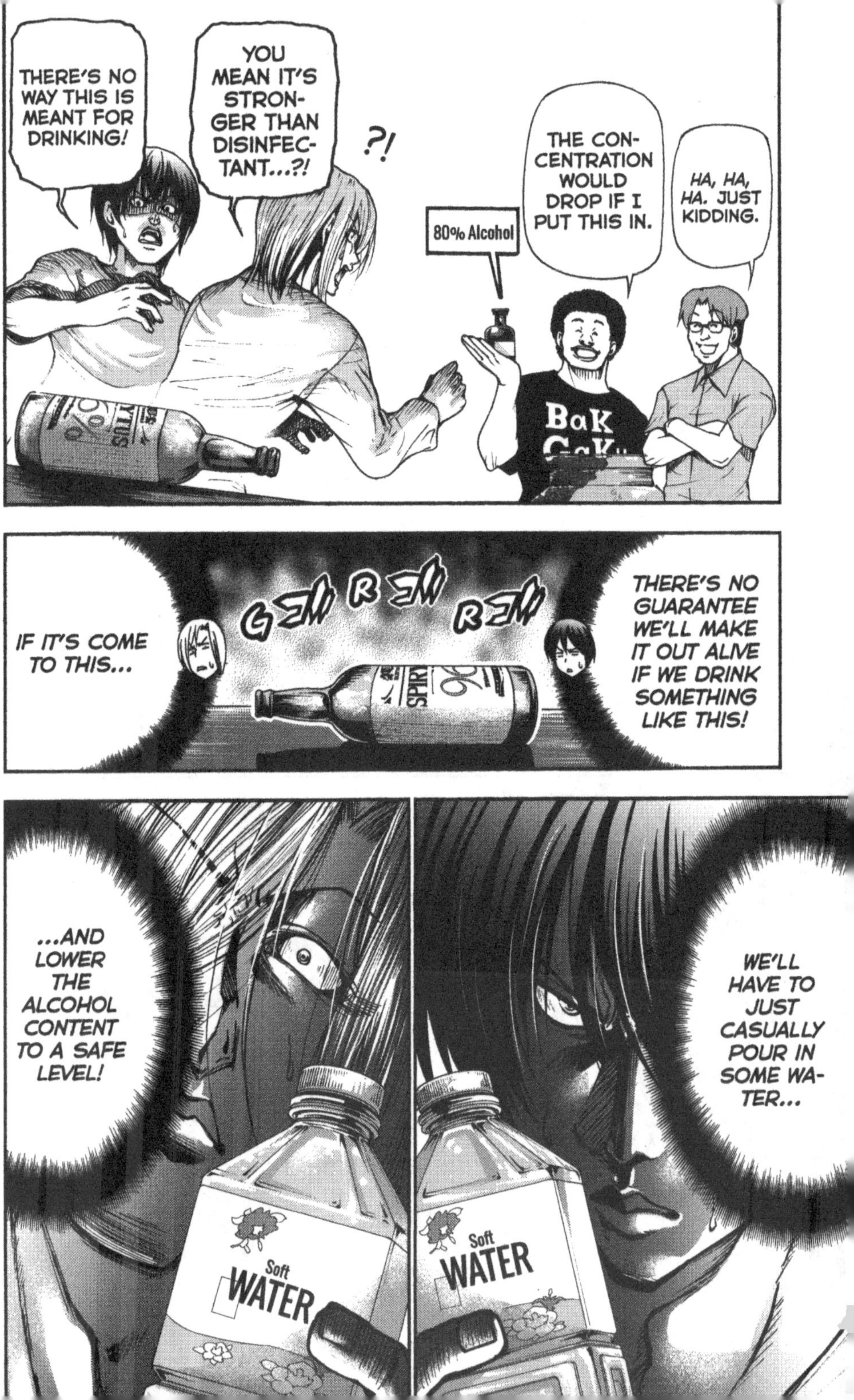
HA, HA, HA. JUST KIDDING.
THE CONCENTRATION WOULD DROP IF I PUT THIS IN.
80% Alcohol
?!
YOU MEAN IT'S STRONGER THAN DISINFECTANT...?!
THERE'S NO WAY THIS IS MEANT FOR DRINKING!
THERE'S NO GUARANTEE WE'LL MAKE IT OUT ALIVE IF WE DRINK SOMETHING LIKE THIS!
IF IT'S COME TO THIS...
WE'LL HAVE TO JUST CASUALLY POUR IN SOME WATER...
Soft WATER
...AND LOWER THE ALCOHOL CONTENT TO A SAFE LEVEL!
Soft WATER

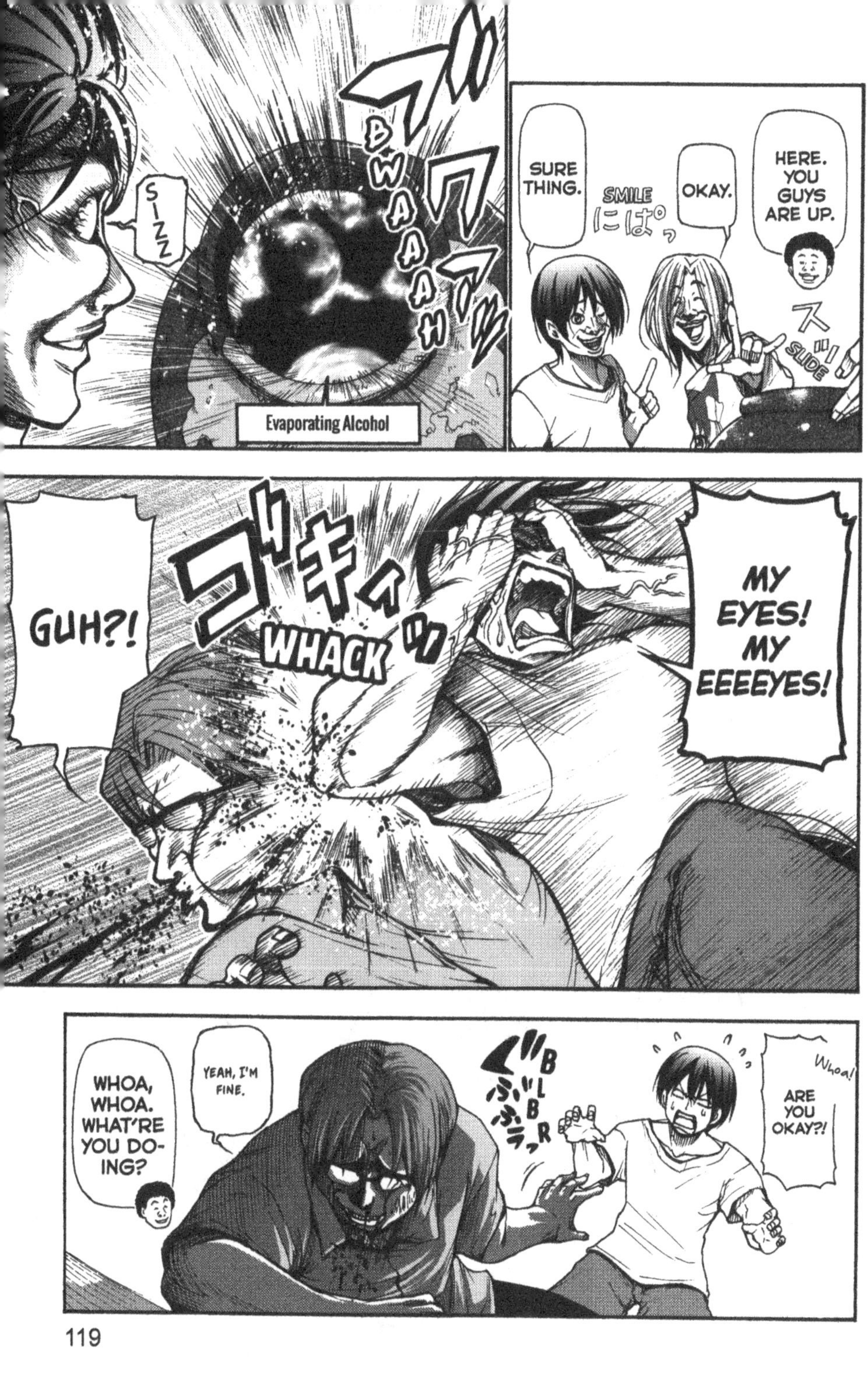
HERE. YOU GUYS ARE UP.
OKAY.
SMILE
にぱっ
SURE THING.
SLIDE
BWAAAAH
SIZZ
Evaporating Alcohol
MY EYES! MY EEEEYES!
WHACK
GUH?!
Whoa!
ARE YOU OKAY?!
BLBR
YEAH, I'M FINE.
WHOA, WHOA. WHAT'RE YOU DOING?

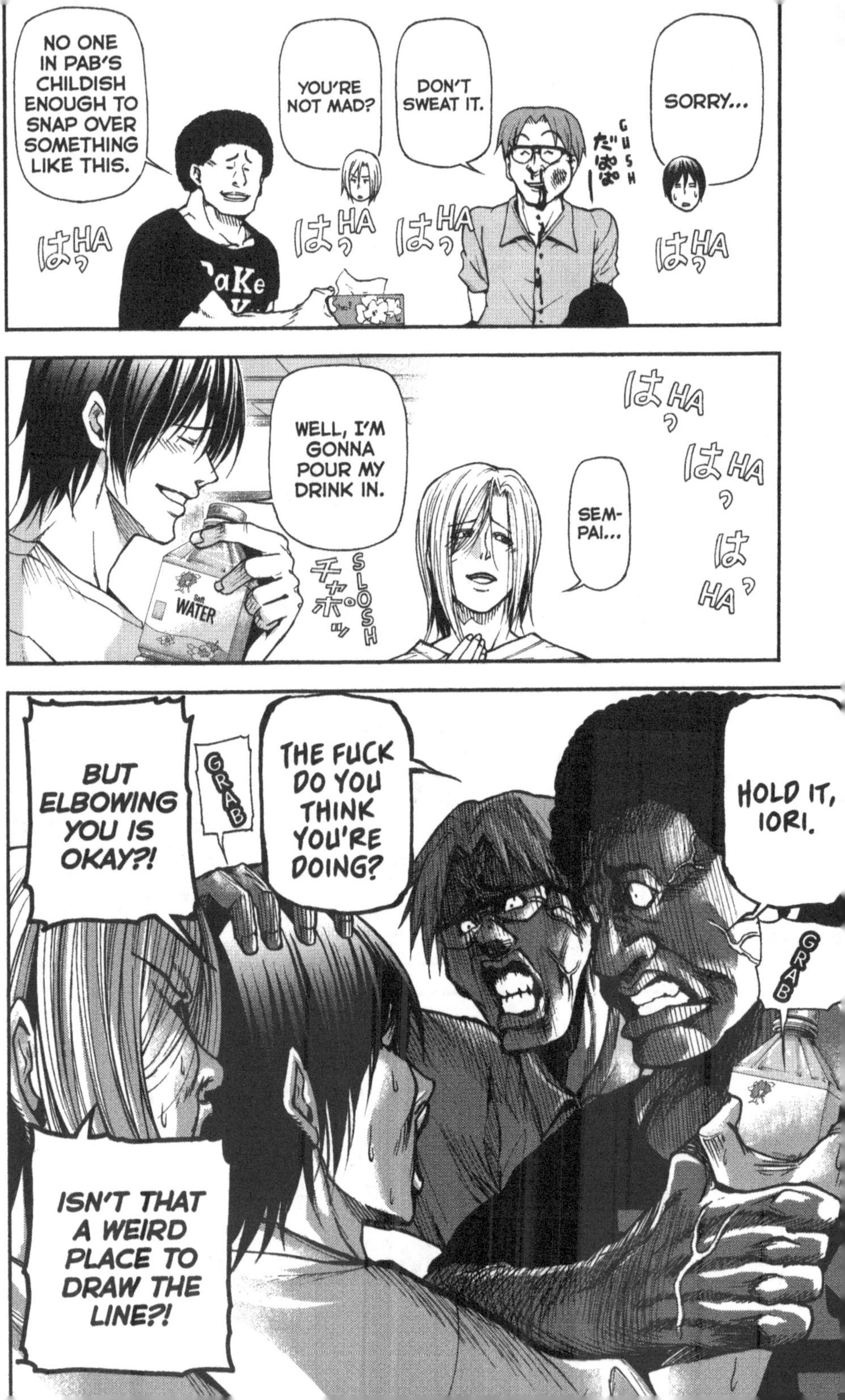
SORRY...
HA
GUSH
DON'T SWEAT IT.
HA
YOU'RE NOT MAD?
HA
NO ONE IN PAB'S CHILDISH ENOUGH TO SNAP OVER SOMETHING LIKE THIS.
HA
HA
HA
HA
SEM-PAI...
WELL, I'M GONNA POUR MY DRINK IN.
SLOSH
SOFT WATER
HOLD IT, IORI.
GRAB
THE FUCK DO YOU THINK YOU'RE DOING?
GRAB
BUT ELBOWING YOU IS OKAY?!
ISN'T THAT A WEIRD PLACE TO DRAW THE LINE?!

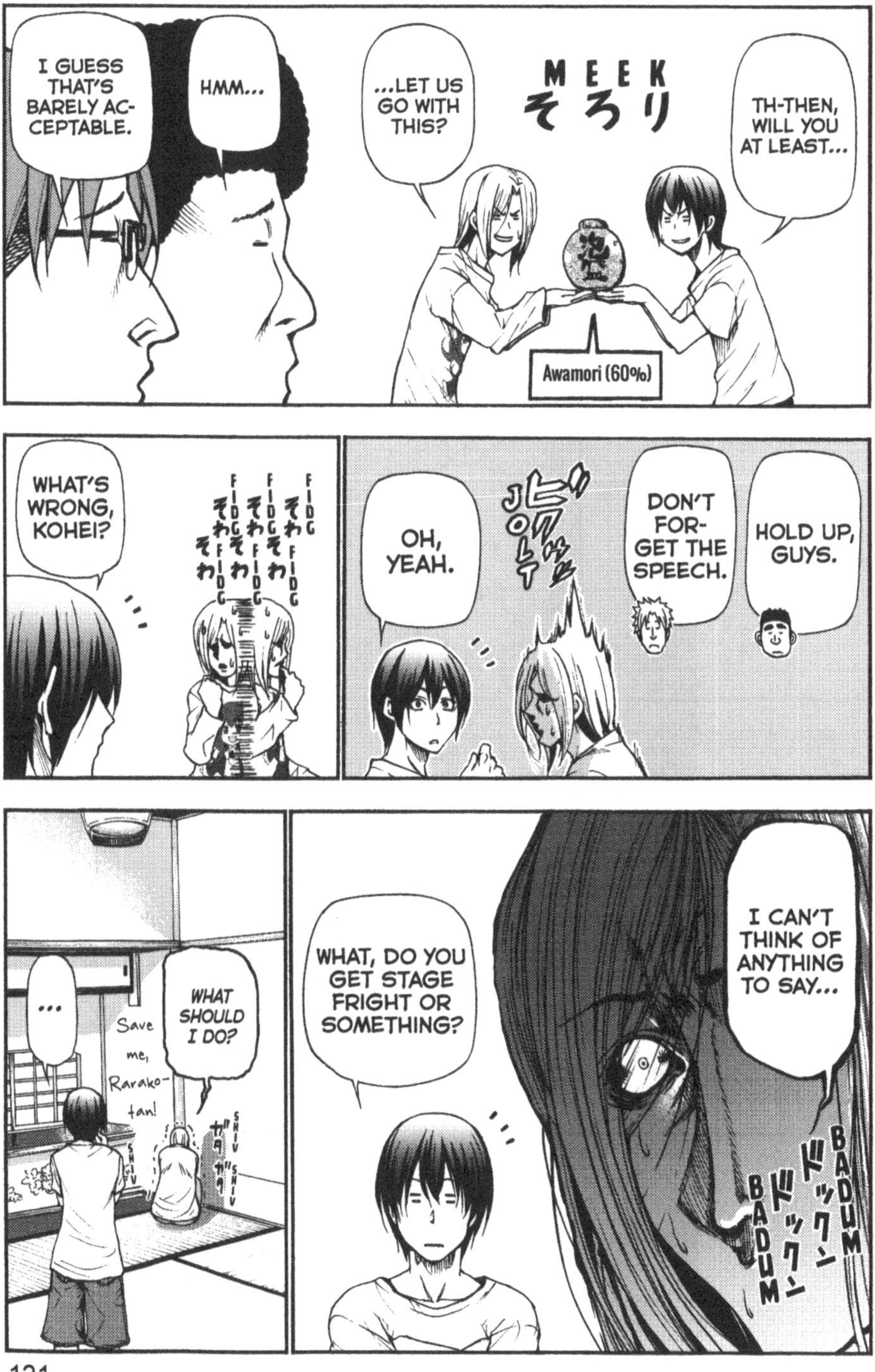
TH-THEN, WILL YOU AT LEAST...
MEEK
そろり
...LET US GO WITH THIS?
HMM...
I GUESS THAT'S BARELY AC-CEPTABLE.
Awamori (60%)
HOLD UP, GUYS.
DON'T FOR-GET THE SPEECH.
JOLT
ビクッ
OH, YEAH.
FIDG FIDG FIDG FIDG FIDG FIDG
そわ そわ そわ そわ そわ そわ
WHAT'S WRONG, KOHEI?
I CAN'T THINK OF ANYTHING TO SAY...
BADUM BADUM
ドックン ドックン
WHAT, DO YOU GET STAGE FRIGHT OR SOMETHING?
WHAT SHOULD I DO?
Save me, Rarako-tan!
...
SHIV SHIV SHIV
ガタガタ

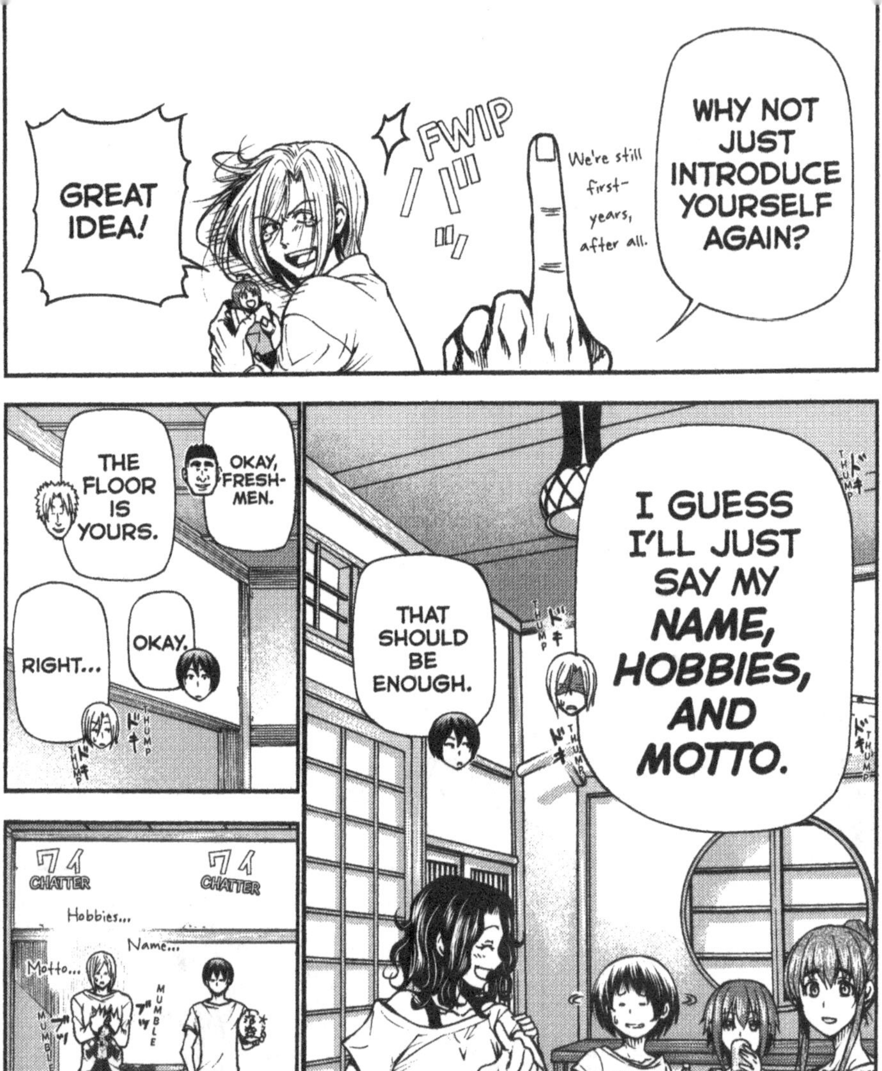
WHY NOT JUST INTRODUCE YOURSELF AGAIN?
We're still first-years, after all.
FWIP
GREAT IDEA!
I GUESS I'LL JUST SAY MY NAME, HOBBIES, AND MOTTO.
THUMP
THAT SHOULD BE ENOUGH.
THUMP
OKAY, FRESHMEN.
THE FLOOR IS YOURS.
OKAY.
RIGHT...
THUMP
CHATTER
CHATTER
Name...
Hobbies...
Motto...
MUMBLE
MUMBLE

*Awamori

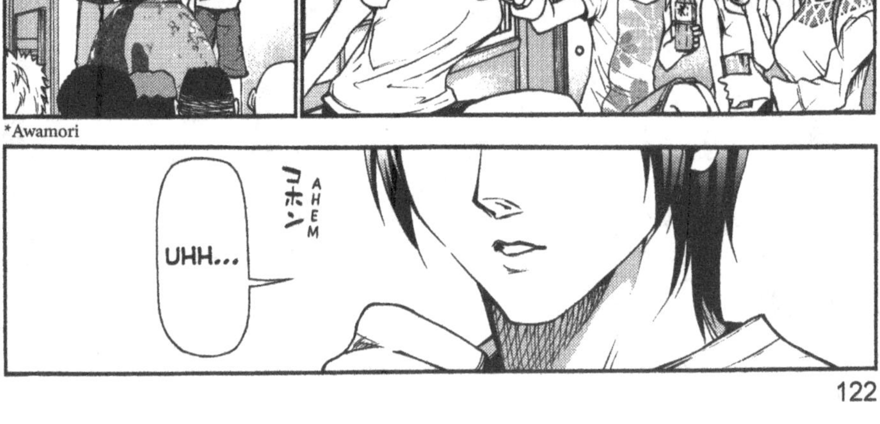
AHEM
UHH...

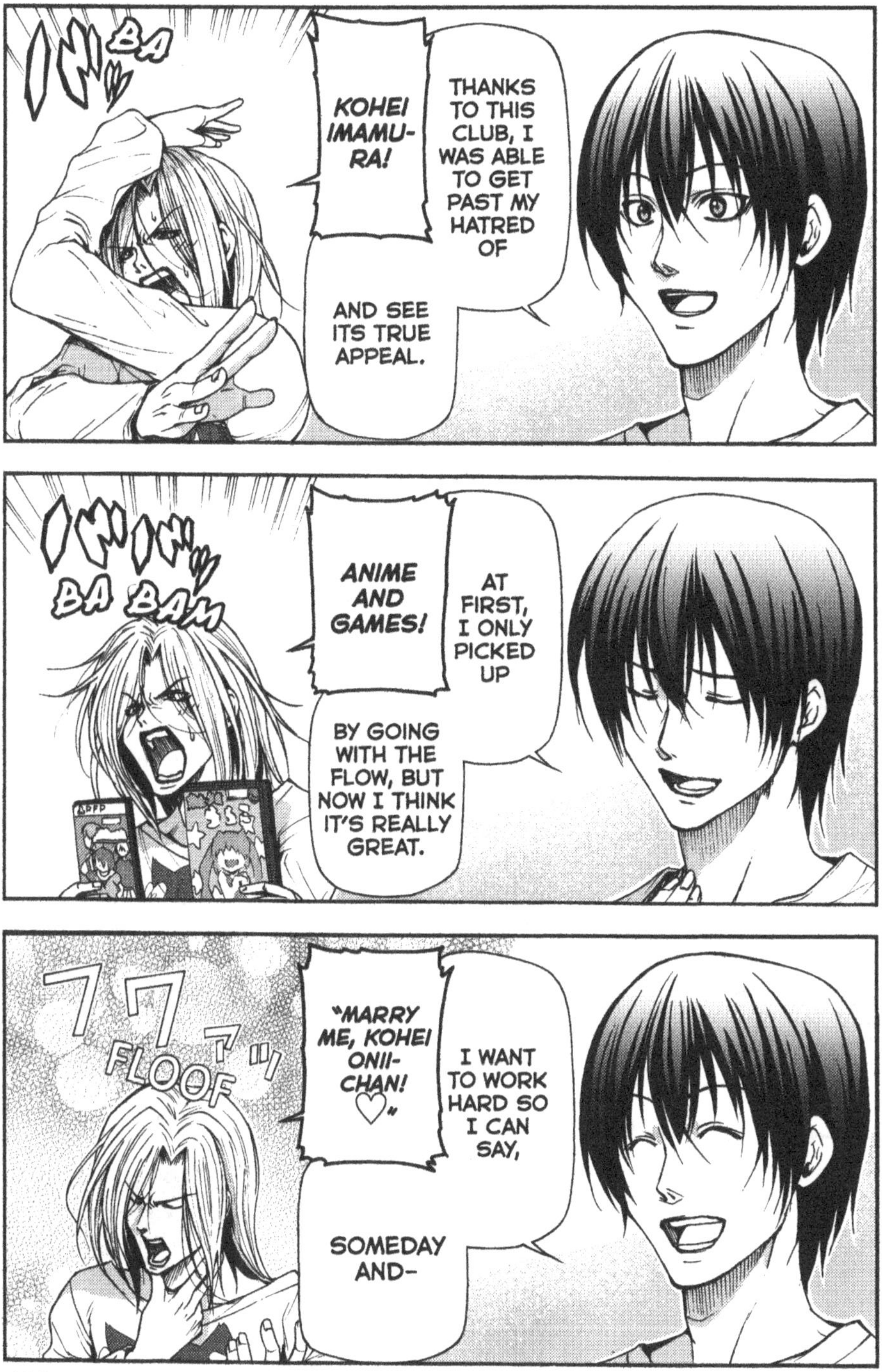
THANKS TO THIS CLUB, I WAS ABLE TO GET PAST MY HATRED OF
KOHEI IMAMURA!
AND SEE ITS TRUE APPEAL.
BA
AT FIRST, I ONLY PICKED UP
ANIME AND GAMES!
BY GOING WITH THE FLOW, BUT NOW I THINK IT'S REALLY GREAT.
BA BAM
I WANT TO WORK HARD SO I CAN SAY,
"MARRY ME, KOHEI ONII-CHAN! ♡"
SOMEDAY AND-
FLOOF

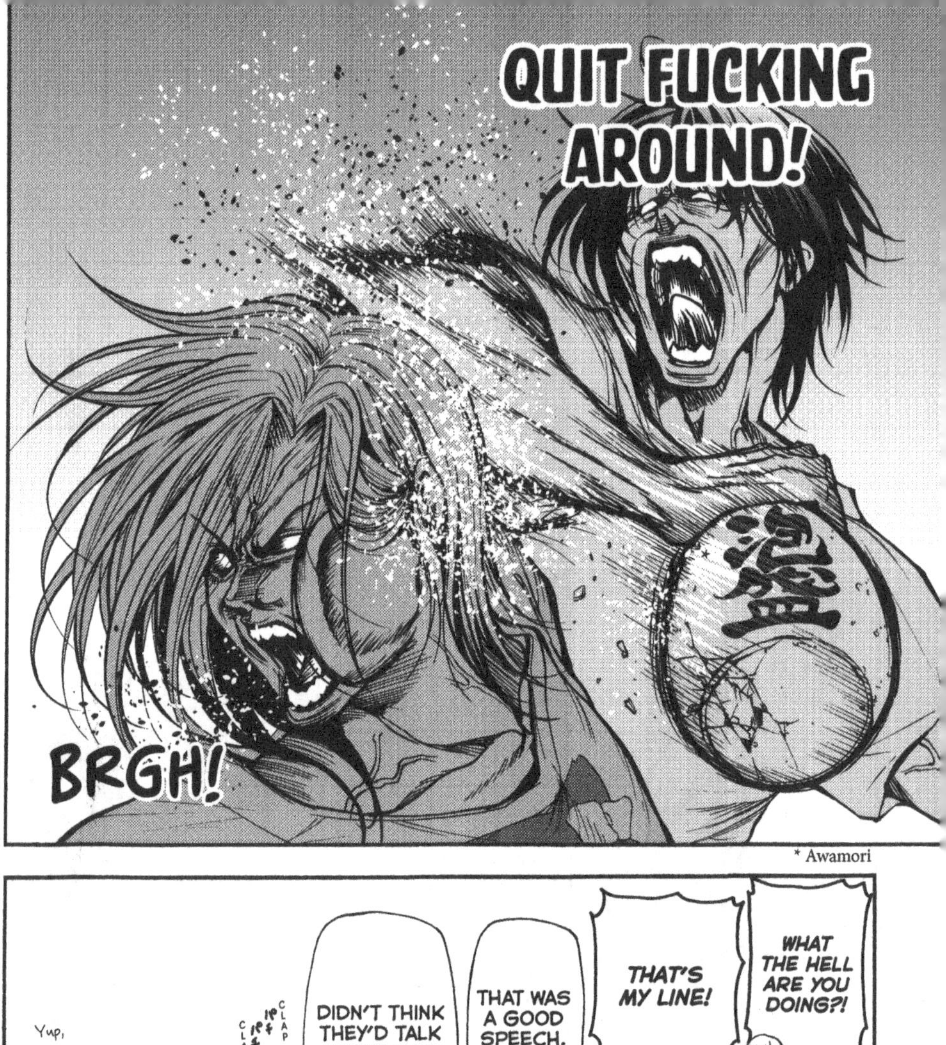
QUIT FUCKING AROUND!
BRGH!

* Awamori

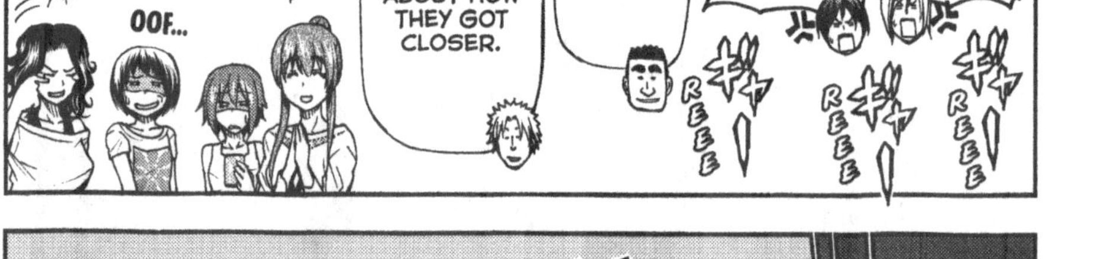
WHAT THE HELL ARE YOU DOING?!
THAT'S MY LINE!
ギャー
REEE
ギャー
REEE
ギャー
REEE
THAT WAS A GOOD SPEECH.
DIDN'T THINK THEY'D TALK ABOUT HOW THEY GOT CLOSER.
パチパチ
CLAP CLAP
OOF...
Yup, yup.

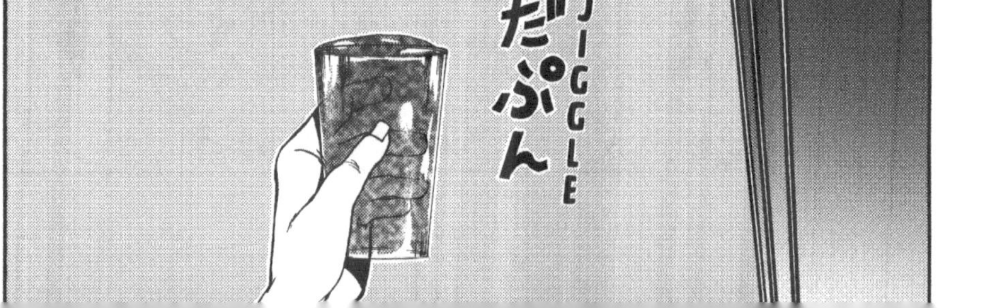
だぷん
JIGGLE

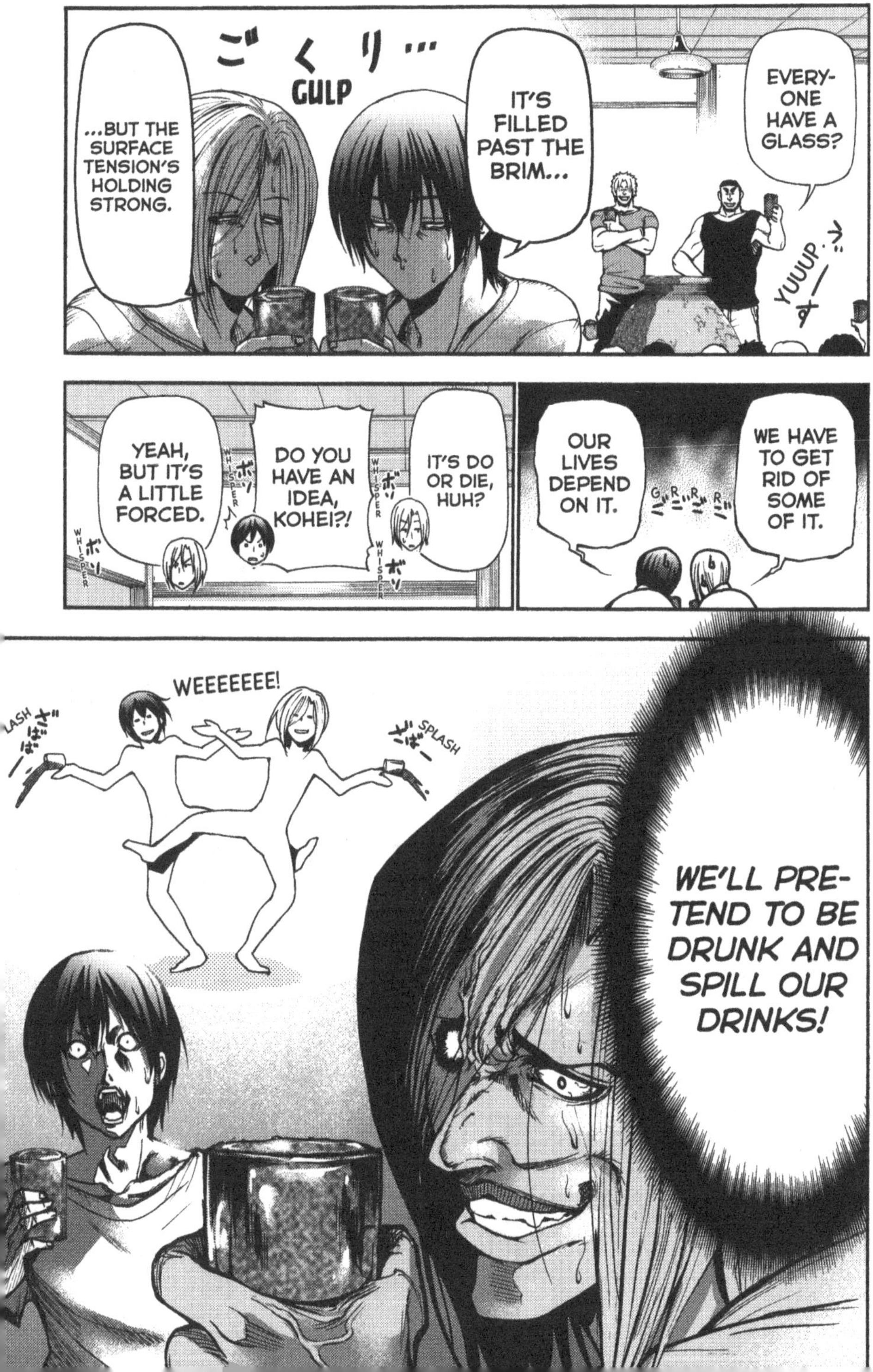
EVERY-ONE HAVE A GLASS?
YUUUP.
すー
IT'S FILLED PAST THE BRIM...
ごくり…
GULP
...BUT THE SURFACE TENSION'S HOLDING STRONG.
WE HAVE TO GET RID OF SOME OF IT.
ごごご
GRR
OUR LIVES DEPEND ON IT.
IT'S DO OR DIE, HUH?
ボソ
WHISPER
DO YOU HAVE AN IDEA, KOHEI?!
ボソ
WHISPER
YEAH, BUT IT'S A LITTLE FORCED.
ボソ
WHISPER
WE'LL PRETEND TO BE DRUNK AND SPILL OUR DRINKS!
ざばー
SPLASH
WEEEEEEE!
ざばば
LASH

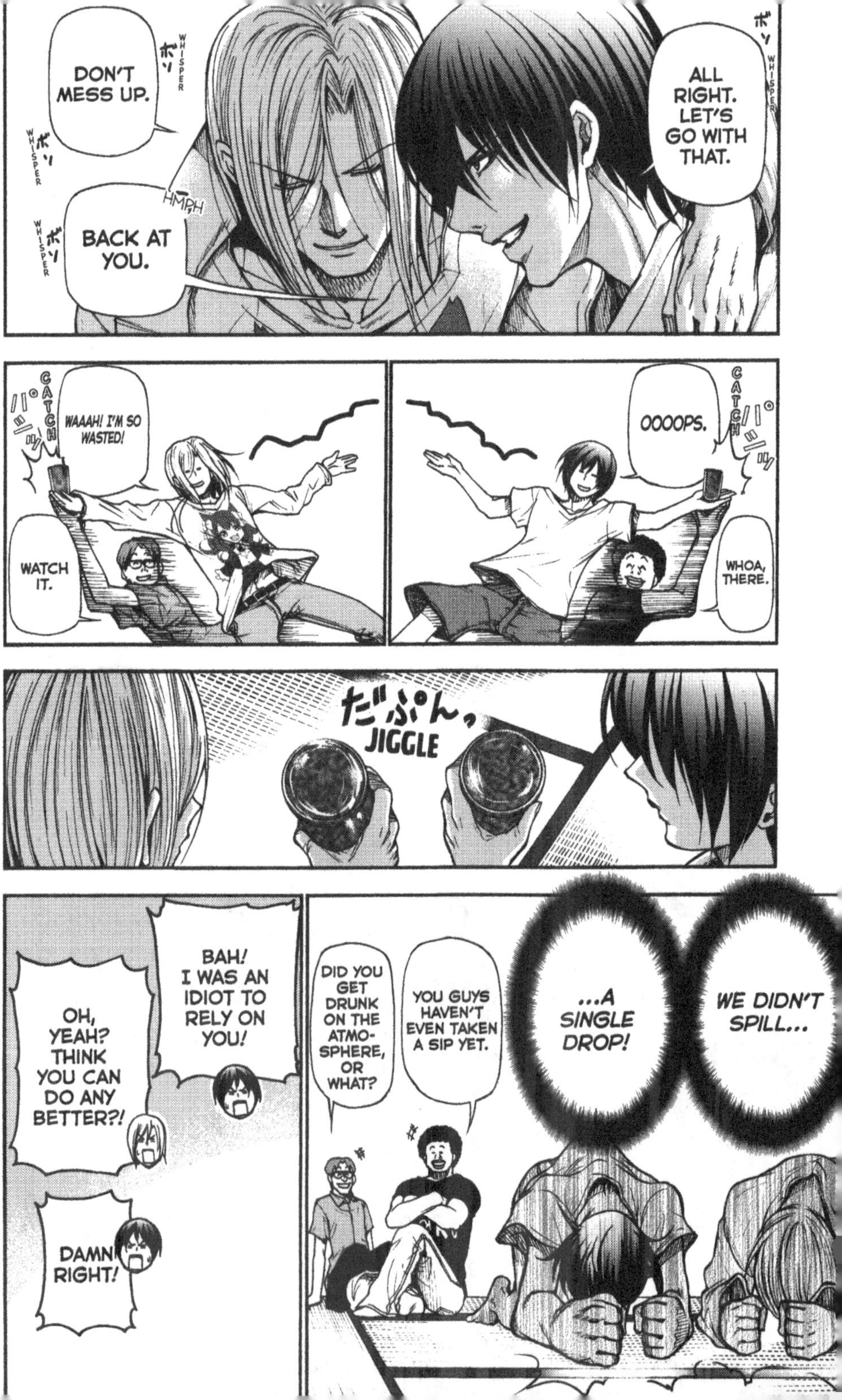
ボソ
WHISPER
ALL RIGHT. LET'S GO WITH THAT.
DON'T MESS UP.
ボソ
WHISPER
ボソ
WHISPER
HMPH
BACK AT YOU.
ボソ
WHISPER
OOOOPS.
CATCH
WHOA, THERE.
WAAAH! I'M SO WASTED!
CATCH
WATCH IT.
だぷん
JIGGLE
WE DIDN'T SPILL...
...A SINGLE DROP!
YOU GUYS HAVEN'T EVEN TAKEN A SIP YET.
DID YOU GET DRUNK ON THE ATMOSPHERE, OR WHAT?
BAH! I WAS AN IDIOT TO RELY ON YOU!
OH, YEAH? THINK YOU CAN DO ANY BETTER?!
DAMN RIGHT!

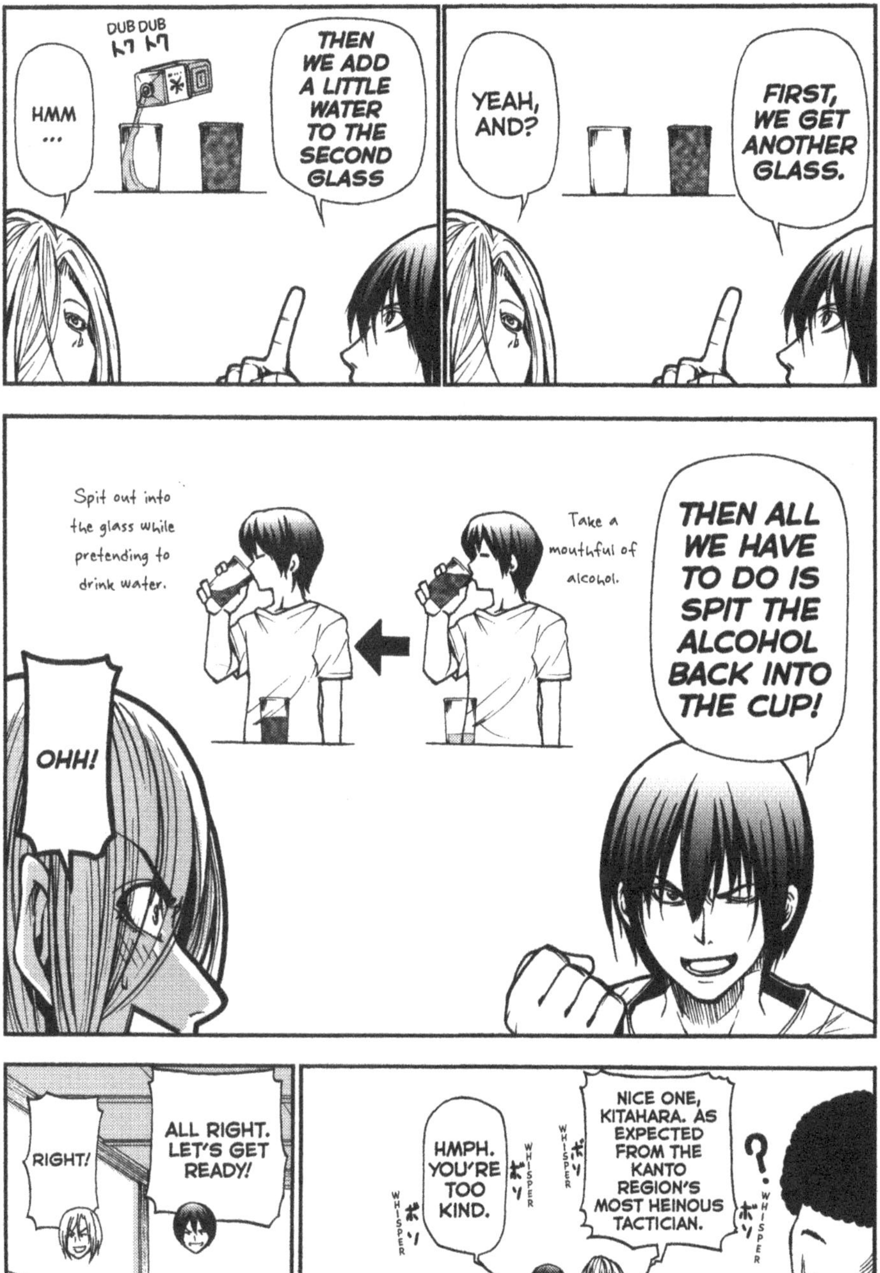
FIRST, WE GET ANOTHER GLASS.
YEAH, AND?
THEN WE ADD A LITTLE WATER TO THE SECOND GLASS
DUB DUB
トク トク
HMM ...
THEN ALL WE HAVE TO DO IS SPIT THE ALCOHOL BACK INTO THE CUP!
Take a mouthful of alcohol.
Spit out into the glass while pretending to drink water.
OHH!
WHISPER ボソ
NICE ONE, KITAHARA. AS EXPECTED FROM THE KANTO REGION'S MOST HEINOUS TACTICIAN.
WHISPER ボソ
HMPH. YOU'RE TOO KIND.
WHISPER ボソ
HEH く HEH く HEH く
ALL RIGHT. LET'S GET READY!
RIGHT!

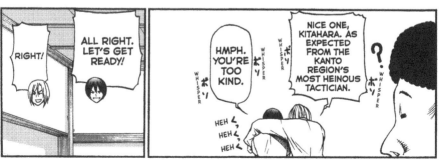

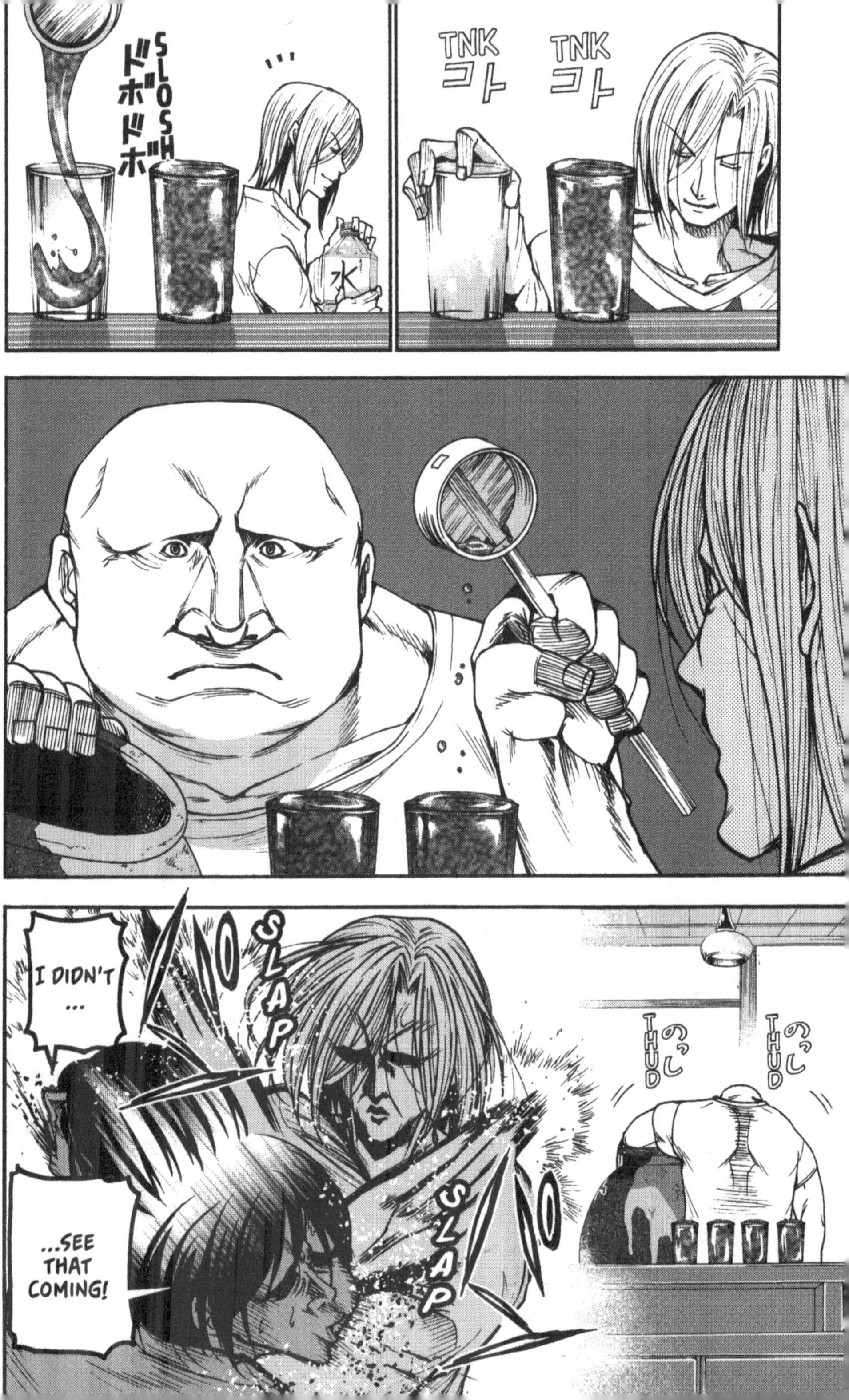
TNK コト
TNK コト
SLOSH ドボドボ
...
THUD のっし
THUD のっし
SLAP
SLAP
I DIDN'T ...
...SEE THAT COMING!

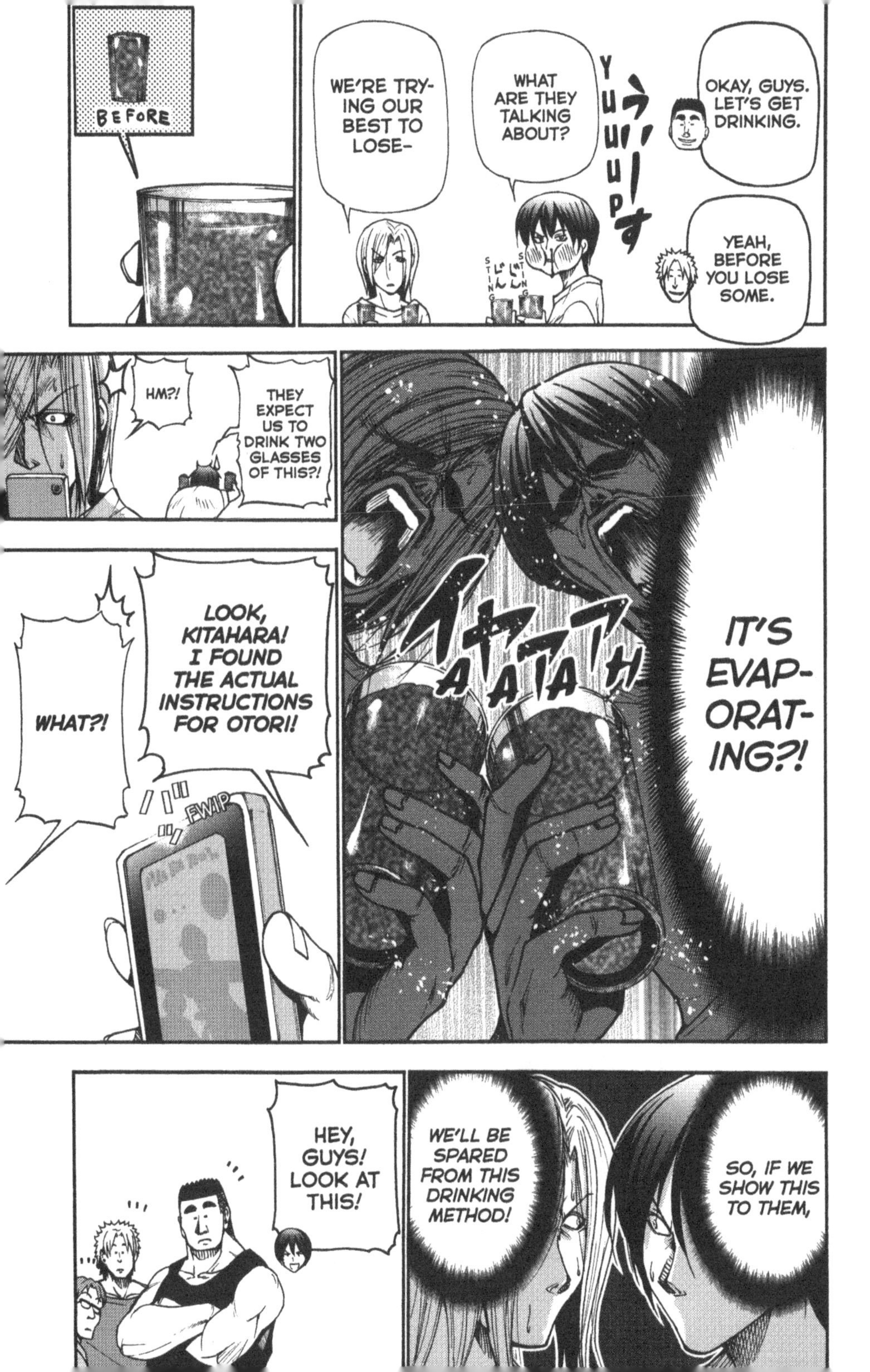
OKAY, GUYS. LET'S GET DRINKING.
YUUUUP
WHAT ARE THEY TALKING ABOUT?
YEAH, BEFORE YOU LOSE SOME.
WE'RE TRY-ING OUR BEST TO LOSE-
STING
STING
BEFORE
IT'S EVAP-ORAT-ING?!
AAAH
HM?!
THEY EXPECT US TO DRINK TWO GLASSES OF THIS?!
LOOK, KITAHARA! I FOUND THE ACTUAL INSTRUCTIONS FOR OTORI!
WHAT?!
FWAP
SO, IF WE SHOW THIS TO THEM,
WE'LL BE SPARED FROM THIS DRINKING METHOD!
HEY, GUYS! LOOK AT THIS!

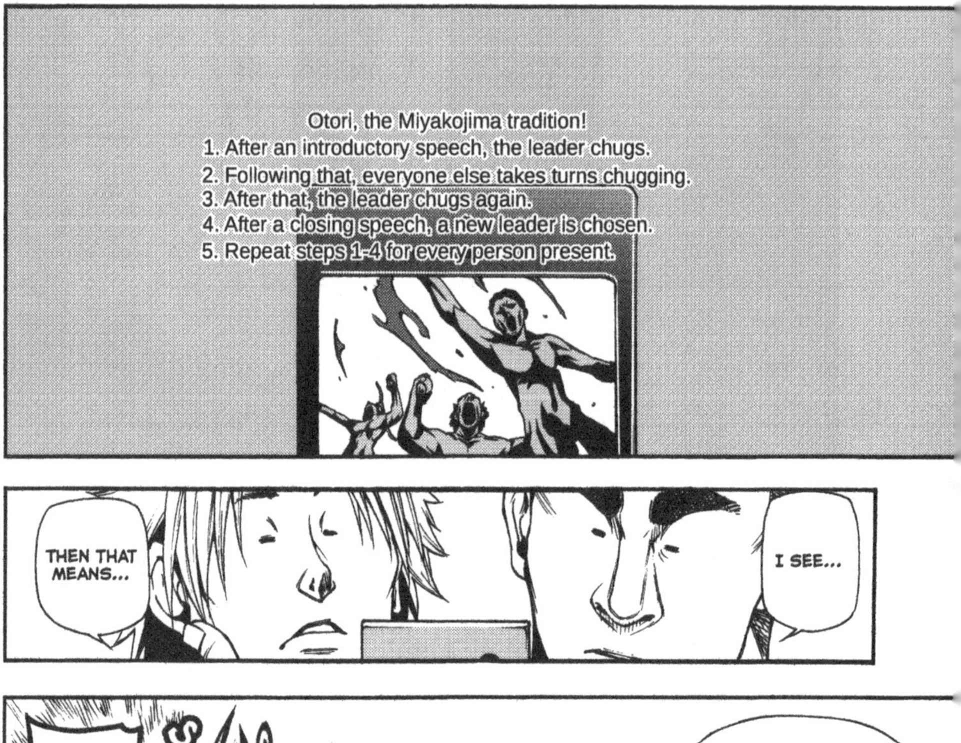

Otori, the Miyakojima tradition!
1. After an introductory speech, the leader chugs.
2. Following that, everyone else takes turns chugging.
3. After that, the leader chugs again.
4. After a closing speech, a new leader is chosen.
5. Repeat steps 1-4 for every person present.
I SEE...
THEN THAT MEANS...
...WE'LL HAVE TO TOAST AT LEAST 12 TIMES.
WE'RE GONNA NEED MORE BOOZE.
LET'S TOSS IN EVERYTHING.
ドポポポ
GLUG GLUG GLUG
SLAP
SLAP
I DIDN'T...
...SEE THAT COMING!

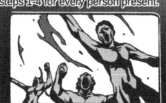

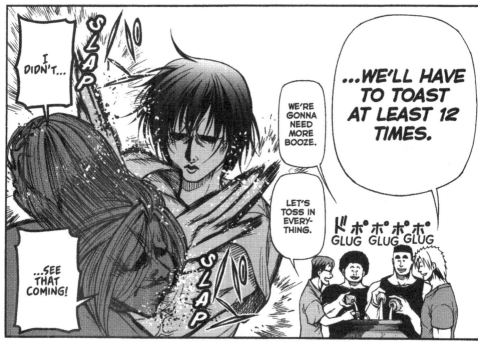

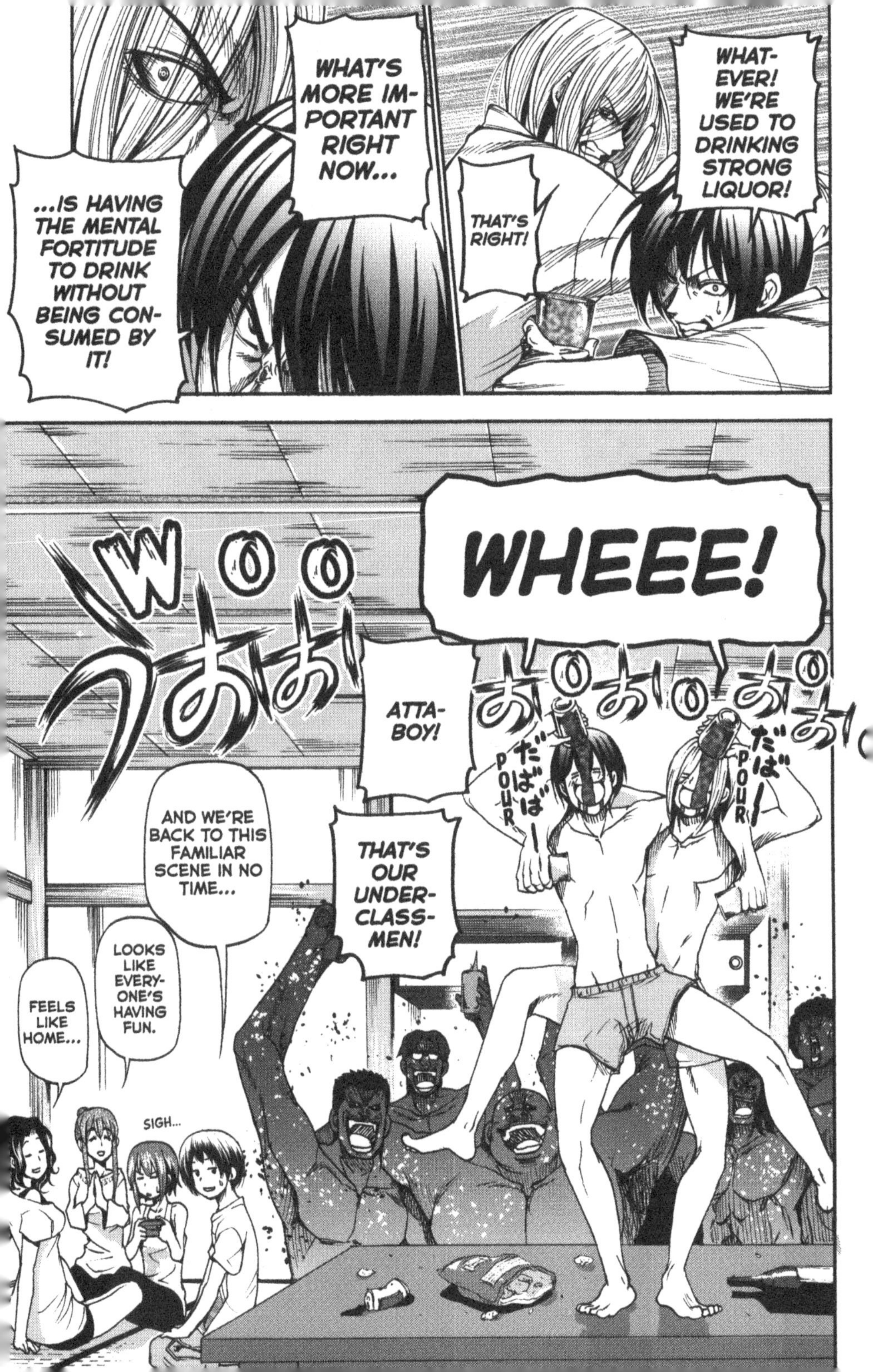
WHATEVER! WE'RE USED TO DRINKING STRONG LIQUOR!
THAT'S RIGHT!
WHAT'S MORE IMPORTANT RIGHT NOW...
...IS HAVING THE MENTAL FORTITUDE TO DRINK WITHOUT BEING CONSUMED BY IT!
WHEEE!
POUR
POUR
ATTA-BOY!
THAT'S OUR UNDERCLASSMEN!
WOO
AND WE'RE BACK TO THIS FAMILIAR SCENE IN NO TIME...
LOOKS LIKE EVERYONE'S HAVING FUN.
FEELS LIKE HOME...
SIGH...

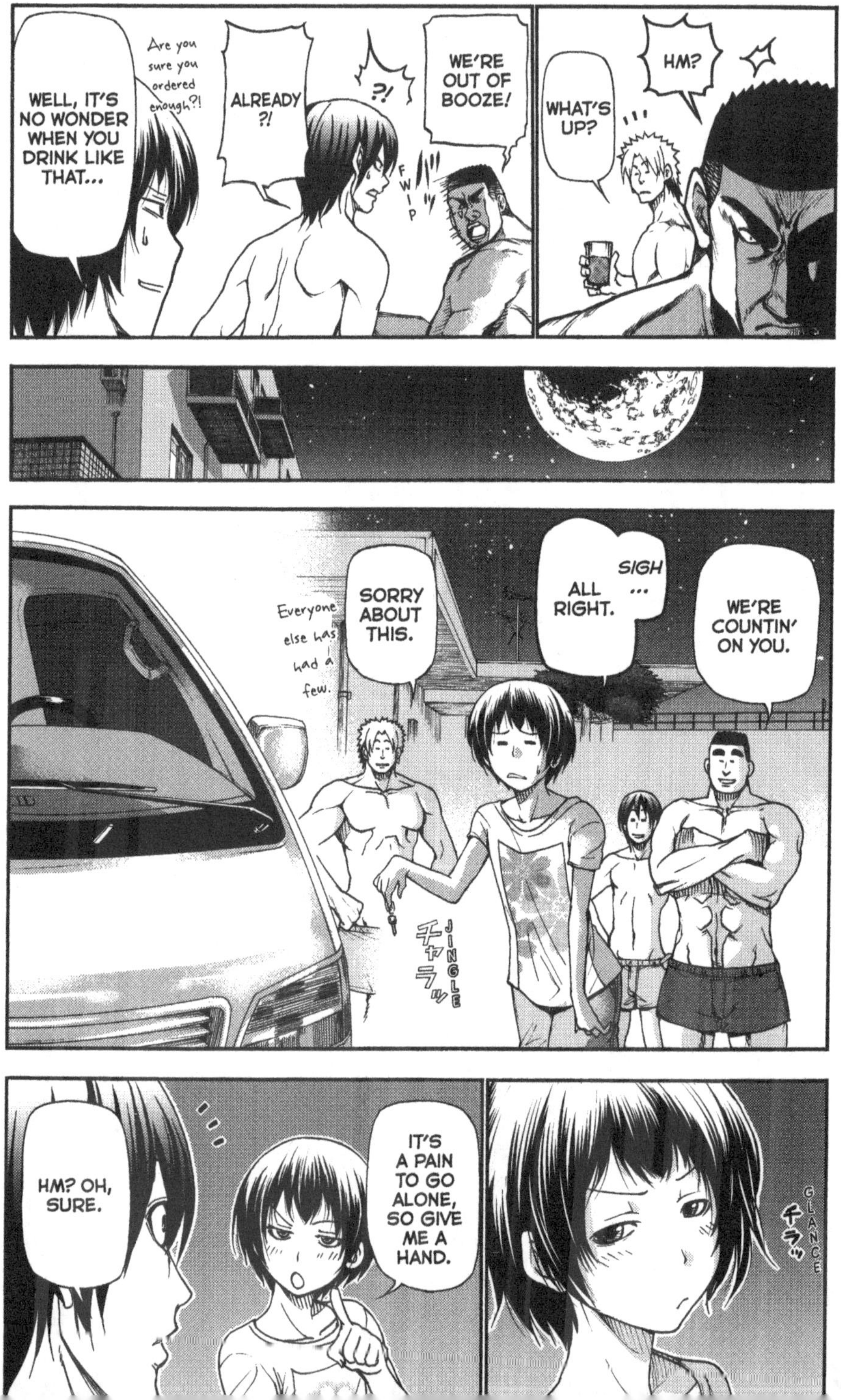
HM?
WHAT'S UP?
WE'RE OUT OF BOOZE!
?!
FWIP
ALREADY ?!
Are you sure you ordered enough?!
WELL, IT'S NO WONDER WHEN YOU DRINK LIKE THAT...
WE'RE COUNTIN' ON YOU.
SIGH ...
ALL RIGHT.
SORRY ABOUT THIS.
Everyone else has had a few.
チャラッ
JINGLE
チラッ
GLANCE
IT'S A PAIN TO GO ALONE, SO GIVE ME A HAND.
HM? OH, SURE.

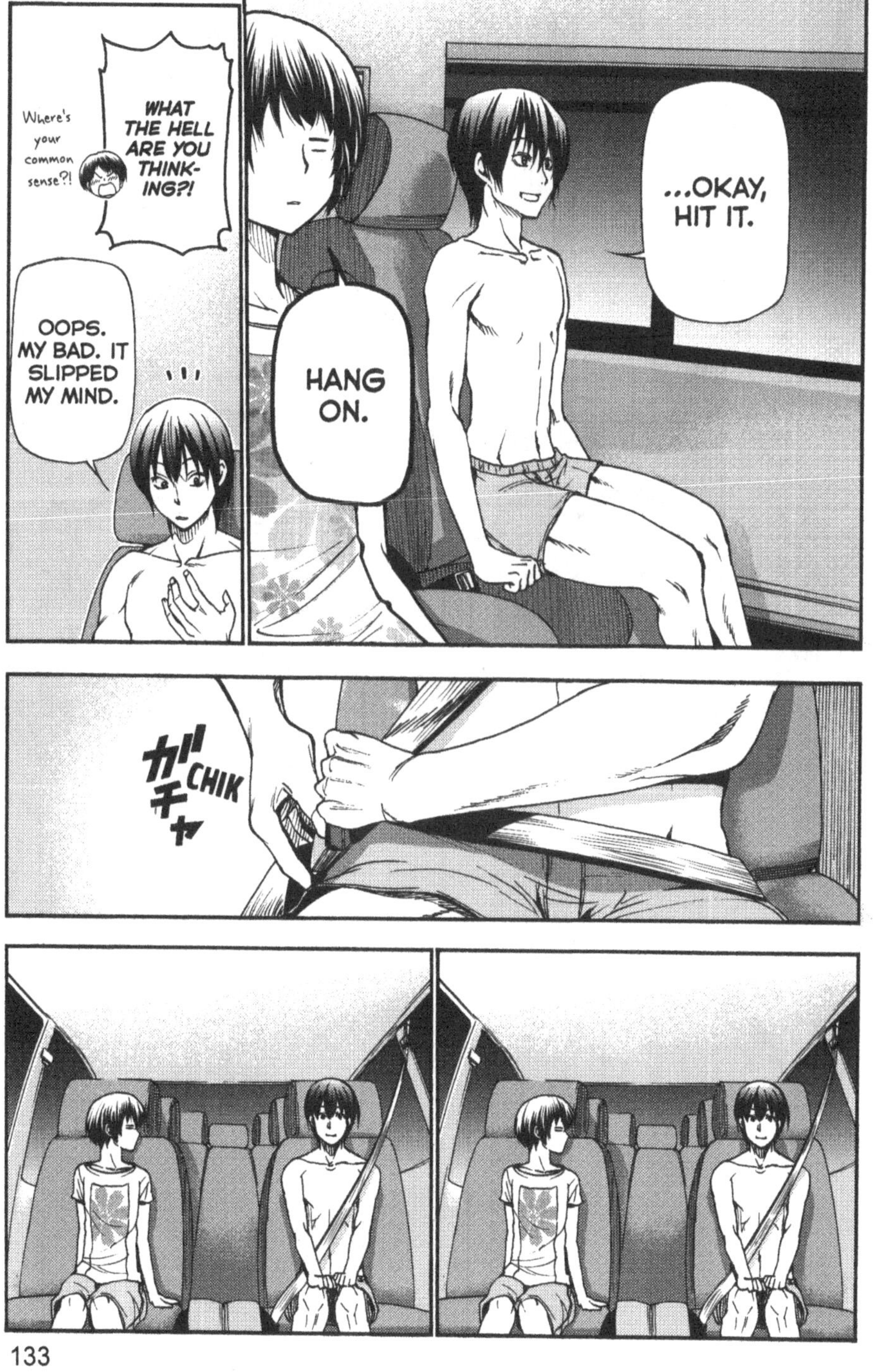
...OKAY, HIT IT.
HANG ON.
WHAT THE HELL ARE YOU THINKING?!
Where's your common sense?!
OOPS. MY BAD. IT SLIPPED MY MIND.
カチャ CHIK

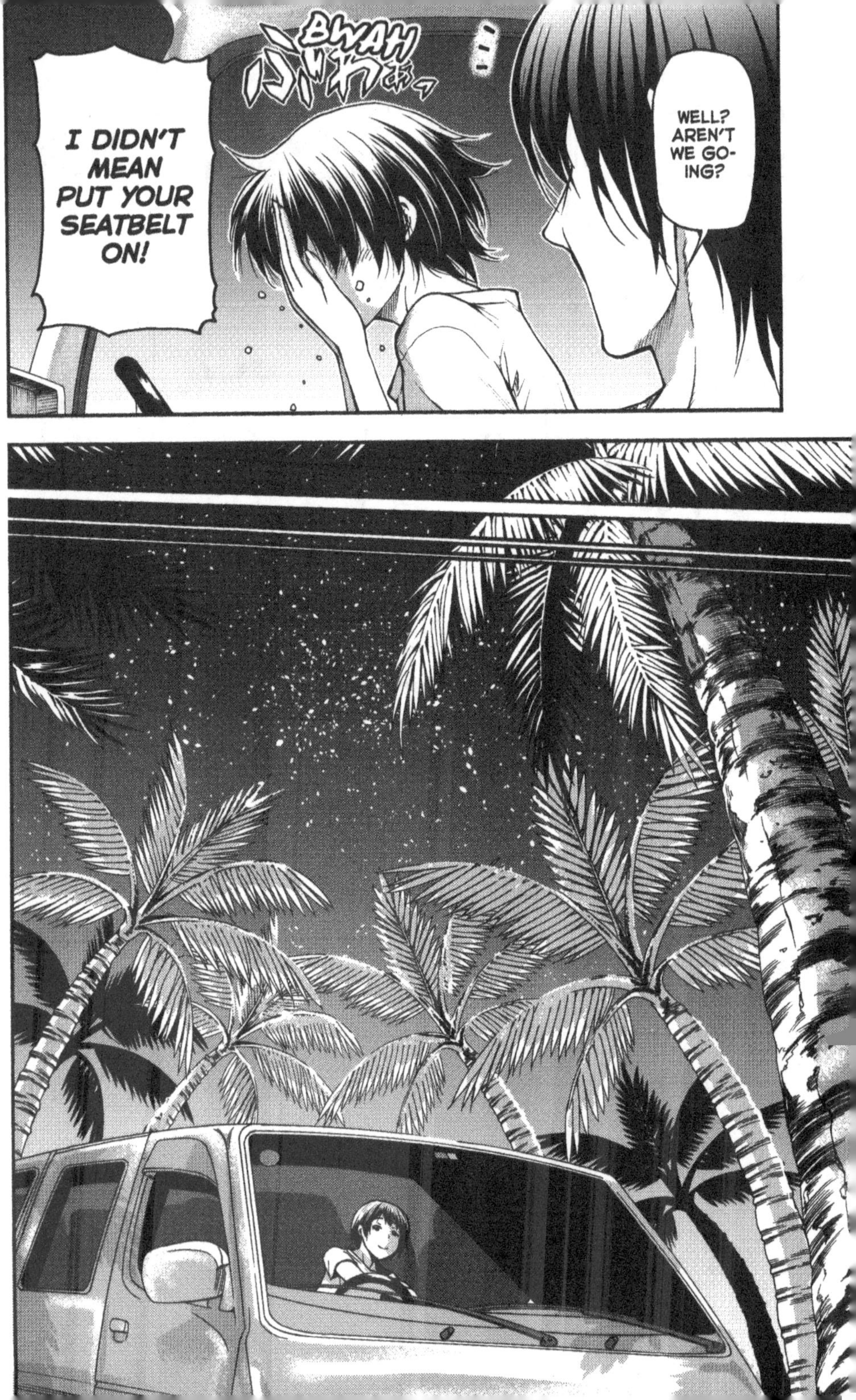
WELL? AREN'T WE GO-ING?
BWAH
I DIDN'T MEAN PUT YOUR SEATBELT ON!

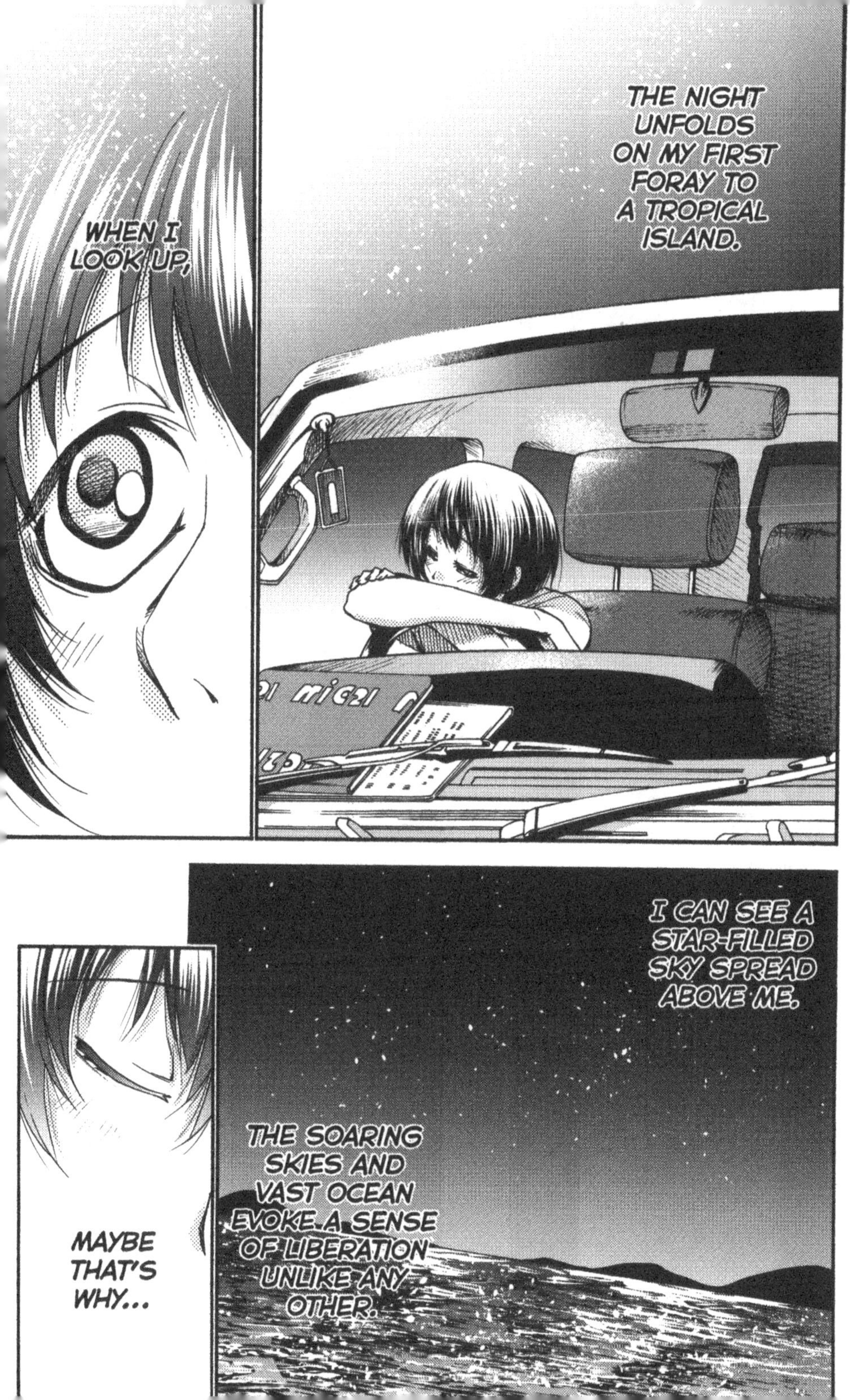
THE NIGHT UNFOLDS ON MY FIRST FORAY TO A TROPICAL ISLAND.
WHEN I LOOK UP,
I CAN SEE A STAR-FILLED SKY SPREAD ABOVE ME.
THE SOARING SKIES AND VAST OCEAN EVOKE A SENSE OF LIBERATION UNLIKE ANY OTHER.
MAYBE THAT'S WHY...

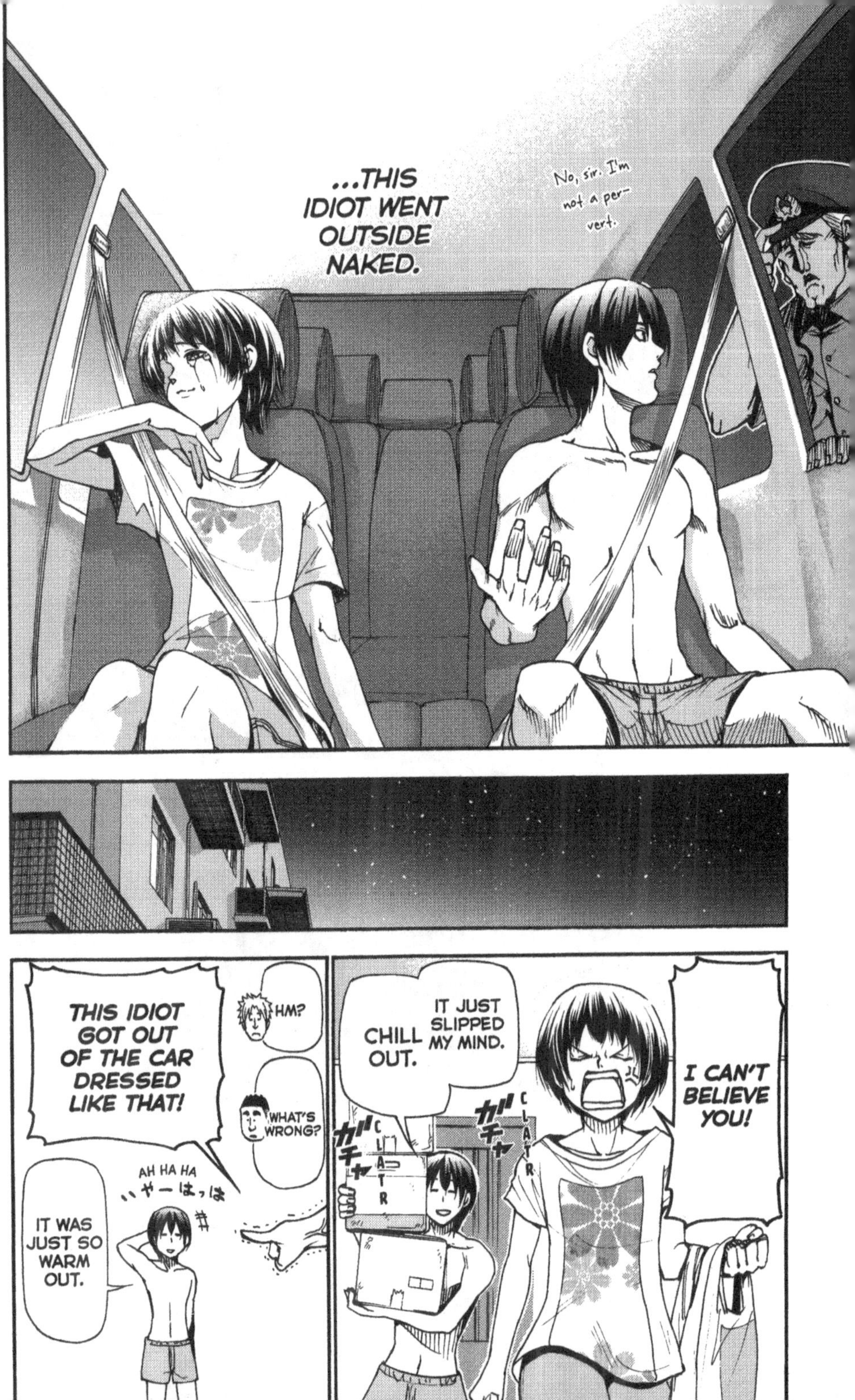
No, sir. I'm not a per- vert.
...THIS IDIOT WENT OUTSIDE NAKED.
I CAN'T BELIEVE YOU!
ガチャ
CLATR
ガチャ
CLATR
IT JUST SLIPPED MY MIND.
CHILL OUT.
HM?
THIS IDIOT GOT OUT OF THE CAR DRESSED LIKE THAT!
WHAT'S WRONG?
いやーはっは
AH HA HA
IT WAS JUST SO WARM OUT.

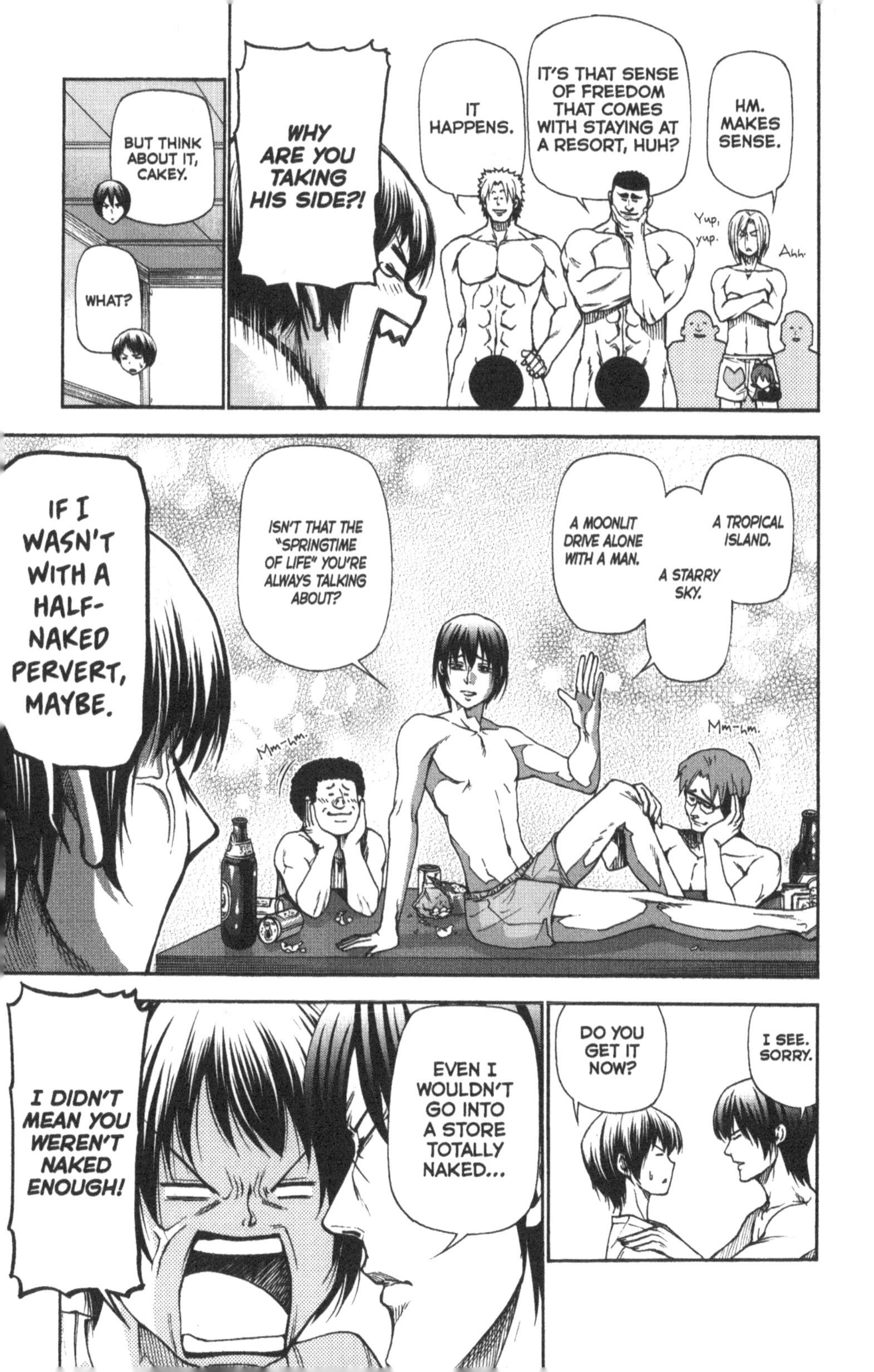
HM. MAKES SENSE.
Yup, yup.
Ahh.
IT'S THAT SENSE OF FREEDOM THAT COMES WITH STAYING AT A RESORT, HUH?
IT HAPPENS.
WHY ARE YOU TAKING HIS SIDE?!
BUT THINK ABOUT IT, CAKEY.
WHAT?
A TROPICAL ISLAND.
A MOONLIT DRIVE ALONE WITH A MAN.
A STARRY SKY.
Mm-hm.
ISN'T THAT THE "SPRINGTIME OF LIFE" YOU'RE ALWAYS TALKING ABOUT?
Mm-hm.
IF I WASN'T WITH A HALF-NAKED PERVERT, MAYBE.
I SEE. SORRY.
DO YOU GET IT NOW?
EVEN I WOULDN'T GO INTO A STORE TOTALLY NAKED...
I DIDN'T MEAN YOU WEREN'T NAKED ENOUGH!

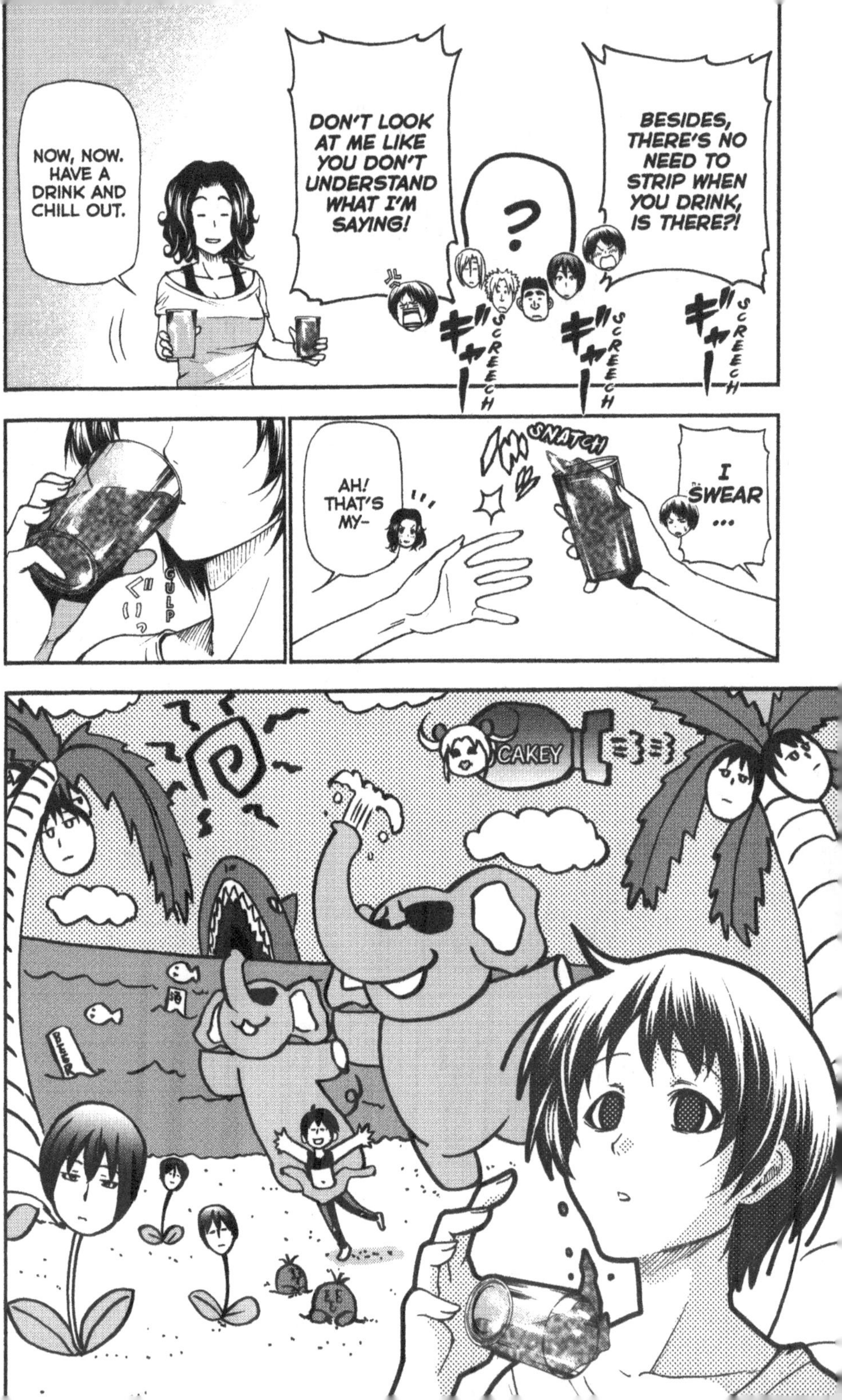
BESIDES, THERE'S NO NEED TO STRIP WHEN YOU DRINK, IS THERE?!
ギャー
SCREECH
?
ギャー
SCREECH
DON'T LOOK AT ME LIKE YOU DON'T UNDERSTAND WHAT I'M SAYING!
ギャー
SCREECH
NOW, NOW. HAVE A DRINK AND CHILL OUT.
I SWEAR ...
SNATCH
AH! THAT'S MY-
GULP
CAKEY

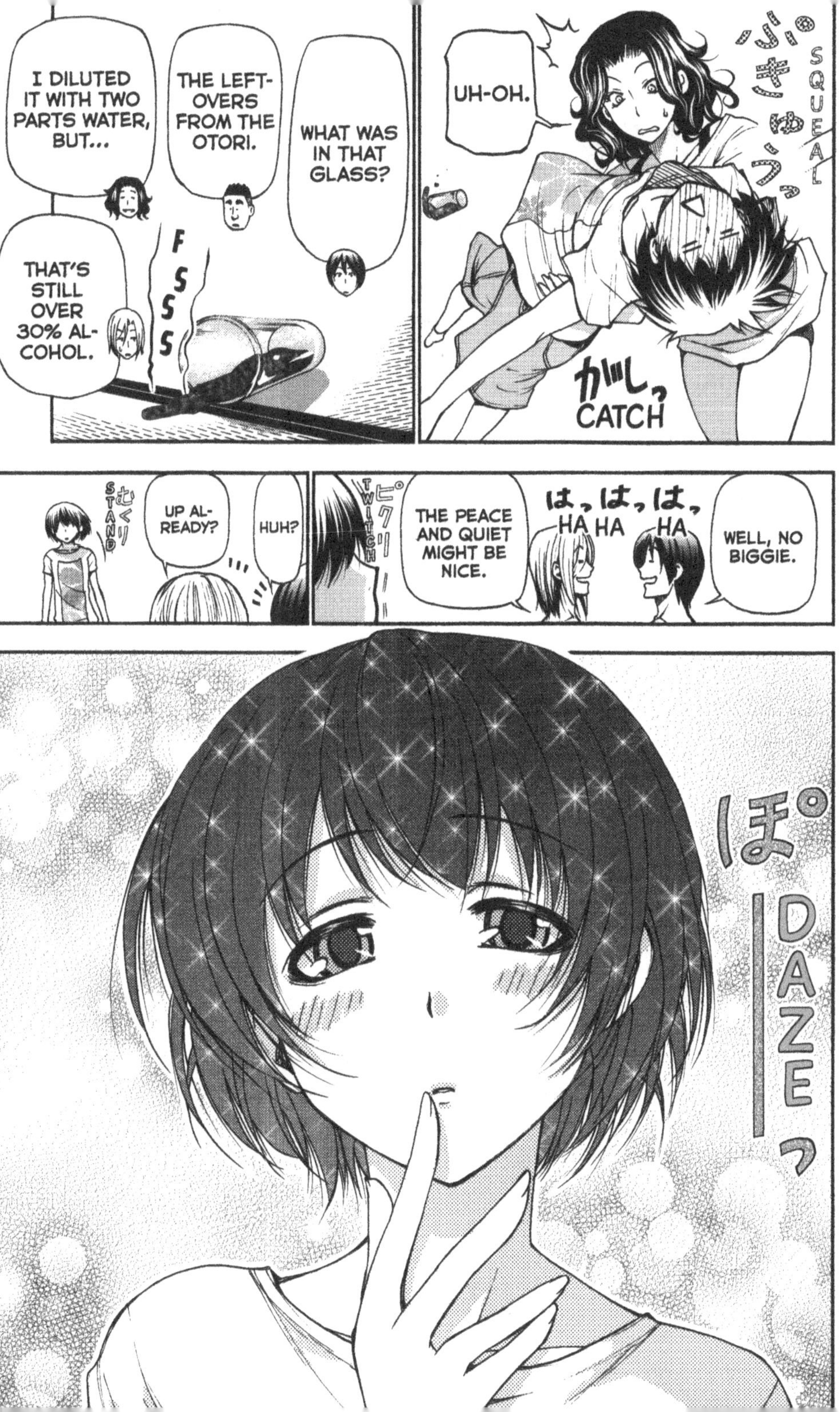
ぷきゅっ
SQUEAL
UH-OH.
がしっ
CATCH
WHAT WAS IN THAT GLASS?
THE LEFT-OVERS FROM THE OTORI.
I DILUTED IT WITH TWO PARTS WATER, BUT...
FSSS
THAT'S STILL OVER 30% AL-COHOL.
WELL, NO BIGGIE.
はっはっはっ
HA HA HA
THE PEACE AND QUIET MIGHT BE NICE.
ピクリ
TWITCH
HUH?
UP AL-READY?
むくり
STAND
ぽーっ
DAZE

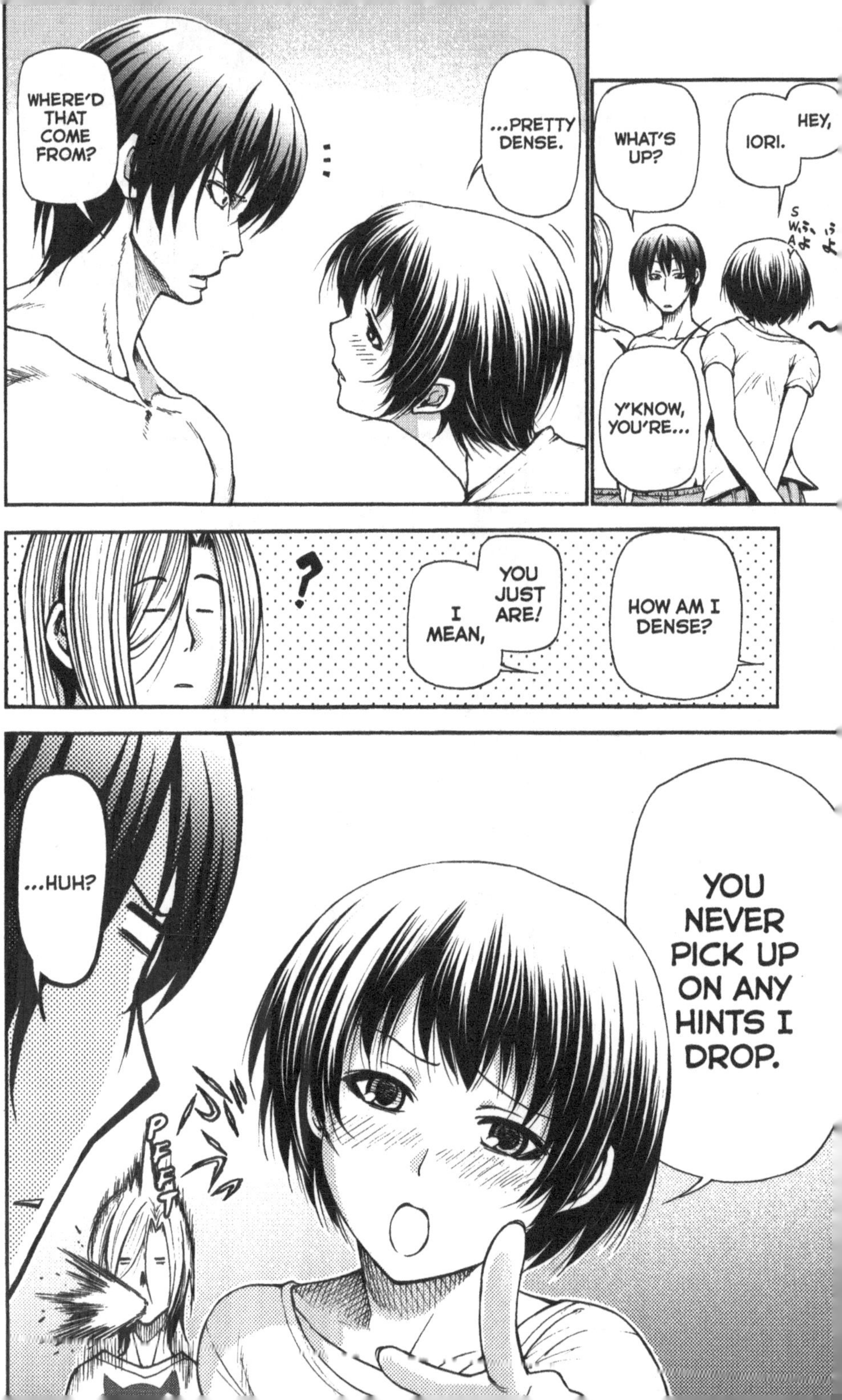
HEY, IORI.
WHAT'S UP?
SWAY
Y'KNOW, YOU'RE...
...PRETTY DENSE.
WHERE'D THAT COME FROM?
HOW AM I DENSE?
I MEAN, YOU JUST ARE!
YOU NEVER PICK UP ON ANY HINTS I DROP.
...HUH?
PFFT

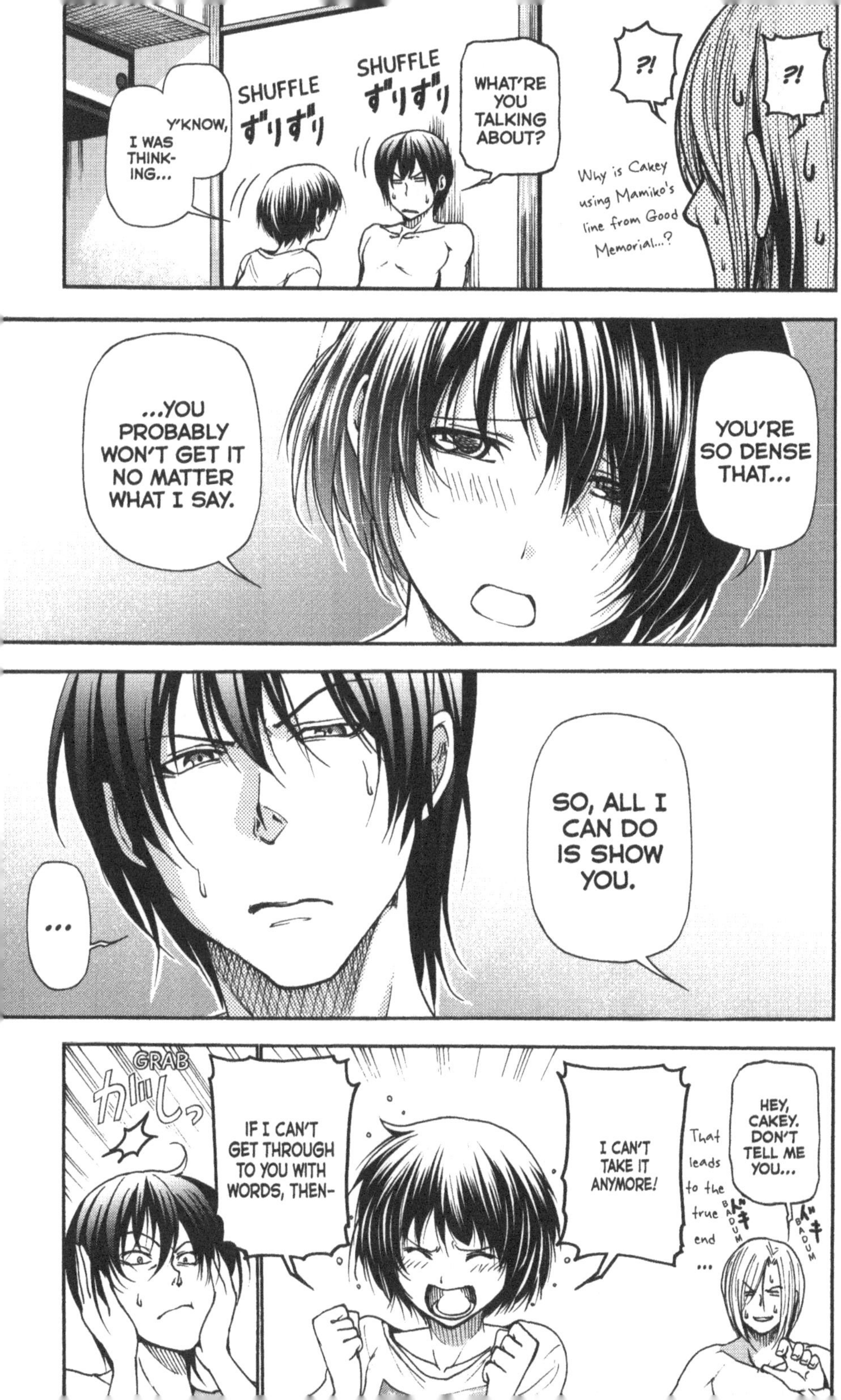
?!
?!
Why is Cakey using Mamiko's line from Good Memorial...?
WHAT'RE YOU TALKING ABOUT?
SHUFFLE ずりずり
SHUFFLE ずりずり
Y'KNOW, I WAS THINKING...
YOU'RE SO DENSE THAT...
...YOU PROBABLY WON'T GET IT NO MATTER WHAT I SAY.
SO, ALL I CAN DO IS SHOW YOU.
...
HEY, CAKEY. DON'T TELL ME YOU...
BADUM ドキ
BADUM ドキ
That leads to the true end ...
I CAN'T TAKE IT ANYMORE!
IF I CAN'T GET THROUGH TO YOU WITH WORDS, THEN-
GRAB がしっ

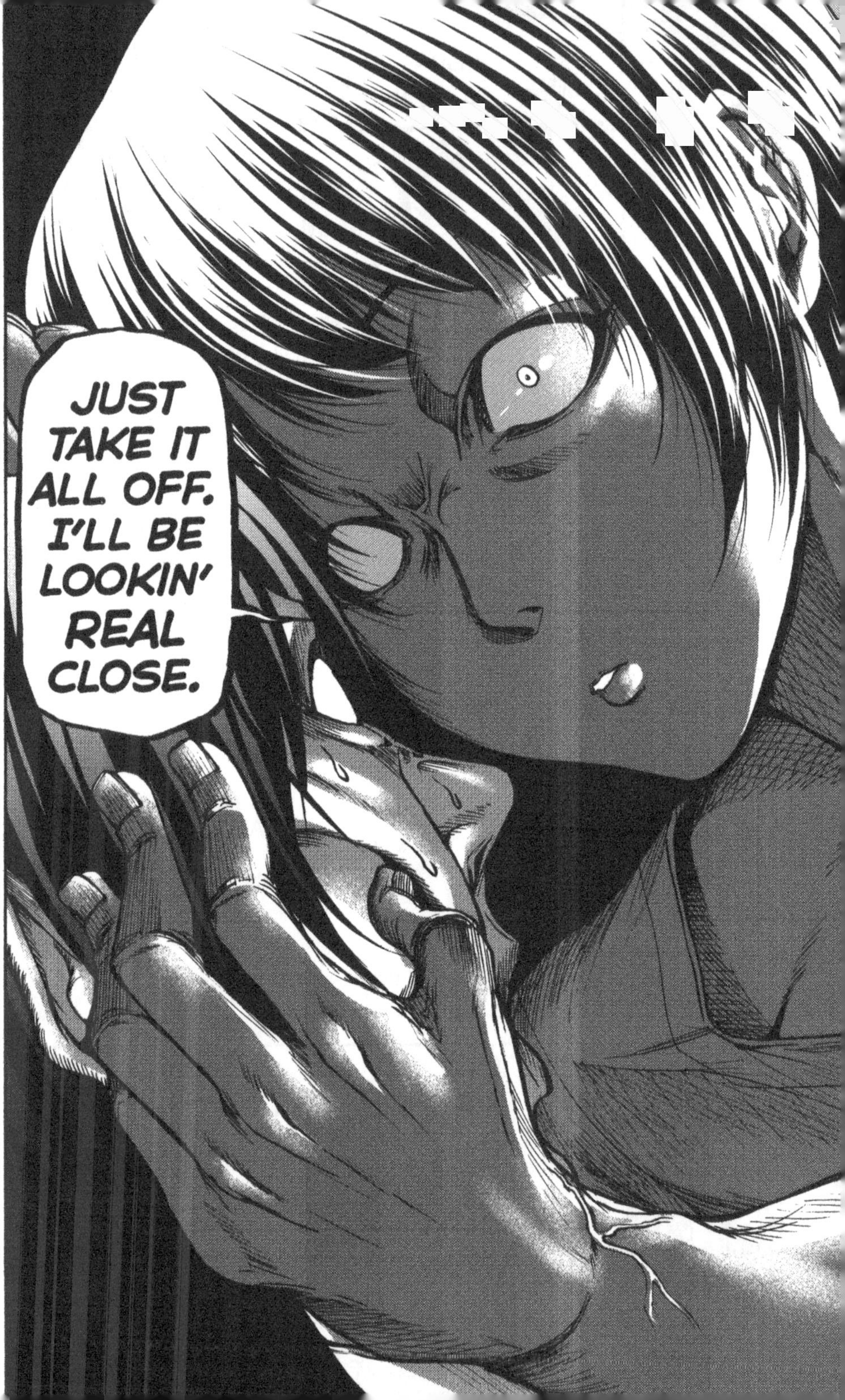
JUST TAKE IT ALL OFF. I'LL BE LOOKIN' REAL CLOSE.

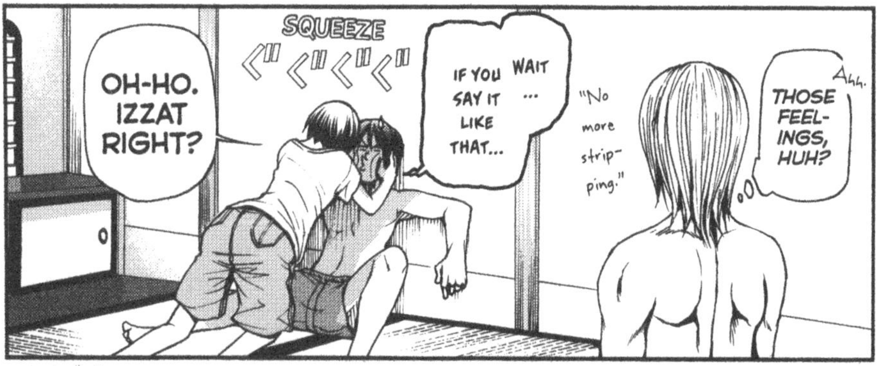
Ahh.
THOSE FEEL-INGS, HUH?
"No more strip-ping."
WAIT ...
IF YOU SAY IT LIKE THAT...
SQUEEZE
OH-HO. IZZAT RIGHT?
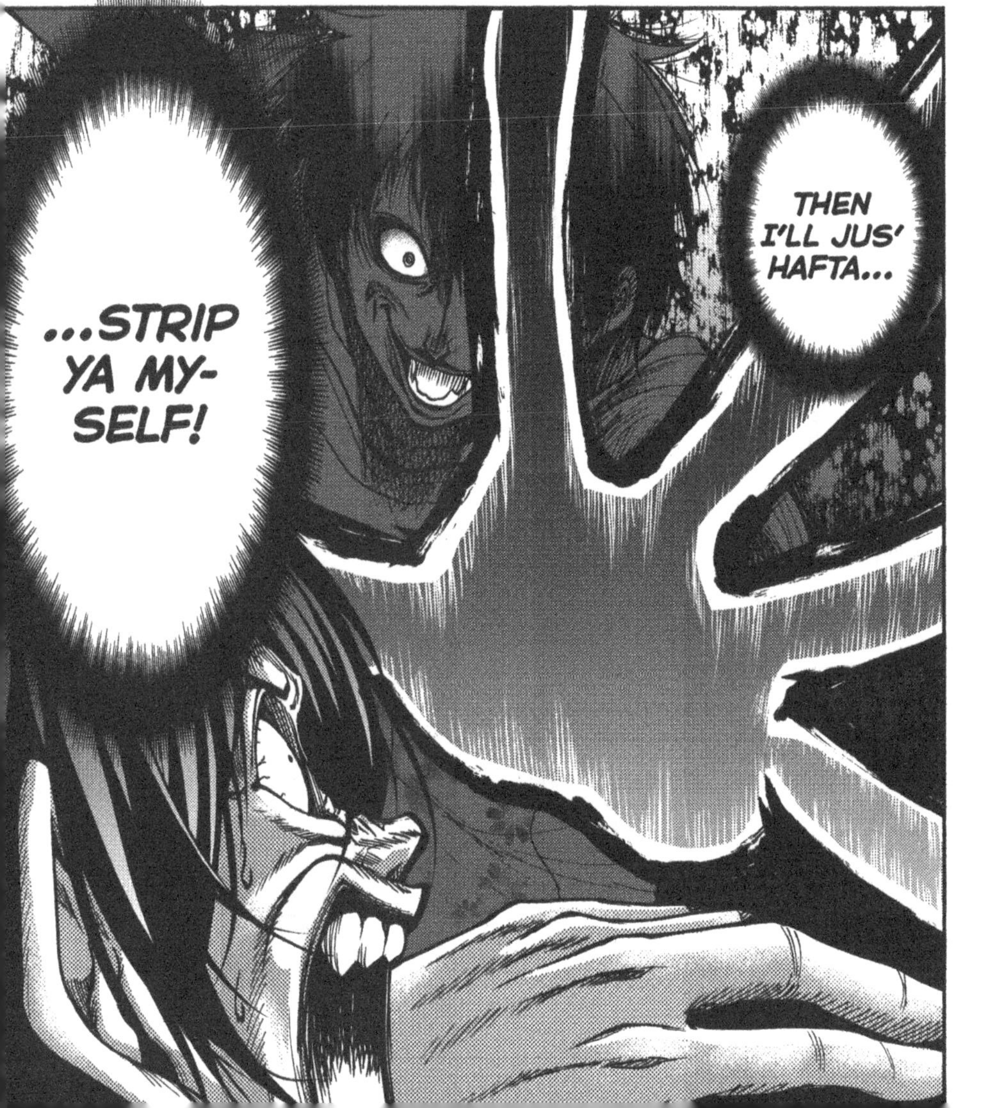
THEN I'LL JUS' HAFTA...
...STRIP YA MY-SELF!

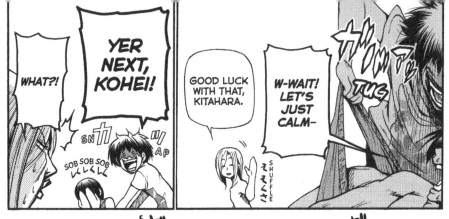

TUG
W-WAIT! LET'S JUST CALM-
GOOD LUCK WITH THAT, KITAHARA.
SHUFFLE
YER NEXT, KOHEI!
SNAP
WHAT?!
SOB SOB SOB
SCREECH
SCREECH
SCREECH
SKRTCH
THAT WAS ROUGH...
WHO'D HAVE THOUGHT SHE'D CHANGE SO MUCH AFTER JUST ONE DRINK?

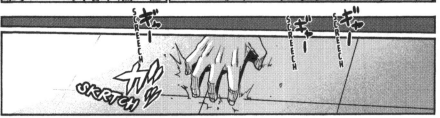

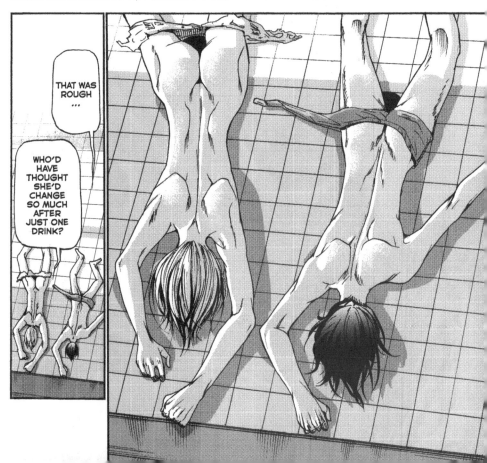

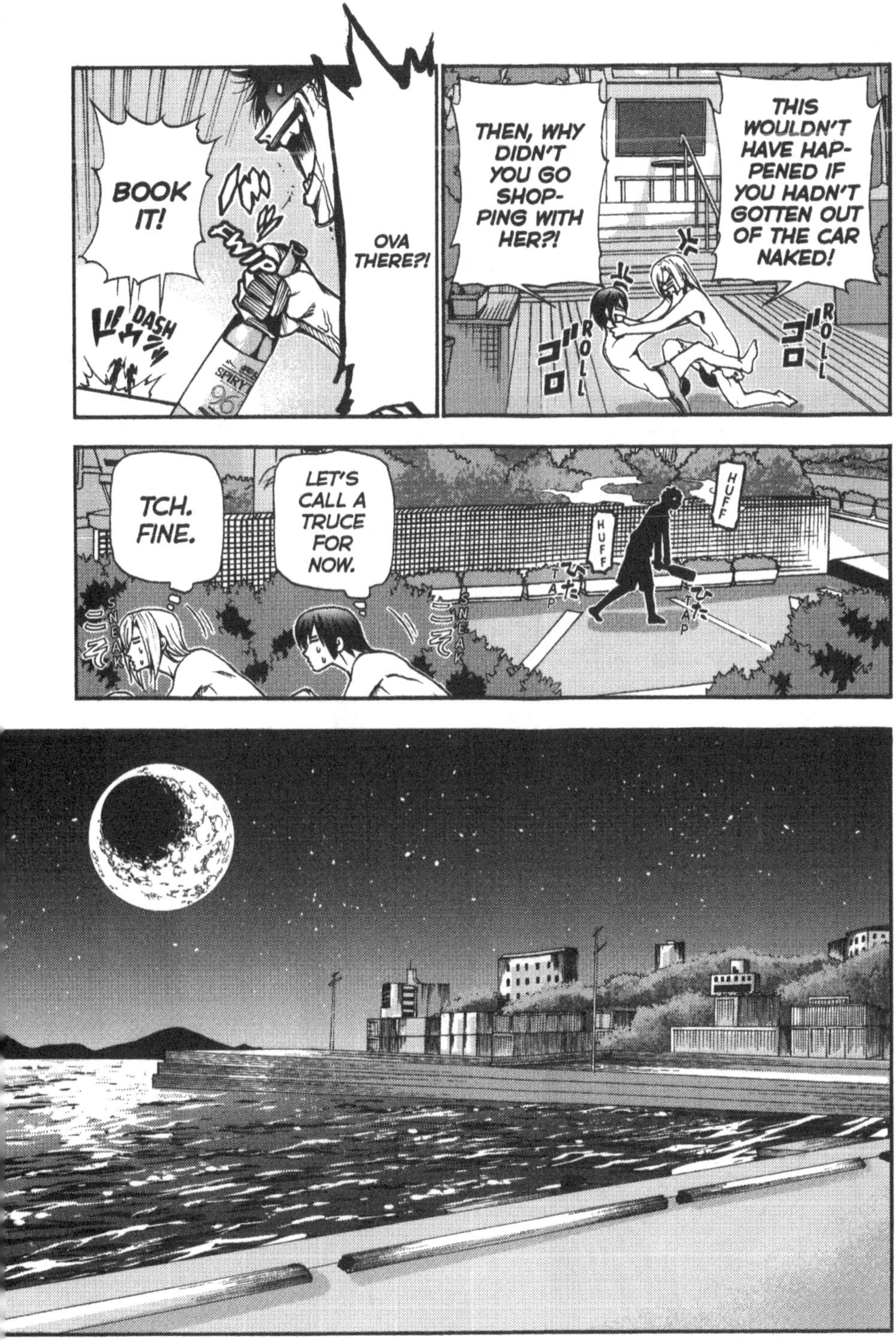

THIS WOULDN'T HAVE HAPPENED IF YOU HADN'T GOTTEN OUT OF THE CAR NAKED!
ROLL
THEN, WHY DIDN'T YOU GO SHOPPING WITH HER?!
ROLL
OVA THERE?!
BOOK IT!
FWIP
DASH
HUFF
TAP
HUFF
TAP
LET'S CALL A TRUCE FOR NOW.
SNEAK
TCH. FINE.
SNEAK

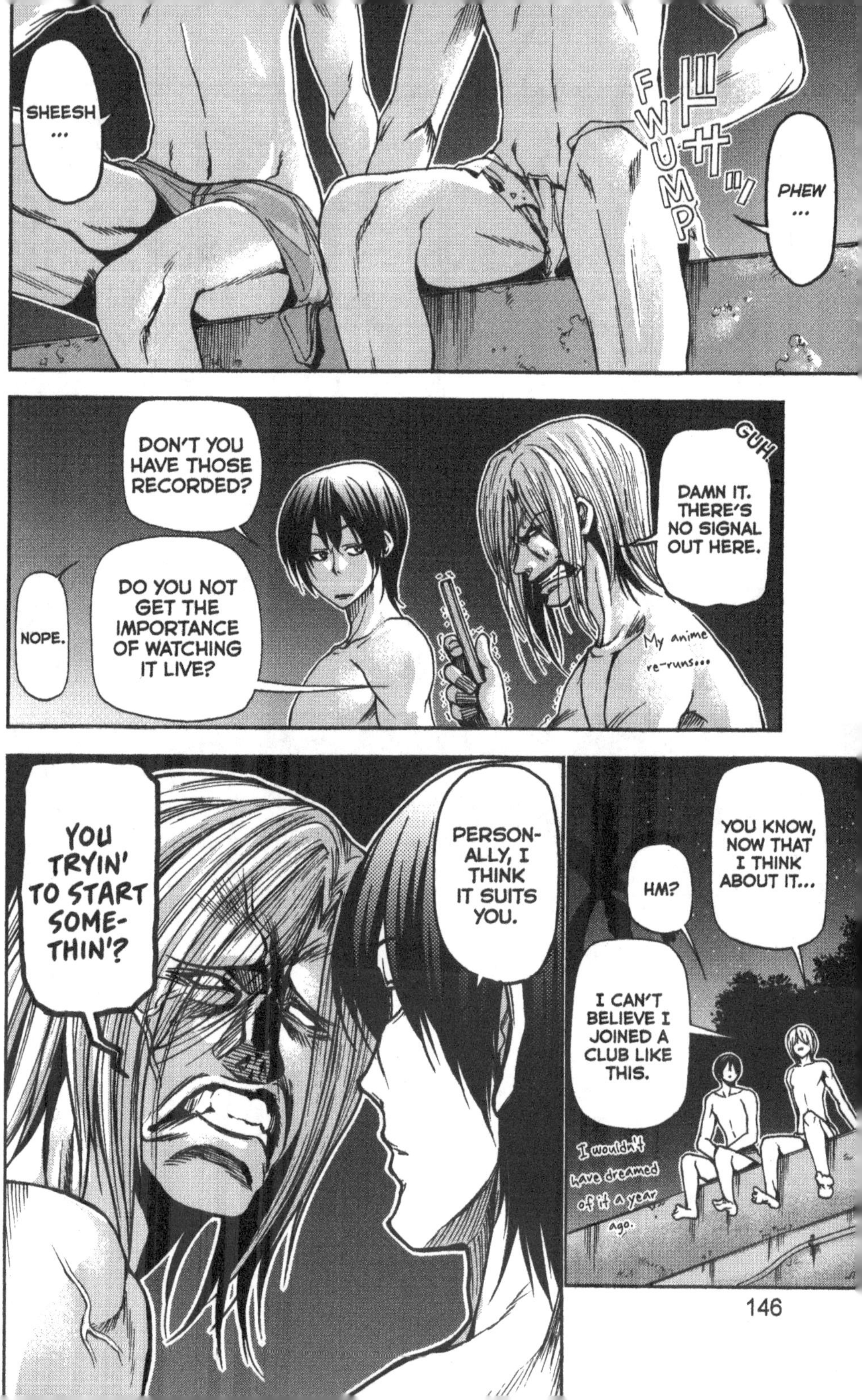
FWUMP
PHEW...
SHEESH...
GUH
DAMN IT. THERE'S NO SIGNAL OUT HERE.
My anime re-runs...
DON'T YOU HAVE THOSE RECORDED?
DO YOU NOT GET THE IMPORTANCE OF WATCHING IT LIVE?
NOPE.
YOU KNOW, NOW THAT I THINK ABOUT IT...
HM?
I CAN'T BELIEVE I JOINED A CLUB LIKE THIS.
I wouldn't have dreamed of it a year ago.
PERSON-ALLY, I THINK IT SUITS YOU.
YOU TRYIN' TO START SOME-THIN'?

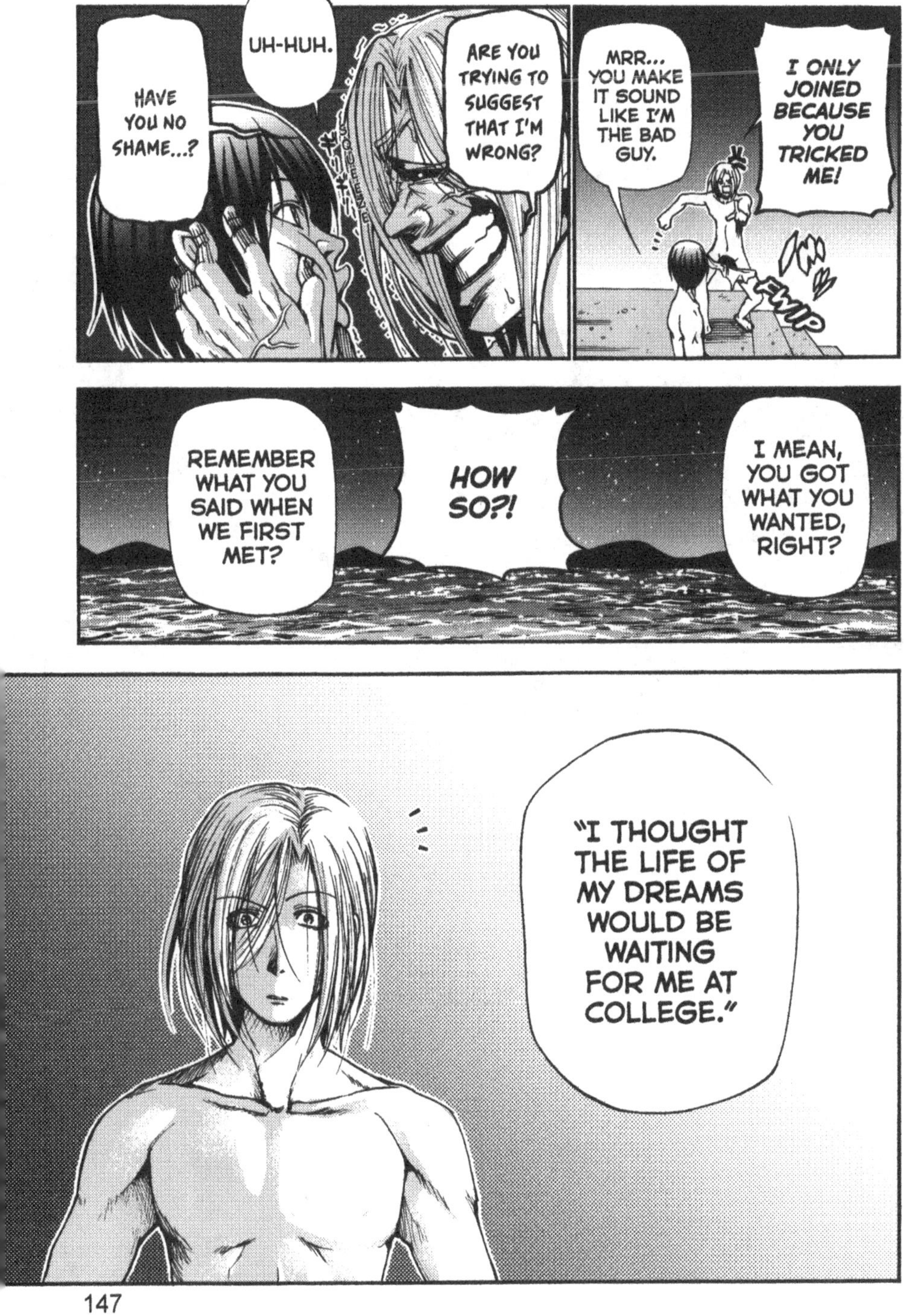
I ONLY JOINED BECAUSE YOU TRICKED ME!
MRR... YOU MAKE IT SOUND LIKE I'M THE BAD GUY.
FWIP
ARE YOU TRYING TO SUGGEST THAT I'M WRONG?
UH-HUH.
HAVE YOU NO SHAME...?
I MEAN, YOU GOT WHAT YOU WANTED, RIGHT?
HOW SO?!
REMEMBER WHAT YOU SAID WHEN WE FIRST MET?
"I THOUGHT THE LIFE OF MY DREAMS WOULD BE WAITING FOR ME AT COLLEGE."

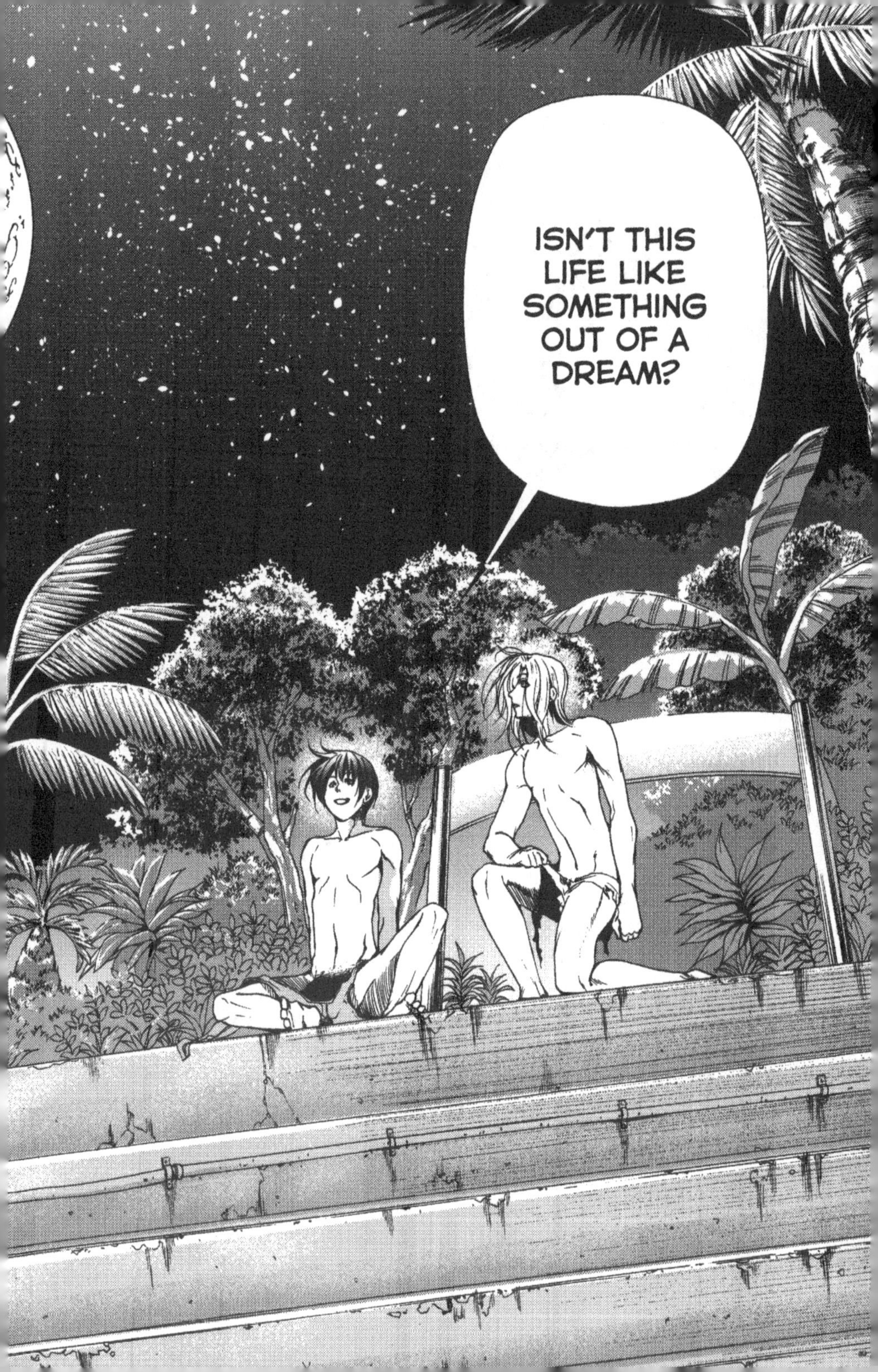
ISN'T THIS LIFE LIKE SOMETHING OUT OF A DREAM?

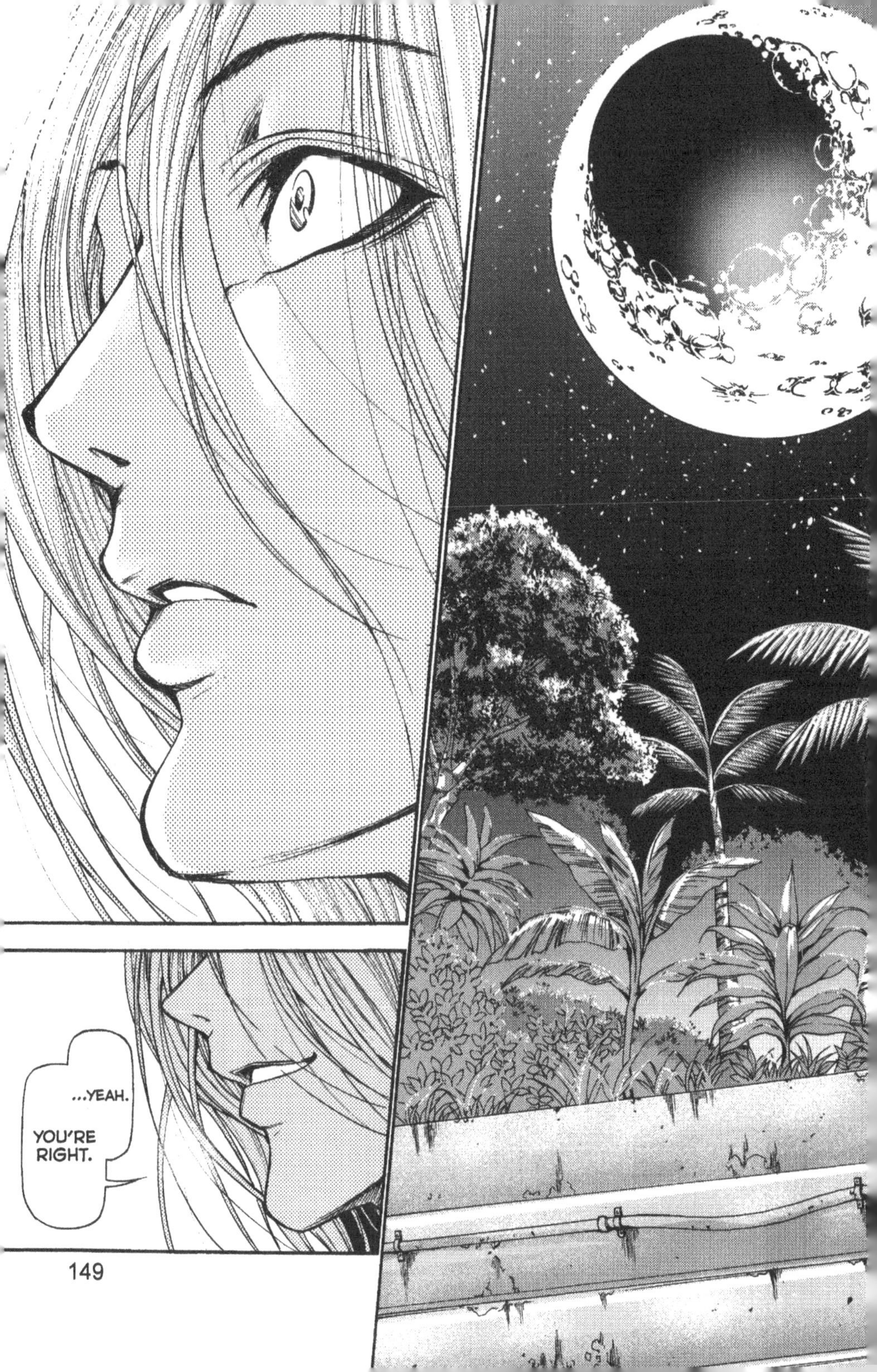
...YEAH.
YOU'RE RIGHT.

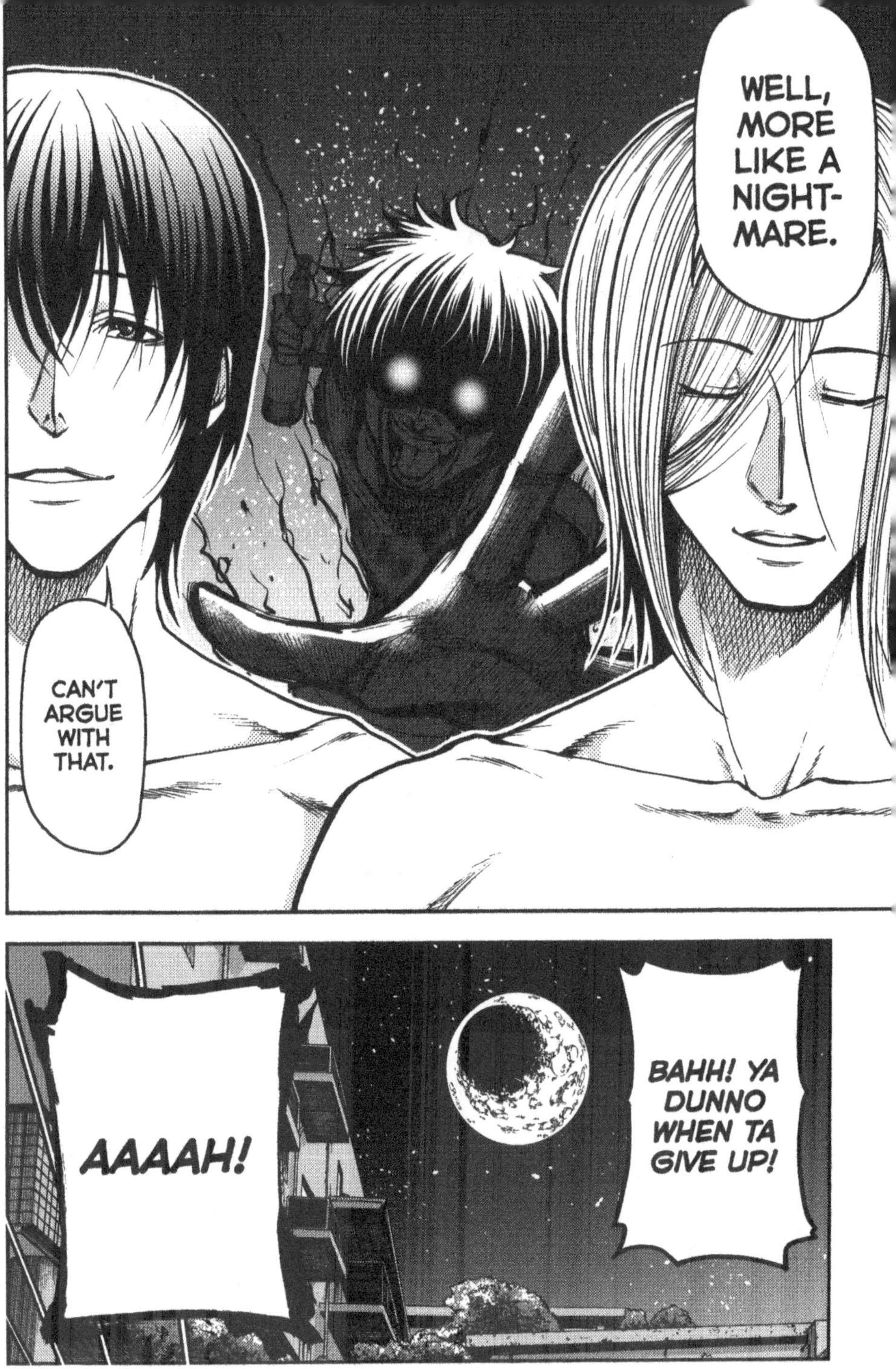
WELL, MORE LIKE A NIGHT-MARE.
CAN'T ARGUE WITH THAT.
BAHH! YA DUNNO WHEN TA GIVE UP!
AAAAH!

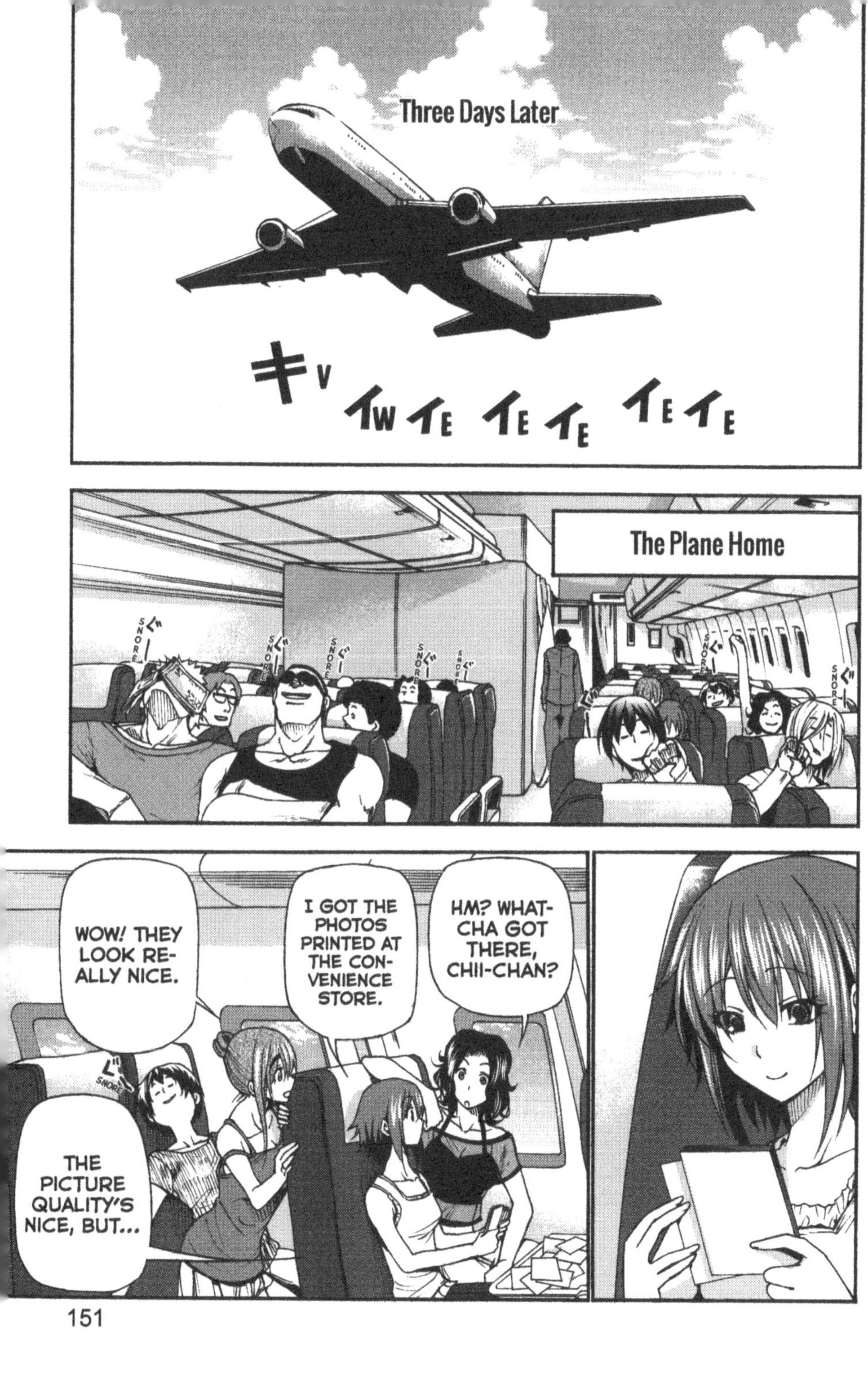
Three Days Later
The Plane Home
SNORE
HM? WHAT-CHA GOT THERE, CHII-CHAN?
I GOT THE PHOTOS PRINTED AT THE CON-VENIENCE STORE.
WOW! THEY LOOK RE-ALLY NICE.
THE PICTURE QUALITY'S NICE, BUT...

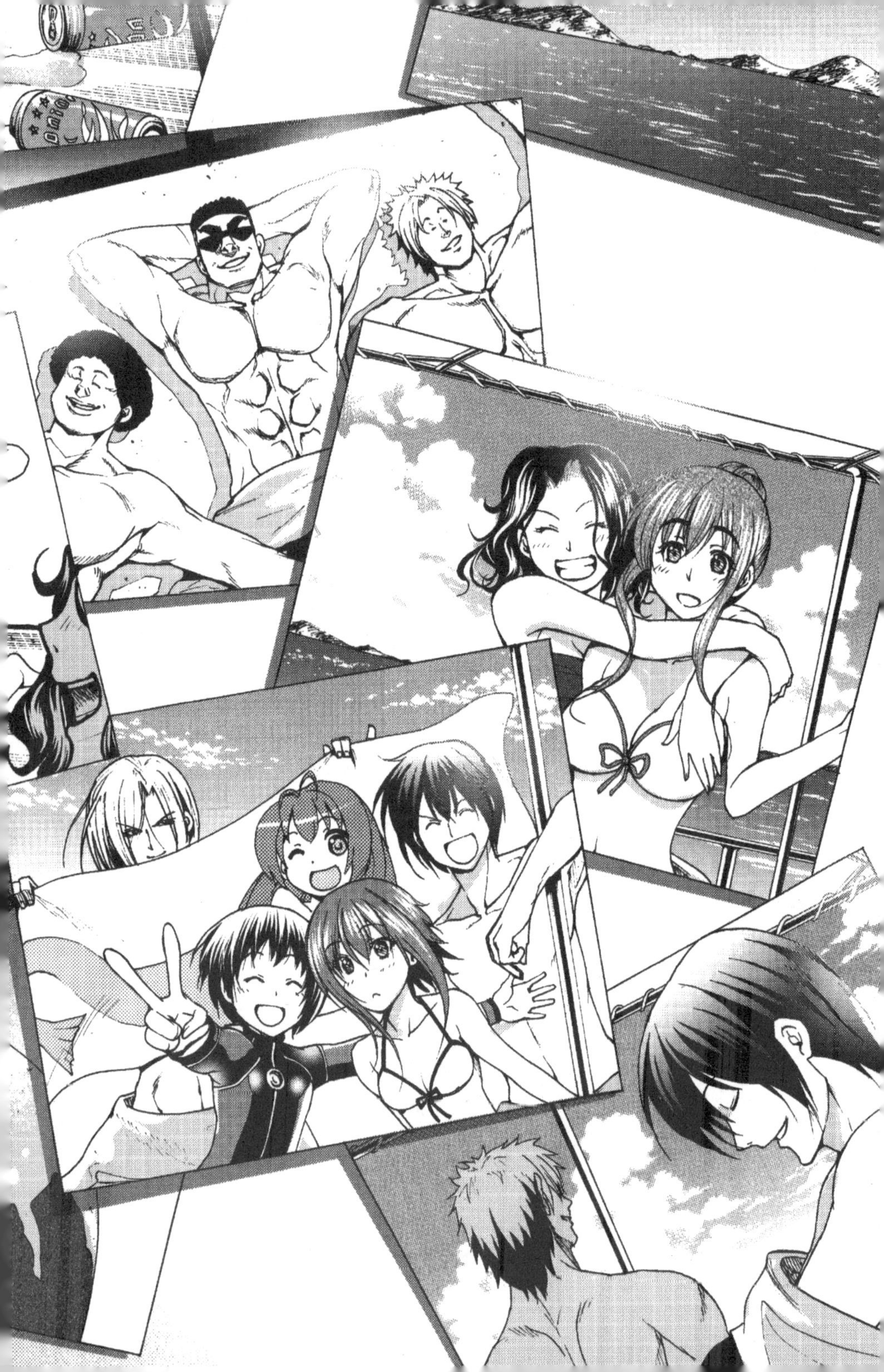

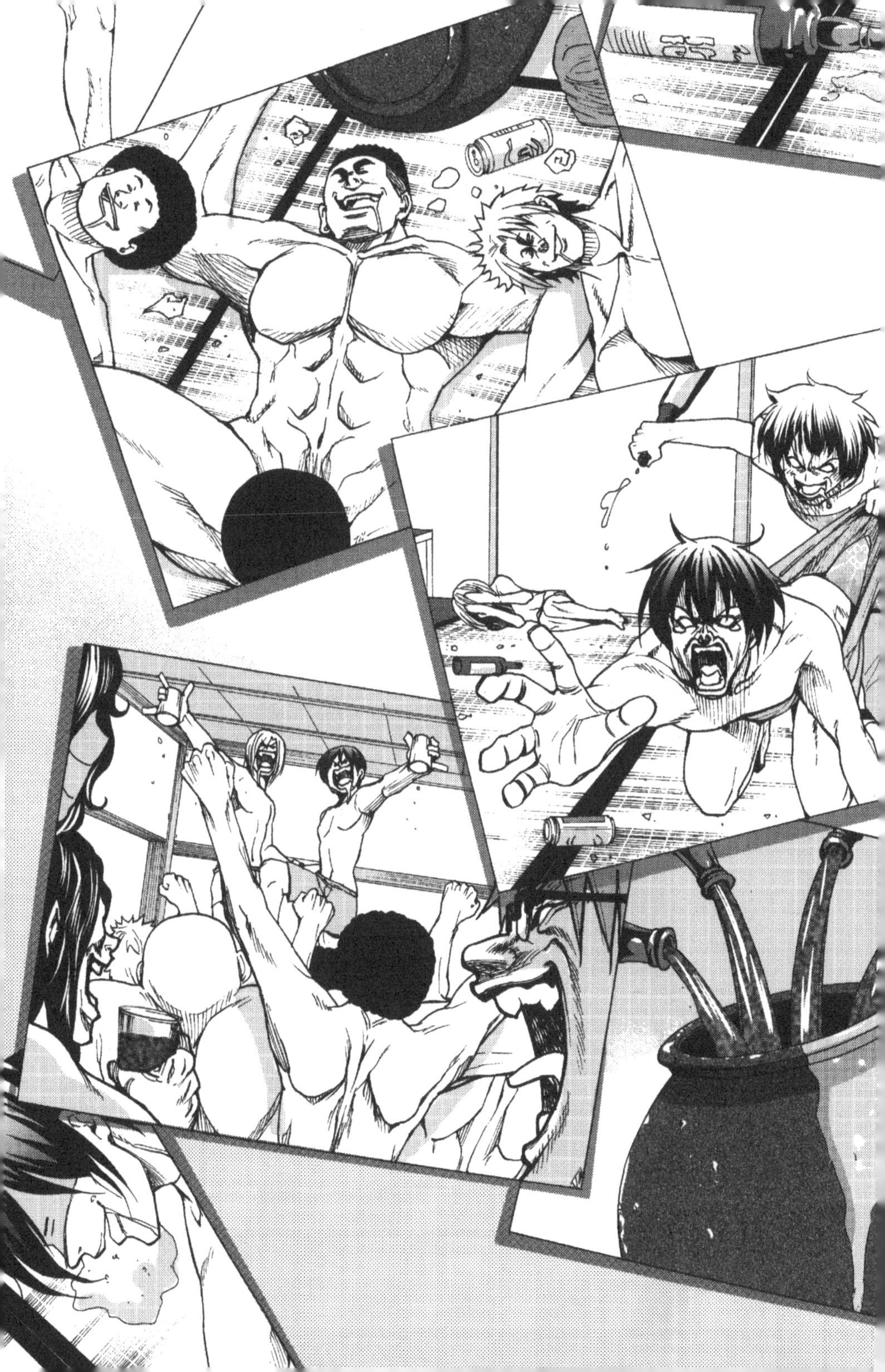

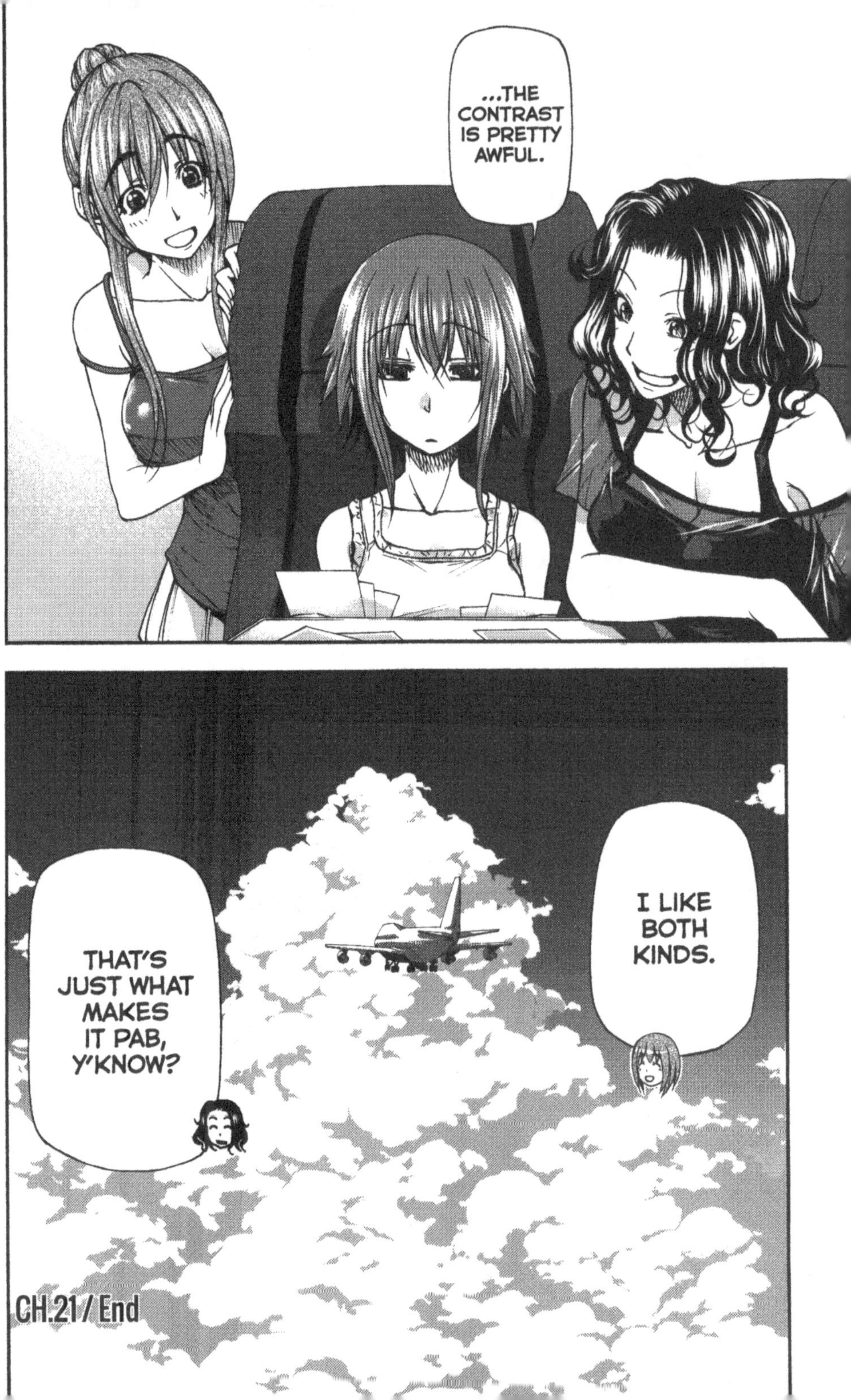
...THE CONTRAST IS PRETTY AWFUL.
I LIKE BOTH KINDS.
THAT'S JUST WHAT MAKES IT PAB, Y'KNOW?
CH.21 / End

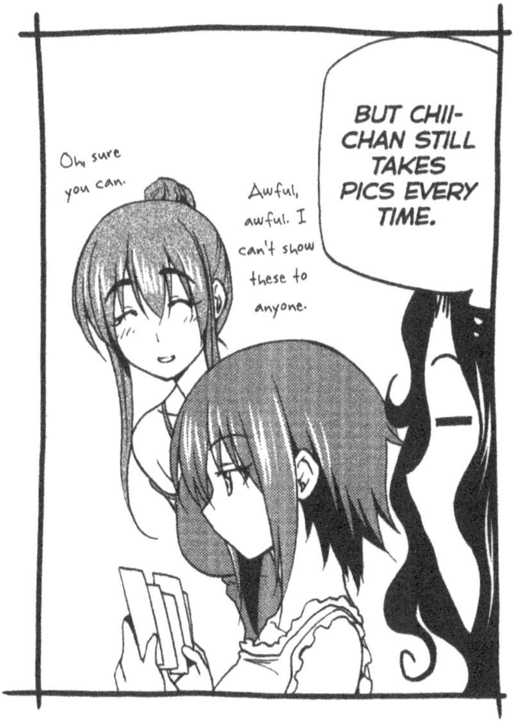
BUT CHII-CHAN STILL TAKES PICS EVERY TIME.
Awful, awful. I can't show these to anyone.
Oh sure you can.

Grand Blue Dreaming

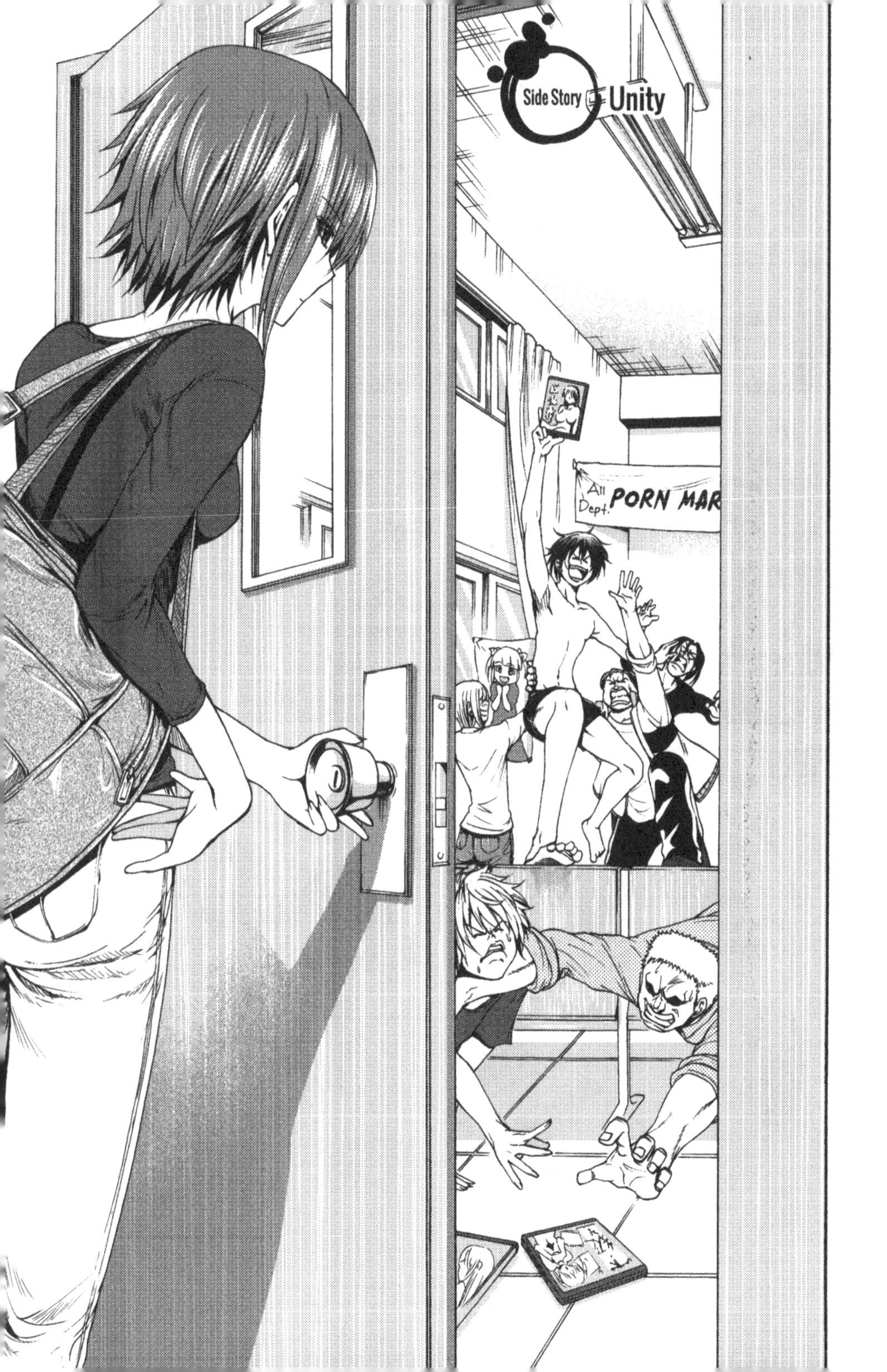
Side Story Unity
All Dept. PORN MAR

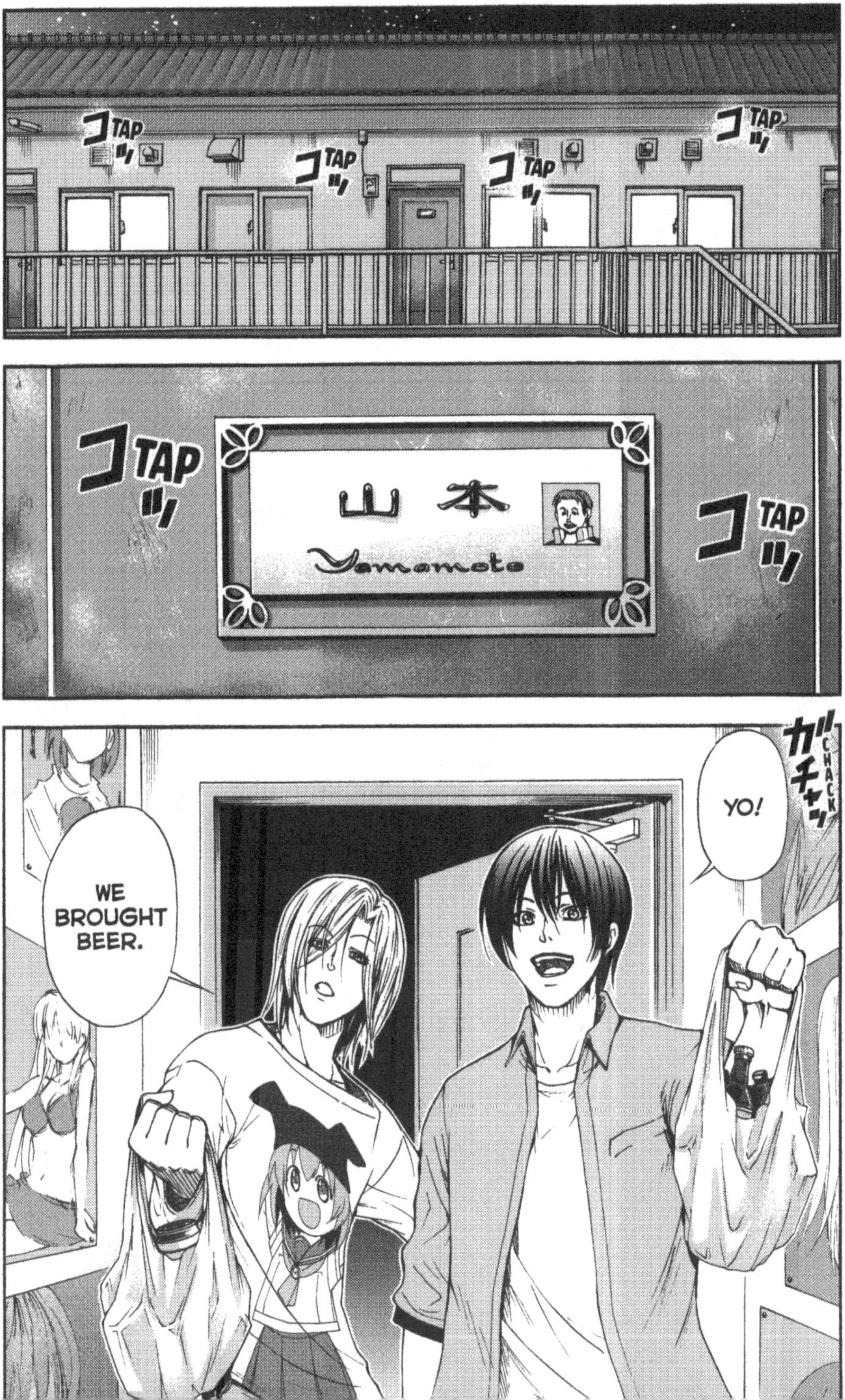
TAP
TAP
TAP
TAP
TAP
山本
Yamamoto
TAP
CHACK
YO!
WE BROUGHT BEER.

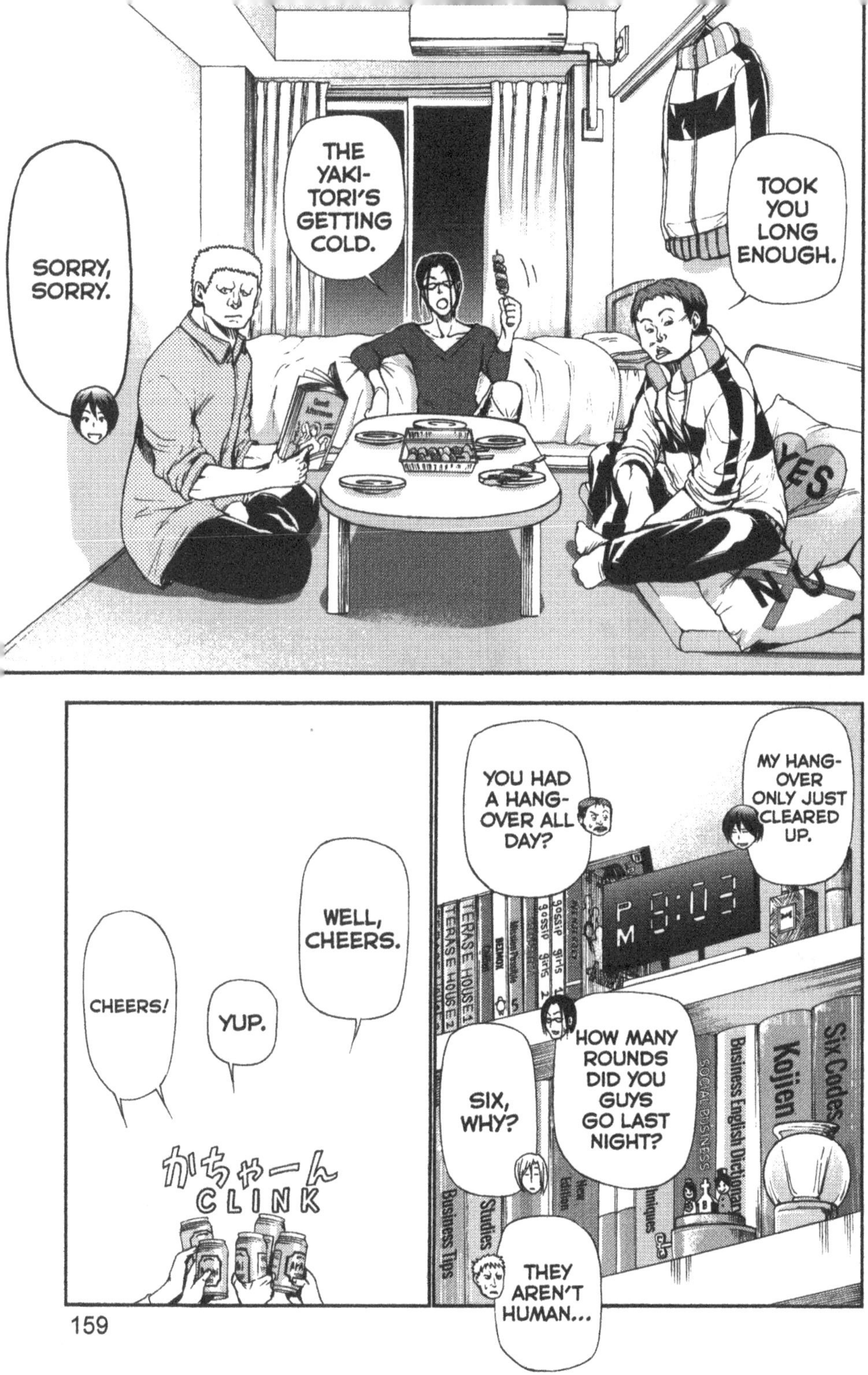
TOOK YOU LONG ENOUGH.
THE YAKI-TORI'S GETTING COLD.
SORRY, SORRY.
MY HANG-OVER ONLY JUST CLEARED UP.
YOU HAD A HANG-OVER ALL DAY?
HOW MANY ROUNDS DID YOU GUYS GO LAST NIGHT?
SIX, WHY?
THEY AREN'T HUMAN...
WELL, CHEERS.
YUP.
CHEERS!
かちゃーん
CLINK

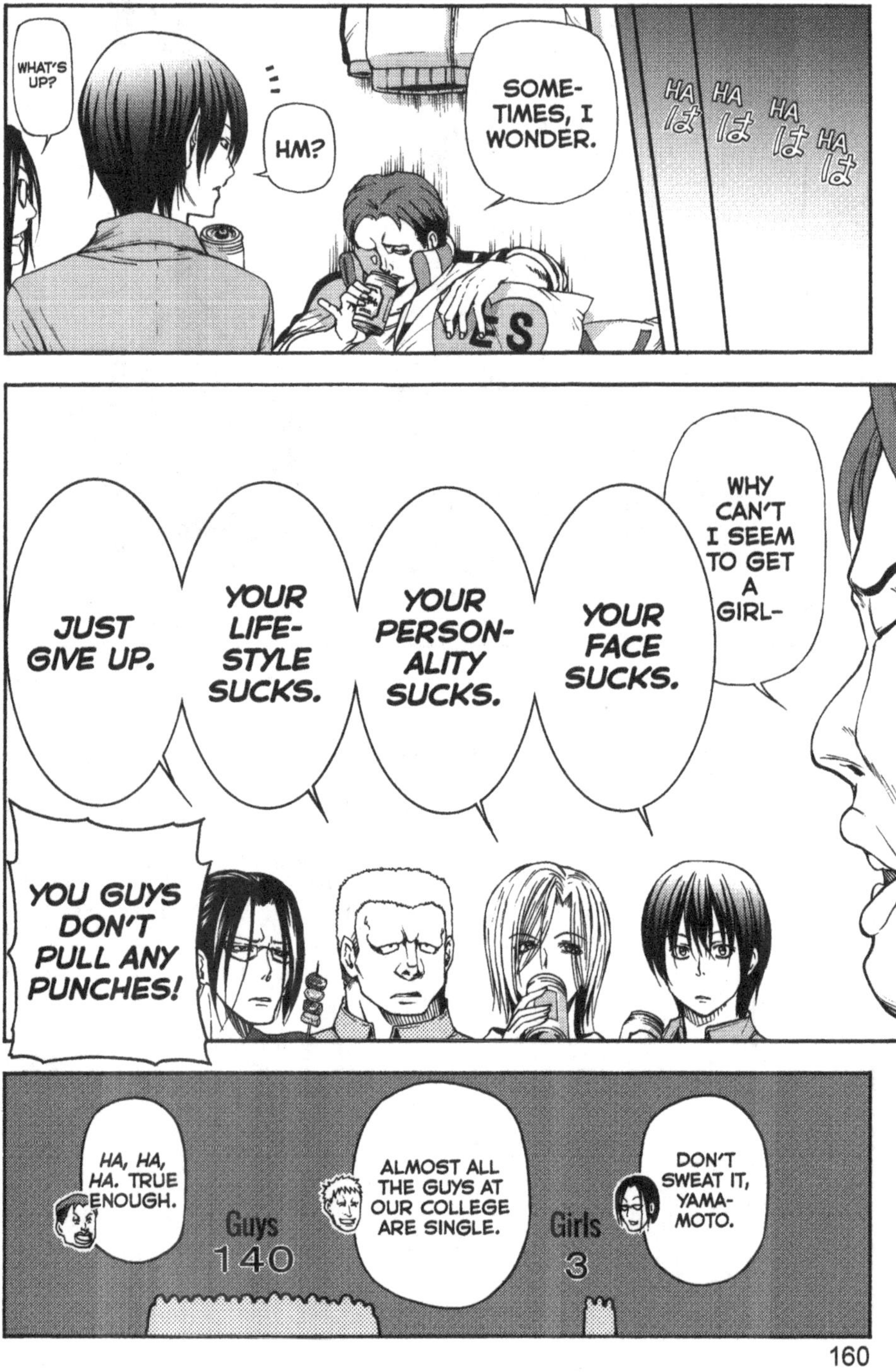
HA は HA は HA は HA は
SOME-TIMES, I WONDER.
HM?
WHAT'S UP?
WHY CAN'T I SEEM TO GET A GIRL-
YOUR FACE SUCKS.
YOUR PERSON-ALITY SUCKS.
YOUR LIFE-STYLE SUCKS.
JUST GIVE UP.
YOU GUYS DON'T PULL ANY PUNCHES!
DON'T SWEAT IT, YAMA-MOTO.
Girls
3
ALMOST ALL THE GUYS AT OUR COLLEGE ARE SINGLE.
Guys
140
HA, HA, HA. TRUE ENOUGH.

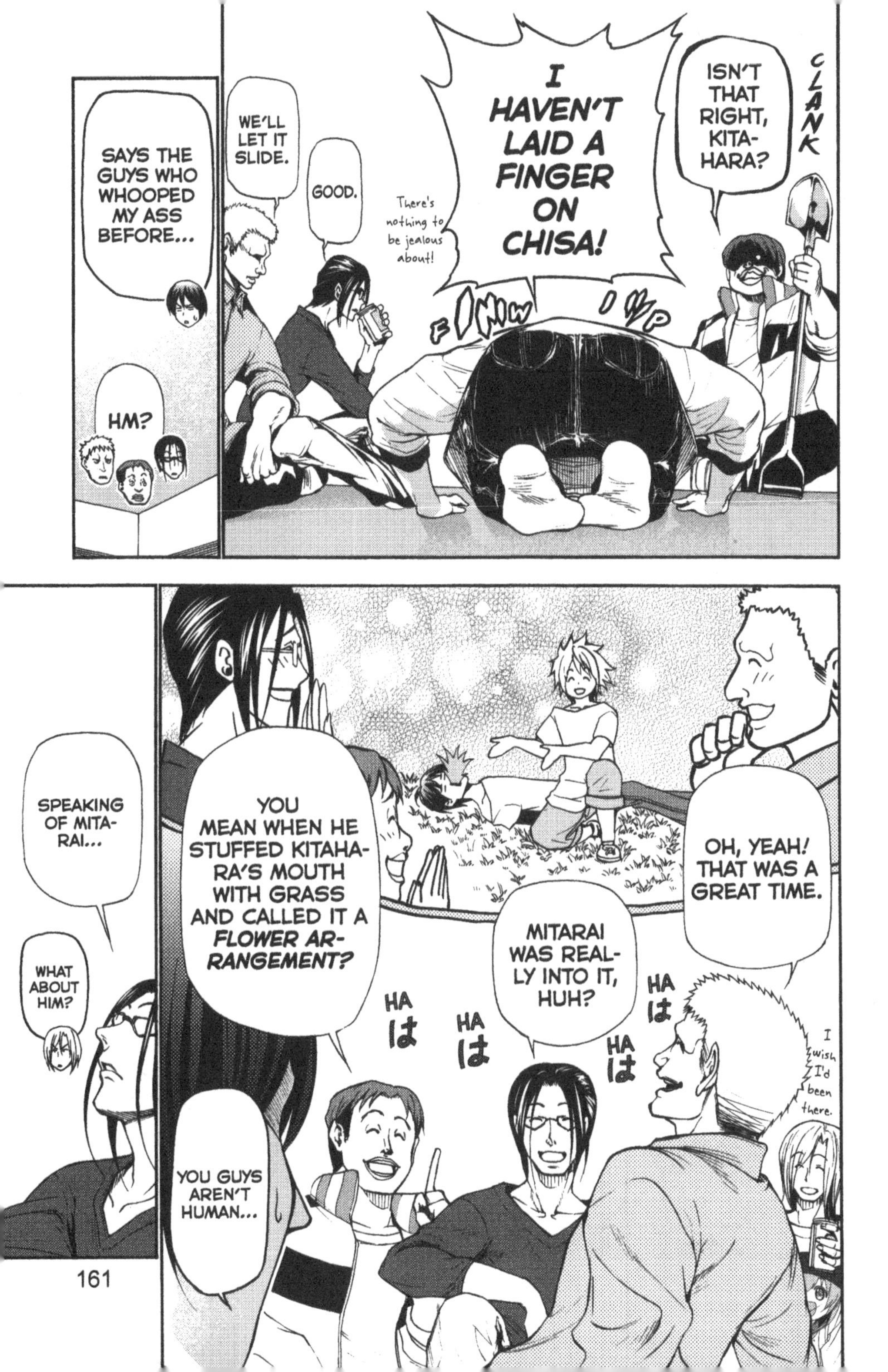
CLANK
ISN'T THAT RIGHT, KITA-HARA?
I HAVEN'T LAID A FINGER ON CHISA!
There's nothing to be jealous about!
GOOD.
WE'LL LET IT SLIDE.
SAYS THE GUYS WHO WHOOPED MY ASS BEFORE...
HM?
YOU MEAN WHEN HE STUFFED KITAHA-RA'S MOUTH WITH GRASS AND CALLED IT A *FLOWER AR-RANGEMENT?*
OH, YEAH! THAT WAS A GREAT TIME.
MITARAI WAS REAL-LY INTO IT, HUH?
HA は
HA は
HA は
HA は
I wish I'd been there.
SPEAKING OF MITA-RAI...
WHAT ABOUT HIM?
YOU GUYS AREN'T HUMAN...

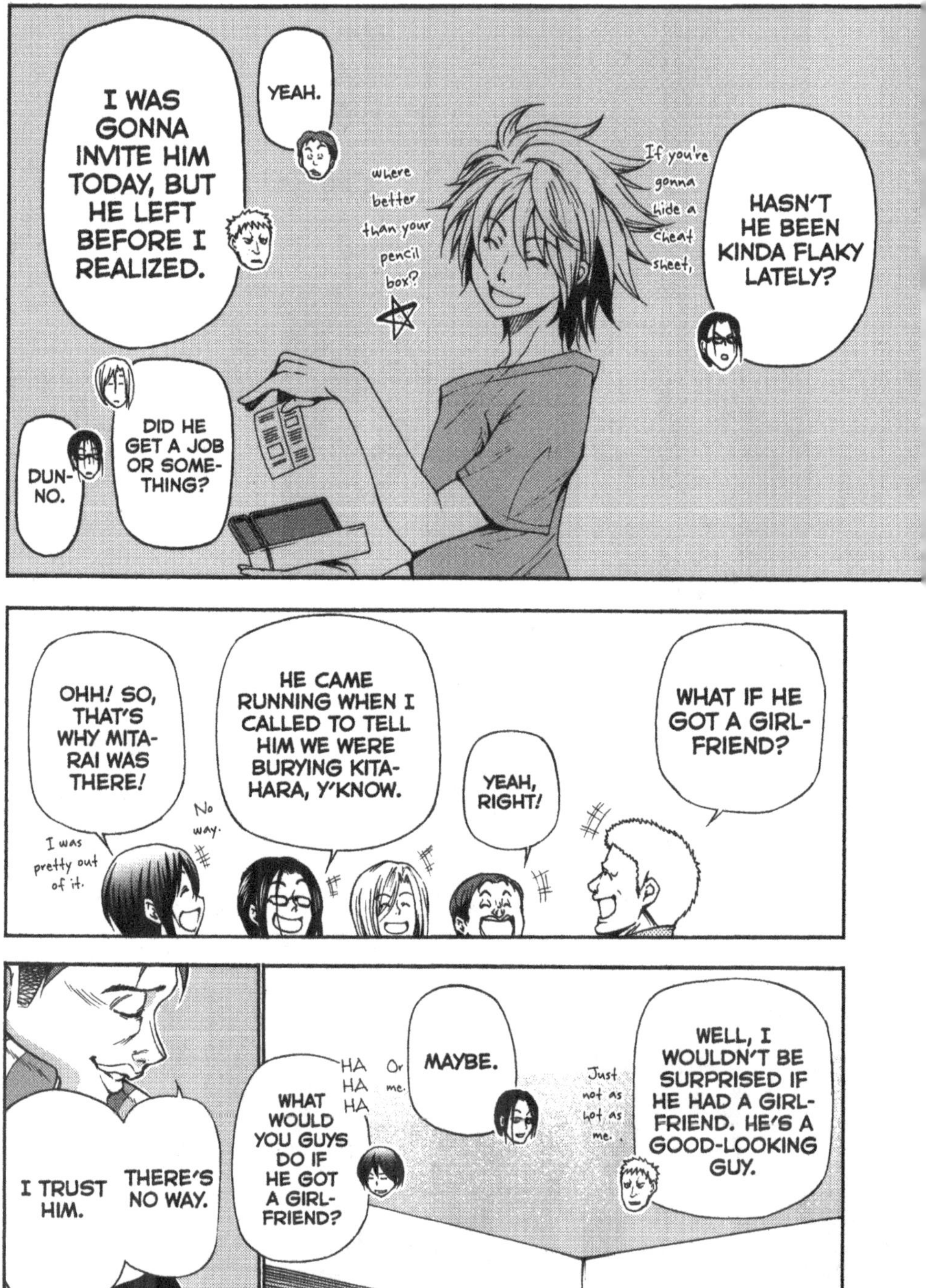
HASN'T HE BEEN KINDA FLAKY LATELY?
If you're gonna hide a cheat sheet,
where better than your pencil box?
YEAH.
I WAS GONNA INVITE HIM TODAY, BUT HE LEFT BEFORE I REALIZED.
DID HE GET A JOB OR SOME-THING?
DUN-NO.
WHAT IF HE GOT A GIRL-FRIEND?
YEAH, RIGHT!
HE CAME RUNNING WHEN I CALLED TO TELL HIM WE WERE BURYING KITA-HARA, Y'KNOW.
No way.
OHH! SO, THAT'S WHY MITA-RAI WAS THERE!
I was pretty out of it.
WELL, I WOULDN'T BE SURPRISED IF HE HAD A GIRL-FRIEND. HE'S A GOOD-LOOKING GUY.
Just not as hot as me.
MAYBE.
Or me.
HA HA HA
WHAT WOULD YOU GUYS DO IF HE GOT A GIRL-FRIEND?
THERE'S NO WAY.
I TRUST HIM.

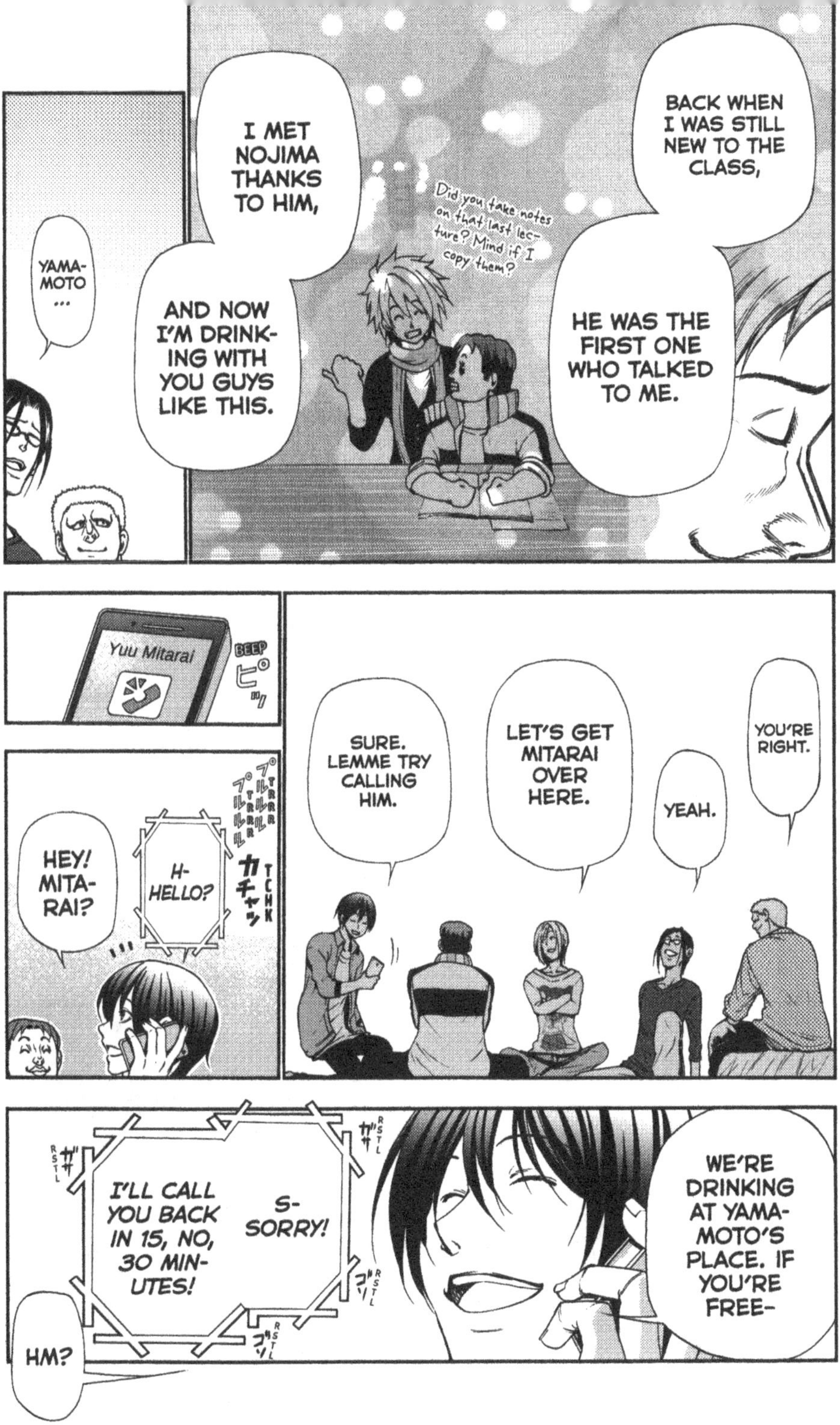
BACK WHEN I WAS STILL NEW TO THE CLASS,
HE WAS THE FIRST ONE WHO TALKED TO ME.
Did you take notes on that last lecture? Mind if I copy them?
I MET NOJIMA THANKS TO HIM,
AND NOW I'M DRINKING WITH YOU GUYS LIKE THIS.
YAMA-MOTO...
YOU'RE RIGHT.
YEAH.
LET'S GET MITARAI OVER HERE.
SURE. LEMME TRY CALLING HIM.
Yuu Mitarai
BEEP
TRRR TRRR
TCHK
H-HELLO?
HEY! MITA-RAI?
WE'RE DRINKING AT YAMA-MOTO'S PLACE. IF YOU'RE FREE-
RSTL
S-SORRY!
I'LL CALL YOU BACK IN 15, NO, 30 MIN-UTES!
RSTL
RSTL
RSTL
HM?

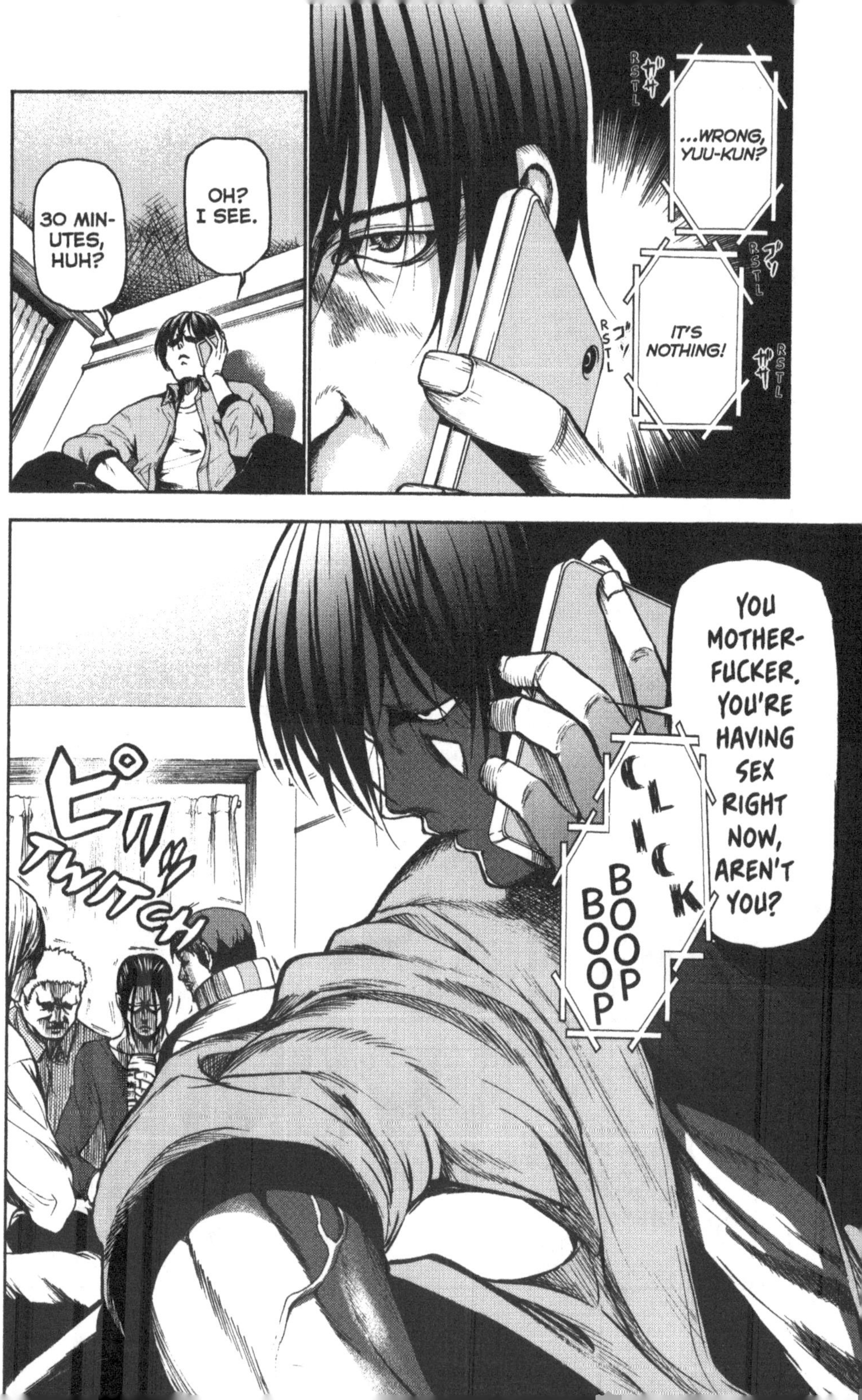
RSTL
...WRONG, YUU-KUN?
RSTL
RSTL
IT'S NOTHING!
RSTL
OH? I SEE.
30 MIN-UTES, HUH?
YOU MOTHER-FUCKER. YOU'RE HAVING SEX RIGHT NOW, AREN'T YOU?
CLICK
BOOP BOOP
BOOP
TWITCH

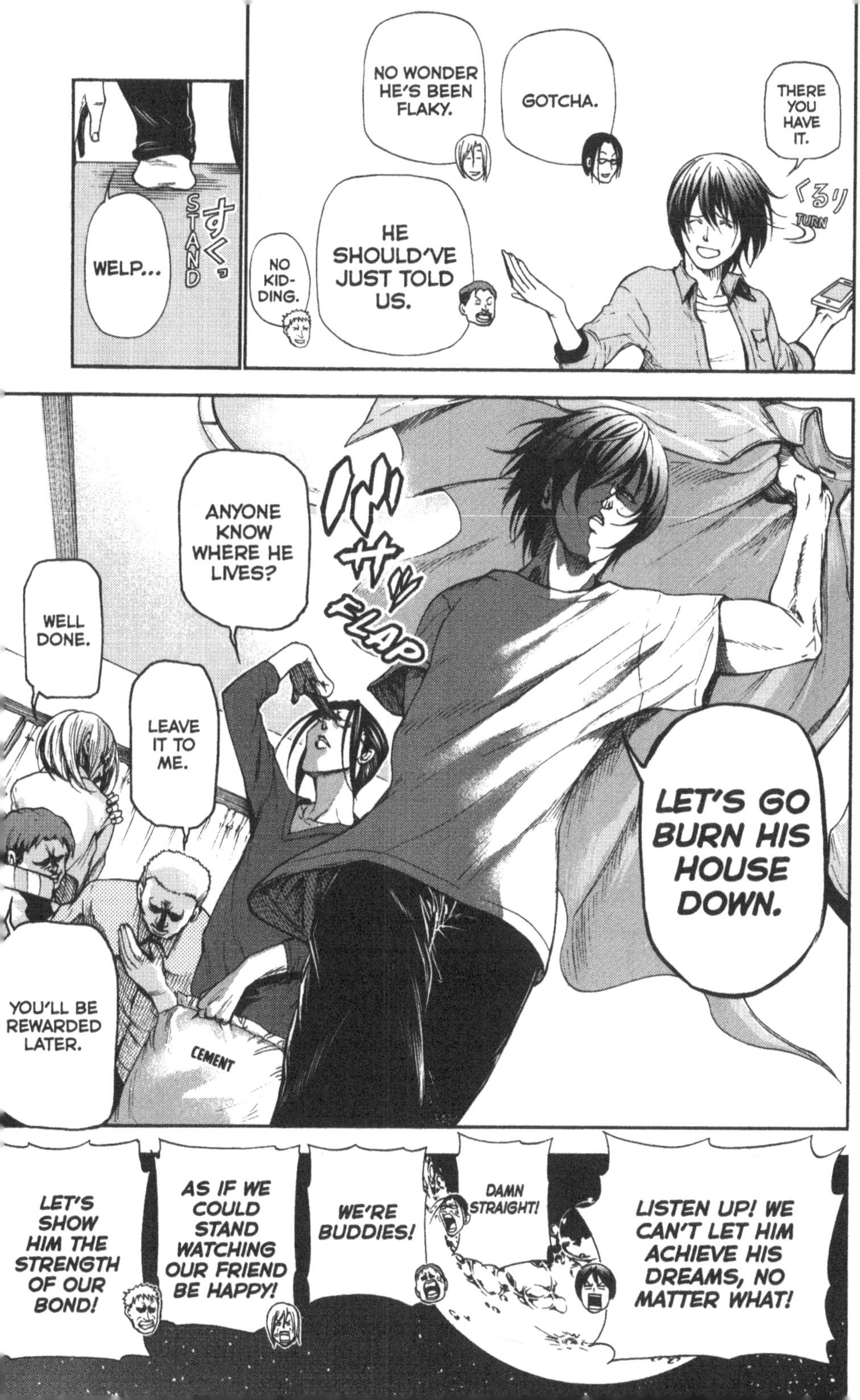
THERE YOU HAVE IT.
くるり
TURN
GOTCHA.
NO WONDER HE'S BEEN FLAKY.
HE SHOULD'VE JUST TOLD US.
NO KID-DING.
すくっ
STAND
WELP...
LET'S GO BURN HIS HOUSE DOWN.
バサッ
FLAP
ANYONE KNOW WHERE HE LIVES?
LEAVE IT TO ME.
WELL DONE.
YOU'LL BE REWARDED LATER.
CEMENT
LISTEN UP! WE CAN'T LET HIM ACHIEVE HIS DREAMS, NO MATTER WHAT!
DAMN STRAIGHT!
WE'RE BUDDIES!
AS IF WE COULD STAND WATCHING OUR FRIEND BE HAPPY!
LET'S SHOW HIM THE STRENGTH OF OUR BOND!

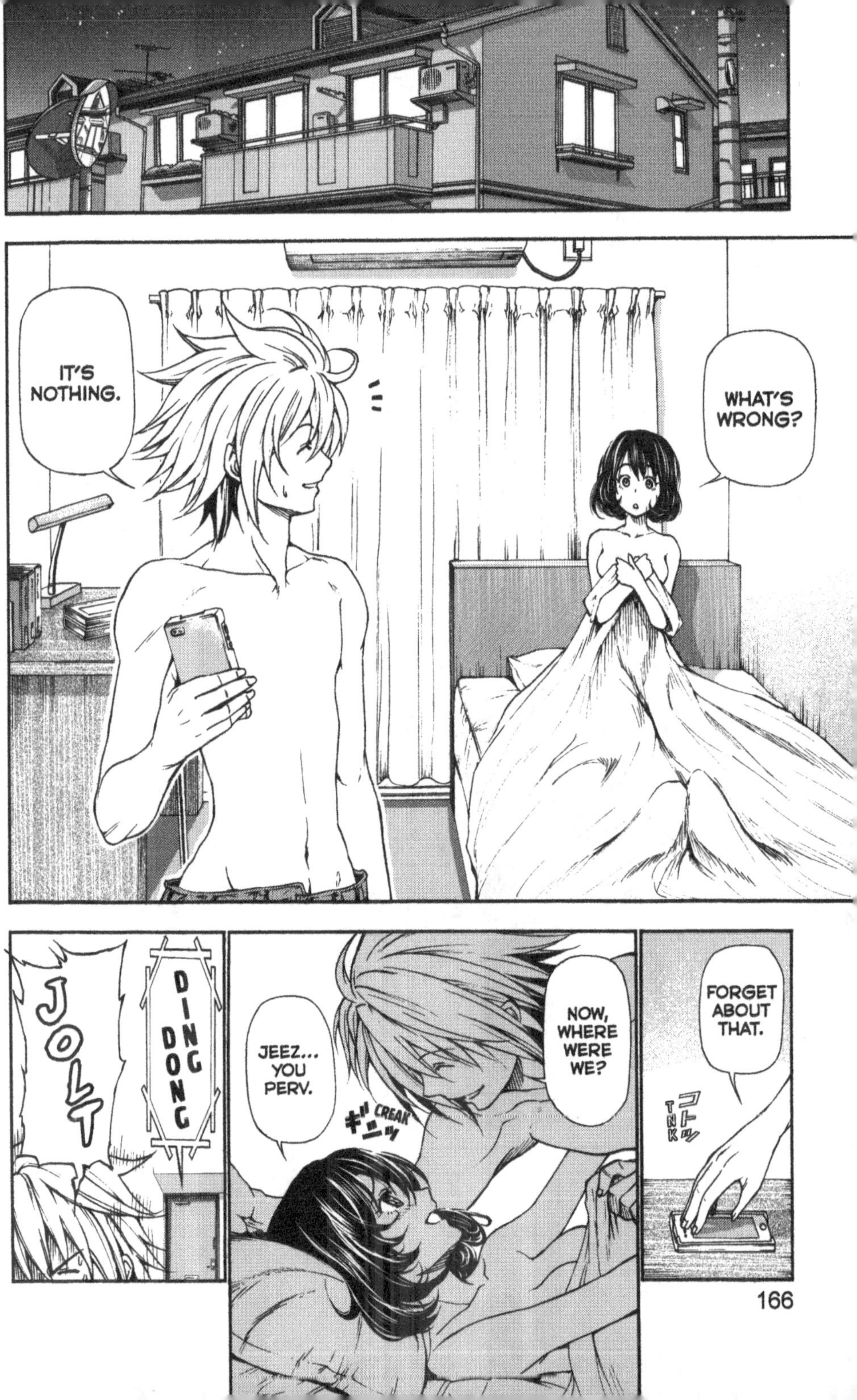
WHAT'S WRONG?
IT'S NOTHING.
FORGET ABOUT THAT.
コトッ
TNK
NOW, WHERE WERE WE?
JEEZ... YOU PERV.
ギシッ
CREAK
DING DONG
JOLT

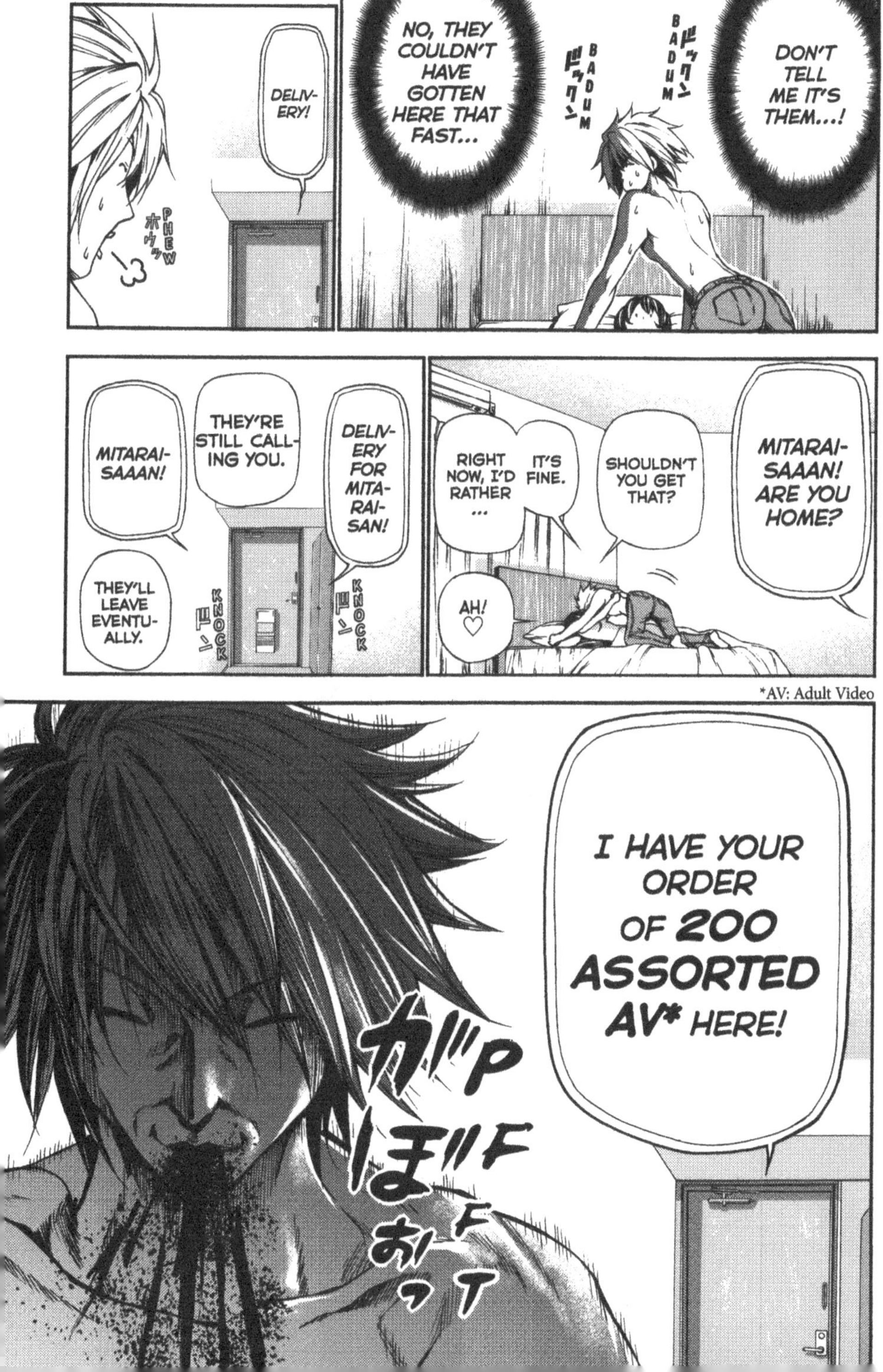
DON'T TELL ME IT'S THEM...!
BADUM
BADUM
NO, THEY COULDN'T HAVE GOTTEN HERE THAT FAST...
DELIV-ERY!
PHEW
MITARAI-SAAAN! ARE YOU HOME?
SHOULDN'T YOU GET THAT?
IT'S FINE.
RIGHT NOW, I'D RATHER ...
AH! ♡
DELIV-ERY FOR MITA-RAI-SAN!
KNOCK
THEY'RE STILL CALL-ING YOU.
MITARAI-SAAAN!
KNOCK
THEY'LL LEAVE EVENTU-ALLY.
I HAVE YOUR ORDER OF 200 ASSORTED AV* HERE!
PFFT

*AV: Adult Video

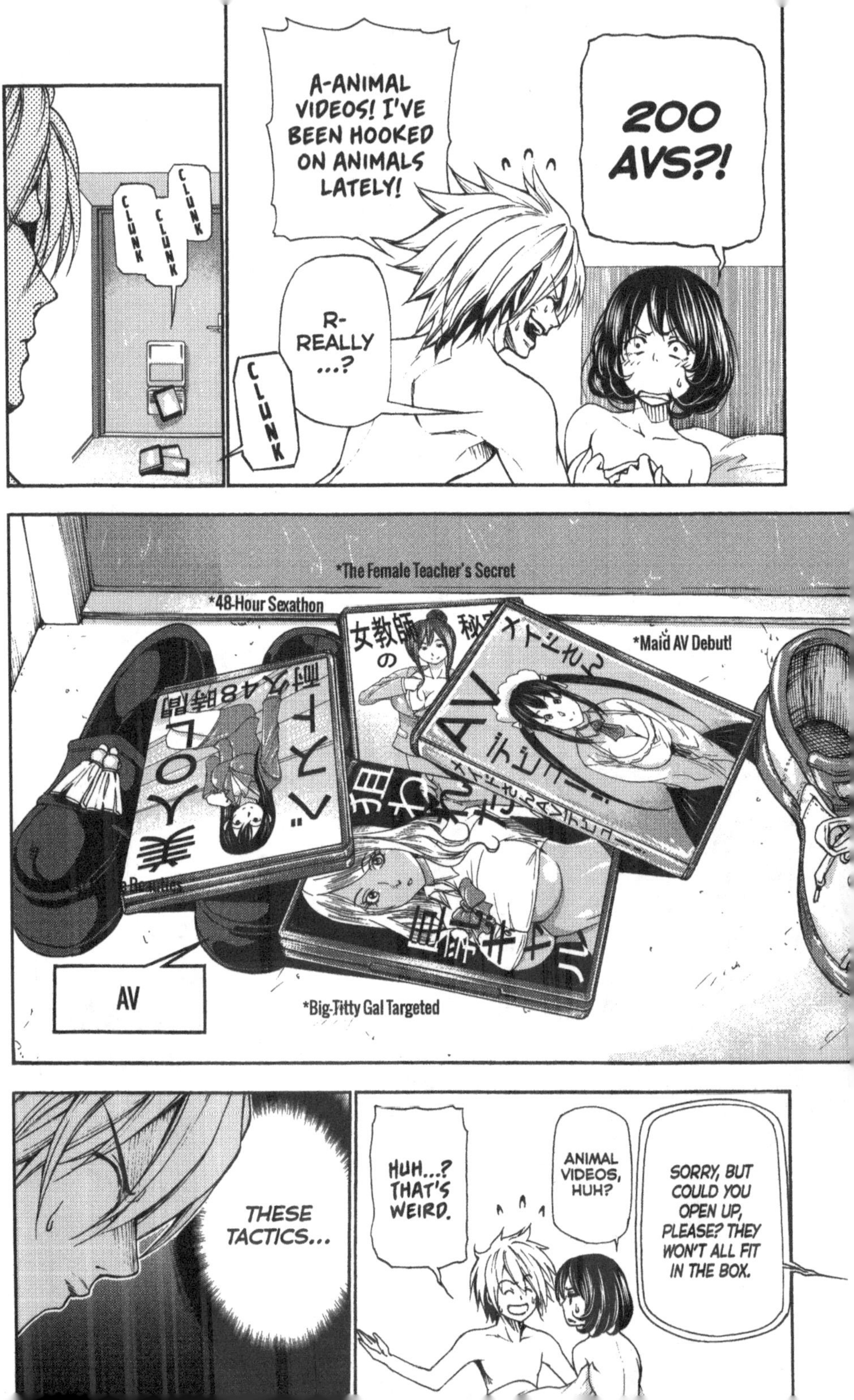
200 AVS?!
A-ANIMAL VIDEOS! I'VE BEEN HOOKED ON ANIMALS LATELY!
R-REALLY ...?
CLUNK
CLUNK
CLUNK
CLUNK
*The Female Teacher's Secret
*Maid AV Debut!
*48-Hour Sexathon
AV
*Big-Titty Gal Targeted
SORRY, BUT COULD YOU OPEN UP, PLEASE? THEY WON'T ALL FIT IN THE BOX.
ANIMAL VIDEOS, HUH?
HUH...? THAT'S WEIRD.
THESE TACTICS...

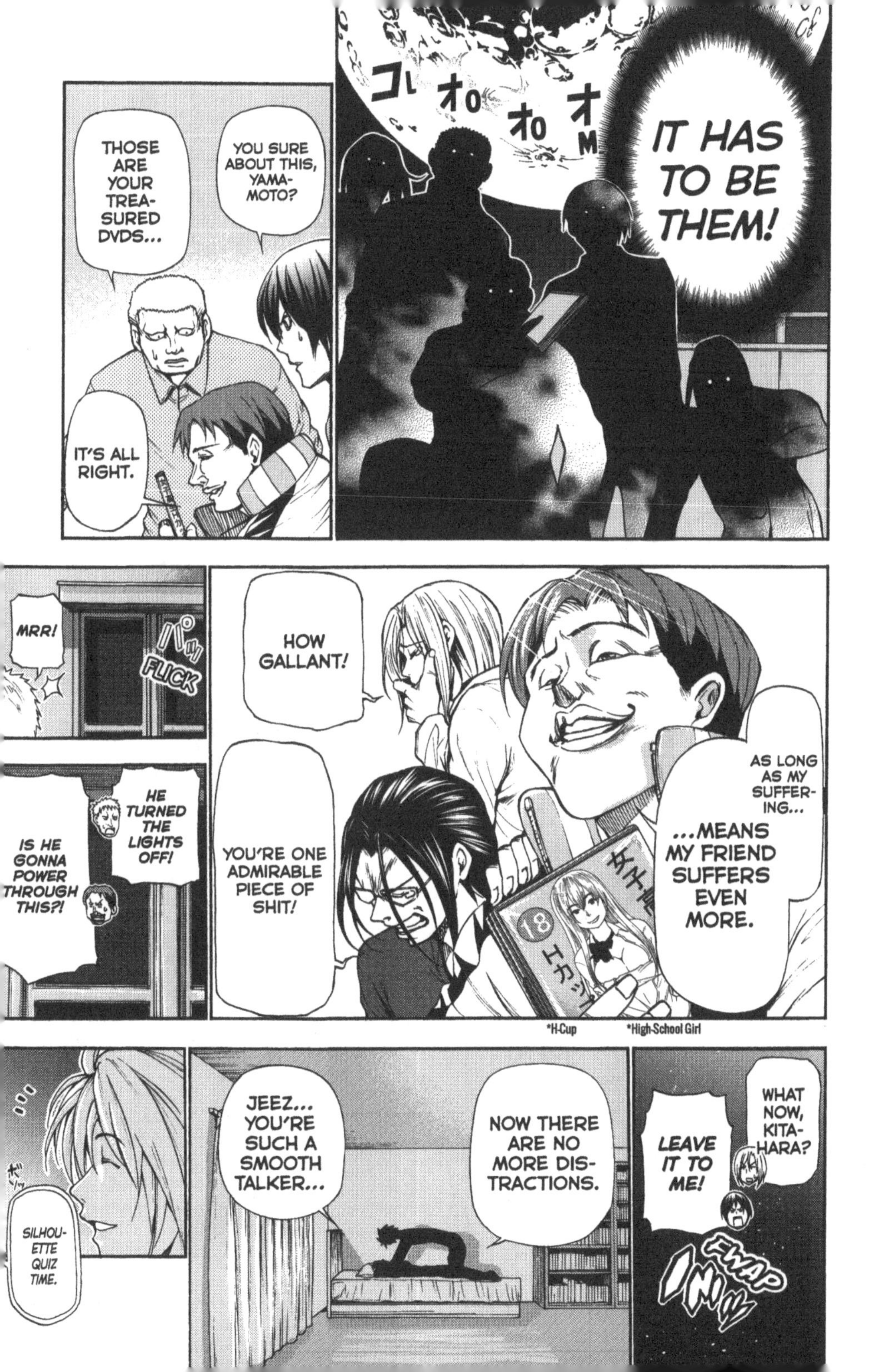

IT HAS TO BE THEM!
YOU SURE ABOUT THIS, YAMAMOTO?
THOSE ARE YOUR TREASURED DVDS...
IT'S ALL RIGHT.
AS LONG AS MY SUFFERING...
...MEANS MY FRIEND SUFFERS EVEN MORE.
HOW GALLANT!
YOU'RE ONE ADMIRABLE PIECE OF SHIT!
MRR!
FLICK
HE TURNED THE LIGHTS OFF!
IS HE GONNA POWER THROUGH THIS?!
*H-Cup
*High-School Girl
WHAT NOW, KITAHARA?
LEAVE IT TO ME!
FWAP
NOW THERE ARE NO MORE DISTRACTIONS.
JEEZ... YOU'RE SUCH A SMOOTH TALKER...
SILHOUETTE QUIZ TIME.

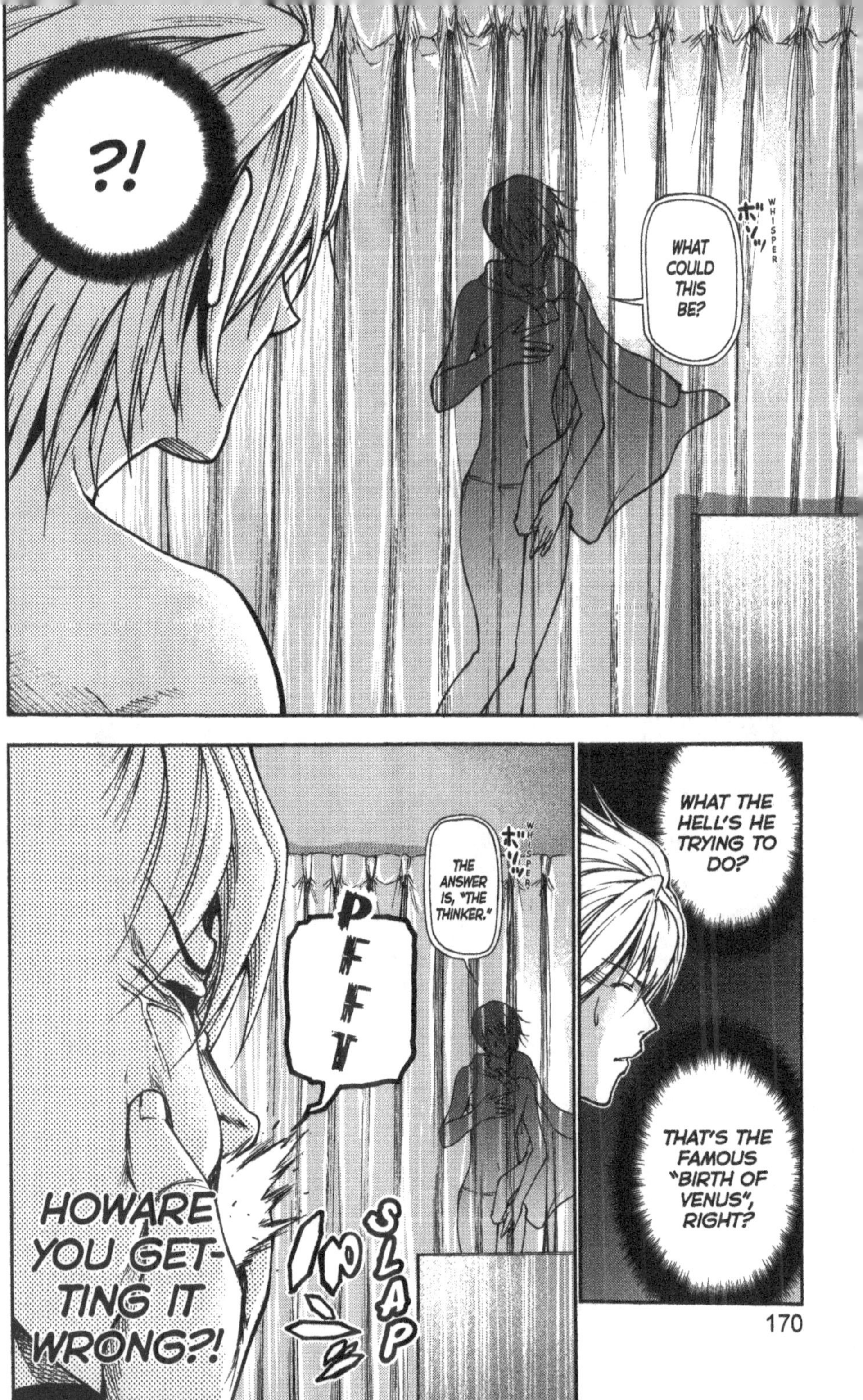
WHISPER
WHAT COULD THIS BE?
?!
WHAT THE HELL'S HE TRYING TO DO?
THAT'S THE FAMOUS "BIRTH OF VENUS", RIGHT?
WHISPER
THE ANSWER IS, "THE THINKER."
PFFT
SLAP
HOWARE YOU GET-TING IT WRONG?!

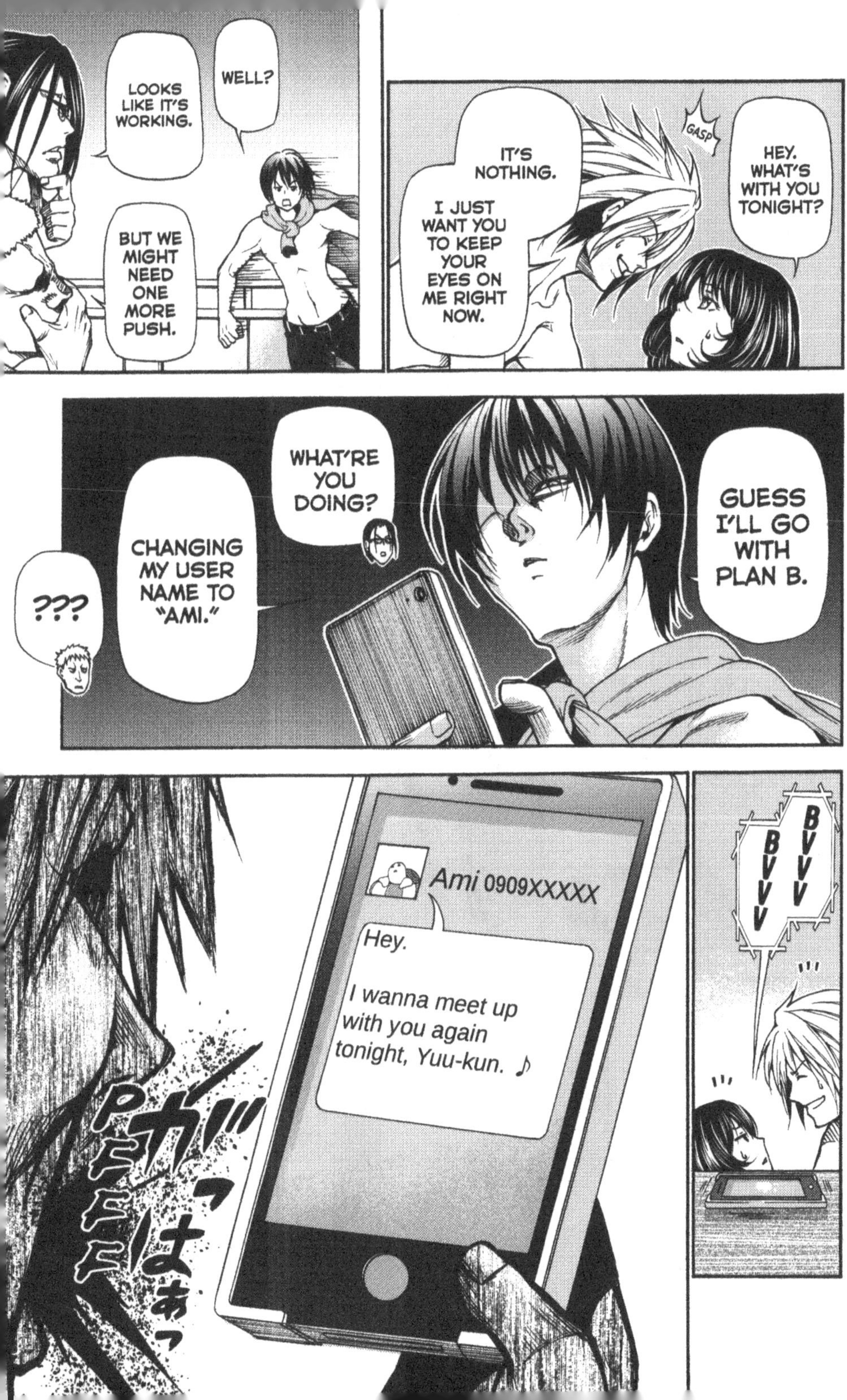
GASP
HEY. WHAT'S WITH YOU TONIGHT?
IT'S NOTHING.
I JUST WANT YOU TO KEEP YOUR EYES ON ME RIGHT NOW.
WELL?
LOOKS LIKE IT'S WORKING.
BUT WE MIGHT NEED ONE MORE PUSH.
GUESS I'LL GO WITH PLAN B.
WHAT'RE YOU DOING?
CHANGING MY USER NAME TO "AMI."
???
BVVV
BVVV
Ami 0909XXXXX
Hey.
I wanna meet up with you again tonight, Yuu-kun. ♪
PFFF
ガッ
はあっ

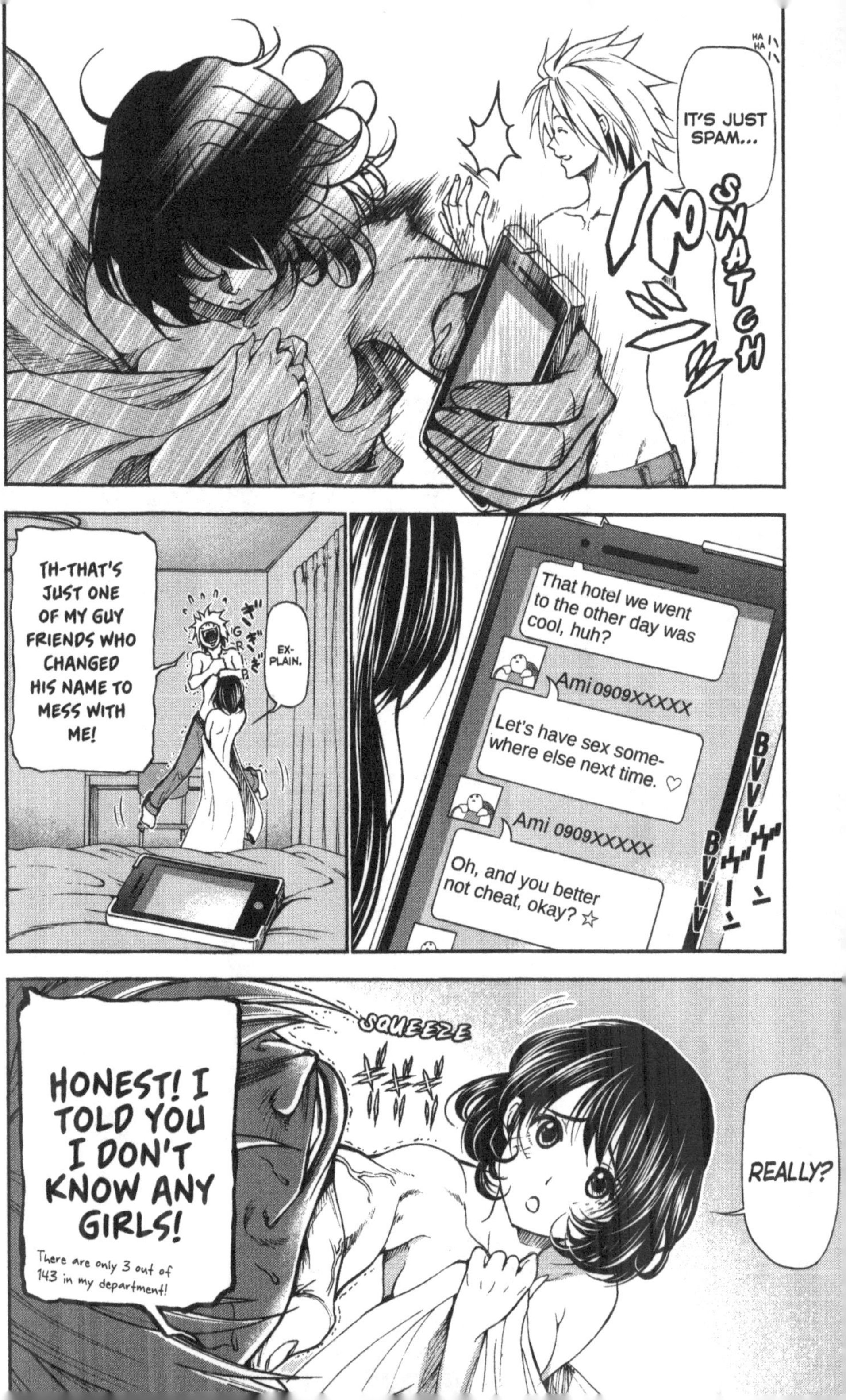
HA HA
IT'S JUST SPAM...
SNATCH
That hotel we went to the other day was cool, huh?
Ami 0909XXXXX
Let's have sex some-where else next time. ♡
Ami 0909XXXXX
Oh, and you better not cheat, okay? ☆
BVVVV
BVVVV
EX-PLAIN.
GRR
TH-THAT'S JUST ONE OF MY GUY FRIENDS WHO CHANGED HIS NAME TO MESS WITH ME!
REALLY?
SQUEEZE
HONEST! I TOLD YOU I DON'T KNOW ANY GIRLS!
There are only 3 out of 143 in my department!

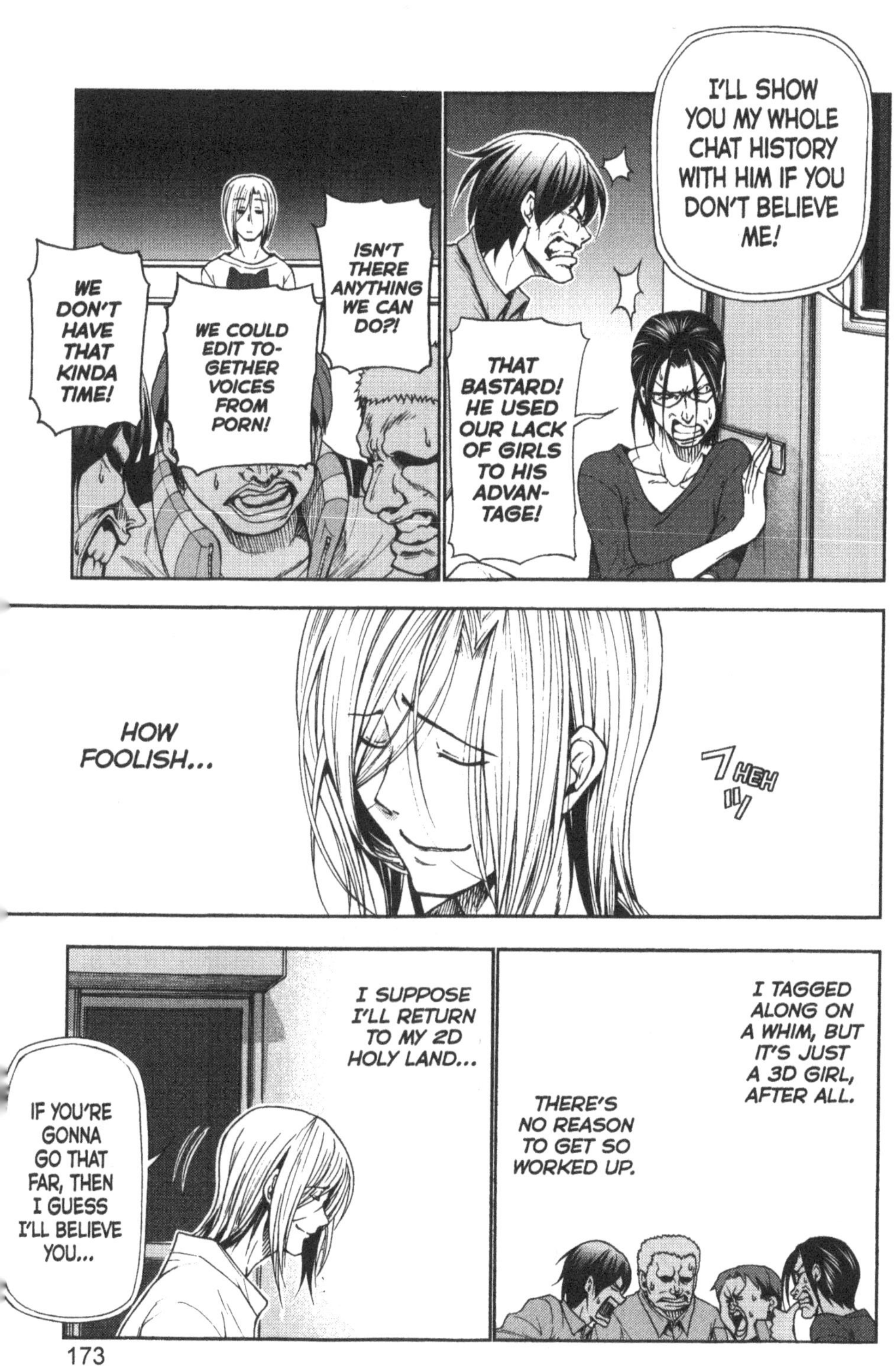
I'LL SHOW YOU MY WHOLE CHAT HISTORY WITH HIM IF YOU DON'T BELIEVE ME!
THAT BASTARD! HE USED OUR LACK OF GIRLS TO HIS ADVANTAGE!
ISN'T THERE ANYTHING WE CAN DO?!
WE COULD EDIT TOGETHER VOICES FROM PORN!
WE DON'T HAVE THAT KINDA TIME!
HEH
HOW FOOLISH...
I TAGGED ALONG ON A WHIM, BUT IT'S JUST A 3D GIRL, AFTER ALL.
THERE'S NO REASON TO GET SO WORKED UP.
I SUPPOSE I'LL RETURN TO MY 2D HOLY LAND...
IF YOU'RE GONNA GO THAT FAR, THEN I GUESS I'LL BELIEVE YOU...

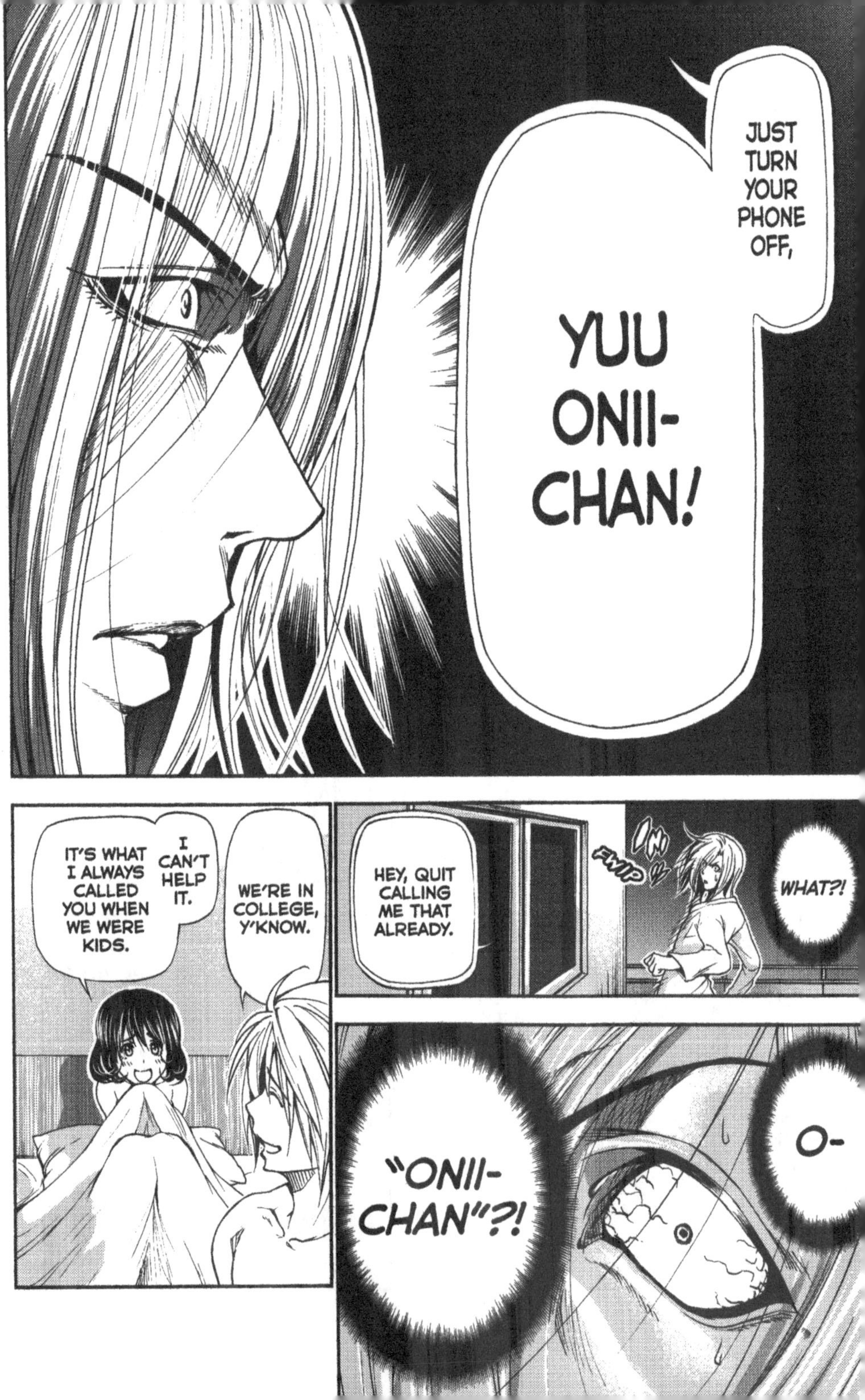
JUST TURN YOUR PHONE OFF,
YUU ONII-CHAN!
WHAT?!
FWIP
HEY, QUIT CALLING ME THAT ALREADY.
O-
"ONII-CHAN"?!
WE'RE IN COLLEGE, Y'KNOW.
I CAN'T HELP IT.
IT'S WHAT I ALWAYS CALLED YOU WHEN WE WERE KIDS.

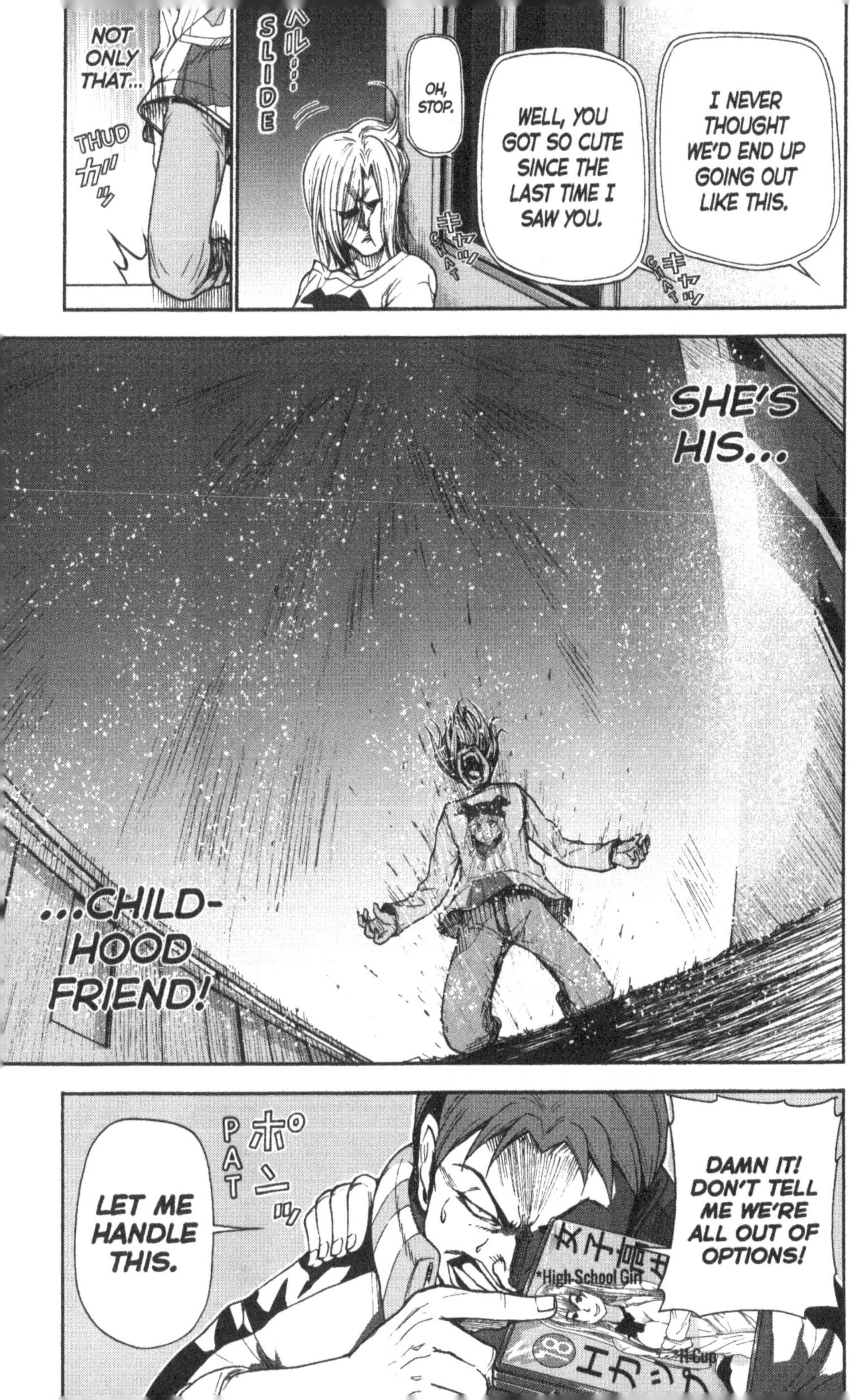
I NEVER THOUGHT WE'D END UP GOING OUT LIKE THIS.
CHAT
WELL, YOU GOT SO CUTE SINCE THE LAST TIME I SAW YOU.
CHAT
OH, STOP.
SLIDE
NOT ONLY THAT...
THUD
SHE'S HIS...
...CHILD-HOOD FRIEND!
DAMN IT! DON'T TELL ME WE'RE ALL OUT OF OPTIONS!
*High School Girl
*H-Cup
PAT
LET ME HANDLE THIS.

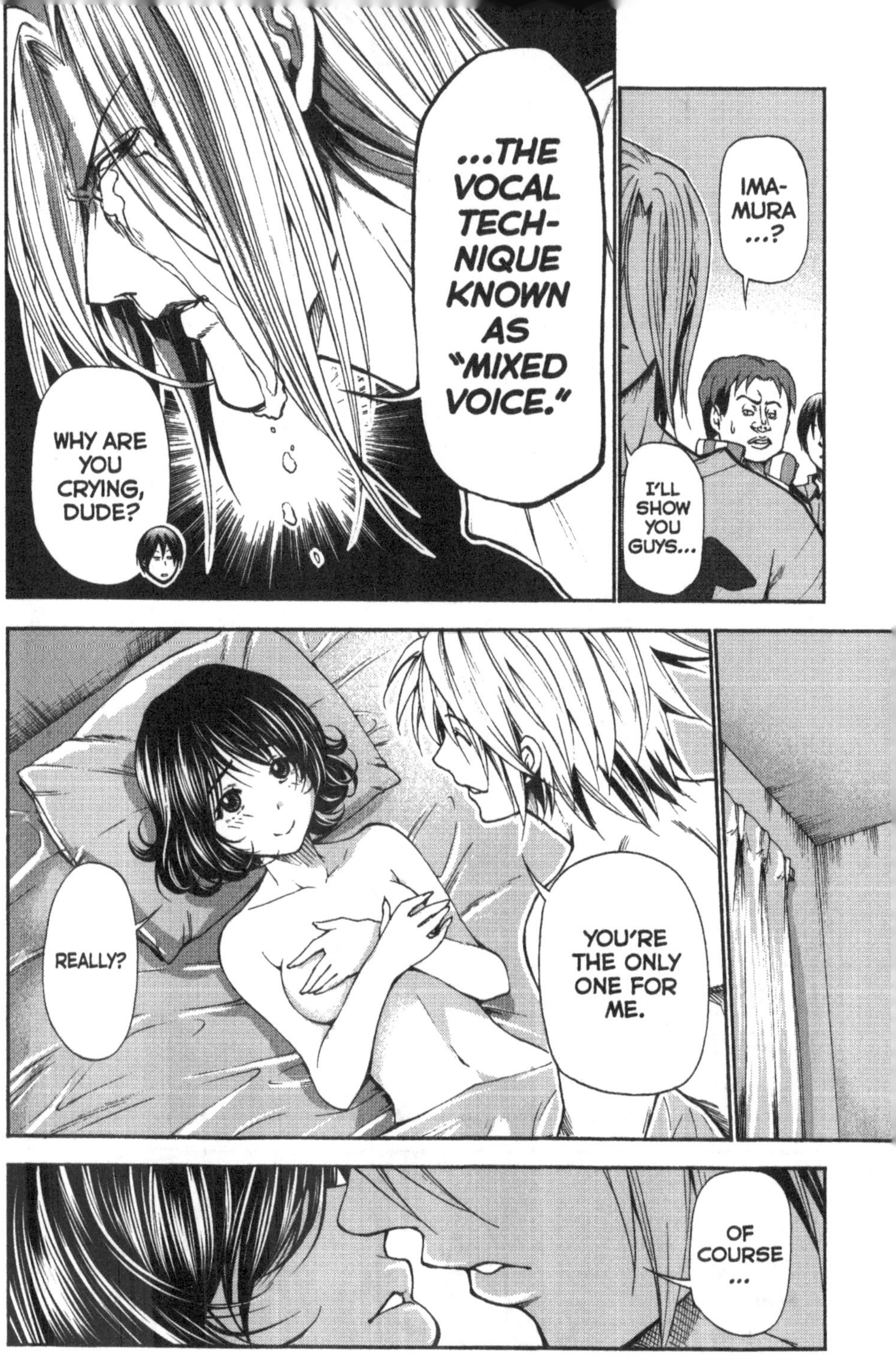
IMA-MURA...?
I'LL SHOW YOU GUYS...
...THE VOCAL TECH-NIQUE KNOWN AS "MIXED VOICE."
WHY ARE YOU CRYING, DUDE?
YOU'RE THE ONLY ONE FOR ME.
REALLY?
OF COURSE...

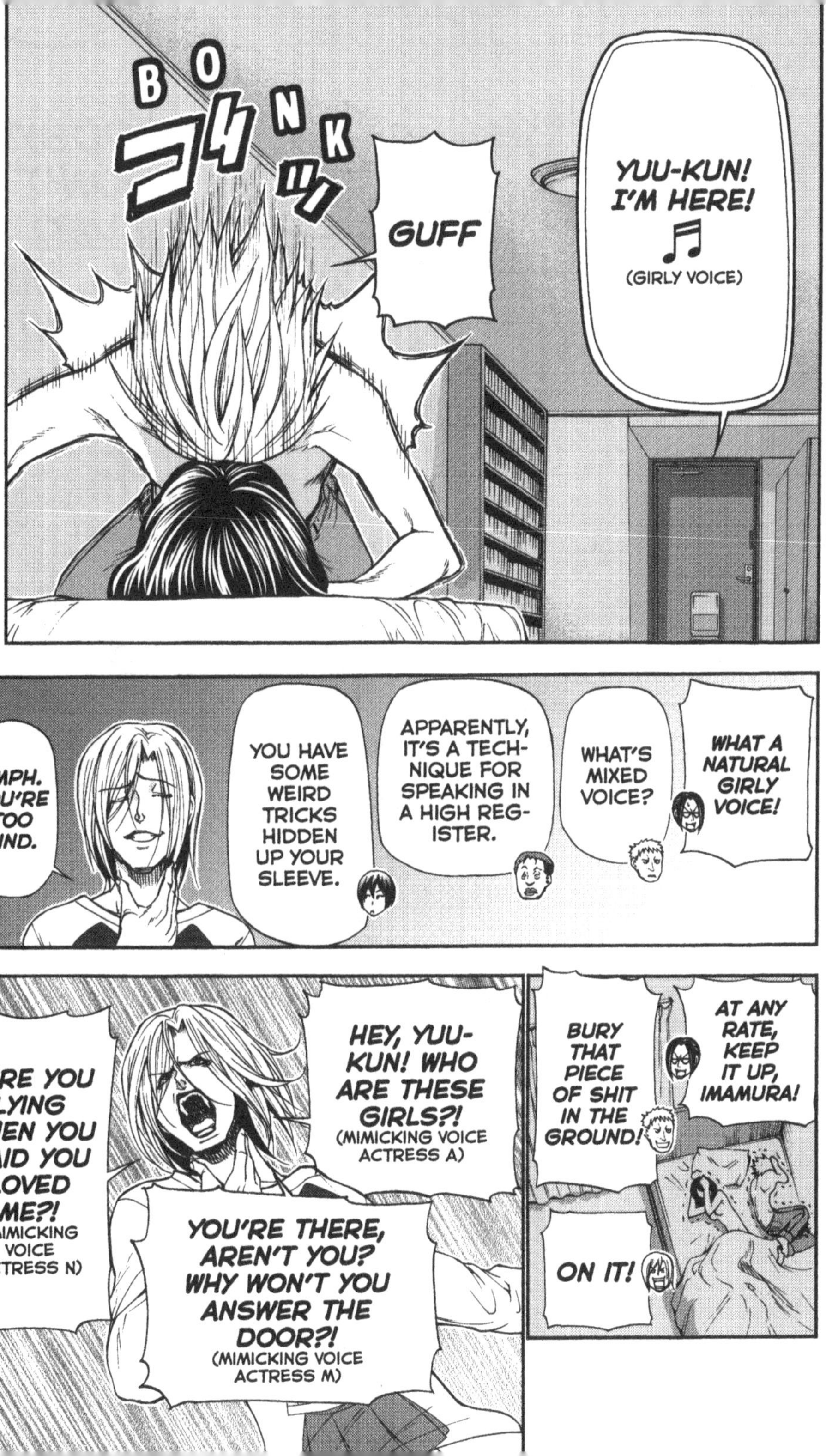
YUU-KUN! I'M HERE! ♫
(GIRLY VOICE)
GUFF
BONK
WHAT A NATURAL GIRLY VOICE!
WHAT'S MIXED VOICE?
APPARENTLY, IT'S A TECHNIQUE FOR SPEAKING IN A HIGH REGISTER.
YOU HAVE SOME WEIRD TRICKS HIDDEN UP YOUR SLEEVE.
HMPH. YOU'RE TOO KIND.
AT ANY RATE, KEEP IT UP, IMAMURA!
BURY THAT PIECE OF SHIT IN THE GROUND!
ON IT!
HEY, YUU-KUN! WHO ARE THESE GIRLS?!
(MIMICKING VOICE ACTRESS A)
WERE YOU LYING WHEN YOU SAID YOU LOVED ME?!
(MIMICKING VOICE ACTRESS N)
YOU'RE THERE, AREN'T YOU? WHY WON'T YOU ANSWER THE DOOR?!
(MIMICKING VOICE ACTRESS M)

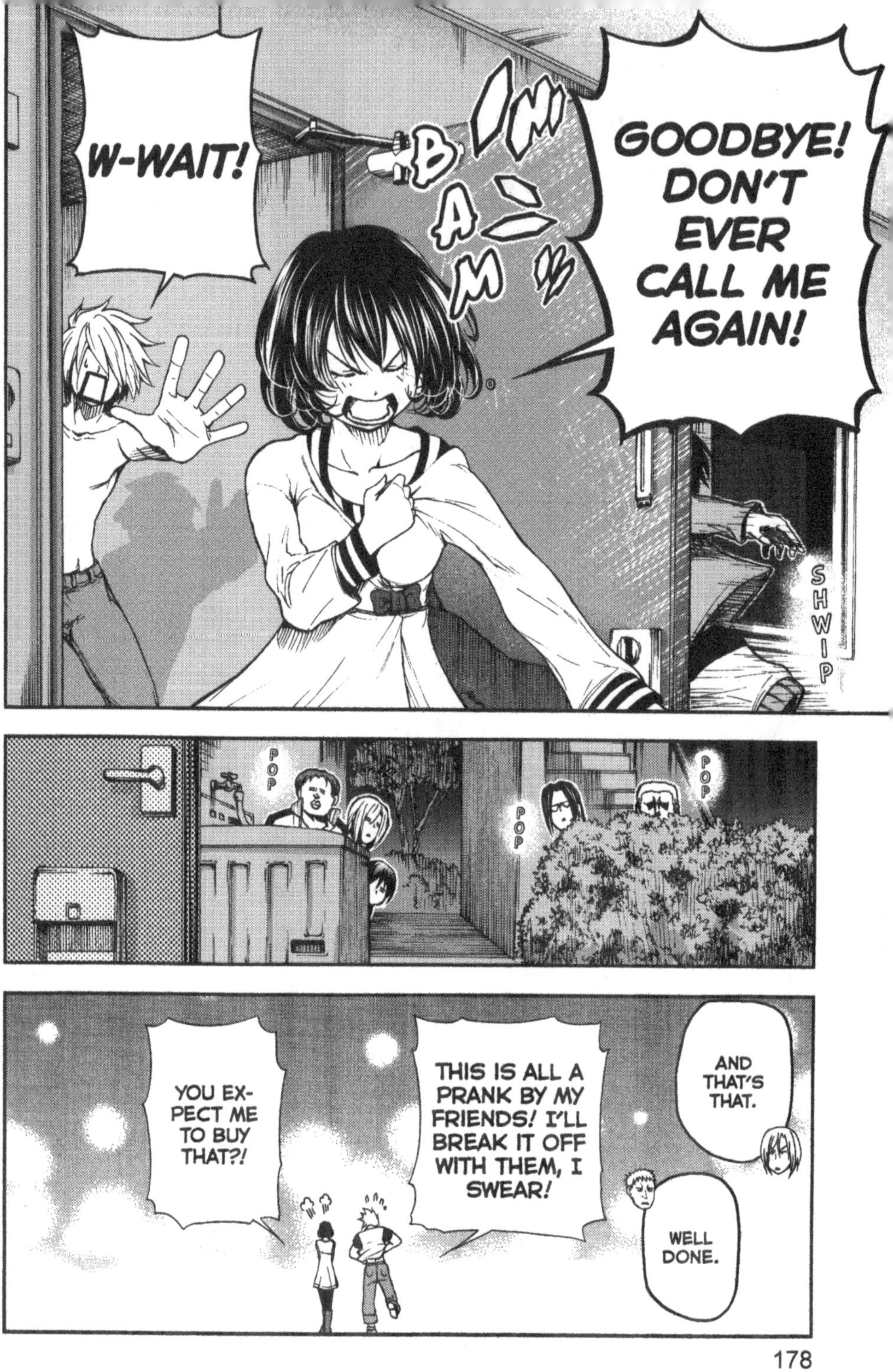
GOODBYE! DON'T EVER CALL ME AGAIN!
BAM!!
W-WAIT!
SHWIP
POP
POP
POP
POP
AND THAT'S THAT.
WELL DONE.
THIS IS ALL A PRANK BY MY FRIENDS! I'LL BREAK IT OFF WITH THEM, I SWEAR!
YOU EX-PECT ME TO BUY THAT?!

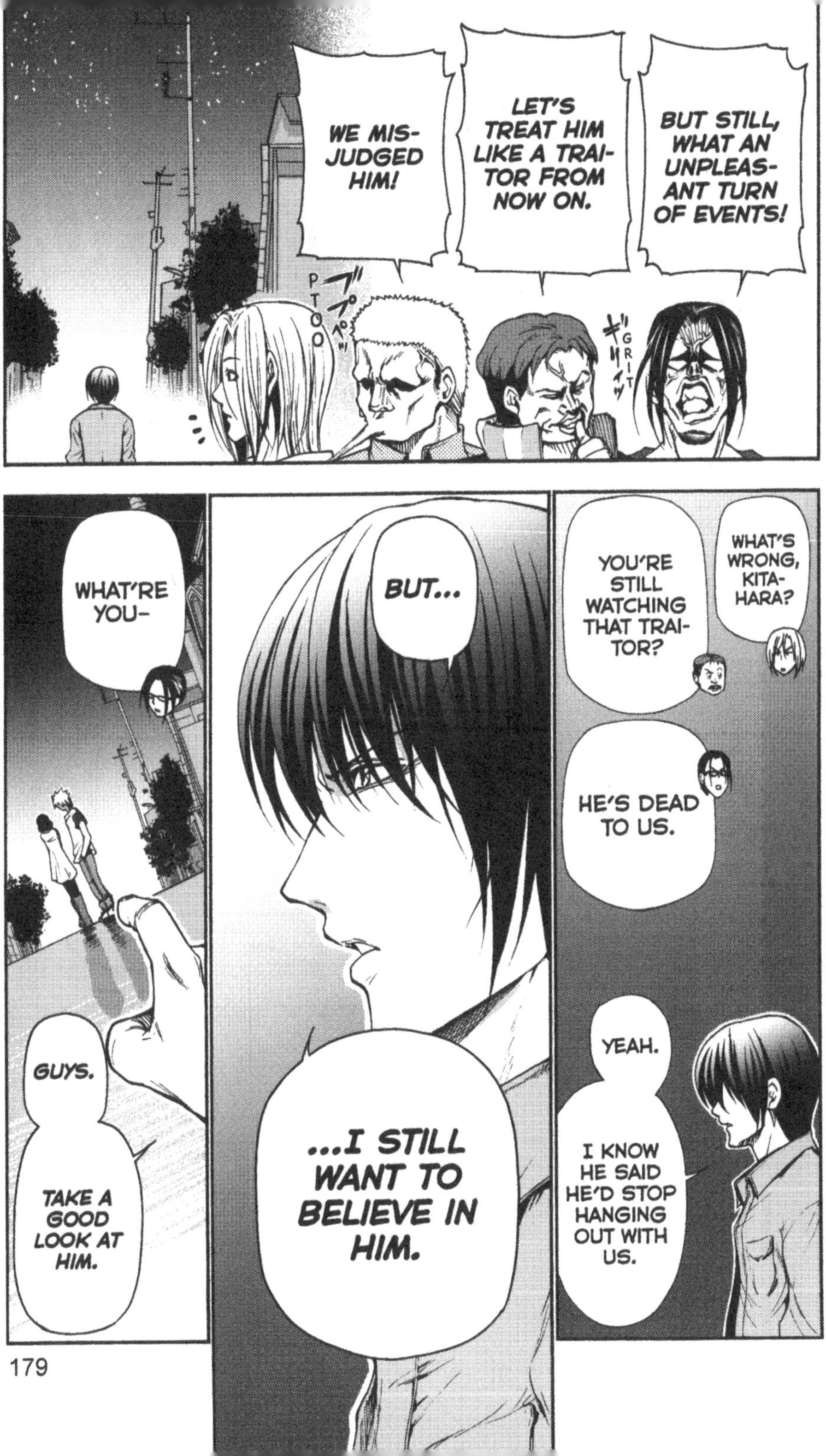
BUT STILL, WHAT AN UNPLEAS-ANT TURN OF EVENTS!
LET'S TREAT HIM LIKE A TRAI-TOR FROM NOW ON.
WE MIS-JUDGED HIM!
GRIT
PTOO
WHAT'S WRONG, KITA-HARA?
YOU'RE STILL WATCHING THAT TRAI-TOR?
HE'S DEAD TO US.
YEAH.
I KNOW HE SAID HE'D STOP HANGING OUT WITH US.
BUT...
...I STILL WANT TO BELIEVE IN HIM.
WHAT'RE YOU-
GUYS.
TAKE A GOOD LOOK AT HIM.

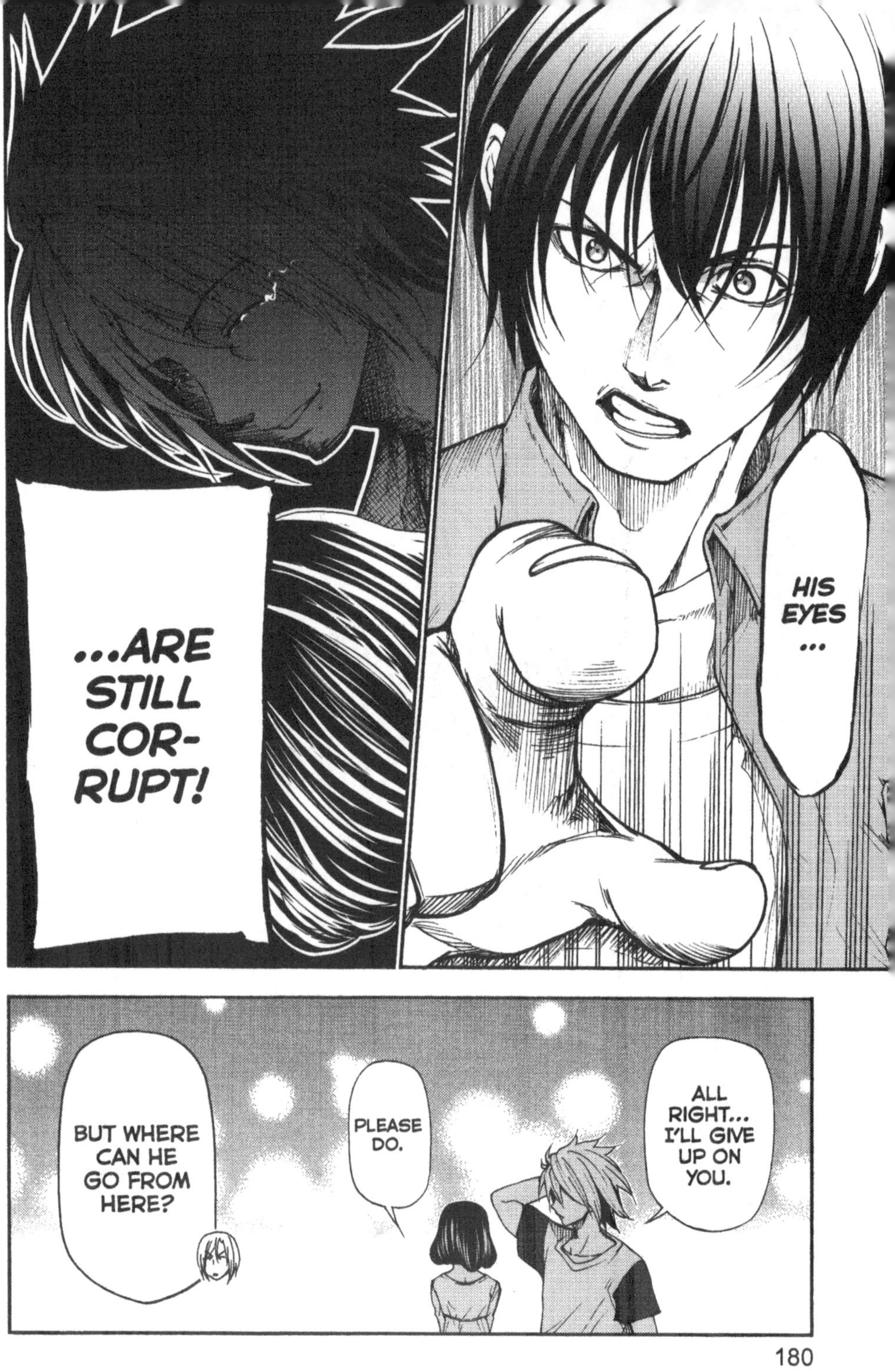
HIS EYES ...
...ARE STILL COR-RUPT!
ALL RIGHT... I'LL GIVE UP ON YOU.
PLEASE DO.
BUT WHERE CAN HE GO FROM HERE?

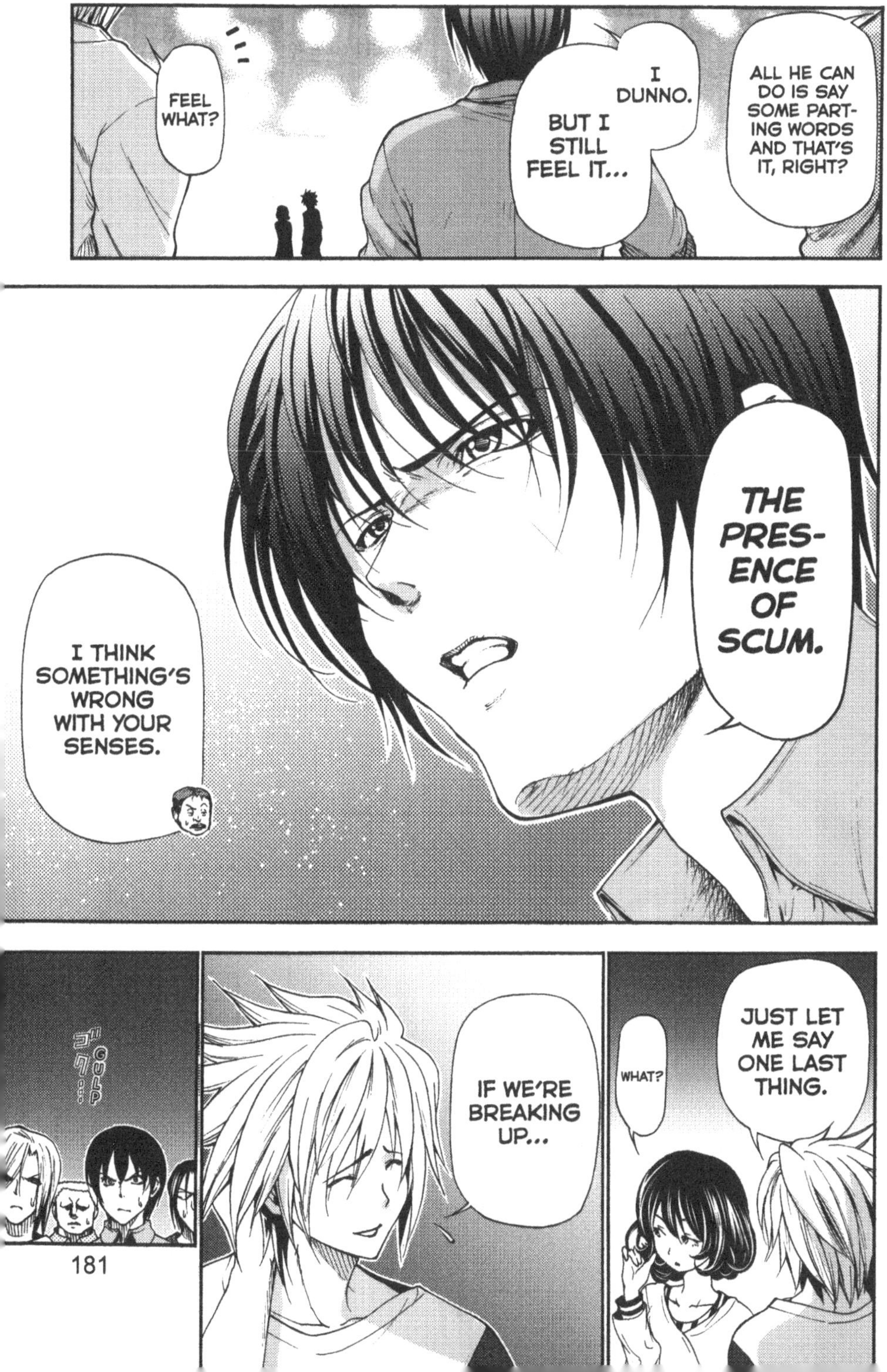
ALL HE CAN DO IS SAY SOME PARTING WORDS AND THAT'S IT, RIGHT?
I DUNNO.
BUT I STILL FEEL IT...
FEEL WHAT?
THE PRESENCE OF SCUM.
I THINK SOMETHING'S WRONG WITH YOUR SENSES.
JUST LET ME SAY ONE LAST THING.
WHAT?
IF WE'RE BREAKING UP...
GULP

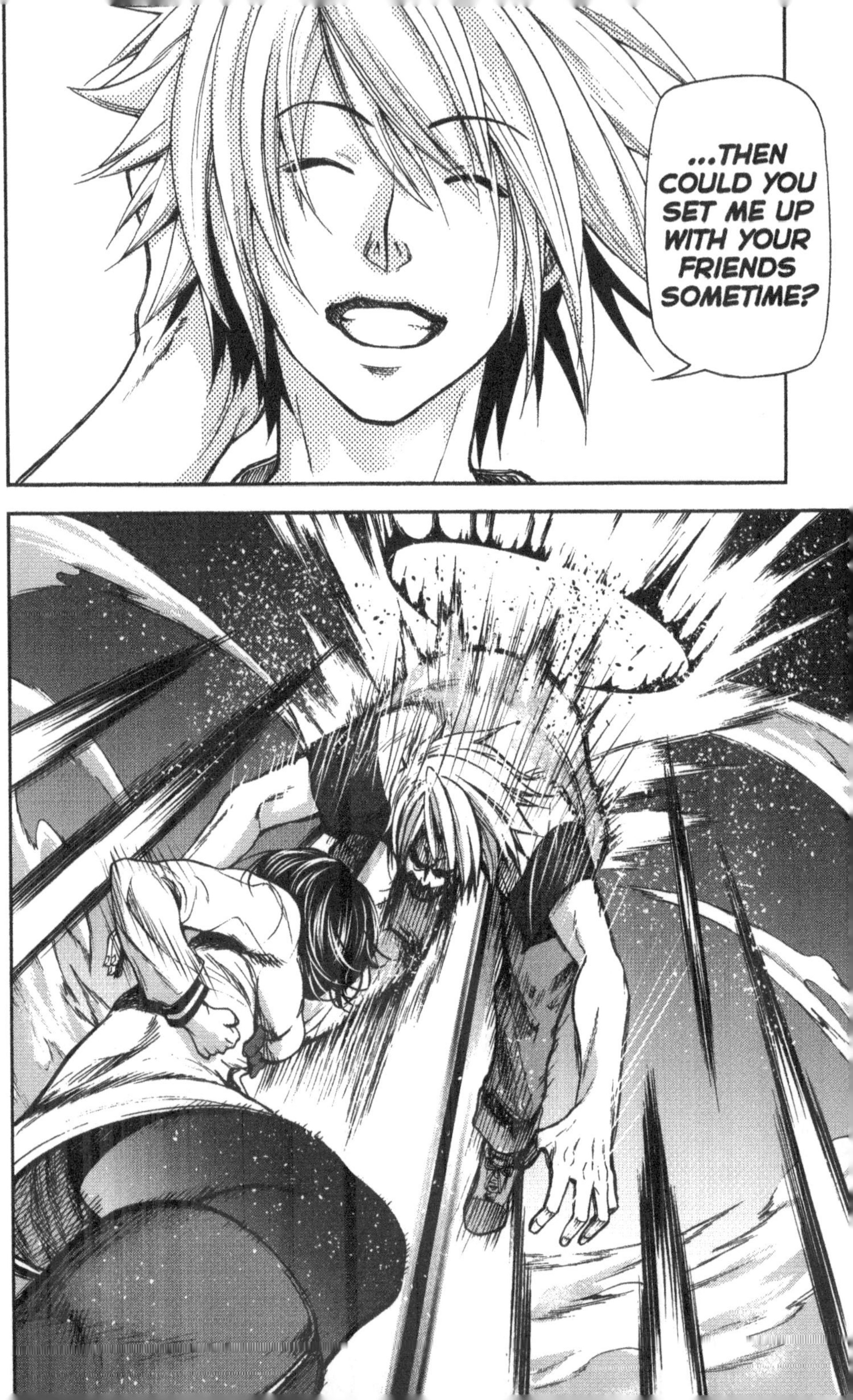
...THEN COULD YOU SET ME UP WITH YOUR FRIENDS SOMETIME?

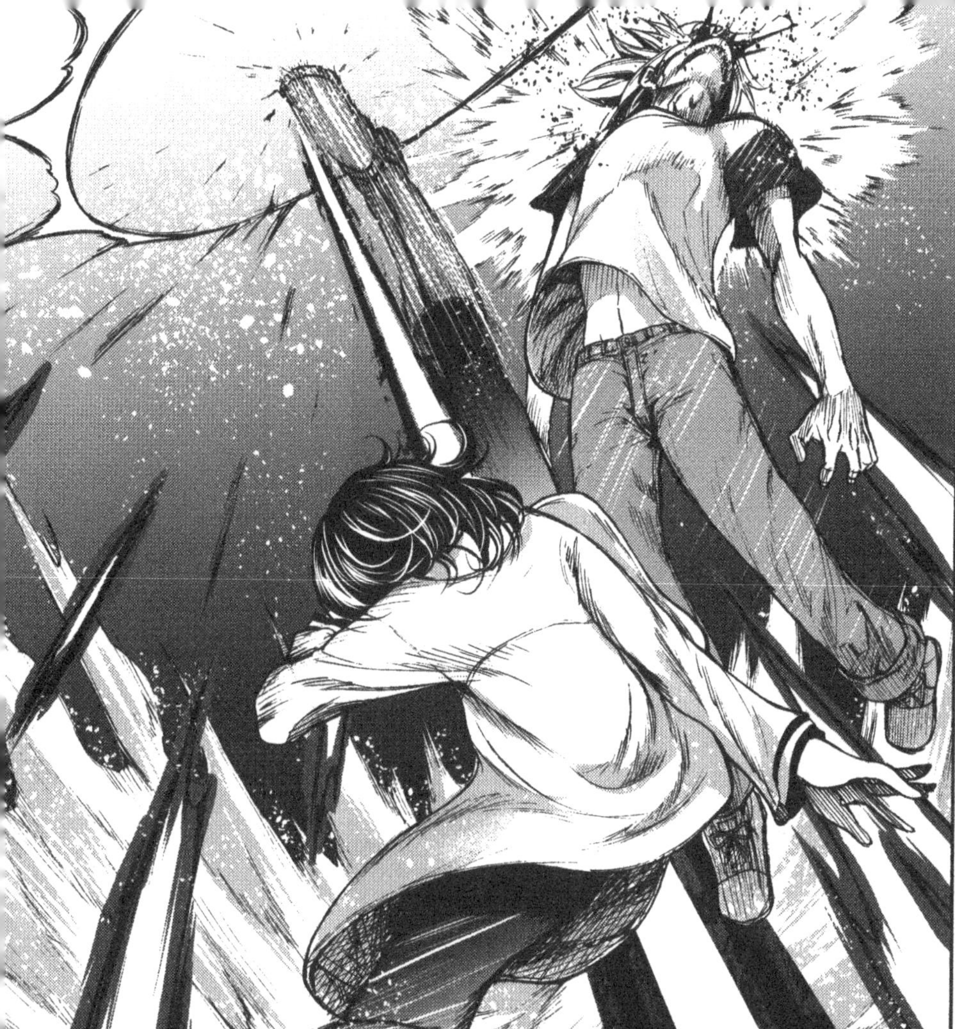
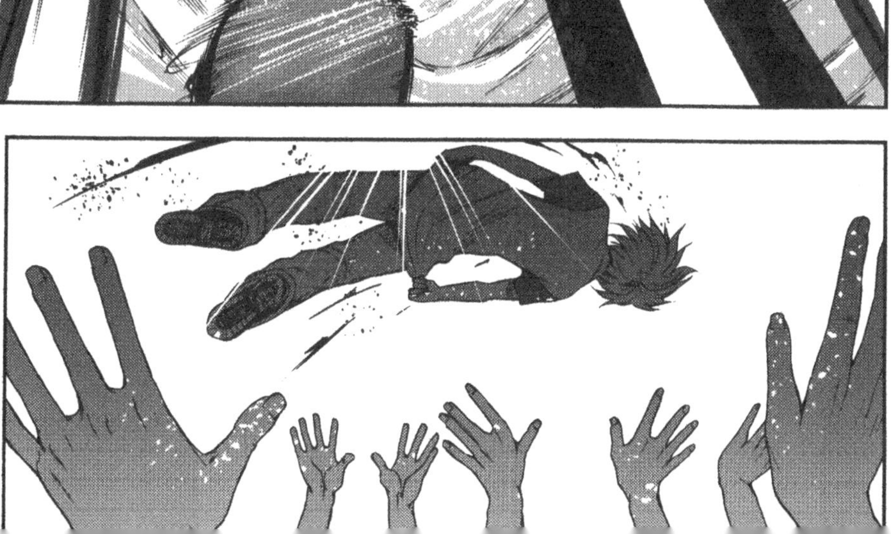

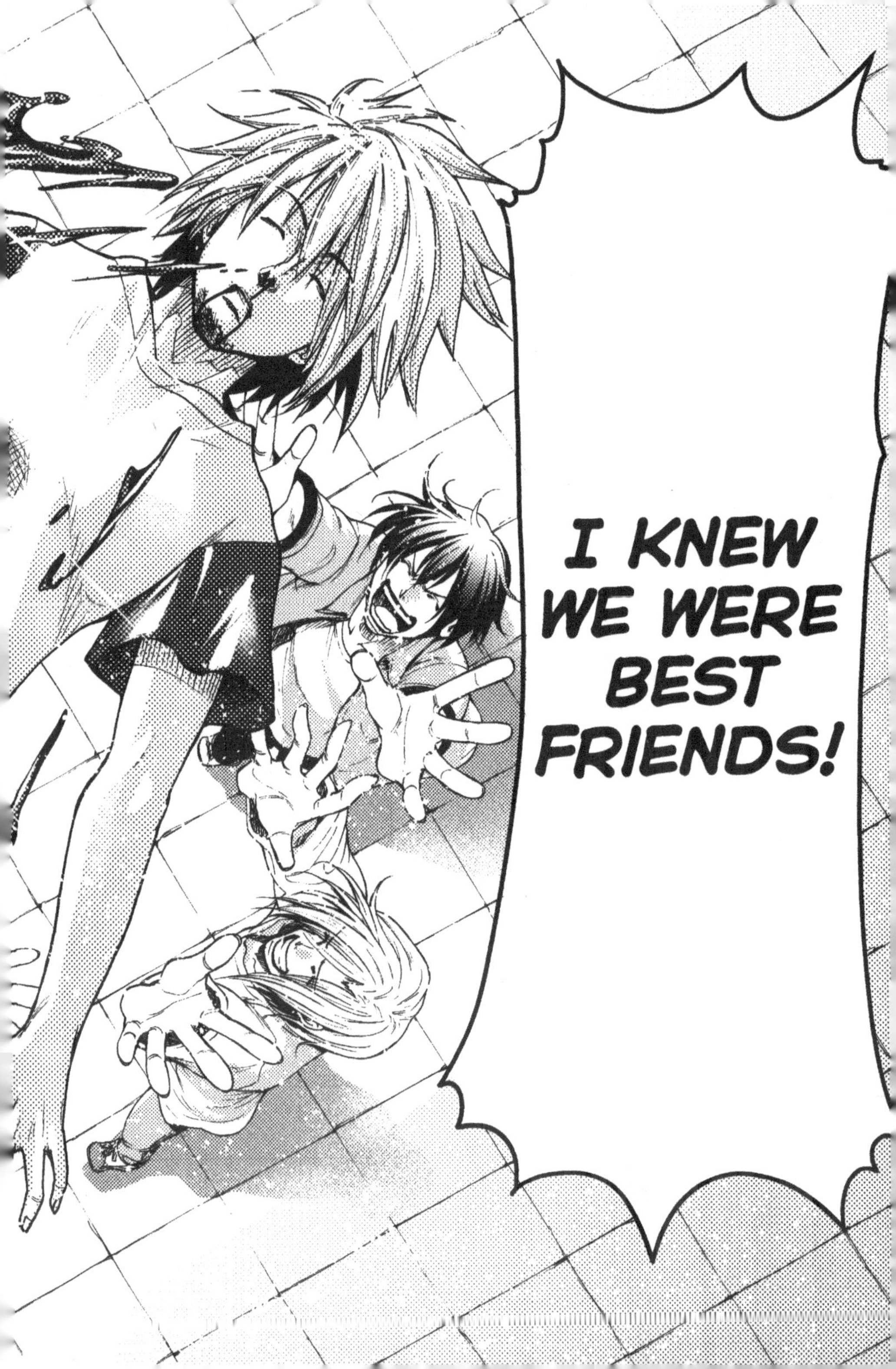
I KNEW WE WERE BEST FRIENDS!

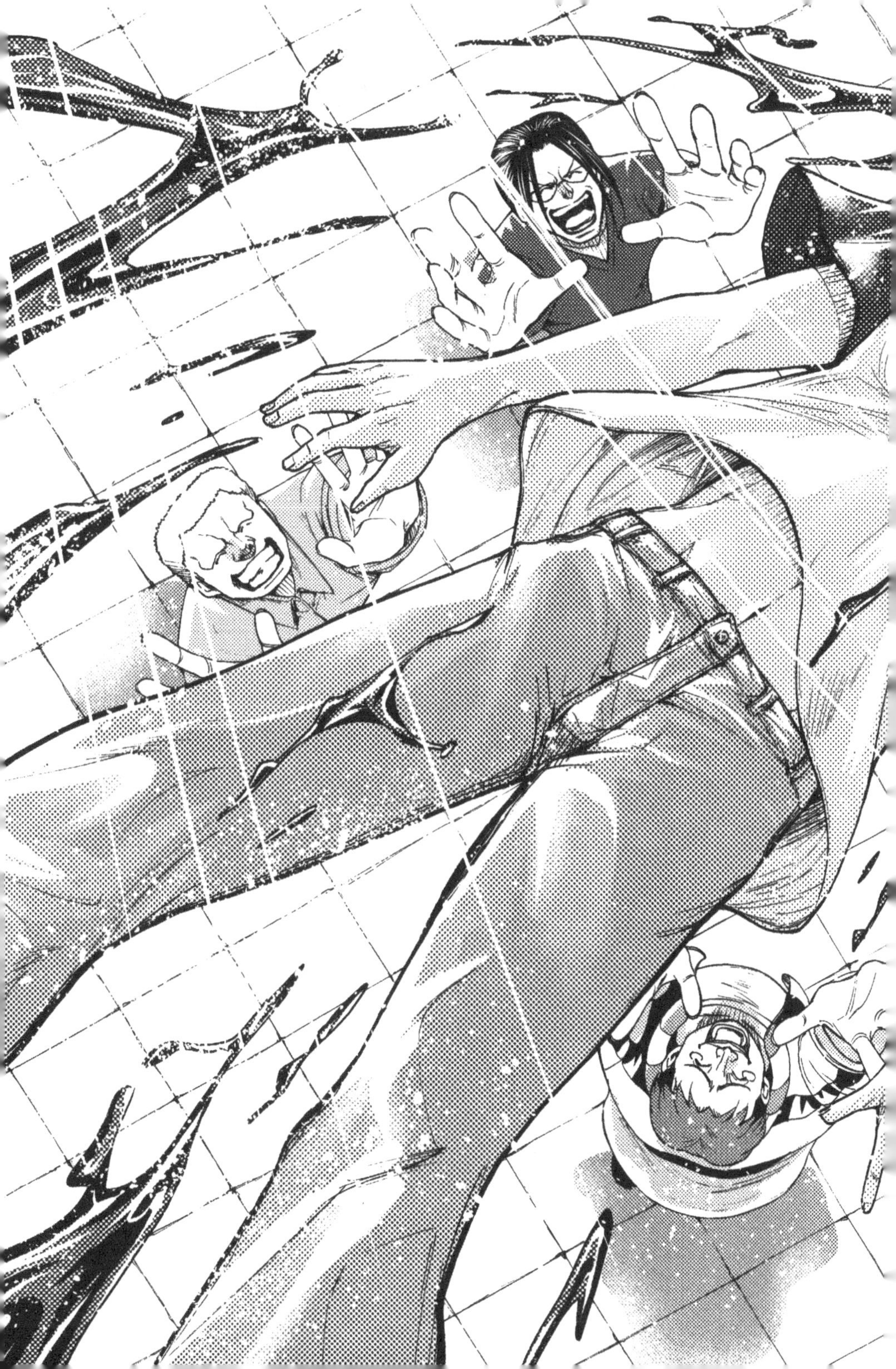

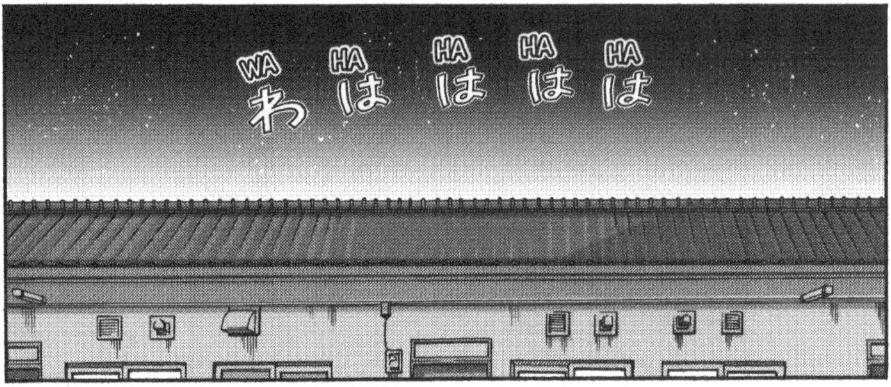
WA HA HA HA HA
わはははは

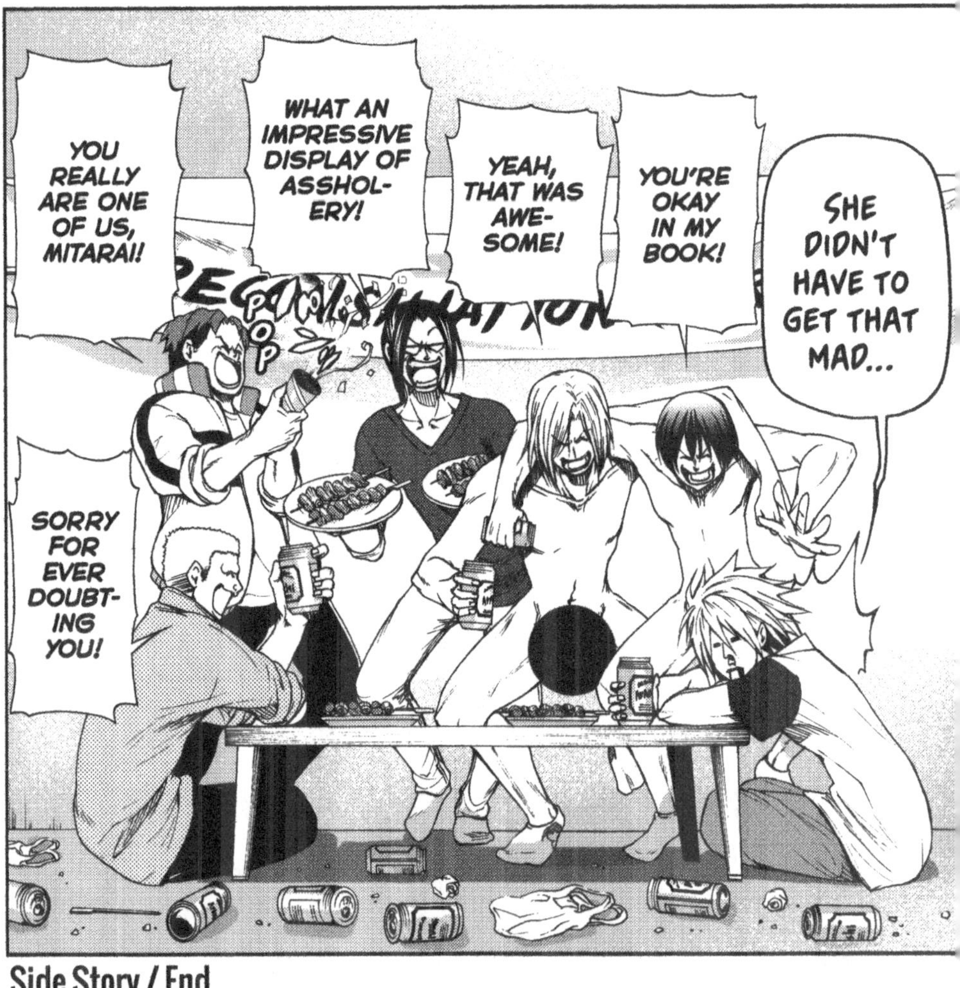
SHE DIDN'T HAVE TO GET THAT MAD...
YOU'RE OKAY IN MY BOOK!
YEAH, THAT WAS AWE-SOME!
WHAT AN IMPRESSIVE DISPLAY OF ASSHOL-ERY!
YOU REALLY ARE ONE OF US, MITARAI!
POP POP
SORRY FOR EVER DOUBT-ING YOU!

Side Story / End

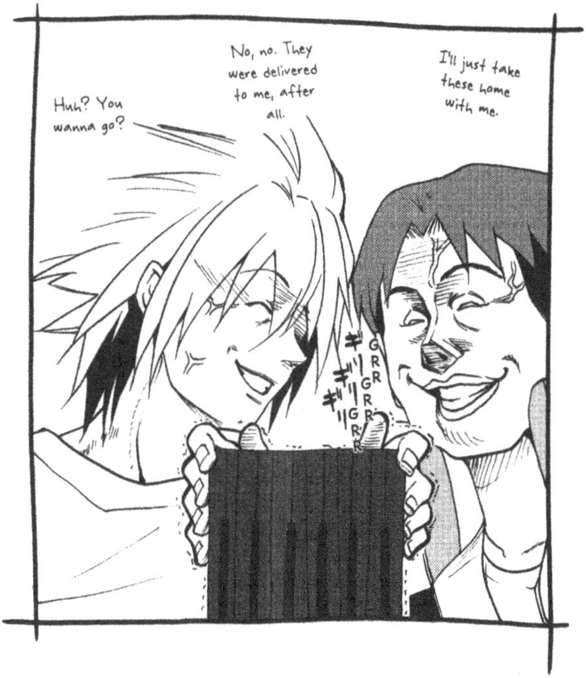
I'll just take these home with me.
No, no. They were delivered to me, after all.
Huh? You wanna go?
GRR
GRR
GRR

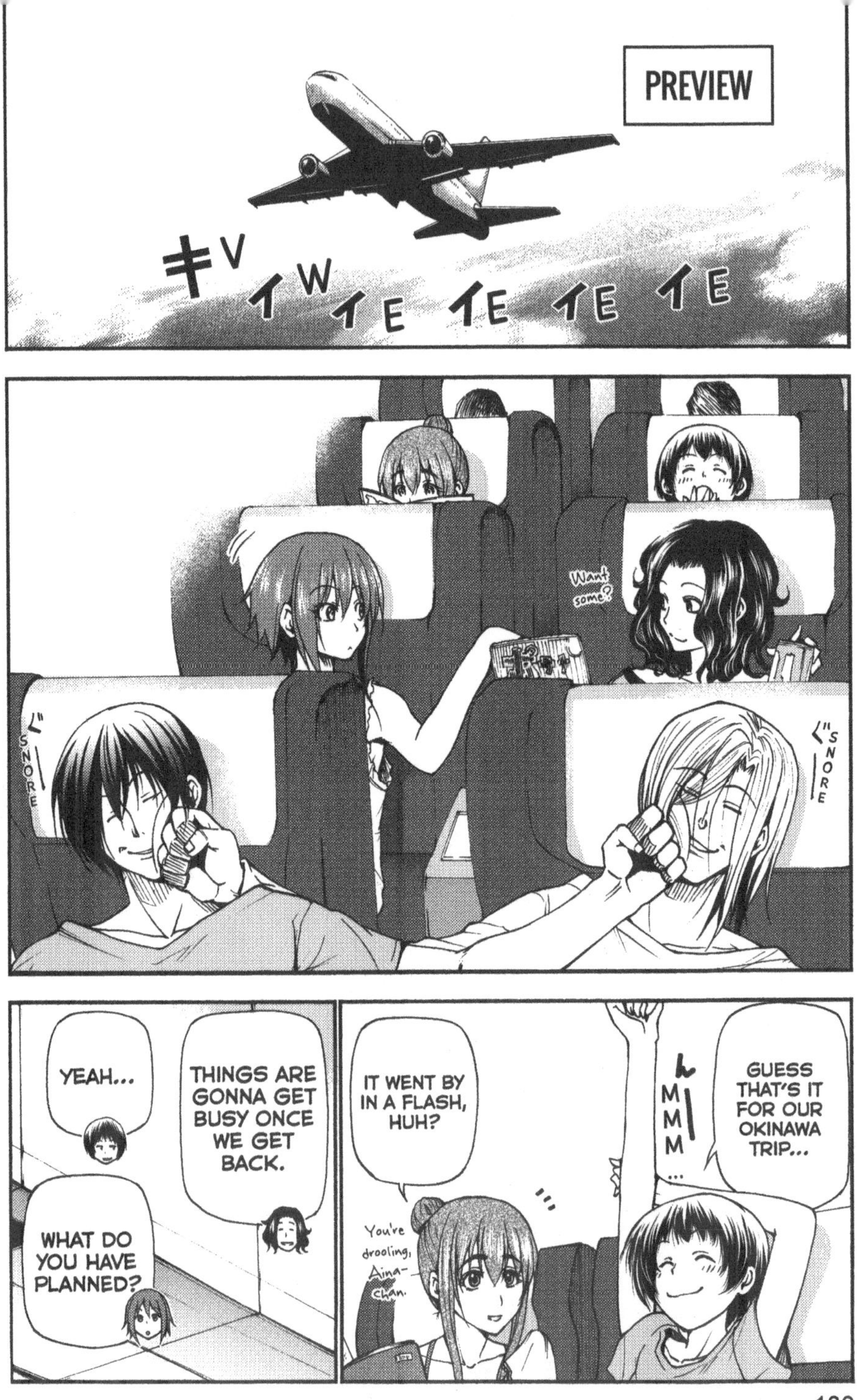
PREVIEW
キVイWイEイEイEイE
Want some?
ぐ SNORE
ぐ SNORE
GUESS THAT'S IT FOR OUR OKINAWA TRIP...
ん MMM...
IT WENT BY IN A FLASH, HUH?
...
You're drooling, Aina-chan.
THINGS ARE GONNA GET BUSY ONCE WE GET BACK.
YEAH...
WHAT DO YOU HAVE PLANNED?

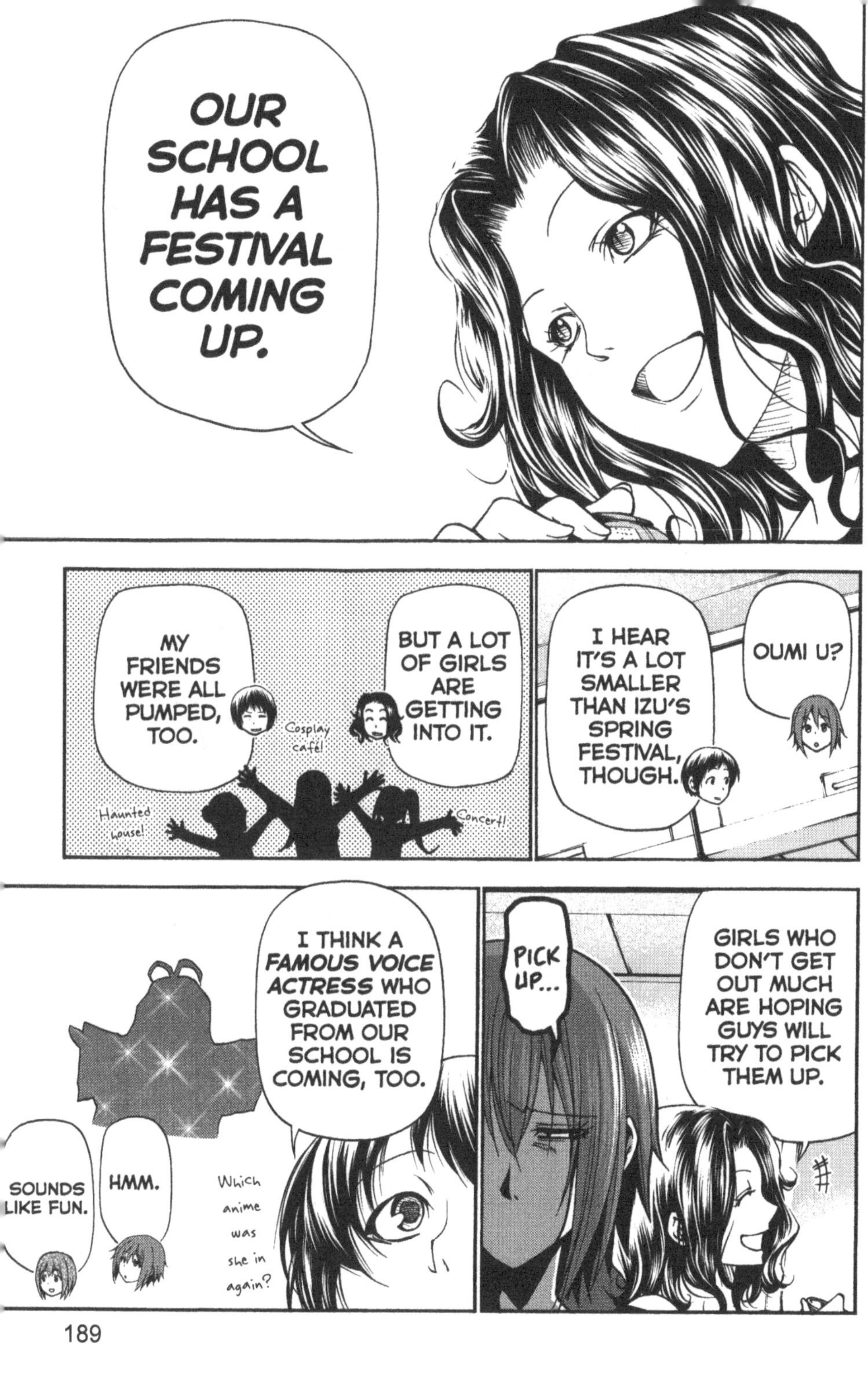
OUR SCHOOL HAS A FESTIVAL COMING UP.
OUMI U?
I HEAR IT'S A LOT SMALLER THAN IZU'S SPRING FESTIVAL, THOUGH.
BUT A LOT OF GIRLS ARE GETTING INTO IT.
MY FRIENDS WERE ALL PUMPED, TOO.
Cosplay café!
Concert!
Haunted house!
GIRLS WHO DON'T GET OUT MUCH ARE HOPING GUYS WILL TRY TO PICK THEM UP.
PICK UP...
I THINK A FAMOUS VOICE ACTRESS WHO GRADUATED FROM OUR SCHOOL IS COMING, TOO.
Which anime was she in again?
HMM.
SOUNDS LIKE FUN.

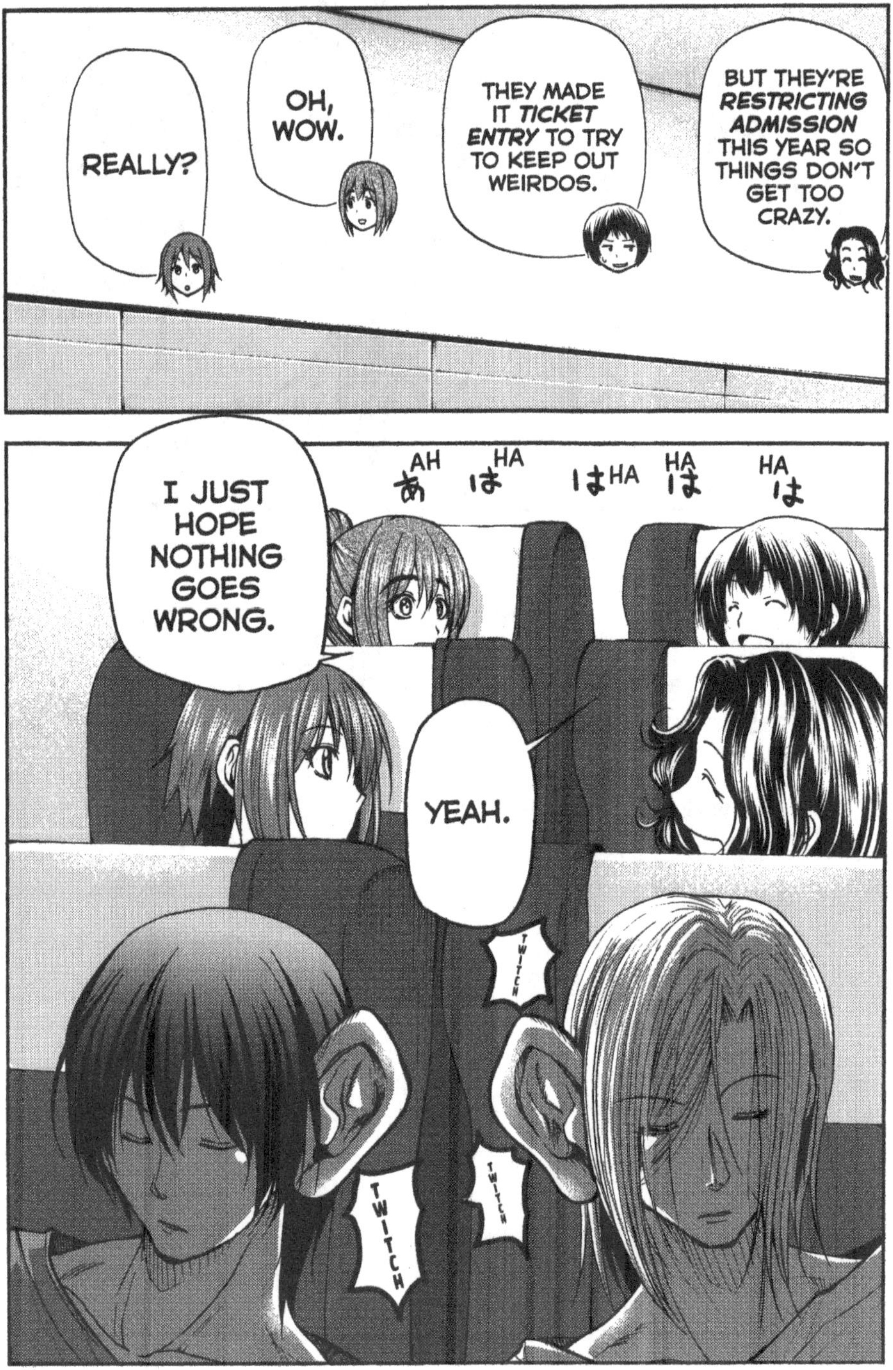
BUT THEY'RE RESTRICTING ADMISSION THIS YEAR SO THINGS DON'T GET TOO CRAZY.
THEY MADE IT TICKET ENTRY TO TRY TO KEEP OUT WEIRDOS.
OH, WOW.
REALLY?
あ AH は HA は HA は HA は HA
I JUST HOPE NOTHING GOES WRONG.
YEAH.
TWITCH
TWITCH
TWITCH

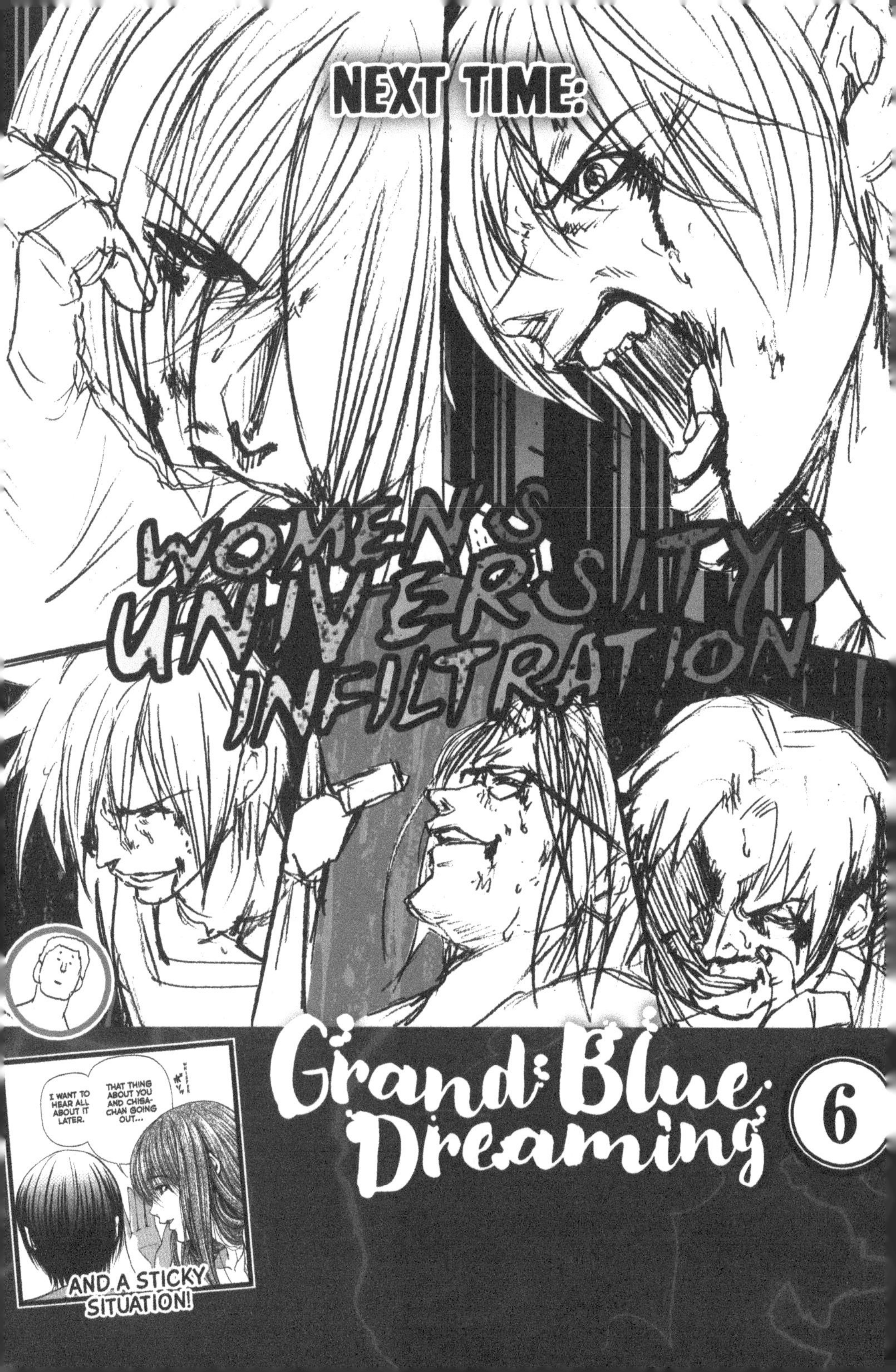
NEXT TIME:
WOMEN'S UNIVERSITY INFILTRATION
THAT THING ABOUT YOU AND CHISA-CHAN GOING OUT...
I WANT TO HEAR ALL ABOUT IT LATER.
AND A STICKY SITUATION!
Grand Blue Dreaming
6

A Kodansha Comics Trade Paperback Original.

Grand Blue Dreaming volume 5 copyright © 2016 Kenji Inoue/Kimitake Yoshioka
English translation copyright © 2019 Kenji Inoue/Kimitake Yoshioka

All rights reserved.

Published in the United States by Kodansha Comics,
an imprint of Kodansha USA Publishing, LLC, New York.

Publication rights for this English edition arranged through Kodansha Ltd., Tokyo.

First published in Japan in 2016 by Kodansha Ltd., Tokyo.

Cover Design: YUKI YOSHIDA (futaba)

ISBN 978-1-63236-724-2

Printed in the United States of America.

www.kodanshacomics.com

9 8 7 6 5 4 3 2

Translation: Adam Hirsch
Lettering: Jan Lan Ivan Concepcion
Editing: Sarah Tilson and DavidYoo
Editorial Assistance: YKS Services LLC/SKY Japan, INC.
Kodansha Comics Edition Cover Design: Phil Balsman